THE GENESIS OF SPORT IN QUEENSLAND

Dr Reet A. Howell, of Estonian heritage, is Associate
Professor in the School of Human Movement Studies at
the Queensland University of Technology. She has de-
grees from the University of Toronto and the University
of Alberta and a Doctorate from the University of California at Berkeley. She plays tennis and is an avid jogger.

Professor Maxwell L. Howell has the Foundation Chair
of Human Movement Studies at the University of
Queensland. He has taught at the University of British
Columbia and the University of Alberta, and was Dean of
the College of Professional Studies, San Diego State University. He plays tennis and represented Australia in
rugby union against New Zealand and was a member of
the 1947-48 Wallabies to the British Isles and France.

THE GENESIS OF SPORT IN QUEENSLAND

FROM THE DREAMTIME TO FEDERATION

Reet A. Howell
Maxwell L. Howell

University of Queensland Press

First published 1992 by University of Queensland Press
Box 42, St Lucia, Queensland 4067 Australia

The typeset text for this book was supplied by the authors in camera-ready form
Printed in Australia by The Book Printer, Victoria

Distributed in the USA and Canada by
International Specialized Book Services, Inc.,
5602 N.E. Hassalo Street, Portland, Oregon 97213-3640

Cataloguing in Publication Data
National Library of Australia

Howell, Reet.
    The genesis of sport in Queensland.

    Bibliography.
    Includes index.

    1. Sports — Queensland — History. I. Howell, Maxwell L.
    (Maxwell Leo), 1927-   . II. Title.

796.09943

ISBN 0 7022 2253 4

Contents

Figures

Tables

Foreword

In September 1979 I spent a weekend at the Gold Coast in the company of the late Professor Julius Sumner Miller of "Why Is It So?" and Cadbury's Milk Chocolate fame. I was honoured to have the opportunity to meet a person of his standing and enjoyed the discussions we had.

Two things he told me caught my interest more than any other.

Firstly, he said that one sixth of a matchbox contained ten to the nineteenth power of molecules. The number ten to the nineteenth power, he explained, would equate with the number of grains in one cubic mile of sand!

The other thing that has stayed with me is the good professor's insistence that sport was merely a meaningless time-wasting pursuit which did little for society. He argued that games and physical education should play absolutely no part in a child's school life. Academic goals could not be achieved, he apparently believed, if children's minds and bodies were occupied with sporting endeavours.

Not surprisingly the statistical data he gave me with regards to the matchbox has proven of little value to my development as a person, and his opinion on the role of sport in our lives is not one shared by many others I know.

Certainly not by the next professor I was to meet in my life — Professor Max Howell. Well before this publication was issued, Queensland sports lovers owed Max and Reet Howell an enormous debt. In line with the current economic climate, that debt is rapidly increasing. As successful sportspeople themselves, Max and Reet's achievements on the inside of their respective sporting arenas, were characterised by four main elements — enthusiasm, selflessness, talent and the capacity for plain hard slog!

As sports historians they continue to get the highest ratings in those particular areas. Their willingness to share the vast knowledge they possess and their deep-rooted love of sport is evident in any conversation with them or in a fifteen minute wander through their library at home.

The Genesis of Sport in Queensland is a history, but sports fans deterred by the word history should not be discouraged to delve into the fascinating information with which this book is filled. I remain curious as to the state of the pitch in the cricket match played in Drayton in 1850. Only two players in the entire game reached double figures, with the top scorer being a Mr Bolton, representing the Drayton Eleven, who carried his bat for an unconquered 14, in his side's first innings total of 24!

From tree climbing to horse racing, the Howells' thorough and, one assumes, at times painstaking research, has covered anything and everything that in one way or other contributed to the sporting history of this state in the early years.

In the preface to the book Max and Reet note that "we all stand on the shoulders of those who preceded us". Thankfully, the Howells have provided a wide and solid foundation for those who take up similar challenges in future years.

Andrew Slack

Preface

This volume deals with the genesis of sport in Queensland, covering the period from Aboriginal times to 1901. It is part two of a trilogy. The first was *The Sporting Image: A Pictorial History of Queenslanders at Play,* published by University of Queensland Press. The final volume will basically deal with sport in Queensland in the twentieth century. When completed, these works will represent the most comprehensive history of sport of any state in Australia.

What is apparent in this study of Queensland is how the need to play inevitably surfaces. A small community would begin in the wilderness, and as soon as the survival necessities were complete there was a virtually unanimous desire to play sport.

Children, of course, never ceased in their play activities, forever exploring and creating in their glorious dream worlds. Adults are more ordered and systematised, and could delay the play process, but beating in their breasts appeared to be this primal need. The individual challenge races, on horse or foot or boat, were followed by the development of race courses and sports grounds, often remarkably soon after a town was formed. They all served as relief from the endless drudgery, monotony and loneliness of a frontier society.

No one, of course, writes *the* history of anything. What is written is *a* history. This volume is modestly presented as *a* history of sport in Queensland in the early years, in the hope that others will take up the challenge in the future.

We all stand on the shoulders of those who preceded us, and this volume acknowledges and honours such pioneering works as Carmichael and Perry's *Athletic Queensland,* written in 1900; Hutcheon's *A History of Cricket in Queensland,* brought up to date after the death of the author; Mahoney's *Wide Bay and Burnett Cricket; Harking Back,* written by journalists J.L. Collins and G.H. Thompson in 1924; W.H. Bickley's *Maroon: Highlights of One Hundred Years of Rugby in Queensland 1882-1982* (1982); N.H. Caswell, Elaine Cook, C.M. Feez,

Mrs W.K. Gunn, H.W. Henricksen and V.J. Rogers for their *Outline of the History of Polo in Queensland;* Rhonda Bushby's *Seventy Years of Sport in Queensland University;* J.R. Winders' *Surf Life Saving in Queensland* (1969).

These books, though occasionally in error, were invaluable as secondary sources as they presented somewhat of an overview to the task at hand. Then there were the contributions of various historical societies, and the centenary histories of many shires which not only included sport in their contributions but portrayed the early settlers and their struggles, transportation difficulties and economic and social changes. There were school centenary histories as well, which often portrayed the sporting successes of some of their alumni; and a few sporting bodies have attempted a history of their sport or a particular club. These are listed in the bibliography.

The main task was the day-by-day reading of Queensland newspapers from the first issue down to the present. Though exhausting at times, such research was exhilarating, for we were turning back the pages of history, and there was an understandable growing feeling of respect and reverence for those individuals who assisted in carving out the beginning of sport in isolated communities throughout this state. The names became familiar over the passage of time. The pattern has changed little, for sport in Queensland to this day is still dependent on the volunteers, who willingly give their time because of the basic conviction that participation in sport can assist not only in the promotion of health but in the development of character. This belief, basically English in origin, still persists as a driving force in the promulgation of sport in society generally.

We have collected enough material for ten books, and so this work has had to be selective. It is a pity, for what has become very obvious is that sport, almost from the outset, has been an essential aspect of society in Queensland. It was eagerly sought after for a host of reasons: as a relief from monotony; for health and fitness; because of a desire to compete; to meet others and enjoy their company in a sporting environment; for altruistic concerns, in the belief that such activity had a greater meaning in strengthening the bonds of Empire; and simply for fun and enjoyment.

Sport, traditionally underrated by academicians, has an undeniably strong role in society. Historians have shown biases for general, political and economic histories, to the detriment of social histories, which tell us more about how people lived and loved, adapted and struggled. The importance of kings, queens, political leaders and outstanding citizens cannot be denied, but neither can the importance of sport be underestimated. Sport is a microcosm of society and it is possible that we may learn more about a society from its sport than from other aspects.

This study of Queensland sport is a minute unravelling of the place of sport in Queensland. It does not begin with white settlement — to do so would be a major disservice to the only occupants of this beautiful and harsh country for thousands upon thousands of years prior to that settlement. It begins, then, with its occupancy by the Aborigines, and then analyses those changes that took place following the arrival of a basically Anglo-Saxon immigrant. That impact is studied, and how adaptations were made by them in a foreign land.

There are countless thousands who have contributed to the rise of sport in Queensland: the Aborigines themselves, the squatters and selectors, the miners, the labourers, the businessmen, the women, the educators and so on. There are those who participated, and those who volunteered to assist in the management of sport: the officials, stewards, coaches, judges, referees and umpires and linesmen. There are also the spectators, who have supported individuals and teams since the first sports began.

Acknowledgments

We must express our thanks to the thousands of Queenslanders who have corresponded with us, and the hundreds we were able to interview. It was heart warming to hear how the feats of deceased members of families had been remembered, and saddening to note how many magnificent artefacts had been destroyed or lost, vital memories of a state's sporting prowess and achievement. An Olympic certificate was found discarded on a rubbish dump, Queensland and Australian "caps" have been destroyed, scrapbooks have been burned, and so on.

There are so many faces we will ever remember: Stan Lord and his scrapbooks and memories of Tommy Lawton, Eddie Gilbert and camp-drafting; Godfrey Morgan, then somewhat bed-ridden at Yeppoon but with a spark in his eye that fully explained the lifestyle he described in *We Are Borne On As A River*; Norm Pask and his reminiscences of early rugby league; Mr F.W. Golding and his analysis of rugby union at Mount Morgan; the delightful Tully and Lehane families, who introduced us to the life of the early squatters and led us to their relative Mary Durack's book *Kings in Grass Castles*; Mrs Turner at Bredou Stud Farm, who spoke of the Baynes and Feez families, and early golfing and fox and dingo hunting; Maurie Vayro of Cranbrook Press, who led us to shire histories and who was most kind in copies that he presented to us; the memorable Herb Steinohrt, whose handshakes will never be forgotten and who showed us his own scrapbooks and the photographs left him by "Nigger" Brown, which are now a collection in the Fryer Library, University of Queensland; Allan Gilmore at Clifton, who led us delightfully through the world of polo; Jim Malcolm of Collinsville, an ex-miner who made an outstanding contribution to sport in his area in his lifetime; Mr E. Cunningham at Strathmore station, from whom we got a delightful gin and tonic and a brief look at a squatter's life; Norman "Mossy" Millar, an ex-rugby league player, 83 years of age when we interviewed him, with a mind like a steel trap; Frank Stewart of

Rockhampton, who has almost single-handedly made racing history respectable in the north; Mrs Catherine Dawes of Julia Creek, who told us of early women's basketball; John Osbourne of Toowoomba, who enlightened us about sport in his area; Norm Wedlock of Gordonvale, who learned swimming in the river and was an early swimmer with the Cairns Club; Jessie and Alan Belz of Bajoor, who kindly presented us with a photograph of the Spartan Ladies' Cricket Club; the unbelievable "Chilla" Seeney, Australian champion in three sports — bareback riding, roping and bronco riding; Keith Tallon, who told us of the Feez family and early motor car racing; Mrs Alice Wood (Burke), who told us she won the first Queensland ladies' championship in running, and in bare feet; Jack Ward, who recounted early sport in Warwick, Mr and Mrs Eldershaw of Alexander Headlands, who told us of Tom Welsby, J.J. Trundle and the founding of the Brisbane Gymnasium; Mrs Evelyn Reeman of Geebung and Marjorie McKinney of Kalinga, who spoke to us of early church leagues in women's basketball; Peter Reaburn, for collecting information around Longreach; Ron Harvey for his voluminous information on sport in Bundaberg; Sid Kelly of Rockhampton for his marvellous contribution and research on rugby league in his area; and so many others who told us stories of their lives and their love for sport.

It is to these and so many others we have not mentioned that we dedicate this book, because it is people like them who have lived through sport in Queensland and have contributed to its continuation. May their sacrifices never be forgotten.

This book is dedicated to S.J. (Spencer) Routh, Principal Librarian (Collection-Development) at the University of Queensland. Spencer is not only keenly interested in all sports, he is a devoted Queenslander who has assisted countless students at the university, displaying a particular delight when they undertake research in sport history. A credit to his profession, he is never too busy to help others, and is ever a loyal and trusted friend.

Introduction

A number of generalisations are offered in this overview of the genesis of Queensland sport.

1. The indigenous games of the Aborigines emphasised stability, perpetuation of culture and a balance with nature. Their games were rich in variety, and reflected the economic, political, social, religious, social-psychological and demographic aspects of the society, and contained both internal and external characteristics. Their activities were, in the main, not perpetuated, but rather were rapidly submerged and obliterated, following the imposition of a new and dominant culture.

2. With a few exceptions, adoption of English sporting values and sports did not overall act as an agent of social mobility or assimilation for the Aborigines. Aborigines have performed well in a host of sports, and many demonstrated outstanding athletic aptitude. There were boxers, cricketers and runners, but few over the passage of time can be said to have increased their social status as a consequence of sporting involvement.

3. Sports in the early years of settlement were essentially a mirror of those in England and were class-differentiated. Cricket, horseracing and hunting in the early years were under the control of the military and government officials, and the landholders. Only they had the leisure time, equipment and money to compete. The lower classes gambled, engaged in boisterous dances in comparison with the balls of the upper classes, fought, and on holidays participated in such activities as climbing greasy poles, chasing a greasy pig, and trials of strength.

4. The leading colonists engaged in symbolic elite activities. These were seen in the early introduction of cricket, the jockey clubs with gentlemen riders, the importance and breeding of thoroughbreds and hunting with the hounds, where dogs and appropriate apparel would be imported for such occasions. The colonists with wealth and position

were engaging in those activities held to be the prerogative and domain of the upper class in England.

5. Sport adaptations by the settlers were occasioned by variant geographic and climatic conditions, as well as by deprivation of specific and essential resources. The absence of the fox and rabbit, for example, found easy substitution through the presence of dingoes and marsupials and the hunt proceeded with local adaptations. Innovations were introduced, such as the herding and clubbing of kangaroos, a substitution for blood sports, such as ratting and cock–fighting and bull and bear–baiting, which had been popular in the home country. These may be termed substitutive–similar sports.

6. The woman's role in sports in the early years was negligible and was mainly confined to spectatorship at socially approved functions. The values enforced by male–dominated sport did little to aid such social restrictions. There were invariably comments in the press in the early years as to the enhancement of most of the social sports by the presence of the ladies, and their fashions would be described in detail. Opinions were unanimous that the "fair sex" added considerably to such occasions. Women were observers in the early years. However, their presence was not condoned at the sports such as boxing and professional athletics. Essentially, in so far as participation in sport is concerned, this was only permissible and approved for men. Women pursued leisure pursuits in the home, such as playing cards and board games, and would ride horses.

7. A mateship and masculinity ethos dominated early society. Essentially sport was the man's domain, and there was a great store placed in supposedly masculine pursuits. Sports of strength dominated over sports of skill, the man who was admired being the one who displayed endurance, who could withstand pain, ride hard, and could handle himself with his fists. Another characteristic that emerged was the mateship phenomenon, stimulated among other things by the reliance on each other under arduous and isolated circumstances.

8. Sports emerged in country areas which reflected the skills of the farmer and bushman. Rodeo activities, ploughing matches, shearing contests, wood–chopping and ultimately activities like sheep dog trials developed which arose out of the skills of the bush. Sports, then, developed which mirrored the society.

9. By the end of the nineteenth century an egalitarian social doctrine permeated Australian society, and sport assisted in that democratisation, in so far as males were concerned. The gold and other mineral discoveries not only occasioned an influx of migrants with varying social doctrines, but emphasised the worth of the individual, and labour

unrest and preliminary organisation of workers started to appear, and this was to have an effect in Queensland. Ability was deemed more important than social status, and this slowly influenced sport. Cricket, for example, by the 1890s, showed downward class mobility.

10. By the end of the nineteenth century, in urban areas, there was a transition from a pre-industrial to an industrial society, with attendant changes in sport complexity. The structural-functional characteristics of folk games were modified towards the characteristics of modern sport. Increased bureaucratisation of sport was a concomitant development occasioned by the diffusion of sport and the necessity for uniformity. Although it is impossible to generalise in Queensland because of the variation in development of population areas, there were obvious attempts in the major centres to regularise sport regulations and to engage in regional, interstate and finally national competitions. These changes were hastened as a result of sweeping technological changes, such as the development of railways, electricity, the telephone and telegraph.

11. State sport successes assisted in establishing a state self-identity and enhanced and reinforced that state image and unity. Success in sport against Queensland's southern neighbours served as verification of Queensland's better way of life, in a similar way that the national self-image was reinforced by victories over the English. This need for justification remains evident today. Such interstate victories acted as symbolic messages about the social structure of Queensland itself, reflecting the underlying tensions felt by Queensland about federal unfairness when dealing with the state.

12. Sporting activities developed by the second half of the nineteenth century which were ultimately to hold the focus of national attention as being essentially Australian. Queensland differed little in this respect. Cricket, in particular, became an expression of Australia's emerging nationalism, as did Australian Rules, though this was mainly in the southern states.

13. Sporting heroes and heroines emerged in Queensland who were in the main reproductive in nature, rather than transformative. A transformative hero or heroine is one who changes a sport by his/her actions, the equipment that is worn or used, or some major sporting innovation. A reproductive hero or heroine is one who epitomises the society as it is, who reinforces the value system. Queensland heroes and heroines, and there were few of the latter in this time period, were almost exclusively reproductive. They endeavoured to sustain rather than change the cultural mores in the sport domain. What is for certain however is that there were heroes aplenty in Queensland, to capture the

imagination of a public eager to worship at the shrine of sporting ability: M.J. Slack, Jack Wieneke, Pring Roberts, Frank Baynes, Arthur Feez, G.E. Markwell, W.T. Evans, R.H. McCowan, Sine Boland, Albert Henry, Charlie Samuels, W.A.D. and C.B.P. Bell, Alick Dennis, George Dawson, Edmonstone Markwell, Peter Corrigan, E.J. Kellett, J.A. Smith, Carl Swensson, Bob Walne, Ben Goodson, and so on.

14. Unionisation affected sport in Australia, particularly through the reduction of working hours. The eight hours' movement, the Shop Assistants' Act and so on were set up to argue for the rights of the working man, and a central issue was to allow more time for leisure activities for the working class. These issues, when resolved, gave the work force more time for sport, and increased sport's democratisation in Queensland.

15. Sport was seen not only to mirror society in some respects but to assist the establishment of important, lasting social relationships, traditions and relationships. Sport in Queensland was not important simply for the activity in and of itself, but also for the fact that it reinforced worthy societal goals and values, bound people together and created lasting friendships.

It may be argued by some that the positive aspects of sport far outweigh the negative in this history of the genesis of sport in Queensland. Modern appraisals, particularly those by sport sociologists, tend to pick the bones of sport, glorying in finding salmonella in the process. This study endeavours to cover by scholarly analysis the origin, diffusion and growth of sport in this state, from before settlement to 1901, and comes out unequivocally on the positive side. To be sure, there was more than occasional exploitation of the Aborigine, little worker's compensation for those who sought it in professional or amateur sport, monopoly of hegemonic positions in sport by the leaders of society at times, occasional fixing of human and animal races, and so on. It is easy to dwell on the negatives, but they are but pin pricks when the total picture is analysed.

This history confirms the overall worth of sport, its role in binding small communities together, its undeniable place in society, the effective manner with which it gives individuals release after a hard day's work in the fields or in the offices of this state. The influence of sport has certainly never been overrated in our society; indeed, in our opinion, it has been grossly underrated. Sport is a social institution of remarkable complexity and importance, which can overshadow by a single deed or in a moment of time other social institutions, such as politics, religion and economics.

Sport in Queensland is, and ever has been, however, more than any of its super-heroes and super-heroines. It is the club bowler, croquet players, the golfer and tennis player; it is the battler, ready to fill a place on any team at a moment's notice; it is the club worker, the secretary, the president, the coach and the supporters; it is the horde of sun and sea-worshippers, the sailors, the canoeists, the fishermen.

Sport has enriched beyond measure Queensland's social history. For some, it is a slave, for others, a pleasure, for a few, a bore, for most, an abiding interest. This analysis of the genesis of sport in Queensland, with all its inadequacies, demonstrates with clarity sport's vital role in this state. It is perhaps impertinent to call sport the soul of the state, but what other social force is of such significance?

In unravelling this history of sport in Queensland in its early years, the authors have been continuously humbled by the discoveries. As the veneer of sport was uncovered, Queensland society itself unfolded: the opening of the gold fields, the movement of the squatter, the creation of towns, the opening of agricultural areas. Sport did not follow a single flag, but understandably people started participating in the activities they pursued as youths wherever they come from: the Irish, the Scots, the Germans, the English, and those migrants from the southern states. Eventually the sports became less insular and more Queensland in concept. Some disappeared, others increased in popularity.

The interstate rivalries, which still persist to the present day, reflect deep societal concerns that have developed since the time of settlement. The tyranny of distance in Australia, lack of communication in the early years, relative isolation, perceptions of unfair apportionment of federal monies to the north, and a host of other factors, have combined to develop a personal consciousness and pride within the state second to none in Australia. Clannish and tribal at times, exaggerated at others, it becomes obvious that the battle on the sports field often has a deeper significance than the event itself. There is historical and social meaning in the event that clearly transcends that event. No one can be precise as to what a Queenslander is, but there is a clarity of expectation within the population when it comes to sport. Courage, pride, persistence, toughness and determination are some of the qualities expected of their representatives, male and female.

Indeed, sport has deep meaning in the state of Queensland, and this treatise points out unequivocally that without sport Queensland would have been a lot sorrier place in which to live. As our tale unfolds, the names keep coming to mind, those thousands upon thousands of glorious athletes and administrators who brought sport in the state to a position of respectability in these early years; Thomas Welsby, Frank

Markwell, the Baynes and Feez families, Fred Lea, Ernest J. Stevens, R.H. Roe, W.B. Carmichael, J.K. Cannan, F.S.N. Bousfield, Thomas Finney, R.P. Francis...the list goes on and on and on. We are left with the feeling that they created a legacy they would never have dreamed of. They were vital forces in making Queensland sport what it is today, and that contribution has been grossly undervalued. It is our privilege to provide this more general perspective to the role of sport and the contribution of some of its athletes and administrators in the founding years.

From the point of view of theory, sport in Queensland might be explained by the utilisation of more than one theoretical model. Perhaps this study supports *evolutionism* more than any other theory, as sport has been analysed in an evolutionary framework, beginning at a point of origin and then diffusing, and changing in its complexity and structure as society similarly changes. On the other hand a *functionalism* model can be clearly seen, for sport in Queensland, it has been argued, is not only ritualistic, it has served a valuable integrative function. Sport has acted in developing the self–concept and in fulfilling deep psychological needs. A *structural–functional theoretical* model could also be represented, for sport can be viewed as reinforcing and supporting other parts of the social system, such as politics, economics and religion. *Cultural materialism* could also be argued, as culture change is viewed primarily as techno–economic change, and certainly sport in the state has changed with the pressures that emanated from the economy and technology. This study, then, is supported by various theoretical positions.

1

Games in Queensland: From Dreamtime to Early Settlement

The story of what is now called Queensland does not begin with the arrival of the white man but with the Aborigines, the first inhabitants of this continent.

For some 35,000–40,000 years the Aborigines had been the sole human occupants of this land. It has been estimated that out of some 300,000 Aborigines living in Australia in 1788, about 100,000, from some 200 separate tribes, were living in Queensland. These small tribal units meant that there was no apparent political framework for white settlers to deal with, which led to their lack of unity and near demise.

Each tribe lived in a strictly defined area as tribal territoriality was one of the fundamental features of their society. These ideas of territory, however, were foreign to the white invaders. The Aborigines were essentially peaceful in nature and were not a war–like people. Only when there were blatant territorial encroachments, or serious crimes or insults, were wars or recrimination resorted to. For most of the time they lived in an orderly, prosperous and dynamic environment.

There was, however, considerable intertribal contact and interaction, and many of them would come together for special occasions. Such meetings at times were used to settle only territorial disputes and matters of revenge, and would include mass and individual fights, corroborees as well as the bartering of products.

During the season of the *bon–yi* (a nut highly prized by the Aborigines), for example, various tribes in the Queensland area would travel considerable distances to engage in a variety of inter–community activities. Such an occasion was aptly described by Petrie in *Reminiscences of Early Queensland*.[1] After the ceremonies were over, there was an exchange of possessions, the inland blacks giving weapons, opossum rugs and so on to the coastal blacks for shells, reed necklaces and other items that could only be obtained from the coastal regions.

The sham fights between the tribes on these occasions were exciting times: "Spears would fly fast, waddies sound with a crash against thick skulls, and blood would flow freely".[2] However, there were set rules and regulations that all had to abide by. At sunset all fighting ceased, and the feasting would begin.

The established lifestyle was that of hunting and gathering, a semi-nomadic existence, particularly in the interior parts of the continent. As they neither grew nor cultivated their foods, they killed, picked or dug it from their environment. Their diet was extensive and included animals and insects of all types, sizes and shapes. The surrounding vegetation also provided food in the form of berries and fruits. Essentially they ate whatever they could find and would usually consume the food soon after its procurement.

As the food supply was more constant in the coastal areas, such tribes led a more stable existence, often establishing semi-permanent settlements. Their diet was supplemented by the yields of the surrounding waters. They developed specialised marine-related skills such as sailing, canoeing and fishing. Occasionally they had contact with other cultures such as the Torres Strait Islanders, the Papuans from New Guinea, and perhaps Macassars and Malays, even Chinese and Japanese seafarers who ventured such distances in order to barter. Some Aboriginal skills and traditions were necessarily modified because of such social interaction.

The Aborigines developed an intimate knowledge and understanding of their environment, upon which their survival was dependent. They placed maximum emphasis on stability within their society and an equilibrium between nature and people. They had a spiritual bond with the land, and an implicit belief in the balance of nature dominated all aspects of their life and culture, which was a concept unfamiliar to the whites.

Although physical survival was the most salient feature of Aboriginal life, they developed a culture which was rich with traditions, religious rites, and ceremonies. They created myths which explained the origins of their society, and life around them, and these myths were passed on from generation to generation. An integral part of their daily life was their leisure pursuits and games. The games played, and the pastimes indulged in, reflected their main societal concerns, which were survival and perpetuation of culture. The need for physical fitness and hardiness was readily apparent to the Aborigines, as the weak did not survive. Hence, the development of physical fitness attributes such as muscular strength and endurance, speed, power, as well as various motor skill abilities, naturally evolved from their habitual daily activities. Running, jumping, throwing and climbing were essential prerequisites for the hunt, but they also provided sources of amusement and pleasure for youngsters and adults alike. Often, it was difficult to distinguish between activities for economic production and those for play purposes. For example, throwing spears accuracy and distance were common games, and children would be taught to play such games from an early age. Other common activities were numerous variations of animal tracking games. All these activities, although they may be classified as play, had a dual function as they served to master and perfect the skills of hunting, necessary in their society for survival.

Dancing, to the Aborigines, was an integral component of their culture, and was nurtured as a serious, usually religious, activity. Their dances served many functions such as evoking the support of the spirits for a successful hunt or needed rain, as well as being part of initiation rites and celebrations. They also served entertainment and amusement functions.

The dances, which were called *corroborees*, were accompanied by songs and musical instruments such as didgeridoos, leaf whistles and boomerangs struck together as well as the clapping of hands and stamping of feet. The dancers would be painted with designs and decorations which were tribe and dance specific. Usually preparations for a dance would occupy the major portion of a day, as such dances were principally held at night, after sunset, and continued until sunrise. Only women's dances were held during the daytime. Often a corroboree would be performed over five consecutive nights.

The traditional games of the Aborigines were not extensively recorded by the early chroniclers of Aboriginal life. At the end of the nineteenth century, W.E. Roth, Protector of Aborigines in Queensland, wrote profusely on Queensland Aborigines and their customs,[3] and he included games and amusements in his research. The most detailed, and scholarly analysis of this subject was undertaken by Salter[4] in the 1960s.

Salter's analysis was based on the theoretical model presented in figure 1. The basis for the motel was his division of the Aboriginal culture into six major external components or characteristics: *economic* activities, *political* activities, *domestic* aspects, *ceremonial* rites, *cultural identification* and *social interaction activities*.

The various games and pastimes of the Aborigines were identified by Salter in accordance with their affinity to these components. The main characteristics exhibited by each of the games and pastimes was determined, and then the activity was categorised according to whether it was mainly an activity of chance, dexterity, enigma, exultation,

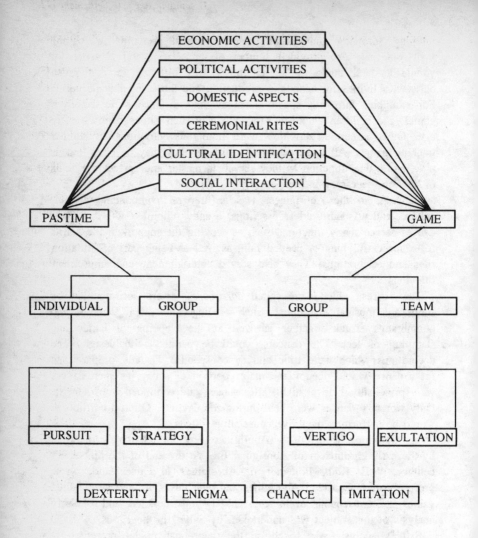

Figure 1   Model employed to classify Aboriginal games and pastimes
(Salter 1967)

imitation, pursuit, strategy and/or vertigo (these were the internal characteristics or components).

The results of Salter's study are too extensive to be presented in totality, however the main points to emphasise are the wide range and the number of pastimes and games indulged in by the Aborigines. Games are thought to be a reflection or microcosm of culture, and as the Aborigine is often classified as "primitive" in the anthropological sense it is assumed that their culture was devoid of games and sports. Yet they indulged in a whole host of games, and some of them were exceedingly complex, innovative and ingenious.

Some 94 different physical activities of the Aborigines were identified by Salter. Ten were considered to be individual pastimes, 42 group pastimes, 33 group games and 9 were team games.

Individual pastimes were such as shooting the petiole or leaf stalk of a grass blade. A piece of blade grass was split away from the petiole until a fair length was exposed and the end of the leaf was held securely in the mouth. A stick was placed under the leaf with the petiole facing away, and the stick was drawn sharply forward to shoot the petiole. Targets could be hit a hundred feet away from the person.

Group pastimes were such as skipping, in which a long root such as that of the white gum was used as a skipping rope. It was held by two players, and others jumped over it as it was swung backwards and forwards, but it was never circled. It was popular among the Northern Mitakoodi and Grenada Kalkadoon tribes.

Group games were exemplified by activities involving the "kangaroo rat" or "weet weet". The idea was to throw the kangaroo "rat", which was made out of a single piece of wood, so that it slid or bounced along the ground. Each person tried to gain the greatest distance.

Team games were represented in their ball games. Roth identified three types of ball games among Queensland Aborigines: catch-ball, stick and stone, and spin-ball. Catch-ball was the favourite and most widespread, and it was played by both sexes. The game involved tossing the ball back and forth, with the aim being to intercept it while it was in the air. The Kalkadoons described it as "kangaroo-play", as the jumping movements of the players resembled kangaroos.

Twenty-nine of the activities in Salter's study were either directly or indirectly associated with economic activities, 13 with political activities, 9 with domestic aspects, 8 with ceremonial rites, 13 with cultural identification and 22 with social interaction.

Of the *economic* type of activities specifically identified in Queensland, only two will be mentioned. One such was tree climbing, which involved competition to determine the fastest to scale and descend a tree. Girls as well as boys were instructed in the skills necessary to perform such feats. As their skill progressed, the elders would increase the climbing difficulty by choosing straighter trees and so on.

Another game was "spearing the prey", in which one or more boys imitated a kangaroo and an emu, while the other players attempted to get close to the "animals". The "animal" would attempt to escape, and in so doing would try to avoid the thrown weapons, which were made of bull-rush stalks and thick reed.

As for *political*-type activities there were, for example, sham fights, in which small boys imitated the arts of welfare as practised by their elders. Toy spears, toy woomeras and toy boomerangs would be used. However, adults also participated in inter-tribal tournaments such as those among the Mallanpara Aborigines of Central Queensland. These were called a *Prun*. Although basically for entertainment, such meetings were also used to settle personal scores and tribal disagreements. An area was designated for the "battle" between the tribes. Spears could only be thrown at the knees or feet. Then boomerangs, and finally clubs, would be thrown at any part of the body. Rest pauses were called every ten to fifteen minutes to allow for physical recovery and weapon collection. Fair play was adhered to at all times.

Domestic-type activities were children's games such as "grown-ups", "marriage" and "house", or even "cooking" over imaginary fires in imitation of their elders. Also, "honey gathering" and "cracking beans" were popular amusements, particularly for girls.

Activities related to *ceremonial rites* were perceived by the use of the "roarer", "whirring stick" or "whirler" by children. A larger bull-roarer, however, was only used on sacred ceremonial occasions and was not a plaything. Play corroborees were also performed by children, and of course tribal corroborees were common.

Cultural Identification-type activities embraced mimicry games. The mimicking of animals and birds was the most common, a most popular form of amusement during leisure hours. The games consisted of imitating the movements of animals, their calls and their tracks.

Social Interaction-type games incorporated a wide variety of diversions, such as games while bathing. Children and adults enjoyed jumping into the water, and "bombing" each other. "Mud sliding" was also popular, and a piece of bark would be used to slide along or down mud banks.

Some 44 of the games and pastimes had as their major component dexterity, 34 imitation, 12 pursuit, 12 strategy, 11 exultation, 8 enigma and 8 vertigo. Only 5 of the activities involved elements of chance, but no activities involving gambling were identified.

Games that emphasised *dexterity* were those such as target throwing competitions for distance and accuracy. A popular recreational game for men was "avoiding the boomerang", in which a boomerang, much smaller and lighter than the fighting boomerang, was used. This toy could be thrown in such a manner as to make three to four complete gyrations, while a team of five or six men, standing in a line with hands on each other's shoulders, moved as a unit following the gyration pattern, but avoiding being hit.

The most complex dexterity activity was the making of string figures, or "cat's cradle". Many an hour was whiled away fashioning intricate designs, and stories were told as the players would move from one creative figure to another. At times, up to eight people would work together and various parts of the body such as the teeth, knees, feet, necks as well as fingers were used. Although both sexes made string figures, the women generally could recall more designs and were able to make more elaborate manipulations. One woman was noted as being able to make over 200 different figures.

Imitation of real-life habits and activities was evident in children's play. In the lower Tully River and at Cape Bedford, girls fixed a forked stick on to the back of their necks, and imitated a mother carrying a baby, with its legs dangling over their shoulders. Imitating "iguanas" was a popular pastime with boys in the Upper Normanby district. One boy would lie down and cover up his forearms in sand. He would poke a finger up through the sand and pull the finger down again. Others would try to hit the finger with small sticks before it disappeared.

Various *pursuit* pastimes were played, such as a game that resembled hockey or, to be more correct, shinny. To play the game wooden balls and sticks were used, and there were few if any rules. The ball was hit from one person and from one place to another, but there were no goals.

Of the *strategy*-type activities, the game "hide and seek" was common, even among adults. Usually there were up to three who would participate and attempt to seek out the others who had obliterated their tracks or created false clues. Wrestling contests were also classified as strategy activities, and were essentially challenge matches.

Exultation was evident in many diverse pastimes such as singing games, corroborees, swinging and swimming. A form of tug-of-war practised among the McDonnell and Batavia River Aborigines also produced great enjoyment.

Memory games were examples of *enigma* activities. A hunter, for example, would hide his catch and players would be asked to guess the animal killed. Another similar game was called "hunt the eye", when the lens of a rat or a kangaroo's eye would be hidden in the sand, and other players had to locate it.

Vertigo activities included tobogganing and tree climbing. Also, Bloomfield River Aborigines enjoyed diving head first towards the ground from great heights. Attached to one leg was a vine which was just shorter than the distance from the top to the ground.

Chance activities encompassed various guessing games, as played at Cape Bedford. A game similar to "I Spy", where one person challenged the others to guess or "spy" what he had seen, was played.

Based on the play classification model, Salter concluded that Aboriginal games were played solely for enjoyment, victory was of minor importance, participation was close to maximum, the less skilful were encouraged to participate, game rules were few and simple, competition did not dominate play, activities were of a group rather than team type, and play was used to solidify tribal relationships and promote goodwill and social intercourse.[5]

In general, Europeans disdained the "primitive", uncivilised Aborigines, however they did occasionally acknowledge and admire some of their skills, such as those of hunting and fishing. Positive cultural exchange also occurred during the early years, in the sphere of games, particularly between the children of the white settlers and Aborigines. Unfortunately, such friendly interactions were not, in the main, recorded, and certainly were not appreciated by subsequent generations.

The first in Queensland to record the pastimes of the Moreton Bay Aborigines was Thomas Petrie. "Tom" Petrie, who as a young child came to Moreton Bay in 1837 with his father Andrew, was highly respected by the Aborigines, doubtless because of his early associations and interactions with them, and played with them and learned their language.

In his youth, Petrie remembered playing many different games with the Aborigines and he recounted such activities as 'kangaroo rat' (*Murrun Murrun*), catch–ball (*Purru Purru*), hoop and pole (*Murri Murri*), swimming and diving, playing with toy boomerangs and the cross (*Birbun–Birbun*), and various mimicry activities.

Their physical prowess, in strength and endurance, was readily apparent to Tom Petrie. He described how Moreton Bay blacks could walk great distances without tiring, even when carrying heavy loads on their heads. He also noted they were very fast runners, and that girls and boys would sometimes run races together.

Summary

Although positive cultural interaction resulted from the playing of games and the sharing of amusements, the lifestyle that the Aborigines had developed and lived with over the centuries was interfered with after white settlement. Indeed, the habits and ways of living of the Europeans were fundamentally in conflict with those of the Aborigines. This conflict was centred around land, its meaning, significance and utilisation.

The spiritual attachment to the land was not shared, nor even comprehended, by the Europeans who settled the land, built permanent settlements and worked the soil to produce products for their European–styled economy. The hunting, semi–nomadic lifestyle that the Aborigines had could not ultimately co–exist with the European lifestyle. Technologically, they were left behind.

The impact of the infiltration of Europeans into Aboriginal cultures throughout the world, including Australia, has been vividly described by Alan Moorehead in *The Fatal Impact*.[6] Diseases such as influenza, tuberculosis and venereal strains decimated whole populations, as such peoples had no resistance to these new scourges. There was abduction of Aboriginal women and children, a virtual trade in children, and prostitution of the women, which left "a legacy of disease". As Dr Roth put it in 1901, venereal disease was "very prevalent in the North–western districts, and along the Peninsula coast–line, especially on its lower Gulf shores, and, of course, is common in the neighbourhood of white settlement generally".[7] Their athleticism virtually disappeared as they became an overwhelmed culture.

Not many settlers shared Petrie's feelings of brotherly love, nor his beliefs in the "noble savage". Indeed, the more prevalent view was that expressed by a writer in 1858 in the *Moreton Bay Courier*, who spoke of the "wretched characteristics of our black civilization – their fearful superstition, their bestial tastes, their undisguised squalor and filth, their indolent habits and their nomadic dispositions".[8] These statements verged on a proclamation of manifest destiny, which essentially argued that as civilisation advanced savages had to be exterminated.

The Europeans and the indigenous society clashed fundamentally in the basic tenets of society, in their societal values and norms from which their particular lifestyle had evolved. The Aborigines lived in a society dominated by a *circle* or static philosophy, in which traditional values and beliefs were maintained, in which change was minimal, and territoriality basically defined. Each generation lived in a manner similar to the preceding generation. The Aborigines knew and understood the delicate balance between nature and their own survival. The *linear* or dynamic philosophy of the European settlers was based on a model of societal evolution and it stressed change, acquisition of property, decimation of animal life for sustenance and had little respect for the territorial rights of the indigenous population or their value system. The Aborigines never recovered from the "culture shock". The days of dreamtime were over, as a more rapacious culture had virtually caused the extermination of another by the dislocation of their natural resources, by slaughter and the forced imposition of an alien culture and its lifestyle.

As games and pastimes are intrinsic components of culture, inevitably when the culture is disturbed, or transformed, such activities would subsequently undergo modification or disappear. Traditional Aboriginal games and amusements had reinforced their culture and promoted goodwill and interpersonal relationships. Over the centuries the skills and techniques essential for survival had been learned and perfected through the playing of games. However, when their natural environment was restricted and dislocated, their food supply was interfered with and the methods of obtaining food had to be altered. Hence their traditional economically–related games lost their relevance. Moreover their games and amusements, which functioned to perpetuate their culture, were at variance with the new, superimposed culture and its differing norms and values. The games and amusements, that had been passed down from generation to generation and had complemented their own culture, were at variance with the modern western culture. The death knell sounded for them, and has lasted to the present day, and more is the pity, as their games were rich and profuse.

2

Early Settlers and Their Cultural Baggage

The Portuguese were the first known Europeans to sight Queensland, mapping Queensland's east coast in the early sixteenth century. Other explorers including the Dutch captain Willem Jansz followed. A Spaniard, Luis Vaes de Torres, late in 1606, made his way through the reefs at Endeavour Strait, and the Dutch under Jan Carstensz returned in 1623. Thus, despite popular belief, James Cook was not the first to sight these lands when he charted the shores and explored the terrain in 1770. However, he did name Cape Morton, the spelling of which has changed to Moreton with the ensuing years.

Matthew Flinders was the next to explore this area in 1799 and later again in 1802. When Sir Thomas Brisbane became Governor of New South Wales in 1821 it was decided to resettle the worst convicts at Moreton Bay or Port Curtis, present-day Gladstone. With this view in mind, Captain John Dingle explored the terrain in January 1822, and later in 1822 Captain William Edwardson carried on the task. The most significant exploration for the future of Queensland was that by Surveyor-General Oxley in 1823. To his surprise, when he arrived at Moreton Bay, he was hailed in English by a white man on the beach. The story of this person's presence was quickly revealed. He, Thomas Pamphlett, had been caught in a storm, carried north and ship-wrecked. Oxley kindly consented to take him back to "civilization" in New South Wales.

The convict settlement in the area was recommended by Oxley following his exploration. The first thirty convicts were sent north in 1824 on the ship *Amity*, and some forty more arrived the following year. A fifty-mile limit was placed on free settlement around Brisbane.

Eight months after the original settlement, Governor Brisbane wrote to Earl Bathurst that convicts who had escaped from Port Macquarie or who had committed minor offences in New South Wales would be "removed as necessary to Moreton Bay, which I should recommend as the Second place of punishment, viz., Port Macquarie for first grave offences; Moreton Bay, for runaways from the former; and Norfolk Island, as the *ne plus ultra* of Convict degradation".[1]

Fitzgerald has provided us with a summary of how the convicts survived:

> Some idea of the life-style of the early convicts of Moreton Bay can be gleaned by examining their rations and working hours. Each week every convict was entitled to 4 lb. (1.8 kg) of salt meat and 10.5 lbs (4.8 kg) of flour. Two shirts, two frocks, two pairs of shoes, and two pairs of trousers comprised each year's clothing provisions. Convicts worked from sunrise to 8 am., from 9.30 am. to midday, and from 2 pm. to sunset, from which one might reasonably suppose that they looked forward to the winter months, when working hours would be considerably shorter. Convicts bathed on Sunday mornings, and when "perfectly clean", were mustered for divine service performed by the commandant.[2]

In March 1826, Captain Logan took over the convict settlement, "and the clank of leg-irons and the whistle of the lash became the background music of the growing township".[3] In his four-and-a-half years' command of the settlement some 330 convicts escaped, indicative of the harshness of his regime. Logan was found dead in 1830, killed by either Aborigines or convicts.

During Logan's reign the Port Macquarie convict settlement closed, and therefore the Moreton Bay convict settlement became the largest on the mainland. The convict population by 1829 was approximately 1,000, increasing to 1,110 by 1832. Included among these numbers were some females, who were first housed in the women's factory near the present Brisbane GPO, and then moved down river to Eagle Farm.

By 1834 the convict numbers declined to 700, by 1839 to 94. No convicts were sent north to Moreton Bay after 1839. Allan Cunningham, in 1827, discovered the Darling Downs, naming the area in honour of the then Governor. Word of these extensive grazing grounds quickly spread, and squatters subsequently followed. Howe and Thomas Crompton, John Campbell, Patrick Leslie and his brothers, Disney Dalrymple, Arthur Hodgson and Gilbert Elliott, Joseph King and James Silbey, Henry Stuart Russell, David McConnell, William Humphreys and William Duckett White were but a few of these first settlers. The Leslie brothers, for example, gained 40,000 hectares for a squatting fee of 10 pounds a year. The concept of the squatter's licence for 10 pounds per annum was introduced by Governor Bourke in 1834. By 1844, there were 26 stations on the Darling Downs. During the next two years this number rapidly increased to 45, with an additional 37 on the eastern side of the range.

By 1841, as the most promising land on the Downs was already claimed, the squatters moved closer to Moreton Bay. With the closure of the convict settlement in 1842, Moreton Bay was opened up for free settlement.

The new settlement grew rapidly as settlers, as well as businesses, moved in to the newly opened lands. The populace became more diversified as it developed. One of the early editions of the *Moreton Bay Courier*, in 1846, reported the results of an extensive census conducted in the settlement.[4]

Both heredity and environment exert their influences on human-kind, and the European settlers who arrived in the land brought their own cultures or "cultural baggage" with them. As the 1846 census showed, the early settlers were predominantly male (1,123 to 476), single (1,110 to 489), from 21 to 44 years of age (985 to 614), born in the colony or came free (1,168 to 431), Protestant (1,019) compared to Roman Catholic (437), English (523) and Irish (425) rather than Scottish (164) or Welsh (3) or "foreign" born (38), and were blue collar (739) rather than white collar (116).

This census was not revealing in so far as the convict population was concerned, but the figures on the adult population of the Northern districts as of March, 1851, are of interest. By 1851 14 per cent of the population were still not free. Of the total population, 38 per cent of men in the Stanley district, 50 per cent in the Moreton district excluding Stanley, 62 per cent in the Darling Downs, 43 per cent in the Burnett, 66 per cent in the Maranoa and 32 per cent in the Wide Bay area had been transported to Australia. There were almost as many males transported (2,117) as came free (2,393). Thus the convict influence was still very pervasive well into the 1850's in Queensland.

Gradually the northern part of the colony grew quantitatively and qualitatively. By the late 50's it became apparent that this northern land should be separated from New South Wales and should stand on its own. Finally, in 1859, statehood was achieved. Holthouse very vividly summarised the culture and the lifestyles of the land squatters and the townspeople at this time.

> The colony's white population of about 28,000 was scattered along a few settlements, mainly on the south-eastern corner and on the Darling Downs.
> In this area there were four towns – Brisbane (which has been proclaimed a municipality on 7th September, 1859), Ipswich, Warwick and the towns of Drayton and Toowoomba...
> To the north of Brisbane were the growing townships of Maryborough near Furber's old store on the Mary River, Gladstone which had become a

port for northern settlers, and Rockhampton which had grown up on the Fitzroy River near the Archers' Gracemere homestead.

Squatters had laid claim to about ten million hectares on which they ran about three and a half million sheep, 500,000 cattle and 24,000 horses. The only roads were dray tracks through virgin bush. They crossed flats that became bogs when it rained, forded creeks that flooded, wound among tall trees between which the drays would hardly scrape, and along stony ridges and mountain slopes where a false step could send bullocks, drays and loadings rolling down to destruction. Wool and stores were often months on the tracks.[5]

The recreational life in the British Isles in the mid–nineteenth century can provide some insight into the recreational and sporting influences of the early settlers. At the beginning of the nineteenth century in the British Isles, the major feature was the village–oriented way of life, its year "generously studded with festivals and holidays".[6] As Crawford summarised it: "Popular leisure was public, boisterous and gregarious, and certain major holidays allowed social restraints to be tossed aside for the time–honoured ceremonies of saturnalia".[7]

This, then, was the pre–industrial period, but the invention of steam power had a profound effect on British social and political life, as it influenced the expansion of factories with resultant urbanisation. By the 1850s transportation was affected as railway lines brought towns within easy and swift access to one another. The character of the land changed dramatically during this period, though vestiges of the past were still there.

Despite the increasing urban character of Britain countless villages and small towns remained. 'But the old village life was losing some of its particular manifestations. Among these were ritualistic, traditional village activities and...village or rural sports and recreations'. The folk festivals of English fairs and Highland Gatherings continued, but more as attractive anachronisms than an embodiment of a pre–industrial culture. At the same time that village cricket went on there were lengthy sports pages in the cheap daily newspapers, telling of the big–time matches and the exploits of English internationals at Lord's. The rural sporting attention of the mid–nineteenth century focused on national and professional sports.[8]

As the village ethos of the British Isles diminished and industrialisation increased, a whole host of changes occurred. The 12 hour work week of the 1830s gave way to the Ten Hour Act in 1847, which became Saturday half–days by the 1870s. Transportation changes, local, regional and national, coupled with increased leisure time, opened up sport and changed its character, as indeed the character of society was similarly changed.

There was, as a consequence, a transition, from the 1850s, away from a pre-industrial to an industrial society. Robertson[9] has endeavoured to summarise some of the social and cultural changes in the transformation. Community size went from typically small villages to typically large cities. Social relationships in the village were personal and intimate, but in the cities these became impersonal and anonymous. The division of labour in a pre-industrial society was not extensive, other than on grounds of age and sex, whereas in an industrial society occupations were typically socialised.

The social structure was relatively simple in a pre-industrial society, but became increasingly complex in the industrial state. Spontaneous community action was a major factor in a pre-industrial society in endeavouring to effect social control, whereas it became more formal, with laws and courts, in an industrial society. The culture moved from a homogeneous one, with similar norms and values, to an increasingly heterogeneous one, with many subcultures, with differing norms and values.

Technology, of course, proceeded from a very primitive type, based mainly on human and animal power, to a more advanced one, based on machines. Social change occurred slowly in a pre-industrial society but became more rapid in the industrial society.

Changes were effected in the pastimes of the people as well, as there was a movement away from folk games to modern sports. Dunning and Sheard[10] described the structural-functional characteristics of folk-games which are seen in a pre-industrial society and those which are characterised by modern sport.

Features of folk-games, characteristic of the pre-industrial society, were informal organisation, simple and unwritten rules, dependency on tradition, regional variation in rules and equipment, difference in territorial definition and number of players, a loose distinction between the players and spectators, social control being informal and handled by the players, an emphasis on physical force rather than skill, a high level of socially tolerated violence, strong communal pressure demanding participation, and the fact that contests were of local meaning only.

The transition to modern sports sees such sport as being highly specific, with formal organisation, with a clear differentiation institutionally at local, regional, national and international levels. The rules became formal and elaborate, legitimated by national-bureaucratic bodies. Change was institutionalised by these controls. Rules, boundaries, equipment and numbers of participants were clearly defined. There was a clear distinction between players and spectators, and formal control was exerted by officials. Physical violence became controllable through the various rules, and skill tended to become more important than physical force. Individual choice became more normal in contrast with communal pressure, and national and international contests developed, with elite players and "monetisation" of sports.

Ingham and Beamish[11] developed a theoretical framework related to industrialisation and the instrumentalisation of sport linkages. This could have relevance for Australian sport. In brief summary, through industrialisation, which is an outgrowth of capitalism, there is accelerated urbanisation, technological innovation, expanded transport and communications. These developments occasion increased discretionary time and income, class restructuration and changes in ideological dimensions of the dominant meaning system. Each of these developments has an effect on sport. Some of these changes will be analysed in future chapters.

The settlers coming to Queensland in these early years, then, had been subjected to a high degree of societal change as a consequence of industrialisation. That change was also evident in sport, and many of the settlers had been subjected to the effects of industrialisation.

It is important to look at the changes being effected in sport in the British Isles, and the rate of progress of sport at the time the new settlers were moving into Queensland.

It is obvious by an analysis of McIntosh's[12] research on the development of national organisations in the British Isles (see table 1) that only horse-racing, golf, cricket and mountaineering developed national associations in the British isles prior to 1859. There was a surge towards the organisation of such bodies from 1860 to 1890. National codification of most sports was to occur after 1859 with the formation of these national associations. Local and regional rules in many sports were common.

However, a whole host of sports was known to at least some of the immigrants. Chariot and horse racing and various ball games had been known in Great Britain since Roman times, and "during the Middle Ages we hear running, jumping, weight-throwing, wrestling, single-stick and quarter-staff, football and golf".[13] Royal or Court Tennis, a forerunner of lawn tennis, was played in the 1400s, there being public courts in the period. Rackets was played between Oxford and Cambridge in 1858. Rackets was an early form of squash.

Archery, bowling, blood sports like bull and bear baiting, and cock fighting were practised by the 1600s, as well as cricket and stool-ball.

The first attempt to publish the laws of cricket was in 1752. The rules of the Marylebone Club (MCC) were published in 1788. The first Oxford-Cambridge cricket match was in 1827. Sussex (1839) and

Table 1. The organisation of British sport (McIntosh, 1968)

Sport	Earliest national organisation	Date
Horse Racing	Jockey Club	c. 1750
Golf	Royal & Ancient Club	1754
Cricket	Marylebone Cricket Club	1788
Mountaineering	Alpine Club	1857
Association Football	Football Association	1863
Athletics	Amateur Athletic Club	1866
	Amateur Athletic Association	1880
Swimming	Amateur Metropolitan Swimming Association	1869
Rugby Football	Rugby Football Union	1871
Sailing	Yacht Racing Association	1875
Cycling	Bicyclists' Union	1878
Skating	National Skating Association	1879
Rowing	Metropolitan Rowing Association	1879
Boxing	Amateur Boxing Association	1884
Hockey	Hockey Association	1886
Lawn Tennis	Lawn Tennis Association	1888
Badminton	Badminton Association	1895
Fencing	Amateur Fencing Association	1898

Source: P.C. McIntosh, *Sport in Society*, (London: C.A. Watts, 1968), p. 63.

Surrey (1844) were some of the early cricket clubs. The first cricket touring team to the United States and Canada went abroad in 1859. It was not until 1861–2 that the first team visited Australia.

As for rowing, the Doggett's Coat and Badge race was founded in 1715, for apprentice watermen. The first regatta was in 1775, for professional watermen. The first Oxford–Cambridge race was in 1829, the Henley Regatta in 1839.

Cowes was the site of the first yacht club in 1815, changing its name to the Royal Yacht Squadron in 1833. Liverpool built the first public swimming bath in 1828, and London had one in 1846.

There had been primitive forms of football since medieval times, with such as the Shrove Tuesday matches, when villages would play villages, with rules minimal and numbers of players variable. Hurling was mentioned in 1602, though it was played in Ireland well before that date. We know that football was played in Ireland in 1780.

What was the game of football was in a considerable state of flux in the 1800s, William Webb Ellis supposedly initiating the running game at Rugby School in 1823. It was not until 1863 that the two codes, association and rugby football, were clearly delineated. Until that time local and variant rules were utilised.

Robert Dover's Olympic Games in the Cotswold Hills were held about 1600, and the sports included wrestling, pitching the bar, throwing the sledge, tossing the pike, cudgel–playing and leaping, and Pepys' Diary in 1663 described a foot–race. Running foot–men were the early professionals. The first Oxford–Cambridge athletic contests were held in 1864, and the events were similar to those of today, only in yards. Walking (or pedestrianism) was another sport which occurred prior to 1850, and cross–country running by 1830.

Bowls is of very ancient origin, but it was codified in Scotland in 1849. Golf was another essentially Scottish activity that diffused rapidly, it being mentioned as early as 1457. Croquet had its precursors as early as 1611, but the term 'croquet' was first put in the Oxford Dictionary in 1858.

Wrestling was another early sport, being mentioned in Chaucer, as was boxing. James Figg opened a gymnasium, which included boxing, in 1720, and James Broughton introduced boxing gloves in 1745. Fencing and archery, of course, were other ancient sports.

As well as these more traditional sports, there were hundreds of recreational activities that were brought with the settlers: card–playing, children's games, billiards and board games, etc. These are summarised in Strutt.[14]

There was also the influence of the schools, particularly the Great Public Schools, such as Rugby, Eton, Harrow, Shrewsbury and so on, and the ethic of Muscular Christianity that was the credo of these schools. This fundamental belief in the world of sport – "the battle of Waterloo was won on the playing fields of Eton" – was an important factor in the introduction of sport to Australia. The concept was basically English. Games followed the flag. Where the Englishman went his games went with him. There was the rise of the new middle class in England, who saw sport as preserving social order and patriotism, as well as creating favourable and worthy personality characteristics such as discipline, obedience and courage. The class relationships of certain sports will be developed in later chapters.

There were also developments in the other areas of Australia that have to be considered.[15] Some sporting clubs had developed in Australia prior to 1859, such as the following (table 2).

Table 2. Some of Australia's first sports clubs up to 1850

Year	Sport	City of Formation
1814	Boxing	Sydney
1825	Horse Racing	Sydney
1826	Cricket	Sydney
1835	Rowing	Sydney
1836	Billiards	Sydney
1836	Sailing	Sydney
1842	Shooting	Sydney
1846	Lawn Bowling	Hobart
1847	Golf	Melbourne

Moreover, intercolonial contests had emerged, with cricket being played by 1851. The New South Wales Cricket Association was formed in 1858, demonstrating the same trend as in the British Isles towards the organisation of sport.

Summary

The immigrants who came to Queensland, then, were mainly in the early years from the British Isles, and they brought their "cultural baggage" with them. A part of that baggage was sport, and when there was available leisure time it was only natural that the activities done in their home–land would be recreated in the new land.

Queensland's First Sporting Industry: Horse–Racing to 1850

As Dunstan so aptly stated, for Australians their "earliest god and the one that calls for the greatest reverence is the horse."[1] Horses were not native to Australia, but were part of the cultural baggage that European settlers brought with them to the Antipodes. On the First Fleet in 1788 there were three mares, one stallion and three yearlings, and within ten years the number had risen to 117.[2]

Australian conditions were ideal for the horse, and by 1800 steps had been taken to improve the stock by importing Arabian horses as well as blood horses from England and America. The first official horse race was organised in 1810 in Sydney's Hyde Park. Since that time horse racing, whether it be in the form of organised racing at the track, challenge matches in the open, picnic races in the country, steeple chasing or trotting, has been the most popular sport for Australians. Collins and Thompson, in their historical overview of the turf in Queensland, reaffirmed this position, stating that Queenslanders "are heart and soul in the support of any horse the State can produce to pit against the cracks of the southern states."[3]

There are numerous factors that cultivated the popularity of horse–racing. Firstly, it was a recreational activity which offered relief from a generally harsh daily life, and it was conducted in pleasant surroundings that were reasonably easily accessible and could be indulged in generally by the whole family. Secondly, it was a pastime that appealed to all socio–economic groups. Thirdly, it provided an opportunity to gamble, which appealed to the basic instincts of many colonists, rich or poor. Fourthly, particularly in the early years, the horse was important in daily life, and there was a particular reverence attached to its performance, tenacity, endurance, speed and courage.

The convict settlement at Brisbane was formed in 1825, after initial attempts at Redcliffe failed. Free settlement was forbidden within a fifty–mile radius until 1842, though a few free settlers were in the area.

The first acres of Brisbane land were auctioned in Sydney in 1842. From 1825 to 1842, then, a period of some 17 years, Brisbane was the domicile for convicts, the military, some public servants and few free settlers. Outside the convict zone, graziers gradually occupied the Downs and were steadily moving on, northward and westward, in a relentless search for good land.

The leisure habits in the Moreton Bay Settlement in this 17–year period are virtually unknown. Doubtless convicts indulged in some gambling games and pugilistic contests, or brawls, but leisure for them was obviously virtually non–existent. The recreational and sporting habits of the remainder of the citizens can only be conjectured, and the soldiers doubtless gambling and testing their strength and endurance in running, wrestling and boxing, and indulging in shooting and fishing when the opportunity presented itself. Card and dice games would have been popular, and the basic desire for leisure would have given cause for invention and modification in the new environment in which they found themselves. The pleasant Queensland climate would have encouraged outdoor activities.

The officer class and other leaders in the society such as Andrew Petrie hunted and fished, perhaps encouraged regiment sports which allowed for activities like boxing and athletics, and above all else indulged in activities related to the horse, as they were the only members of Brisbane society that owned them. Horse–racing, then, would have been one of the earliest amusements for those in Brisbane, and most certainly for those outside of the restricted area, in the area of free settlement. Friendly challenge races would have been soon in evidence. Gradually, races that were held became more organised and definite race programs were established. "The Rambler" opined about those early days.

> Squatters and officers of the military regiment stationed in Brisbane – dare-
> devil fellows with silken beards and gallant moustaches and side burns –
> raced their spirited mounts over the tracks and the jumps on Saturday
> afternoons and holidays. There were gay doings in the little town on those
> festive occasions, when the dignified matrons of Brisbane and demure
> maidens in voluminous skirts and lace bonnets tripped gaily through the
> tree–stumps, attended by gallant swains, with picnic baskets on their arms.[4]

The First Races: Prior to 1846

It is generally believed that the first race–course in Brisbane, and Queensland, was established at Cooper's (or Cowper's) Plains in 1843, one year after Brisbane was opened up for settlement. Petrie, however, takes us back earlier than this generally-acknowledged date.

> The very first racecourse in Brisbane was started by the squatters on the ground occupied by the present Post Office, etc... Well, the course was from the corner of the old wall surrounding this building (just where the Telegraph Office now stands), down as far as Albert Street, and it was about here that a three-railed fence and a ditch some feet wide were jumped. Then the course continued round towards the Gardens, the same ditch and fence being jumped again lower down; then up round by the R.C. Cathedral, and back to the corner of the wall. The ditch mentioned was cut as a drain to carry water (for the land was swampy) into a small creek that ran into the river at the present Post Office wharf. The place all round was fenced in cultivation paddocks, where the prisoners worked.

> When people commenced to settle a little and build, a man named Greenyead built a house at South Brisbane, at Kurilpa (pronounced in English, Kureelpa) – that we now call West End. This man obtained a license for a public house, and the squatters then started a racecourse there. The next one was at Cooper's Plains, and the next at New Farm.[5]

There appear, then, to have been at least two race-courses utilised in Brisbane before the one at Cooper's Plains, one near the present Post Office, and the other at Kurilpa. The squatters, then, came into the restricted convict area at certain times, with permission, doubtless to buy goods, to trade and to participate in any leisure pursuits that were available, from drinking to horse-racing.

Much of the preceding is conjecture. What is for certain is that the first mention of horse-racing, or for that matter of any sport, in the Moreton Bay Settlement area, was on February 22 1843 in the *Sydney Morning Herald*. This report, then, occurred the year following the opening up of the territory for free settlement.

Brisbane, February 15, Moreton Bay (1843)

> We have had a meeting of several sporting men of this district, at Bow's, "Victoria", North Brisbane, towards establishing annual races at this place, the result has been, that in June next, the first of their meetings on the turf will take place at Cooper's Plains, a beautiful spot for the young bloods to make their first appearance, about six miles from the settlement. A considerable fund has already been subscribed, and a steeple chase on the intervening day will come off at North Brisbane; further information will appear in your advertising columns for the information of the up-country gentlemen.[6]

It should be emphasised that the steeplechase race on the second day was scheduled for North Brisbane, and it is possible that this was the first experimental use of the New Farm site.

This newspaper report was followed by another notice that the first meeting would indeed be at the New Race Course at Cooper's Plains, under the jurisdiction of the Moreton Bay Racing Club, on the 12th, 13th and 14th of July. The colonists felt that because of this event they "may be considered almost out of pale of civilized society",[7] that is, they equated the organising of horse races as an indicator of having achieved a 'civilised' state. The complete program was presented, and it was noted that the "new race-course is in a pretty spot, and by the time of the meeting will be wholly cleaned and stumped, the length, one mile and a distance".[8] The stewards for this historic meeting were announced: C. Mackenzie, Esq., Walter Leslie, Esq., and Lieut. Johnstone, 99th Regiment, Judge – D. Hunter, Esq., Clerk of the Course, D.B. Hawkins, Esq. Apart from Johnstone, the others were members of the squattocracy, and their names were to figure prominently in the early history of horse-racing in the city. Because of the importance of the initial meeting, the report is reproduced in its entirety.[9]

Owing to the very hot weather we have had lately, the maiden meeting of the Moreton Bay Jockey Club did not come off until the 17th instant, when some excellent sport was afforded; but I am sorry to say that scarcity of cash was the general cry, so much so that usual animation of the race week was out of the question. Annexed is an account of the three days' sport. The members of the Jockey Club, and their friends, wound up the festivities with a dinner at Bow's Victoria Hotel, on the evening of the last day's racing. Every one stands pledged to make the next meeting an out-and-out concern, but it is to be wished that next year an earlier period will be fixed, as the present month is certainly the dullest time of the year in Brisbane. An affair of honour was nipped in the bud, by our active Chief Constable placing his bunch of fives on one of the belligerent party, on the evening before the meeting was to have taken place. The next morning, Captain Wickham, the Police Magistrate, bound them over to keep the peace: at present, so the matter stands.

MORETON BAY RACES
MONDAY, JULY 17

The Brisbane Town Plate of 30 sovereigns, with a sweepstake of 3 sovereigns each added, for all horses-weight for age – heats

Mr. Hawkin's Whig, aged 1
Mr. Hunter's Conservative (by Grates) 4 years 2

Betting – five to one on Conservative

The Maiden Plate for 25 sovereigns, with a sweepstakes of 2 sovereigns each added, for all horses that never won before the day of that race – weight for age – heats

Mr. F.W. Bigge's Splinter, aged 1
Mr. Marriott's Paddy, aged 2
Mr. Smyth's Charcoal, 5 years 3
Two others started, but were not placed.

Betting – three to one against the winner

The Welter Stakes of 20 sovereigns, with a sweepstakes of 2 sovereigns each added, for all horses carrying 12 stone – three miles.

Mr. Bigg's Satellite, aged 1
Mr. Mackenzie's Old Jerry, aged 2
Three others started, but were not placed.

Betting – three to one against Satellite, and five to one against Old Jerry.

TUESDAY, JULY 18

The Hurdle Race of 30 sovereigns, with a sweepstakes of 3 sovereigns each added, for all horses – weight for age – three miles.

Mr. Hawkin's Billy, aged 1
Mr. Dalrymple's Ebony, aged 2
The others not placed.

The Hack Hurdle Race of 10 sovereigns, with a sweepstakes of 2 sovereigns each added, for untrained hacks – catch weights – mile heats.

Mr. W. Leslie's Buck's – foot 1
Mr. Bigge's Stump 2
Mr. Hawkin's Niche 3

WEDNESDAY, JULY 19

The Publican's Purse of 30 sovereigns, with sweepstakes of 3 sovereigns each added, for all horses – weight for age – heats –

Mr. Bigg's Splinter, aged 1
Mr. Marriott's Lizard, aged 2
Mr. McKenzie's Governor, 4 years 3
Mr. Hunter's Whipcord, 4 years 4

Betting – six to four against the Lizard; three to two against Splinter; and two to one against Governor. The first heat Splinter made running at a good pace, and at the post had disposed of all his opponents except Lizard, who challenged him but lost a splendid race by a head.

The Tally-Ho Stakes of £20, with a sweepstakes of 2 sovereigns each added, for all horses carrying 11 stone 7 – three miles.

Mr. Hawkin's Whig, aged 1
Mr. Bigge's Satellite 2
Mr. McKenzie's Blue Beard 3

Betting – Five to two on Whig

The only two entrances for the Beaten Stakes were –

Mr. Smyths' Charcoal 1
Mr. McKenzie's Governor 2

Mr Bigge's horses ran in at least five races at this historic meeting, and he was the most successful owner, with three wins and two seconds. Both Hawkins and Mackenzie were in four events, with Hawkins coming up with three firsts and a third, and MacKenzie being winless on the day. Other owners, well known in the colony, were Hunter, Marriott, Smyth, Dalrymple and W. Leslie.

This interest in horse–racing in the emerging settlement was enhanced when news broke of a highly prized purchase. "Our stud masters have received a valuable acquisition this season by the introduction of the entire horse Mentor into the district, by Messrs. Hunter and Fyfe, who it must be admitted deserve every encouragement for their spirited speculation."[10]

A further notice some five months later alerted turf enthusiasts that the second meeting of the Moreton Bay Jockey Club would be held in May 1844, an attempt being made to escape the bad weather of the previous year. It was noted that the newly acquired Mentor was favourite for the Plate, and that it had been purchased from Hunter and Fyfe by the wealthy squatter–businessman, Evan Mackenzie.[11]

Brisbane Town's second race meeting was considerably more organised and was again extensively covered by the Sydney paper. Such precise, detailed coverage of the occasion was indicative that such races were highly ranked for newsworthiness, not only for the local populace but also for Southern Turf enthusiasts.

The races were held on May 13, 14 and 15 at "Cowper's" Plains,[12] and as well as the Brisbane Town Plate, the Maiden Plate and the Publican's Purse, each best–of–two heats, there were single races such as the Welter Stakes, the Tally–Ho Stakes, The Hack Race and the Beaten Stakes, and two steeple–chase events, the Hurdle Race and the Hack Hurdle Races. There were several private matches and a number of sweepstakes each day, and a race dinner was held at the Brisbane Hotel.

A new owner, Mr Campbell, entered four horses in this Second Race Meeting – Spitfire, Bachelor, Harkaway and Champion – in nine races, gaining two firsts and four seconds. Evan Mackenzie, with the acquisition of Mentor, and perhaps smarting from his lack of success at the meeting of the previous year, raced twice for two firsts. Both Bigge – one win, one second and two thirds – and Leslie – two wins and two seconds – showed the consistency that was to be demonstrated in their stables in the years to come.

What was clear, from this meeting, was that if the owners themselves were not the jockeys, then other owners would race for them. MacKenzie was aboard Mentor in its two wins; Bigge raced Splinter and Satellite; Campbell was Harkaway's jockey once, but depended on McDonald on the other occasions, at least showing confidence in Scottish heritage in his jockey selection; W. Leslie raced one himself, but relied on G. Leslie and C.J. Mackenzie for his other entries; owner E.B. Harkins rode mounts for Mr Humphrey, whereas G. Burgoyne and George Leslie acted as jockeys for Hawkins. In all, Bigge and McDonald rode in four races, Evan Mackenzie, Burgoyne and C.J. Mackenzie three each.

In addition to such annual races, there were occasionally other forms of racing, such as a steeple-chase which was held on April 22 1845 at North Brisbane. It was, reportedly, "got up by a few of the right sort."[13] Owner-riders competed: Mr McKenzie on Cinderella, Mr J. Campbell on Giggler, Mr Whitting on It-can't-be-done and Mr Hawkins on It-must-be-done, the latter winning. Campbell's horse hit one of the rails and rolled over him, causing him to drop out, and McKenzie's horse tripped and threw him, but he remounted and finished second. The excitement was such that these two horses raced again, with the result being a dead heat.

The *Sydney Morning Herald* carried the announcement that the Third Annual Meeting of the Moreton Bay Jockey Club would be held on June 17 at "Cowper's Plains Racecourse".[14] It was actually held on the 18th, 19th and 20th of June that year.[15]

The 1846 Races

The venue for the Fourth Annual Meeting in 1846 was designated as being at New Farm, not Cooper's (or Cowper's) Plans. This meeting marked the first newspaper reporting of a sports event in the colony itself, as the race meeting was described in the inaugural issue of the *Moreton Bay Courier*, Queensland's first newspaper.

THE RACES

The Annual Meeting of the Moreton Bay Racing Club, took place at the Race Course, New Farm, on Tuesday and two following days in the past week. The attendance on the course was not only numerous but boasting more than an average of respectability. The sun shone brightly, and judging from the happy faces of the holiday folks, it was evident that all came there to enjoy themselves, and to take part in the amusements. The greater part of the assembled throng consisted of pedestrians, who like ourselves, chose to make use of that far-famed animal known as Shanks' mare for the occasion. Included (?) were a goodly number of the fair sex dressed out in holiday attire, which with the bright costumes of the gentleman jockeys, gave a most animated appearance to the scene. It only wanted a bank of music to add to the harmony of the proceedings, and make the mirth and excitement complete. Some of the booths were gaily decorated with flags; others with drapery, while the less ambitious were ornamented with the productions of nature, which gave them a rustic appearance. The spread at the several tables was very substantial, and ample justice was done to the many good things provided for the visitors. Our friend "David" at the Victoria, as such, got a large share of patronage.[16]

By 1846, the sport of horse-racing was firmly ensconced, this being the fourth annual meeting. These meetings were traditionally three-day affairs and, in 1846, they were held on Tuesday, the 16th of June, and then, presumably, on Wednesday the 17th and Thursday the 18th.

The program that emerged over these years was somewhat uneven, with four events on the first and second days and six on the third. It was, however, a varied program with distances ranging from once around the course to three times around the course. There were races for established racing horses, for maidens, for untrained hacks, for beaten horses, and for horses carrying different weights. There were two hurdle races, on the middle day, as well as those of the more informal variety, such as the Hurry Skurry Stakes, in which any horse could be entered. Heats were conducted in about fifty per cent of the races.

A detailed description of each individual race was vividly recounted in this first edition. For example, in the very first race: "A charge of foul riding was brought against the rider of Toby; and the Stewards, having heard evidence, *pro* and *con*, decided that it had been substantiated. Toby was accordingly adjusted to be distanced, and Mr. Bigge became entitled to the stakes."[17]

There appeared to be problems in virtually every race. In the Hurdle Race, one of the riders was unseated, another horse refused to jump and "threw his rider with fearful force against the hurdles [which] placed him hors de combat."[18]

In the Hack Hurdles Race, which followed,

> ...Cantab, in baulking at the third leap, turned a complete sommerset [sic] over the ropes, fortunately without any serious injury to poor Sandy [the black rider], who immediately remounted, and cleared it beautifully amidst the plaudits of the company. A subscription was shortly afterwards entered into by the gentlemen present, and the amount was handed over to him, by way of encouragement, for his spirited conduct.[19]

In another two-horse race, one of the riders was thrown. "Mr Hawkins, in witnessing this untoward event, pulled up his horse, and coolly waited until his friend Colin had picked himself up and remounted."[20] This was an excellent example of sportsmanship which obviously had not been the case in the Brisbane Town Plate Race. In that race an adjudgment of foul riding was given.

An amusing account was related by Knight about this 1846 Meeting.

> While intensely interested in the proceedings he (Russell) was approached by Mr. Frank Bigge's French groom, Douyere, who thus accosted him:
>
> "I vas to ask you, sare, if you would ride Voltigeur for Mr Frank in the hurdles, sare? His veight is too mush, he will take de'velters' himself on de old horse"
>
> "Oh, yes! Douyere," said I.
>
> "Thank you, sare! Now I will tell you, sare! Voltigeur can jump well like de gangaroo! You do ride, I tink, some ten stone. He will carry you like von monkey! But, sare, I must tell you: Voltigeur do not talk the Inglish. Ven you come to de hurdle you touch him on de shoulder vid de vip, and cry 'hoopela!' in his own language."
>
> "Ay, ay! Douyere, I'll remember."
>
> Out of the scales into Voltigeur's saddle – sweet little horse he was! "Mind, sare!" were the last words I heard after "off" – "mind, sare, he talk de Francais!"
>
> "Hoope-la!" shouted I with the prescribed touch on the shoulder, and over he went :like a gangaroo." "Hoope-la! at the second; "Hup!" at the third – forgetting myself in the heat – Voltigeur caught the top bar, and making a complete somersault, rolled over, me under! Somewhat confused by the "pip", the voice of Douyere brought me to me senses.
>
> "Ah! sare, you did call de 'hop!' not de 'Hoope-la!' Voltigeur did not – ne comprehend pas l'Anglais!"
>
> "For years after," writes Mr. Russell, "I was greeted with a 'Hop!' by my friends. This was my last lesson in French."[21]

There were a few administrative and organisational problems related to the conduct of the races. A decision with respect to the right to the stakes was deferred in the Ladies' Purse, it being alleged that the age of one of the horses was "not correctly entered".[22] A false start occurred at the commencement of The Hack Stakes, "in consequence of some unauthorised officious individual giving the word 'off'."[23] The Publicans' Purse resulted in a walk-over, as only one horse entered.

The report of the annual meeting of 1846 concluded with the following remarks.

No serious accidents occurred to mar the pleasures of the sports, and every thing passed off exceedingly well. The stewards, as well as the Clerk of the Course, gave general satisfaction. The Race Dinner took place on the 28th Ult., at the Victoria Hotel, and we understand the entertainment was first rate – the worthy host and hostess having spared neither expense nor pains in making a display suitable to the festive occasion.[24]

After the dinner, however, "some of the exhilarated squatters celebrated...by removing signs, and indeed, everything moveable, not even forgetting the Government flagstaff and belfry, which stood somewhere opposite the present Town Hall".[25] Obviously, when some of the squatters came to town, there was a little hell to pay. Knight also reflected on these early days at New Farm when one would "liquor up at Bow's or McAdams Hotel. Foot races were run out on the streets"[26] and there was generally a convivial atmosphere.

The majority of the riders continued to be, in 1846, "gentleman" jockeys, mainly owners and "amateurs". However, they readily accepted the purses for victory! Many of the same names recur in the major races, such as Messrs Bigge, Burgoyne, Berkeley, Hawkins, Furber and Whitting. These names also appeared in the committee positions in racing and other sporting activities throughout early settlement. A marked exception in this 1846 meeting was one rider in the Hack Hurdle Race, the jockey of Cantab, who was noted as being Sandy, black boy.

The population statistics of 1846 provide an interesting insight into the make-up of the population. From table 3[27] numerical dominance of males is readily apparent, with males comprising about two-thirds of the total population at the time.

What is more relevant from the quantitative data is that there were in this year[28] only 55 individuals in the district who had a voter's qualification, that is, had the "possession of an estate in freehold in lands or tenements, situate, of course, within the district, of the clear value of £200 above all charges and encumbrances, or the occupancy of a house rated at a rent value of £20 a year." those who merited the voter's qualification and most were to loom largely in the district's history, were: Thomas Adams, David Ballow, Arthur Binstead, David Bow, John Burgess, John Boyland, David Bunton, Kersey Cannan, Richard Cannan, John Campbell, Richard G. Coley, William M. Dorsay, Robert Davidson, Robert Dix, George Edmondstone, Andrew Graham,

Table 3. Population of southeast Queensland in 1846

District	Males	Females
North Brisbane	299	180
South Brisbane	209	137
Ipswich	64	39
Squatting Stations	390	92
Military & Government Stations	160	25
Totals	1122	473

John Gregor, Thomas H. Green, Jacob Goode, John Harris, Thomas Horsman, William Handcock, James Hill, Henry G. Isaac, John Kelly, Edward Lord, Benjamin Lee, Henry Lynch, Patrick Leslie, George Little, Louis F. Layard, John McConnel, David McConnel, Thomas Moore, John Ocock, Richard F. Phelan, David Peattie, Andrew Petrie, Daniel Petersen, William Pickering, John Richardson, Robert Rowland, John Shepherd, William Sheehan, Michael Sheehan, Daniel Skyring, George M. Slade, John Smith, George Thorne, William H. Thomson, Henry Wade, John C. Wickham, Alex Wright, James Warren, John Williams.[29] Surprisingly few of these "voters" were the owners of the horses, with the Cannans, Edmonstone, the Leslies and David Bow the publican being the only ones. The clear explanation is that most of the leadership in horse-racing, then, came from the squattocracy, who up to 1846 had their principal residences outside of the area originally designated as the convict settlement.

It became obvious by 1846, then, that although improvements could be made in the organisation of the meetings conducted by the Moreton Bay Racing Club, the races represented a considerable social occasion for the leading citizens. They dressed suitably on these occasions, mimicking those at the race meetings in Europe. Over and above the social attraction, the races presented an opportunity for the squatters, and other horse owners, to test their horses in organised competition. For poor colonists the races gave them a respite from their daily toils, as well as an opportunity to gamble.

The Races: The Struggle for Control in Brisbane

The 1846 races, in spite of the apparent problems, had been a success, and the concept of conducting annual races for the community was clearly established. However, the Brisbane Races, instead of growing in strength after 1846, actually declined because of the factional in-fighting that ensued. By 1847, it was apparent that there had been criticism of the Club by the sporting public. The Club members reserved the right for races to be run for by Club subscribers only; it was simply a matter of a desire for exclusiveness by the subscribers to the Club. With egalitarian philosophies prevalent among many of the citizens, such class control of both a sport and an entertainment was not received in a kindly manner, particular as the size of purses grew, as well as the crowds in attendance.

There was a battle for control going on between the racing fraternity and the public. The Hon. Treasurer and Secretary of the Moreton Bay Racing Club, Mr Patrick Leslie, resigned, presumably over the issue. The Leslie family, owners of a stud farm at Canning Downs, represented the squattocracy and their desire for elitist control. Leslie was replaced as Treasurer and Secretary by Dr Cannan, another owner. The significance of the issue provoked the editor of the newspaper to take a stand:

> We believe that the Club now comprises upwards of sixty—four members, who have agreed to subscribe £3 3s. each towards the racing fund to be appropriated for prizes, which will have to be contended for by horses owned by members of the Club. It is generally understood that in consequence of some unpleasantness between the sporting gentlemen and some of the inhabitants of Brisbane, at the last meeting, no subscriptions will be solicited from persons residing in the town. If any of the inhabitants wish to contribute towards the fund their subscriptions will, however, be very acceptable, as the Committee will then be enabled to make the stakes larger than last year, and, of course, of more consequence than formerly. However this may be, it is very desirable that one or two of the stakes should be enlarged to create greater emulation; for it is hardly worth any one's while to train a horse to contend for such comparatively small sums. We throw out these hints for the consideration of the committee of management, with the hope that they will not allow the funds to be frittered away into numerous small stakes, which always have a prejudicial effect, particularly where country races are concerned.[29]

Subsequently a compromise position was adopted, which allowed individuals other than subscribers to contribute to the racing fund.[30] However, as was later evident, such a compromise was not sufficient.

The 1847 annual races were organised and conducted without any major problem. However, their overall success did not approximate that of 1846. Such was evident by the *Courier's* comment that "the attendance was more select than numerous."[31] This statement reflected the continuing animosity and controversy that surrounded the running of the Brisbane Races, many of the squatters demonstrating their displeasure by staying away. The issue of elite subscriber's versus public control was complicated by the 'townspeople' versus 'squatter' rift. The townspeople had come to resent the squatters, who did not have their principal residence in Brisbane Town, but wished to dominate and control the town's affairs in racing and other matters. Moreover, many townspeople were chagrined "by squatters coming roaring into town and racing their horses up and down the streets".[32] Many squatters were in disagreement that Brisbane should be the major port and the commercial centre of the settlement. They preferred Cleveland, which they considered to be a superior port, or Ipswich, which was closer to their properties. Many refused to support anything related to Brisbane and indeed "the people of Ipswich and the back country refused to countenance the proceedings. Had the races been held at Cleveland Point they would, perhaps, have subscribed liberally".[33]

The controversy continued to fester and surfaced again for the 1848 races. The advertisement for the annual races that year announced a significant change, which appeared at the end of the program. It was noted that the "Brisbane Town Plate and the Publicans' Purse are open to all horses and riders. In other races, members of the Club alone are permitted to ride and enter horses."[34] The opening of only two races to the public, however, did not meet with public approval, as the announcement came only two or three days prior to the meeting. The editor continued to argue the case and warned the club: "either let the races be public, or strictly private, otherwise a death blow will be given to legitimate racing in the district. {A combination is] not compatible with good sport."[35]

The racing committee, the next year, 1849, perhaps swayed by the criticisms of the previous year, shifted in its stance and it was announced on March 24 1849, that the Brisbane races would forego their previous restrictions. "The principle upon which they go is that the course will be open to all horses entered by a subscriber to a certain amount, and that the horses are open to all riders."[36] This was a considerable change in philosophy, and moved racing towards democratisation. The races were now renamed the 'First' Brisbane Races, and a new executive was elected. Although the principle of public control was established, there appeared to be still some questions related to the involvement of working men in the races. At the 1849 races, there were claims that the horse Forester had been disqualified as it was "backed by working men,"[37] and in the Hurry Skurry race special mention appeared to be made of the fact that the black gelding was "the property of a working man."[38] However, as the 1849 Races drew a much greater crowd than the previous year it indicated "the experiment [was] proving successful."[39]

In spite of this apparent success, the controversy was not settled to the satisfaction of the parties, and as a consequence, in 1850 the 'annual' races were not organised in Brisbane.

Diffusion of Racing: 1846–1850

Prior to 1848, organised race meetings were held only in and around Brisbane Town. As the settlement grew and increasing numbers of colonists settled further from the town centre, the accessibility of the race-course became of paramount concern.

In 1846, when the move was made to New Farm, and the majority went by foot, there were complaints of "the great distance combined with the dreary nature of the road."[40] The entrepreneurial owner of the steamer 'Experiment'[41] – which had acted as the flagship for the 1848 Regatta – realised the viability of providing transport service for race-goers, and organised special 'race' excursions for the 1847 Races:

RACES! RACES!

THE STEAMER *EXPERIMENT* will ply between Brisbane and the Race Course at New Farm, on each day of the Races.
Fares to and fro: Cabin, 3s; Steerage, 2s.
Refreshments will be provided on Board.
N.B. – Parties residing in Limestone [Ipswich] desirous of attending the races may make such arrangements as will suit their convenience regarding the time of going and returning by the steamer, on application to Mr Elkins, at Ipswich.[42]

These excursions were a success, and a tradition was thereby established. For the 1848 Races, the 'Experiment' even added to the festivities by providing a band for the passengers during their journey to and from the races.[43] Knight was particularly appreciative of the music, as the drumming marked the ship's "position on the river when the deepening shades of evening rendered her form indistinct to optical perception, and if it was not exactly what the poet meant by the expression 'music on the waters' it was, as Sam Weller said on a rather different occasion, 'a very good imitation of it'."[44] These steamer excursions proved to be so successful that another steamer, the 'Raven', joined the 'Experiment' in the race passenger trade in 1849. Even with the availability of two boats the demand was such that "they seemed to be crowded."[45]

The sport of horse-racing, and the industry associated with it, was not confined to the Brisbane area. In May, 1848, it was noted in the *Moreton Bay Courier* that the horse Meteor was at Drayton racing, and he had just competed at the Armidale races. This was the first indication that a "horse-racing" circuit was being established. In the same article it was noted that "the Drayton folks have it in contemplation to get up races themselves, upon the same principle as those forthcoming at Brisbane."[46] Such a desire became a reality with the formation of the Drayton Racing Club. Its initial two-day program was announced in the *Moreton Bay Courier* on May 20th, 1848, the main event being the Drayton Flats, worth thirty sovereigns.[47] Interestingly, the Drayton Committee limited participants to subscribers, except for the Hack Race.

The Drayton Races were an immediate success and were well patronised by gentlemen and ladies from surrounding districts. The *Courier's* reporter vividly recounted this grand occasion.

> ...shortly afterwards [spectators] arrived on the course, where only last year the whole was a waste, but which was now thronged with several hundred pleasure seekers, either in stylish landaus or other vehicles, on horseback or on foot. What a change had a few months wrought? Here was a scene which in many of its features reminded us of old times in England. An excellent course, situated on a fine plain, with "all the appurtenances thereunto belonging", which together with highly trained and thorough-bred horses of the same stamp as winners of the principal stakes in England, afforded a field of attraction rarely met with in a newly inhabited country.[48]

In 1850 Ipswich became the next centre to organise separate races. On March 20, 1850, the *Moreton Bay Courier* announced the race meetings for that year: at Warwick, on the 23rd, 24th and 25th of April; Drayton, on May 14th, 15th and 16th; and Ipswich, on the 11th and 12th of June. A racing circuit had been established in the colony, Ipswich organisers selecting their dates so as to "enable the horses running at Warwick to come on to Drayton, and from thence proceed to Ipswich."[49] Unfortunately not all the meetings followed the same regulations, there being variations in weight-for-ages and other specific rules. The Warwick and Ipswich Rules followed those of the Newmarket Jockey Club in England, while the Drayton Rules followed those of Homebush. There was, however, gradually increasing sophistication with respect to the rules and organisation.

These race meetings served a local integrative function, for they brought the community together and offered an avenue for the development of local pride. At these meetings local horses were displayed and their prowess was compared to those from other areas. Newspapers were utilised to boost local feelings, and these were manifested in letters to the editor.

> ...It is not certain yet what horses are to contend for the prizes, as the Drayton sportsmen have hung fire in a most unaccountable way. Are they afraid of meeting the Warwick maidens? If so, I can assure them the latter will not be at all backward in showing their brazen faces at the Springs;— brazen I say, for I think it does show a little brass in the four-year-old untried filly, just eight weeks since first mounted, coming forward to vie with old standards. We yet hope that we may have the pleasure of their, as well as other, society and support... Great disappointment was manifested at the apparent cowardice of the Drayton sportsmen. The fact that a four-year-old untried filly cantered round for the Warwick Stakes, when there were three tried horses within 50 miles of the course, speaks for itself. Shame on ye, Draytonians![50]

Sectional rivalry became apparent when Ipswich was described as "this go-ahead remote village."[51] In spite of this burst of jealousy, a frank admission was made that Ipswich's race-course was "about, if not actually the best in the colony."[52]

In addition to scheduled races at race meetings, private challenge races were run, sometimes shortly after an official program had ended, or on the next day. However, many 'sporting' gentlemen were not satisfied with races being held only once a year and hence arranged private matches throughout the year to maintain their's, and other's, interest. Campbell and Leslie, two prominent squatters, were ones who frequently indulged in such challenges.

> Yesterday a private match was run between Mr. Archibald Campbell's Julius Caesar against Mr. G. Leslie's Harlequin, for £10 a side; heats once round and a distance; which was won easily by the former. Mr. Russell rode the winner. Notwithstanding the heavy shower of rain which fell in the morning, several other private matches took place on the course, and afforded a good deal of amusement.[53]

These contests often attracted a sizeable crowd, with bets waged liberally 'on the side'. Such matches, in addition to providing occasions for gambling, served as an opportunity for an owner to display his prowess and enforce his position in the community. Private matches were not restricted to the upper classes, as all segments of the colony indulged in such pursuits. Occasionally challenges would be proclaimed in the press.

CHALLENGE

BARONET is open to run TOBY round the new Farm Course, one mile and distance, Heats, or twice round the Course, carrying 11 stone 10 lbs., within two months from this date, for fifty Pounds. D. Bow.[54]

Although it was not as popular as horse–racing, trotting also captured community support. Such events were offered in Ipswich in 1850.

With such an intense interest in horse–racing, as well as the primary economic and social needs of owning a horse, it was obvious that a stud industry would soon emerge. Stud breeding became very specialised, stallions being used for specific needs. Although early advertisements were confined in Brisbane studs, squatters in outlying areas soon realised the market potential. Advertisements started to appear from Brisbane River properties such as Kilcoy, as well as from Canning Downs and the Darling Downs. These advertisements were often a response to the large number of horses that at times were needed. For example, the East India Company announced their intention of purchasing 120 horses, to be sent to Calcutta.[55] Newspaper advertisements aptly demonstrated how specialised the stud market had become, as there were four distinct categorisations: (1) draft horses; (2) horses for the Indian trade; (3) roadsters; and (4) race–horses.[56]

The major interest was associated with the fourth category, that is, race horses. Patrons of the turf were most concerned with improving the blood lines. The areas of the country where the farms were located are of considerable interest, as are the owners, who became leading figures in promoting thoroughbred racing. Mr. Bigge, for example, rode and owned horses in the first Brisbane meetings and his stud was on the Brisbane River. The Leslies were at Canning Downs, another owner was at Glengallan on the Darling Downs, and another was at Kilcoy on the Brisbane River. Two examples of advertisements are;

TO STAND THIS SEASON,
AT CANNING DOWNS

The following STALLIONS, the property of Messrs W and G Leslie –
KNAVE OF CLUBS – a brown–black Horse, standing 16 1/2 hands high, got by the thorough–bred horse Tros, (imported by H.H. Kater, Esq., in 1839); dam Lady Mary (imported in 1839) by Redlamite – her dam by Woful, grand dam by Orville, out of Tempetta by Trumpator.
Terms – Five Guineas a Mare
EAGLE – a bay Horse, standing 16 hands 1 inch high: foaled in 1843; got by the thorough–bred imported horse St. George – dam by Old Whisker, her dam by Steeltrap, out of a mare by Hector.

Terms – Four Guineas a Mare.

ST. ANDREW – a roan Horse; foaled in 1841; stands 15 hands 3 inches high; got by St. George – dam by Stride, her dam by Champion – g. dam by Sheik, out of an imported mare.

Terms £2.12s. 6d. a Mare

CONSERVATIVE – a dark-brown Horse; foaled in 1839, got by Gratis – dam by Theorem, her dam by Cammerton – g. dam by Champion, Gt. g. dam by Sheik, out of an imported mare.

Terms – £1. 2. 6d. a Mare.

Every attention will be paid to Mares sent, but the proprietors will not hold themselves responsible for accidents or losses.

TO STAND THIS SEASON,
AT KILCOY, BRISBANE RIVER.
THE THOROUGH-BRED RACE HORSE
MENTOR
By Toss out of Penelope

Mentor is a Bay with black points, and a sure foal getter. His performances on the Turf are too well known to need any lengthened description, he having beaten the crack horses of the day, viz., Jorrocks, Blue Bonnet, The Colonel, Zephryrine, & c.

Terms – One Mare £3.10s; three Mares, £3 each. Every attention paid to Mares, but no responsibility incurred.[57]

As the stud industry expanded rapidly, the sophistication among the stud owners increased. For example, the Leslies decided to sell their outstanding race horses Eagle and Conservative, and further announced that The Knave of Clubs and an "Imported Arab Horse [would] cover mares only on their ninth days."[58] It was apparent, very readily, that the market was such that the stud owners had to be progressive and keep up with the latest developments in breeding. Owners were continually attempting to secure the best progeny to improve their holdings.

As was apparent, the horse-racing industry was of considerable significance, with large sums of monies being involved. Thus, individuals who could help, or who claimed they could help, in promoting and preserving a horse's well-being were surfacing. This was exemplified by an advertisement placed by an individual who could "cut horses...cure all diseases to which horses are subject..., and break them in."[59] That there was a need for knowledge of how to combat horse diseases is seen in the death of Toby, "one of the best horses belonging to the Moreton Bay Turf",[60] of tetanus, or locked jaw. The owner was Dr Cannan, the then Treasurer and Secretary of the Club.

Specialised needs related to horse-racing brought forth astute individuals ready to capitalise on the situation. Stables, paddocks and feed were made available. It was noted that there were 13 horses in regular training for the Moreton Bay Races of 1848,[61] and such developments created a need for specific facilities.

RACES! RACES!
STABLES, PADDOCKS, AND OTHER ACCOMMODATIONS
FOR THE ENSUING RACES.

WILLIAM CRABB begs to announce to the inhabitants of Moreton Bay and Darling Downs districts that, in addition to the very superior accommodation for Horses he already possesses in South Brisbane, he has especially rented for the Races

A WELL-FENCED AND BEAUTIFULLY
GRASSED PADDOCK

at New Farm (adjoining the Race Course), where, on the Race days, Horses will be carefully attended to; also, the superior Stables of Mr. Powers, Sovereign Hotel; the Stables of Mr. Peattie, at the Sawyers' Arms, where SINGLE BOXES for Racing Horses can be obtained on reasonable terms; and the Stables of Mr Wm. Sheehan, at the St. Patricks Tavern.

W.C. having received a large supply of Oats, Maize, Bran and Hay, from Sydney, his charges will be extremely moderate, and the greatest attention will be paid to Horses entrusted to his care.[62]

In Drayton, when its race meetings were held, similar accommodations were made available, with eight boxes for racehorses at the Bull's Head Inn, with plenty of hay and corn on hand for the horses, and a reminder of excellent wines and spirits for the guests.[63]

The horse races were also a means for publicans to make extra monies. They could set up stalls at the race-course and sell their liquid refreshment. But, for this privilege, they had to apply for a special licence. "On Tuesday, the Magistrates granted permission to William Sheehan, James Powers, and Jacob Goode, licensed publicans, to pursue their calling on the race-course during the ensuing sports. No other applications were made to the Bench."[64]

That many interests had to be catered for at race meetings was evident in the declaration that there would be a Temperance Booth at the Brisbane Races, with lemonade at 6d. per bottle, ginger-ale at 3d. per glass and coffee at 3d. a cup. History does not record whether it was successful.[65]

For the majority of colonists horse-racing, gambling and drinking were all 'one and the same', and frequently celebrations would get out of hand! Such an occasion was vividly described in the *Courier*.

In the evening the "boys" kept it up in North Brisbane in grand style under the able leadership of a gentleman well known to the sporting fraternity. It so happened on this particular night that a hogshead of beer was quietly reposing under the veranda of the Victoria Hotel, when it was observed by the boys aforesaid. The word was passed, and the cask was set in motion down Queen Street as far as the corner of Albert Street. Finding the amusement highly exhilarating, our heroes commenced rolling it back again up the hill, and got it as far as the green opposite the Post Office [then located between the site of the present Town Hall and George Street]. Here a council of war was held, and it was decided to make a manful attack upon the head, as being the most vulnerable part of the cask. This was soon accomplished, and a general invitation was given to imbibe the contents, which was accepted by numbers who had assembled to witness the fun. "Capital stuff, Ned, is it not?" said one. "Old Tooth is a brick", said another; and all agreed that it was an excellent remedy for a cold. Suffice it to say that nearly the whole was drunk by our Bacchanalians and their guests without the slightest compunctious visiting of wry faces."[66]

A considerable economic industry, then, emerged around the horse, and horse-related activities such as horse-racing, hunting and riding. An advertisement in the first issue of the *Moreton Bay Courier* described the various horse-related implements and equipment that were for sale: "Jockey and Hunting Whips, Bits, Spurs, Girths, Princes' Check and Jersey Saddle Cloths, Headstall and Plain Bridles, both English and Colonial, Horse Brushes, Curry and Mane Combs, Breaking Tackles, Hunting Saddles, English and Colonial, Harness and Every other article necessary for either the road or the field."[67]

The extent of the horse-racing industry, generally, and its promotion may be seen from newspaper reports of race meetings in Australia and elsewhere. From the extent of coverage it is obvious that the editor of the *Moreton Bay Courier* had concluded that such sporting news was of prime importance to the reading public. A race at Homebush was reported in 1846,[68] as well as a steeple-chase at Five-Dock. Although the news was seven months late, the venerable Epsom Races in England also received ample coverage. The Petersham Races were reported in 1847, as were the Longford Races in Van Diemen's Land and Melbourne.[69]

Summary

Horse-racing, by 1850, had clearly emerged as Queensland's first sporting industry. Race courses were constructed at the major towns, and infra-structures were created to handle the organisational aspects; committees, judges, clerks-of-the-course, and so on. Circuits were established, specialised quartering facilities developed and studs were initiated to accommodate the demand for improved breeding. Public pressures also increased during the time period to "open up" racing for a wider clientele. In seven short years, from 1843 to 1850, the sport had come a long way. Problems were already apparent, but horse-racing was clearly Queensland's leading sport.

4

Sports of the Early Colonists to 1850

By 1842, when Moreton Bay was open for settlement, there were only ten buildings in existence of any consequence and life would have been very primitive for the colonists. However Thomas Dowse, reflecting on life in these formative years of Brisbane Town, maintained that although the colonists lacked many of the pleasurable attractions of other more established centres, their days were not devoid of amusements, or recreational pursuits.

> Well, the fact is, it was very hard work – as those in the "settlements" of the present day are aware – to occupy the mental faculties between the departure and arrival of the mails. Library or reading–room not contemplated; the expensive luxury of billiards not yet introduced...
>
> But we had the river and the glorious bay, two fields for our bodily and mental gratification, far in advance of either billiards, football, or cricket.
>
> Anyone in the full vigor of life who can shut his eyes to the benefits to be derived from a boating excursion to the bay or a day's going down the river, must be, in my opinion, less advanced in civilisation than a South Sea Islander.[1]

As the settlement expanded and more free settlers moved into the area, social institutions, similar to those in Sydney and Melbourne, emerged. The sport and recreational pursuits were patterned after the background of the arrivals, although availability of equipment would have hampered the immediate implementation of some activities.

Pertinent to any historical analysis is the establishment of the 'origin' of a social institution, event or pattern. The specific intent of this chapter has been to attempt to ascertain when the first sports, games and recreational activities occurred in Moreton Bay Settlement. An attempt has been made to locate the first reference, or references, of such events, and to reproduce them in totality. In so doing, it is hoped at the same time that a feeling of how the early colonists perceived such activities can be gained. In this specific analysis, the research has been primarily dependent, but not exclusively, on the recording of such developments in newspapers. However, the *Moreton Bay Courier* did not come into existence until June 20 1846, which was four years after the area was declared open for free settlement. Obviously, colonists would not have awaited the opening of the newspaper to initiate their sports, and hence it is entirely possible that the activities described on the following pages would have begun before the dates cited. Fortunately, some of the happenings in the Moreton Bay Settlement received some coverage in the *Sydney Morning Herald*, and hence certain developments earlier than 1846 have been ascertained. Additional sources, such as letters and diaries, have been sparse in their observations re sport, little attention being accorded games and recreational activities by such authors.

Cricket

One of the first competitive sports to be played in the Moreton Bay Settlement was cricket. The most authoritative historical work on Queensland cricket was written by E.H. Hutcheon, who stated that the "earliest records of cricket in Brisbane relate to the year 1857."[2] However, the present research clearly demonstrates that cricket began in Brisbane in 1844, thirteen years before Hutcheon believed it to have occurred. The *Sydney Morning Herald* of April 19 1844, noted the historic development in its Moreton Bay column, two years before the first edition of the *Moreton Bay Courier* in 1846.

> The lovers of the manly and exhilarating game of cricket, will soon have an opportunity of displaying their prowess, a club having been formed at South Brisbane, designated as the "Albion" Cricket Club, Mr D. Bunten, of the Woolpack Inn, acting as treasurer, and Mr John Payne, secretary, and Messrs Hopkins, Smith, Mather and Love, as a committee for carrying the arrangements into effect. Parties are admitted members by paying a small fee to the secretary, and the field operations will commence as soon as the bats, ball, and stumps, are received from Sydney.[3]

No other information exists about the Albion Club during this time period.

The first cricket match actually reported in the Queensland press was on Saturday, June 27 1846:

> CRICKET – As a finale of the amusements of the race week, a challenge from eleven of the working men of Brisbane to play an equal number of gentlemen, for £5.10s a side, was accepted by the latter, and the match came

off on the Terrace leading to the Government Gardens. The gentlemen were successful, beating their opponents easily. The stakes were generously handed over to the winning party. Arrangements were made for another match to come off in the next year's race week.[4]

There are several interesting aspects to this first-described match. Firstly, it was a contest between "working men" and "gentlemen". The gentlemen were understandably superior in the game's skills, as would be expected from their background and schooling. Next, the match was played for a rather substantial wager, and yet all the players would have considered themselves amateurs. Also, the location of the event was near the Government Gardens, and for many years to come this area was to be used for the playing of cricket and football.[5] It should be noted, moreover, that the match was one of the many amusements indulged in during Race Week.

The newspaper reported the formation of the first cricket club in Ipswich, which was on the 23rd of October in 1848. Inter-town rivalry immediately surfaced, as the Ipswich club immediately proposed a challenge to the senior club which was playing the game in Brisbane. "A Cricket Club has been established here, and commenced its first game on Monday last, it already numbers about twenty members, who, when sufficiently practised, intend challenging the Brisbane Club. Such a pastime as this ought to meet with encouragement, as it certainly tends to the preservation of health."[6]

The diffusion of the sport to other centres became readily apparent. For example, there was a match organised at Drayton in 1850, occasioned by an early termination of the races. The match pitted the Squatters against a team of men from Drayton, and Mr Bigge and Mr Bell were but two of the more well-known squatters who played.

DRAYTON CRICKET MATCH

In consequence of the races having terminated at a very early hour on the afternoon of the first day [Tuesday], a Cricket Match was got up on the afternoon of the two following days, between eleven Squatters and eleven Draytonians, which was attended with the following results:–

SQUATTERS ELEVEN

FIRST INNINGS

Bigge, bowled by Hopkins	6
Burgoyne, knocked his wicket	3
Houghton, bowled by Knights	0
Pinnock, bowled by Knights	3
Wiggins, bowled by Knights	6
Vaughan, bowled by Hopkins	1

Fairholme, not out   2
Coxen, bowled by Knights   2
Hodgson, bowled by Knights   3
Bell, bowled by Hopkins   7
Davidson, bowled by Hopkins   0

                                          Byes 7
                                    Wide balls 1

                                       Total 40

SECOND INNINGS

F. Bigge, bowled Knights   1
S. Burgoyne, bowled by Knights   5
R. Houghton, bowled by Knights   2
Pinnock, bowled by Knights   5
Wiggins, caught by Lloyd   13
Vaughan, bowled by Knights   5
Fairholme, stumped by Knights   7
Coxen, bowled by Hopkins   0
Hodgson, caught by Cox   0
Bell, bowled by Knights   6
Davidson, not out   0

                                          Byes 3
                                    Wide balls 1

                                       Total 48

DRAYTON ELEVEN

FIRST INNINGS

Bolton, not out   14
Lord, bowled by Bigge   0
Lloyd, bowled by Bigge   0
Hopkins, caught by Burgoyne   2
Samuel Milner, bowled by Hodgson   1
Knights, bowled by Hodgson   0
Sutherland, bowled by Hodgson   2
J. McLelland, caught by Hodgson   2
Thomas, run out   2
Cox, bowled by Hodgson   2

                                    Wide balls 2

                                       Total 24

SECOND INNINGS

Bolton, run out, Hodgson   1
Lord, not out   1
Lloyd, bowled out by Hodgson   0

Hopkins, caught out by Houghton	0
Samuel Milner, run out by Hodgson	4
William Gurney, bowled out by Hodgson	2
Knights, caught out by Houghton	4
Sutherland, bowled out by Hodgson	2
J. McLelland, bowled by Bigge	0
Thomas, caught out by Vaughan	4
Cox, bowled out by Bigge	0
Byes	2
Wide balls	1
Total	21[7]

Later, at the Ipswich Races, the Squatters who won in Drayton took on the Ipswich Cricket Club, the latter being victorious.[8]

From the newspaper coverage it appears that the most common, or popular, time for the holding of cricket matches at this period was in conjunction with horse races. However, celebrations such as those associated with New Year's Day included cricket matches as well. A restrictive factor for the playing of the game would have been that, on other than on special occasions, there was often difficulty in fielding enough players to conduct a proper match. Indeed, the playing of single wicket cricket might have been a reasonably common format, and these might have occurred as spontaneous informal games. Limitations on the game were also placed by a lack of proper equipment and the varied skill levels exhibited by colonists from diverse educational and social backgrounds. Moreover modifications in the playing of the game would have resulted from the variegated sun–baked pitches and hard grounds available in tropical Queensland.

The Regatta: Rowing

The only treatise that has been written on the formative years of the sport in Queensland is that published at the turn of the century by Carmichael and Perry.[9] Although these writers place "Queensland's First Regatta" as occurring on December 10 1860, the *Sydney Morning Herald* reported that the colonists celebrated the beginning of the New Year, 1844 with a regatta.

> We had a regatta in miniature on New Year's Day, when the lads who "can feather the oar with skill and dexterity" had an opportunity of exhibiting their various qualifications on the bosom of the gently flowing Brisbane.[10]

The *Sydney Morning Herald* of December 4 1843 announced that an annual regatta would be held on January 26 1844.[11] So the evidence is clear that regattas were held in Brisbane at least by 1844, some sixteen years before the date advanced by Carmichael and Perry. Also, as the latter announcement designated it as an 'annual' event, it could be assumed that such an event might have occurred in 1842, or even earlier.

The first Brisbane Regatta to be covered by the newly-established *Moreton Bay Courier* was that held on December 20 1846. The program, entrance costs and prizes were described in the announcement.[12]

BRISBANE REGATTA

First Race

Whale boats, five oars...

Entrance 10s. First prize, £5. Second £1.

Second Race

Four-oared boats...

Entrance 10s. First prize, £5. Second £1.

Third Race

Two-oared boats...

Entrance 5s. First prize, £4. Second £1.

Fourth Race

Scullers...

Entrance 2s.6d. First prize £3. Second 10s.

Fifth Race

Dingy and gig, or any other four-oared boat...

The race to be decided in fifteen minutes;

"the man in the dingy must be caught by the bowsman of the gig".

Entrance, free. Prize £2.[13]

The program reveals some noteworthy details. There were prizes for all the races, and there appears to be no distinction between amateurs and professionals. From the type of races advertised we know the diversity of boats in usage at the time. From the announcement it is also apparent that the organisational level of the sport was relatively advanced as the courses, and the boats, were specifically defined, a Flag Ship was present to control the race, entrance fees were established, an Umpire was present to ensure that rules were followed, and there was a committee with a Treasurer and Secretary in charge of the events.

The results of the Regatta were duly reported in the first issue of the *Moreton Bay Courier* in the New Year, 1847. It was noted that it "turned out to be a very sporting affair [and that the] aquatic amateurs and the inhabitants of Brisbane generally appeared to take great interest"[14] in the day's proceedings. The steamer Experiment was the flag-ship for the occasion, being "gaily decorated with flags [and there was music] to animate the scene."[15]

Interestingly, a more extensive coverage in the same newspaper was devoted to the Sydney Regatta, organised to commemorate the 59th Anniversary of the colony.[16]

Considerable advance notice was provided of the intention to hold another regatta in 1848, with the announcement being made on February 6 1847. This regatta, duly held on January 26 1848, was a festive occasion.

...we saw a very large assemblage of spectators, who seemed determined for once to make holiday, and enjoy a day's amusement. Most of the stores were closed, and we were agreeably surprised at the number of gay boats – "their streamers waving in the wind" that danced upon the surface of our beautiful river. Through the kindness of Capt. Morris, the fine schooner *Ebenezer* was anchored in the stream, and used as the flag ship.[17]

The appearance of Dr Cannan as Treasurer was of interest, as he was also Treasurer and Secretary of the Moreton Bay Racing Club. At the races his own horses competed, and he was a "gentleman jockey". He also participated in the race for four-oared gigs, or at the very least was the owner of the craft, the Flying Fish. He was also a competitor in the race for amateur scullers.[18]

Knight, writing prior to the turn of the century, described the 1848 Regatta with such exquisite finesse that the entire narration is reprinted in detail.

A topic more pleasing than the rehearsal of the sorrows and misfortunes of a deserving colonist was the regatta with which the people commemorated the foundation of the colony on the 26th January. Something like £40 was collected for prizes, and the few stores were closed to give the place a holiday appearance. Indeed the whole affair is spoken of as being of a most agreeable character. A respected citizen, Dr Kersey Cannan...acted as treasurer, while Captain Freeman filled the important position of umpire. The first race was for whaleboats pulling five oars, for which there were three entries. This was won by John and Walter Petrie's boat, the Lucy Long, the two brothers fully maintaining their well-earned reputation as oarsmen. Poor Walter Petrie did not, however, live long to enjoy this honour, for a few months later he was accidentally drowned in the creek which ran across Queen-street by Creek-street. The next race was for four-oared gigs pulled by amateurs, though why this stipulation was made is not very apparent. Two boats, the Flying Fish and the Pirate, entered. The Flying Fish, manned by squatters, came to the scratch, but although her opponent Pirate was also to the fore no crew could be found for her but blacks, who, after a little persuasion, were got to try the mettle of the squatters. The Flying Fishes rowed over their course with dignified composure and proved their superiority by permitting the natives to show them the way round. Though last, the Flying Fish was declared the winner, and her gallant crew reposed upon their laurels! The Dart and Spring–heeled Jack entered for the event for amateur scullers, but the former being invisible at the starting point the spring–heeled gentleman "walked" over the course. Owing to the fact that he had rounded the boundary boat on the wrong side, however, he had to try again, and doing it this time with better success won the prize – £2.10s. For the two–oared amateur event there were three starters – the Eclipse, Kipper, and Dart. This is described as having been a good race between the first two boats. The Kipper, however, lost some way by breaking a rowlock, but the deficiency was supplied by the steersman, and the Eclipse might herself have been eclipsed but that one of the Kipper's pullers being unaccustomed to the short rapid stroke required became fagged and changed places with the steersman. The Kipper was thus disqualified, and the "pace" being too hot for the Dart the Eclipse was allowed to get in a good first. The seventh race was between Spring–heeled Jack and Moonbeam, but at the start the latter was invisible, and he of the spring–heels having no substantial antagonist was pulled by blackfellows against his own shadow and was pronounced victorious. The best race of the day was that for blacks, the prize–money being expended in clothing. The Pirate and Swiftsure were entered, the former being the boat given to the Amity Point natives for their exertions in rescuing the "Sovereign" survivors. The efforts of the sable oarsmen simply delighted the spectators, who became most enthusiastic when the Pirate came in. A second prize of £1 was subscribed by three of the spectators, the amount representing their bets won on the race. The proceedings terminated with a race for a dingy and a four–oared gig, the bowman of the latter to catch the man in the dingy in twelve minutes after the start. Any thought of amusement that might have been anticipated from such an event was quickly dispelled when the barque of the fugitive was brought out. This was a ship's jolly–boat, and consequently was far too unwieldy to show much sport. After a vain attempt to dodge the gig round the flagship the "dingy" was overtaken and the occupant obliged to leap overboard. The gig's bowman followed him, but was soon compelled to return to his boat, which soon overtook the victim, who was making for the shore. The bowman now pounced upon him, and thus finished the race in five minutes. There was much festivity on board the barque "Ebenezer", which did duty as flagship.[19]

Because of the extensive detail with which these regattas were described, it is obvious that they were of considerable interest to the early colonials. Thomas Petrie was another to offer lengthy expositions of the races, in which Walter and his brother John were keen participants.[20] Two of the Petries, then, engaged in these early races, as did Mr Bigge, a squatter and a member of a prominent horse–racing family. The involvement of certain families in a host of social and cultural activities not only demonstrates the social control that was being exerted by the upper classes, but also the fact that their occupations provided them with the leisure time to participate in such activities. Such occasions offered the gentry opportunities to overtly display their status.

There was a general exodus from Brisbane in 1849 as news reached the city on January 6 about the discovery of gold in California. The effect was such that, "Even a meeting to consider the question of holding a regatta could not be got together, while the subscriptions were equally difficult to get, and must have thoroughly disgusted the organisers, the chief of whom was the late Dr Kersey Cannan."[21] The 1849 Regatta was finally announced on January 20 1849, though the events were scheduled for later in the month on January 26th. The organisational failings did not augur for success, but the occasion seemed to have been satisfactory to the participants.[22]

Sailing

As Moreton Bay Settlement, and Ipswich, were located on the water way and roads were very primitive, boat travel was an economic necessity for survival. Also, contact with Sydney and other parts of the world was primarily maintained by sailing ships. As well as serving economic and communication purposes, ships and boats were also used for recreational and competitive races. The first reference to the sport was in the *Sydney Morning Herald* of December 4 1843. The report discusses the possibility of the northerners sending a boat to the Sydney Regatta, a forerunner of future inter–state competitions.

> If the citizens of Sydney should be able to muster funds enough in these short–of–money times to get up the annual regatta on the 26th of January, we hope to surprise them with a clipper to contend for the prize in the first–class sailing boats, she is in a great state of forwardness in the building shed of Mr W. Underwood, of South Brisbane.[23]

Apparently Mr. Underwood's boat building yards in South Brisbane produced boats of such superior workmanship that they were exported to Sydney. Any developments in his yard were reported in the Sydney press.[24]

With the easy accessibility of water, pleasure sailing was understandably indulged in by the elite in particular, as they had boats available for such leisure. One of the additional pleasures associated with sailing was the sport of turtle catching. In the early issues of the *Moreton Bay Courier* various references were made to pleasure sailing and, in the advertisement section, there were announcements regarding the availability of pleasure boats for purchase.[25] The first sailing challenge match to be reported by the *Courier* was not until 1850. "We understand that a sailing match, between two boats belonging to gentlemen amateurs, will come off on Tuesday or Wednesday next, in the reach near Breakfast Creek." It was stipulated in the advertisement that the competition was only for "gentlemen amateurs". Although amateurs, these gentlemen had no compunction about accepting the £5 prize. Amateurs accepting money prizes in sports competitions were also seen in cricket, rowing and horse-racing. By twentieth century standards, all these 'gentlemen' would have been classified as professionals.[26] A brief description of the result of the match appeared shortly after the event.[27]

Swimming: Bathing

The preponderance of water in the Antipodes, as well as the generally hot climate, at least in comparison with that in the 'home' country, understandably made swimming very popular, particularly in the summer months. The activity was generally referred to as 'bathing' rather than swimming, and was recommended for hygienic purposes. Unfortunately the majority of the colonists possessed limited swimming skills and hence drownings were frequent. The incidents received considerable press coverage, and an example of a drowning report was that of "Old Jemmy", a hutkeeper at Coal Reach, who fell in the river endeavouring to secure a log.[28]

By 1847 the number of drownings had reached such a level that community concern was raised.[29] Another reported death by drowning in the Condamine River provoked an all-out attempt in Brisbane to get bathing houses for the safety and health of the citizenry.[30]

The bathing campaign continued in 1849, with a definite plan proposed for a floating bath, the plans courtesy of Mr Andrew Petrie. As Andrew's son Walter was drowned in 1848 when he was twenty-two years of age, and John Petrie's son, also named Walter, was drowned in Creek Street, a mere twenty-two months of age, Andrew had a deep personal interest in the campaign.

BATHING – In a warm climate like this, few things are more conducive to a sound state of health than regular bathing. Independently of the actual purification so necessary to the skin, the bath has an invigorating effect upon the whole system, most delightful and refreshing after the lassitude produced by a hot summer day. Every evening, during the summer, at least, the bath should be taken in these latitudes. But bathing in the river Brisbane is prohibited at present, and would be absolute madness, in consequence of the number of sharks in the river. This circumstance, and also the reflection that many persons are unable to swim, even if there was no such danger, have led us to consider the expediency of endeavouring to establish a floating bath; for after consulting with practical men upon the subject, we have been persuaded that the plan would be better than a fixed bath on the verge of the river. We have obtained, from Mr Andrew Petrie, plans for a floating bath, which could be moored at any part of the river, and removed from time to time to different parts of the town, as might be required. Mr Petrie has also made an estimate of the probable expense. The plan comprises two separate baths, with eight dressing–rooms, and other requisite arrangements. We invite our readers to inspect the sketches at our office, as it is most desirable that their opinions should be ascertained before any further reference is made to the subject.[31]

The response for contributions from the Brisbane public for the building was disappointing. The pledged subscriptions did not allow for the construction of a floating bath, which had been the original intent. A fixed bath was then settled on and work began immediately. The site selected was at the old wharf at Government Gardens.[32] The completion of the bath was announced on March 19 1849, with some criticism being directed at the public for its lack of support.[33]

Sharks were more profuse than at present in the Brisbane River and their presence limited the enthusiastic bather who ventured outside the Baths. A warning was issued to bathers on November 27 1847, however it was not heeded and, within a month, tragedy again struck, a nine foot six inch monster attacking a Mr James Stewart.[34] The Editor of the *Moreton Bay Courier* kept up his public campaign, continually expounding the perils of sharks in the Brisbane River.

SHARKS – CAUTION TO BATHERS – We have more than once reminded our fellow–townsmen of the danger they incur by bathing, and we cannot help reiterating our advice. The river absolutely swarms with sharks. We are informed that two were hooked on Thursday, but one, about seven feet long, got away. The fact of so many of these voracious monsters being in the river imperatively calls for the establishment of bathing–houses, and we feel certain, as we have before stated, that such a speculation would pay well.[35]

Boxing: Pugilism

The criminal background of many of the settlers, as well as the harsh and primitive environment, resulted in a societal emphasis on such attributes as physical strength and courage. The ability to protect oneself was an obvious necessity. One's fists were often a means of settling a dispute, but they also served as a means of providing entertainment. Boxing was an established sport in England, being one of the first sports to be organised, and had spectator appeal. Boxing, or pugilism as it was referred to in the early days, was a sport that appealed to many of the settlers. However, pugilism did not meet with the favourable approval of the powers–that–be, not so much because of the possibility of physical injury, but because of the gambling involved. A report from the Magistrate's Court described the results of one illegal match.

> The defendants it appeared had made arrangements to settle an old grudge existing between them by an appeal to arms, on the morning in question. Accordingly at the appointed hour a number of their backers, as well as a great many other persons, assembled to witness the contest. As we were not present on the occasion, it is out of our power, even if we had the inclination, which we have not, to furnish an account of the hits and knocks which were exchanged between the pugilists in about forty rounds of hard fighting; suffice it to say, that as soon as the Chief Constable got information of what was going on, he proceeded to the scene of action; his appearance with the other "traps" was the signal for an immediate cessation of hostilities and the parties retreated to the scrub, where they finished the battle. The combatants appeared before the Bench on the following morning, with their frontispieces beautifully decorated with cuts, as the publishers say, and each with one eye in mourning. "Well", says the Police Magistrate to the defendants, "you appear to be two very reputable characters, what have you got to say for yourselves?". One of the parties thus questioned replied, "that he and his friend did not fight for money – nothing so low as that – besides", says he, "there is no one in court can say that our noddles have not been disfigured by accident" [here the speaker tried to wink with his damaged eye, but failed most lamentably in the attempt]. His friend then put in a word, and said that they were both perfectly satisfied *now*, and were the best of cronies, having "buried all unkindness". Whereupon, the Bench ordered them to find bail to keep the peace for three months, themselves in £10, and two sureties in £5 each.[36]

Due to official condemnation of such contests, many were not reported in the press. A detailed account, given of a contest in Ipswich in 1848, reveals a match considerably more organised than previously reported fights.[37] The interesting aspect of this match, in comparison with the Brisbane ones of 1846 and 1847, is that the stakes were announced, and these were substantial, considering the time period, £50 a side. There is also a reference to the "Fancy", which denotes that there was in existence a group of men who followed the activities of the ring and other sporting engagements. The match would appear to be a bout between two professionals, called "Black Bill" and the "Native". There were rounds, some 32, which took approximately 42 minutes.

Quite often the 'fights' that took place were not contests, but rather "brawls" and, as occurred in Sydney Town, such brawls occurred quite frequently in and around taverns, and after such events as races: "Several pugilistic demonstrations [occurring] after the racing [of 1848] was ended".[38]

Duelling

Although the most common method of settling disputes was with one's fists, duelling with swords was at times resorted to. However, this European pursuit, popular among aristocratic young bloods, was also not tolerated by the law. Despite this, its existence was substantiated by newspaper reports. For example, a case of duelling was dealt with in Brisbane in 1848, and the Editor of the *Moreton Bay Courier* argued against mitigating punishment, stating that justice could not favour "class or station".[39]

> DUELLING – PUNISHMENTS – Mr Munro's sentence has been pronounced. A year's imprisonment is deemed sufficient to expiate his offence... But this imprisonment is, the paper tells us, to be made as "comfortable as possible"... The Crown has been advised to award a very mitigated punishment... But the imprisonment being awarded, it should be such as other misdemeanants suffer. There should be no effort to make it comfortable to the culprit. And that, too, not for the purpose of the mere infliction of pain upon the individual, but for the sake of that principle of equality before the law; the belief in which can alone render the law respectable or efficient. Favour to class or station is the last thing which should be exhibited in the administration of justice.[40]

Hunting and Shooting

It would be expected that the traditional sport of the English upper classes, hunting, would be pursued in the colony, particularly by the military and government elite. There were, however, no mentions of hunting in the first two years of the publication of the *Courier*. This does not mean that hunting as a sport did not exist, but only that at the time it occurred possibly on an individual basis rather than as an organised activity. Although in Adelaide, for example, a Hunt Club was formed as early as 1842, in Brisbane such formal organisation did not eventuate until the late 1860s.

The first mention of shooting as a sport did not appear until mid–1848. There was, at this time, an influx of birds after recent rains, and so there was ample opportunity for shooters to practise their skills.

> WATER FOWL – For several weeks past, numbers of various descriptions of water fowl, comprising ducks, ibises, white and grey cranes, &c., &c., have frequented a small sheet of standing water left by the rains in a marshy hollow immediately in the rear of Queen–street. Several persons, possessing more or less of ornithological lore, assert that many valuable specimens of rare species of water fowl are often to be picked up in this flooded hollow. A considerable number have been shot during the last week or two, a matter by no means difficult, for although the margin of the marsh is quite denuded of trees or bushes, yet such is the tameness of the fowl, that it is very easy to get within range of them, provided the most ordinary precautions are used.[41]

Pedestrianism

The first athletic event to achieve competitive sport status was foot racing. The term used to describe this sport at the time was 'pedestrianism', which was an established spectator sport in the British Isles. The men who competed in these events were called 'professionals', as all the races were for money prizes. Many made their living from such contests, travelling from town to town and even country to country. Carmichael and Perry, the most authoritative source on pedestrianism in Queensland in the early days, state: "The first pedestrian events in Queensland that would be of any interest were those held by the old Brisbane Football Club in the early 60s."[42] However, "interest" occurred much earlier. Indeed, the first mention of pedestrianism in the *Moreton Bay Courier* was in 1847, at least thirteen years earlier than those described by Carmichael and Perry. "ON TUESDAY NEXT, at One o'clock, a Foot Race will take place at Kangaroo Point between William Harrington and James Davis, *alias* the Dorrom Boy, for £20 a–side. The money is staked in the hands of Mr John Campbell, Highlanders' Arms. Mr Bow, Mr. W. Sheehan, Mr Lord, and Mr John Campbell, have consented to act as Umpires on the occasion."[43] Interest in the event was obvious from the extensive coverage accorded it in the press in the following week's issue.

PEDESTRIANISM – The match between Harrington and Davis to run 300 yards, for £20 a-side, came off on Tuesday, at [Main Street] Kangaroo Point, and attracted a strong muster of spectators. The men had a fair start, and kept tolerably well together for about 150 yards, when the Dorrom Boy began "to rock", and allowed his competitor to forge ahead. It soon became evident that he had no chance with Harrington, who kept himself well together throughout the race, and came in an easy winner, his opponent having "coughed" when he reached the "bricks and mortar", and finding he had no chance, gave up the contest. Harrington is evidently an old stager at this kind of sport, and did not appear the least distressed on coming in. He offered to run any man in the two districts the same distance, and stake £50 to £10 on the event. There was very little betting, although Harrington's friends would have sported their money freely.

We have been requested by Mr Lord to state that he never authorised any person to make use of his name as one of the umpires at the foot-race announced in our columns last week; the advertisement was the first intimation he had of the match.[44]

James Davis, the 'Dorrom Boy', is a fascinating case, being described by Petrie in *Reminiscences of Early Queensland*. A former convict, he had escaped to the bush where he lived with an Aboriginal tribe some fourteen or fifteen years. They named him 'Duramboi', hence his later alias 'Dorrom Boy'. Andrew Petrie, on a journey in 1842, during which he discovered the Mary River, brought back Davis ('Duramboi') and another escapee, Bracefield ('Wandie'). In his diary Petrie gives a vivid picture of 'Duramboi':

I shall never forget his appearance when he arrived at our camp – a white man in a state of nudity, and actually a wild man of the woods, his eyes wild and unable to rest for a moment on any object. He had quite the same manners and gestures that the wildest blacks have got. He could not speak his 'mither's' tongue, as he called it. He could not even pronounce English for some time, and when he did attempt it, all he could say was a few words, and these often misapplied, breaking off abruptly in the middle of a sentence with the black gibberish, which he spoke very fluently. During the whole of our conversation, his eyes and manner were completely wild, and he looked at us as if he had never seen a white man before. In fact, he told us he had nearly forgotten all about the society of white men, and had hardly thought about his friends and relations.[45]

The members of his tribe "missed him very much... He was a great man to hunt for game, and was always lucky in spearing kangaroo, and was a good hand at spear and boomerang throwing. He could also climb splendidly [and] was a great fighter."[46] The Aborigines had come to respect, and look up to, their friend, Duramboi. Davis was a blacksmith by trade, and when he returned to civilisation he re-established himself in the profession. He married and lived a long and eventful life among white society. Davis, then, as 'Dorrom Boy', goes down in Queensland's and Brisbane's sporting history as participating in the first organised foot race that we know of.

Some months after the Dorrom Boy race, the same Mr Harrington was competing in another race, only this time the location was in North Brisbane and the stakes were for only £5 a-side.[47]

A year passed before another pedestrian event was mentioned in the *Courier*. This time it was W.F. King, the celebrated *Ladies' Walking-Flying-Jumping-Running-etc.*, *etc.*, *Pieman*, who visited the town of Ipswich. The "Pieman" was renowned throughout the Colonies, having displayed his talents in Sydney, Melbourne, and any other centres that he could find.

> WEDNESDAY, SEPT. 13 – The dull monotony of our Town was to-day a little enlivened by the arrival of W.F. King, the celebrated Ladies' Walking – Flying – Jumping – Running, &c., &c., – Pieman. This extraordinary character, who, I am informed, arrived per last steamer from Sydney, has come to this district for the purpose of exhibiting a few of his wonderful feats, intending to proceed overland to Adelaide and Swan River, and eventually return to Maitland, to perform that which he declares to be the sole ambition of his erratic career, namely, to beat the celebrated pedestrian Barclay by "a long chalk"; in other words to perform the almost superhuman feat of walking *two thousand* miles in *one* thousand hours. After which, if he survives, to "settle down" a domesticated character, should he be so fortunate to meet a damsel duly qualified to enable him to have an heir to perpetuate the memory of the pedestrian champion of the *world*!!! Disdaining the common place conveyance of the *Experiment*, he nimbly footed it yesterday from Brisbane, carrying on his shoulder, to oblige a friend, a carriage pole, weighing about 100 lbs, and beating the equestrians who accompanied him by upwards of an hour; yet this he calls a mere bagatille.[48]

The "Pieman's" skills were such that it was suggested by the Ipswich correspondent that he might gainfully be employed to carry the mail.

> WEDNESDAY, SEPT. 20 – Through the instrumentality of the Flying Pieman, we received your last publication far earlier than we ever did before – that is to say, at noon on Saturday last, the day of its issue; and had it not been that he lost his way, there is not the slightest doubt that we could have enjoyed the perusal of the *Courier* at the same time that we were partaking of our toast and eggs, at nine a.m. "Pity it is" that we cannot secure his services to the districts. After arriving here, instead of resting as ordinary

mortals would do, he kept travelling round our little town at the rate of knots, carrying with him a tray full of "kisses", which he readily disposed of, – and at six p.m. again took his departure for Brisbane, so as to arrive there in time for supper, a distance which, at a moderate calculation, could not have been less than seventy miles in sixteen hours, – but this he designated a mere stroll.[49]

In order to increase public interest in his performance, the "Pieman" did some self promotion by placing a public announcement in the local press:

PEDESTRIANISM

QUESTION TO THE PUBLIC

How many miles shall I have to walk, being engaged to wind, whilst walking, a piece of common tape around a pitchfork handle, or 1½ inch diameter, the tape being 100 yards in length? This task was undertaken many years ago by the celebrated Captain Barclay, who failed in the attempt, and lost a considerable sum of money, which he was of course obliged to hand over to a noble Lord who had challenged him to a bet on the event, and was never game to undertake the same task again.

I am resolved, should my life by the blessing of God be spared a few years longer, to accomplish every task of pedestrianism the gallant Captain Barclay undertook, by which *I mean to give him a triumphant licking*, being determined to make good use of the excellent pair of legs I have.

I purpose to undertake the above extraordinary pedestrian feat at South or North Brisbane, provided the inhabitants consent to subscribe for a new pair of boots, my present pair being nearly worn out: therefore I announce that I will hold a Public Meeting on Thursday Evening next, at half past Seven o'clock.

LADIES' WALKING, FLYING PIEMAN[50]

The appeal was successful and interest in his feats was engendered. The "Pieman" was soon in Brisbane to display his exploits at various venues such as Kangaroo Point, Queen Street and the Brisbane Hotel.

PEDESTRIANISM – We cheerfully comply with the request of King, the *Flying Pieman*, by inserting a programme of pedestrian performances, which he proposes to undertake on Thursday next, three times successively, viz.: at Kangaroo Point at 10 A.M. At Queen–street, Brisbane, 12.50 P.M., and near the Brisbane Hotel, South Brisbane, at 3.50 P.M. The feats at each place will be the same, and upon each occasion, will be concluded in ninety–five minutes. He is not likely to have much spare time, we imagine, as the following are the tasks he undertakes to perform within that period viz. – To run, wheeling a barrow, half a mile – To run backwards half a mile – To run forwards, half a mile – To pick up, separately, fifty stones, placed one yard apart, and place them in a basket or box – To walk a mile – To draw any lady, weighing from 10 to 14 stone, for one mile, in a gig, or spring chaise–cart – And to take fifty flying leaps, 2 feet 6 inches in height, having ten yards to run between each leap.[51]

His exhibitions, however, left much to be desired, as the *Moreton Bay Courier* was quick to point out to its readers.

KING THE PEDESTRIAN – Our illustrious acquaintance, the *Flying Pieman*, has twice or thrice disappointed the townsfolk and others, by failing to keep his promises. We are sorry to bring so grave a charge against such a master of the science of natural locomotion, but it is his own fault. After leading us to expect an exhibition extraordinary, on Thursday week last, he left the whole of the walking to be performed by those who came to look at him, and found him not; and on two subsequent occasions he has broken his appointments. Our flying visitor must stick to his engagements, or else the people may be led to think that there is a slight tincture of the humbug in his composition which would considerably tarnish his laurels.[52]

In spite of the criticism and the broken engagements in Brisbane, the "Pieman" was welcomed again in Ipswich.

The Flying Pieman performed here yesterday the feats which he proposed performing at Brisbane, viz.,: wheeling a barrow half a mile, running forward half a mile, running backward half a mile, walking one mile, picking up fifty stones one yard apart and placing them in a basket; as a gig could not be procured, he, instead, carried a large goat half a mile; and made thirty–eight leaps 2 ft 10 in. high, – fifty leaps were the number he intended having made, but as the bars were put four inches higher than he ordered, he was foiled in the remaining twelve, – he, however, completed the whole undertaking in 86 minutes, being ten minutes less than his stated time, although the day was very sultry. He now talks of trying the tape feat; that is, to wind, while walking, a piece of tape 100 yards long, around a pitchfork handle, one inch and a half in diameter, and placed perpendicularly in the ground. This will, however, depend upon the encouragement he receives.[53]

Although it may have appeared occasionally as if the "Flying Pieman" were only a fraud, and travelled from place to place exploiting the gullibility of the public and their thirst for entertainment, he did set several authentic records.[54] Knight provided some additional insight into the character of this roving 'ped':

The Flying Pieman's proper name was William Francis King. Strange to say, he was educated for the church, but his love for boisterous recreations and sport caused his father to pause before he finally placed him. He at last bought for him a share with a firm of London stockbrokers. But even this did not suit young King, and he soon sold out and accepted a clerkship in the Treasury office in the Tower of London, only to again shortly remove –

this time to New South Wales, where he landed in 1839. His family connections enabled him to bring excellent letters through which he hoped to obtain a Government appointment. He was not, however, successful, and his fate like that of many more well–connected Englishmen who have come to the colonies led him into strange places. He became in turn school-master, clerk, private tutor, and barman, winding up with a roving life under the strange *soubriquet* and performing the most extraordinary and difficult feats. Eventually he became the dupe of sporting men who backed him and pocketed the winnings, and eventually (in 1874) he died in the Liverpool (N.S.W.) Asylum.[55]

From these newspaper accounts it is evident that 'pedestrianism' was used to denote not only race walking but also a wide variety of almost 'semi–acrobatic' locomotor feats. At times, perhaps, some of these performances could be considered as simply entertainment, rather than sporting contests. Essentially the people were so hungry for entertainment that they eagerly supported virtually any kind of show that visited their town. Whatever, all performers and racers were expected to be paid for their efforts, so they were definitely professionals.

Billiards

Billiards was a traditional English "gentleman's" recreational pursuit and it would be understandable that the gentry, in attempting to replicate an English gentleman's life, would pursue this game. The biggest problem was the difficulty in acquiring the correct equipment which, of course, had to be imported at great expense. The hotels became the main venues for the playing of the game. Its promotion was advocated in an advertisement in the *Courier* in the second month of its publication:

BILLIARDS

The lovers of the gentlemanly and scientific game of Billiards, will receive every attention and civility at the Room adjoining the "Sovereign" Hotel, the proprietor of the Table having made arrangements to have the Billiard Room conducted in such a manner as to merit, he trusts, the approbation of all.

The Room is in no way connected with any Public House; gentlemen may, therefore, enjoy a game of Billiards at any hour. The Table is well known, being one of Thurston's best, and fitted with every requisite.

Lemonade, Ginger Beer, Soda Water, and Coffee will be provided at a reasonable rate for parties patronizing the Table.[56]

In this advertisement there was a definite attempt to disassociate the game from alcohol, as well as from the hotel itself. However, hotels were only too aware of the potential of the game in attracting customers to their rooms. Ipswich, in 1848, reported on the development of a "long–talked–of billiard room, opposite the Queen's Arms, which promises to be a great acquisition"[57] to the town.

The hotels became the social centres for the local inhabitants and numerous recreational pastimes were played in and around these venues. The *Maitland Mercury* summed up the pastimes that were officially permitted to be pursued at hotels. "Billiards and bagatille to be allowed in licensed houses; and skittle and quoit grounds may be attached, except to the public–houses situated in Sydney or Melbourne, without any additional payment."[58] However, in Brisbane, hotels were required to obtain a licence in order to offer billiards: "On Tuesday the magistrates granted renewal of the billiard licence for the room at the Victoria Hotel, with permission to keep it open until two o'clock in the morning."[59]

The cost of a billiard table was considerable, particularly because the table and all the necessary accoutrements had to be imported from England. Some private individuals did, however, own their own tables, but that was a rarity. Occasionally second hand ones were obtainable in the colony, as that offered in an auction in 1847 along with 20 bullocks, and some 19 superior breed of horse stock.[60]

Celebrations: Public Holidays

Public holidays were times of considerable festivity at which many old English holiday customs were practised. For the majority of colonists such occasions offered not only a day of rest but also an opportunity to pursue recreational and joyous pastimes. The first mention in the *Courier* of such celebrations was on Boxing Day in 1848 in Drayton, the occasion a "Christmas Sports" day. Although the majority of events were horse races, reference is made to ending the day with the "usual Christmas pastimes, viz., catching the pig by the tail, &c., &c.,".[61]

Similar holiday celebrations were also noted at Ipswich, with events such as climbing the greasy pole and shooting, as well as horse–racing, being highlighted.[62] The country regions seem to have preceded the city in the conduct of such celebrations. It is possible that such events were held earlier, however the first mention of Brisbane's Christmas Sports was not until December, 1849.

CHRISTMAS SPORTS – At North and South Brisbane and Kangaroo Point, yes even to the extremities of the township, and beyond the boundaries thereof, Christmas was seen and felt. At Kangaroo Point, there was the difficult pole greasy, surmounted by the usual prize, and there was also a pig whose tail had been anointed with fat – even the fat of the candle. These things much rejoiced the multitude. In the evening there was dancing, to the sound of the pipe and tabor. At South Brisbane, men brought certain horses to a place of titillation – even the scratch – but, behold! they were alone! Nevertheless, on the second day, which was the day after that of St. Stephen, horses did run, and much merriment was created thereby. On that side of the Brisbane which looketh to the northward two horses raced for a saddle, the distance being half–a–mile, and the race was won by a grey steed, whose owner was named Kelly, and whose rider was Lewis. Verily this race was fiercely contested. There was another race for certain stakes which were called Sweepstakes, and it came to pass that, although six horses started, only one came in first, and the same was a black gelding, the owner of which owned also red whiskers, but did not proclaim his name. Yet a third time there was a race, of three horses, and the same was won by a chestnut hack with much ease. On the following day an innocent pig was released from a bag, and many men hunted the animal, striving to seize him by the tail; but lo! he took to the water, where he dodged his hunters for a season; but many persons having plunged into the water–hole the brute was confused, and, certain of his enemies taking advantage thereof, he was at length made captive by Evans, even Andrew Evans, who useth the saw.

Windmill Reporter[63]

By 1850 Drayton's Christmas Sports program had expanded to include such diverse events as hurling and pigeon shooting.

CHRISTMAS SPORTS AT DRAYTON – We learn from the communication of a correspondent that the Draytonians are preparing for some sport during the festive season of Christmas. Besides the races, already advertised, and which would appear to show a great march of fashion amongst the shearers, there is to be a hurling match, for which it is expected that a few "Tipperary boys, Corkonians, and Dubo's" will contend. The squatters are to have a cricket match, and birds have been sent for to Sydney to furnish "food for powder" in a pigeon match. A large attendance is expected, and the sporting community on the Downs seem determined to keep up the "merrye Christmas tyme" with right good will.[64]

Other public holidays that provided the public opportunities for sports competitions of all kinds were New Year's Day and the Monarch's birthday. Cricket, for example, was one of the main attractions on New Year's Day in Brisbane in 1849.

NEW YEAR'S DAY – The first day of the new year was not suffered to pass like ordinary days in Brisbane. On the north side of the river, horseracing, cricket, and other sports enlivened the day. Amongst other actions, a hogshead of ale was exposed for general use in front of the *Saint Patrick Inn*, and received many friendly calls in the course of the morning. At South Brisbane much amusement was afforded by the amateur races that were got up, and, in all parts of the town, pleasure for the day triumphed over the usual propensity to business.[65]

Although some questioned any allegiance to the crown, various festivities were conducted on "Her Majesty's Birthday".

HER MAJESTY'S BIRTHDAY – On Thursday evening last there were the usual explosive demonstrations of loyalty on the part of our juvenile population, which were joined in by some of the seniors. Mr Hocking's store at South Brisbane was illuminated with a crown, star, and V R, in variegated lamps, being the first time that such an illumination had been exhibited in Brisbane. We are informed that the ships *Chasely* and *Eleanor*, lying in the bay, fired a Royal Salute, and were dressed in their gayest colours on the occasion. Three persons were fined 10s. each, and costs, at the police office yesterday, for discharging fireworks on the previous evening, an offence which would, perhaps, have been sufficiently punished by an admonition. Demonstrations of attachment to an amiable and virtuous Sovereign are not very numerous at the present day, and utilitarians ask what is the use of such displays? Simple as they appear, their influence in a political point of view is very considerable, and it rather strikes us that the present condition of the colony does not call for their suppression – The detachment of H. M. 11th regiment, stationed at Brisbane, did *not* fire a *fue–de–joie*, which, we hear, was in consequence of their not being provided with any but ball–cartridge.[66]

Other Leisure Activities

If one utilises a broad definition of sport and includes recreational activities pursued in leisure time, then mention must be made of leisure time amusements which were observed by the public as spectators. Acrobatics and various comic performances would be placed in this category, and perhaps even the infamous "Pieman" should be so classified.

The performances at the Brisbane Amphitheatre were discussed by the *Courier's* editor, who was concerned that the standards of decency be properly observed, and particularly castigated a Mr Croft's troupe, which essentially was a tight rope exhibition, with clowns of obvious poor wit.[67] The editor's criticism went further at a following performance, advising Mr Croft "not to suffer such gross impropriety in the future."[68]

Even in the 1840s the value of walking as a healthy form of exercise was recognised, and praised: "to such as those rational and healthful recreations, which while they invigorate the body, exalt and delight the mind."[69] For many, walking was a pleasurable leisure activity, and a means of viewing the beauty of the local scenery. The editor of the *Courier* in 1847 particularly recommended the walk and view from the summit opposite Kangaroo Point.

Additional Observations

The previous comments relate to the various sports that were emerging and were pursued prior to 1850. However, there were also other topics that should be included in this analysis: the Aborigine's adaptation to sport in the white settlement, sport and the ladies of the colony, the amateur and professional situation, and the role of the newspaper *vis-a-vis* sport. These are discussed in turn.

The Aborigine's Adaptation to Sport in the White Settlement

At the first recorded race meeting in the Moreton Bay Settlement one of the jockeys, 'Sandy', was a black. It was obvious that there was no attempt to cover up or hide the fact that a rider was an Aborigine. However, it is surprising that such was permitted because of the class control exerted by the Moreton Bay Racing Club, combined with the emotional issue of public versus subscribers' control of the races. There were occasional mentions of the participation of black jockeys in other races as well, "Black boy Jimmy", for example, winning the Maiden Plate in 1848 at Drayton.[70]

Aborigines also competed in the sport of rowing. For example two of the Regatta races of 1848 involved Aborigines, the first being the race for four-oared gigs and the second being for four-oared boats:

> The *Flying Fish*, manned by squatters, came to the scratch, but although her opponent, the *Pirate*, was also "to the fore", no crew could be found for her but blacks, who, however, seemed determined to try the mettle of the jackeroos. The flying fishes rowed over their course in dignified composure, proving their superiority by *permitting the natives to shew them the way round. Flying Fish* was declared the winner, and her gallant crew reposed upon their laurels!...
>
> EIGHTH RACE
>
> For four-oared boats, manned by aboriginal natives. First prize £2.10s; second ditto £1 - to be expended in clothing. Entrance free.
>
> *Pirate* Aborigines...Scull and cross bones...*Swiftsure* Aborigines...Red Cross...
>
> This was the best race of the day. The so-called *Pirate* is the boat which was given to the blacks of Amity Point for their exertions in rescuing the

survivors of the unfortunate *Sovereign* steamer, and her sable crew exhibited skill and emulation in the race. The *Swiftsure*, though not nearly so fast a boat, pressed her antagonist so hard that we are inclined to believe she had the best crew. Bets were even until both had rounded the upper boundary boat, when the black flag fluttered foremost in the race. On nearing the *Ebenezer* the *Swiftsure* made a bold push, but the piratical hero came in first, by little more than his own length. Great praise is due to the Committee for arranging this match, as a means of convincing the blacks that, if we punish criminality, we can always reward merit; and we trust that the example will be followed in all future Regattas on this river. The spectators expressed their pleasure at the result of the race by loudly cheering both boats, to the evident delight of the natives. The second prize was subscribed by Messrs Hawkins, Archer, and Tucker, being the amount of bets won by them on this race.[71]

It is of interest that prize money was not given to the Aborigines, rather they were given clothing.

Pedestrianism was another competitive sport in which the Aborigines competed and, in later years, many of the best in the colony were Aborigines. As part of the 1849 Brisbane Horse Races, a "foot–race between aboriginal blacks was then got up. Six natives started, and the prize was won by a well–known Amity Point black, called 'Jack the Lagger'."[72]

There also appears to have been no overt discrimination against the blacks with respect to admittance at public entertainment centres, although there could be obvious racial prejudice demonstrated by a reporter. It was noted that at the comic and acrobatic performances at the Amphitheatre, for example, that a "number of the aborigines were admitted in to the arena, and stared in stupid amazement at the proceedings."[73]

When the 'Flying Pieman' came to Brisbane to ply his trade of professional pedestrianism, the *Courier* announced that a black with the unlikely name of Major Morriset was in training to challenge the professional.

PEDESTRIANISM – A correspondent from Drayton, who, we strongly suspect, is a wag, says that "a blackfellow called Major Morriset is in active training, under the hands of one Tom Bailey for the purpose of running or walking the *Flying Pieman* for any sum his friends may be included to stake." He adds that Bailey "is prepared to post the needful" if the aeronautic vender of pastry accepts the gallant Major's challenge.[74]

Whether the two ever met in head–on confrontation is not known, as no further mention of the encounter was carried by the *Courier*.

Sport and Ladies of the Colony

In the main, the ladies' involvement in any sporting event was limited to that of being a spectator. The horse races, in particular, welcomed the female spectator, and for many ladies they were a time for social interaction as well as an opportunity to display the latest fashions. A description of the 1847 Race Meeting provides a typical example of how woman's patronage was viewed at the time.

> The animated scene could boast a fair proportion of colonial charms, and some goodly specimens of the Moreton Bay lasses, decked out in handsome holiday attire, graced the course with their presence, and added considerably to the cheerfulness of the proceedings. The presence of ladies always gives additional life to such stirring scenes, and it was highly gratifying to find that such numbers of fair colonists attended the sports.[75]

They were also most welcome as spectators at the Regattas. Indeed, there was a special appeal made for the ladies of Brisbane to support the 1850 Brisbane Regatta: "A day's gratification for the ladies and juveniles may be cheaply purchased, and we trust that the heads of families – we mean, of course, the wives – will take care that their lords be not niggardly upon the occasion."[76]

However, there appeared to be limits as to the extent of their patronage of sports events. The editor of the newspapers, and many others, questioned the propriety of their attendance at certain sports and they most certainly maintained that a pugilistic match was one that ladies should not grace their presence with.

> PUGILISTIC DISPLAYS – A correspondent in calling our attention to a desperate fight which took place in North Brisbane on Tuesday last, between a soldier and a sawyer, says:– "I counted no less than *eight women* who were present, looking on with great interest; and one disgrace to her sex was actually cheering and goading the men on by applause, oaths, and shouts! This virago was the wife of one of the combatants." *O tempora, O mores!*[77]

The only actual involvement of women in a physical activity that is mentioned in the *Courier* is that of walking. A Brisbane walk that is recommended is one that is "...within the compass of a lady's walk".[78] Dancing would also have been another "physical activity" that would have been socially acceptable. However, not only were the ladies restricted by existent social mores, but also by the clothing that they wore. The ladies of Brisbane adopted the fashions of London, which were not conducive to any physical activity. Nor were their dresses and other attire appropriate for the climate. Only hats were of benefit, as the wide brims protected their faces from the hot, tropical sun.

Little is known of the daily life of the working women except that she led a very difficult existence, living in primitive surroundings. Her daily household chores were physically demanding and required considerable strength and stamina. A poor colonists' wife would have had little time or energy for recreational pursuits.

The Amateur–Professional Situation

The amateur–professional problem did not seem to be a vital issue in the early years; indeed, it seemed to be of no concern whatsoever. In most sports matches and contests prizes were given and monies won, and these were accepted by all competitors.

In horse–racing, from the outset it was the gentlemen who were the jockeys as they often entered and rode their own horses. These 'amateur' gentlemen jockeys would, of course, accept the purses. As has already been mentioned, gradually a major problem evolved at race courses, which was that of the 'subscribers' – who constituted in the main gentlemen jockeys – versus the 'public', over the control of the races. The subscribers wanted to keep the races to themselves and not permit 'professional' jockeys to ride. This controversy was first evident in Brisbane, and then elsewhere.

The Drayton Races of 1850 caused a sensation, as in the first race *War Eagle* "was brought on the course, but not stripped, owing...to his owner being objected to as a gentleman rider."[79]

Many are very much chagrined that *War Eagle* is not to be down [to Ipswich], his owner, having left the district in disgust at the very injudicious rule passed at the Drayton meet, of allowing none but gentlemen riders for the Welter Stakes. This was the rock the Brisbane Club split upon, and it is evident the Drayton people dread the same fate, from the sly hint they have given of wishing to prop their falling cause by an union with the Ipswich Racing Club.[80]

Rowing was another sport in which we see the term amateur being used. At the first Brisbane Regatta there were amateur rowers competing for the money prizes, while at the 1848 Brisbane Regatta it was stipulated that four races were for amateurs only.[81] In sailing, also, we see a separate race for "gentlemen amateurs."[82]

In the sport of pedestrianism the 'peds' were all considered professional. For example, the contest between the famous William Harrington and James Davis ('The Dorrom Boy') was contested for £20 a–side.

Another instance of the utilisation of the term amateur was as part of the Amphitheatre, where there was a "performance of two amateurs who displayed much agility and considerable muscular powers."[83]

The Role of the Newspaper vis-a-vis Sport

The *Moreton Bay Courier* did not merely report the news, sports and so on, it campaigned, and expressed specific view-points. The town-country relationship for example was a recurrent theme, and there was an evident attempt to encourage unity and common goals over a broadening geographical area. The editor offered his opinions in 1847 following the annual Moreton Bay Club Races.

> We were, however, disappointed of finding so small an attendance of Squatters. Our Ipswich friends, too, were very backward in coming forward on this occasion. This is not as it should be. Country races are excellent things in their way, got up to encourage horse-breeding and for a day's amusement, and for horses in the neighbourhood, most of which, without being first-rate racers or regularly trained, can give a good day's sport. In a small community like ours racing ought to be well supported to prevent the sports losing their character of local emulation. The residents both in town and country should have a common interest in such matters; and as the races only take place once a year, and at a time when the settlers are not busily engaged with their shearing, they should give them every encouragement, for there cannot be a doubt but that they afford a good deal of rational amusement, and are beneficial to the district. Neither first-rate racing nor first-rate horses need be expected next year if the turf is not better supported by our country friends.[84]

This theme was further expounded in later issues. "It is expected that a great number of gentlemen and others from the bush will visit the settlement about the time when it is proposed the regatta should take place, and we have no doubt that they will willingly take part in the days amusements."[85] An interesting principle of journalism was questioned at the 1849 Brisbane Races. The correspondent was not exempted from a charge at the toll gate because of his profession: "a trifle in itself, but it involves a principle."[86]

Other instances when the editor offered his opinion have already been mentioned. These involved issues such as whether females should attend boxing matches, being critical of the "Pieman's" performances, and campaigning for better bathing facilities.

Summary

When the first European inhabitants arrived they were, in the main, convicts, with military personnel to control them. Gradually, settlement and town life formed around the penal colony, with skilled workers slowly coming to the area. The discovery of inland grazing areas led to settlers moving inland from the southern settlement to establish grazing properties. These individuals who settled on the big properties came to be known as "squatters". Eventually a town–country rivalry developed between the squattocracy on the land and the monied townspeople, and this rivalry was reflected in sport.

The majority of historical records contain very few accounts of the social life of the early Moreton Bay Settlement, and hence the main source for references has been the newspapers. Life was hard; the environment was harsh, survival from one day to the next was of primary concern, work was mainly physically demanding and exhausting, and was generally dawn to dusk. Very little time, or energy, would have been left for leisure or sporting activities. However, in spite of this, there would have been recreational pastimes whenever the time permitted, and certainly on public holidays. The upper class, and the military, of course, unquestionably had more time, money and energy to devote to pleasurable activities.

For the purposes of this section, sport has been viewed from an all-encompassing perspective to include all types of play, games of low organisation, leisure or recreational pursuits, physical activities and dance, as well as the early forms of modern competitive sports. It is acknowledged that when analysing the social life of the early colonists perhaps play, recreational activities or leisure pursuits would have been a more suitable designation.

There were emerging patterns evident in the sport and leisure activities of the colonists, up to 1850, in the area that is now Queensland.

Horse–racing became the most dominant sport in the colony, and its dominance has perpetuated to the present day. Industries developed around the horse: the production of equipment such as saddles, whips, bits, spurs, brushes and combs; specialised studs for horses for export to India, for "roadsters", for draft horses, and for racehorses; the licensing of publicans at the course; and stables, paddocks and feed which were all associated with the racing industry.

Despite the fact that courses and grandstands were constructed and maintained, that officials with specialised tasks were connected with the organisation of racing, that there was a consistency of rules within a particular racing club, it might be argued that horse-racing, prior to 1850, had not attained full sport status, if this implies acceptance of national and international rules. There was however a progression from local rules to acceptance of the rules of an external authority. In 1850 Homebush Rules were accepted by one racing club, and Newmarket Rules by two others.

Chapter 2 outlined the major structural-functional characteristics of folk-games and modern sports. In trying to evaluate the progression in the evolution of horse-racing this concept can be useful.

It is clear that the situation with respect to racing was undergoing considerable change up to 1850. There was informal organisation in challenge races, there was existence of simple rules, regional variations, there were no precise limits on the size of courses, and there was strong communal pressure to participate, more particularly with respect to the "gentlemen jockeys". There were, however, patterns of change, and these occurred more particularly after 1850, with the decision to conform to national rules. There were Homebush, Newmarket and local rules up to 1851. The norms of equality were also being debated as the public demanded participation in the organisation of racing, as well as the right to ride as jockeys in such races. The elite still endeavoured, in this time period, to maintain control over racing. There were commonly accepted norms of fairness and sportsmanship and low levels of socially tolerated physical violence.

In summary, racing was the only sport in the settlement that attained near-sport status up to 1850. It does not, however, conform to a majority of the structural-functional characteristics as developed earlier, though the level of sophistication did increase from year to year.

The hegemonic control of certain sports, such as horse-racing and the regatta, was evident. The squatters were particularly visible in horse-racing, certain families showing their social and sporting commitment and perhaps their desire for power. The races provided the squatters with opportunities to display their wealth and status. There were societal undercurrents which endeavoured to break down this elitist control, and this egalitarian movement appeared to be succeeding, particularly in horse-racing, as the year 1850 ended.

Social distinctions were evident in the labelling of certain riders as "gentlemen jockeys" and certain sculling races being open only to "amateurs". Amateurism was essentially a social classification as these "amateur gentlemen" competed for and accepted money prizes in horse-racing, in sculling and cricket matches. In cricket, gentlemen would compete against workers and, if they won, which they usually did because of their greater skill, they would accept the prizes. Pedestrians, who appeared to be from the lower classes, were however referred to as "professionals", as they made their living from their prizes.

The cultural background of the convicts, the military and the settlers undoubtedly influenced the social habits and customs that evolved in the Antipodes. As most were from the British Isles, more particularly from England, the play patterns that emerged were generally those of the home country. The predominance of sports such as horse–racing, cricket, the Regatta, and pedestrianism, as well as the Christmas sports and billiards and other pub–related games, are evidence of this cultural infusion. English customs appeared to be dominant.

Sports events were seen as social occasions, as periods of fun and relaxation when men and women could enjoy a break from the arduous and at times tedious nature of life in the new settlement. It is clear, with respect to sport, that ladies were encouraged to participate as spectators, but few avenues were available to them as active participants. They "graced the course",[87] their presence secured total social acceptance of the event, and they added colour to the proceedings by their finery. They were at times appealed to, by the editor of the *Moreton Bay Courier*, to make certain their husbands would participate in the Regatta.[88] As well as their appearance value, the picnics that were associated with the horse races and the Regatta added to the festivity of the occasions, and these were considered the more proper domain of women. There was a limit, however, to their involvement, even as spectators. For example, a pugilistic encounter was not deemed acceptable for female attendance. The sole extent of active participation in physical activities by women – except by the lower class women who worked physically as hard as the men did – was to walking, dancing and to a limited extent horse–racing. Up to 1850, the sport patterns in the Moreton Bay Settlement reflected its male–dominated society. Even in quantitative terms there was a male dominance. In the county of Stanley, which included Brisbane, there were some 476 females compared to 1123 males.

The effects of transportation were clearly evident as refinements in the use of steam and the development of roads increased sporting participation. Despite these communication changes, local affiliation weighed more heavily than regional affiliation, during these formative years.

There were acceptable and non–acceptable tavern sports, billiards being acceptable, and card–playing being considered illegal. There was little evidence of blood sports, but the two that did appear – boxing and duelling – were dealt with severely by the law.

Conclusions

There were, then, a number of sports practised in what is now Queensland up to 1850. Activities related to the horse were dominant, with regatta activities being secondary in importance. However, cricket, hurling, Christmas activities, dancing, billiards, card playing, pedestrianism, pugilism, sailing and shooting were other recreational or leisure activities that were pursued in leisure time. The social life of the inhabitants of the Moreton Bay Settlement was not devoid of pleasurable activities. Moreover, many of the sports such as horse-racing, cricket and pedestrianism were being competed in at a much earlier date than previous literature has resolved.

The sport patterns in the settlement reflected the society. Firstly, in organisational patterns, they were in their formative and growing stages, as was the colony itself. Secondly, with respect to social organisation, the class structure and societal mores were manifested in the various sports. The recreational activities served as social integrative forces, as such occasions brought people together and allowed them to interact with each other. Except for horse-racing, the primary motive for involvement in these activities was of participation, as success and victory were not deemed overly significant. In these formative years, recreational and sport activities had particular social value for the pleasure and enjoyment that accrued for participants and spectators alike.

5

The Diffusion of Major Sports:
1850s to 1890s

From 1850 to 1890, Queensland underwent considerable development economically, politically and socially. In 1850 the last convicts were brought to Moreton Bay, marking the end of the convict era for Queensland. Formal recognition of this northern part of Australia was accorded by Queen Victoria on June 6 1857, when the land north of the twenty–ninth degree of latitude (except for a slight deviation at the coastal end) was designated as Queensland. For the next three decades the new colony experienced intensive regional development which Wilson has summarised into seven inter–related strands:

    (a) Successive stages of pastoral advance, retreat and re–occupation,
    (b) Differentiation into a sheep region in the centre and a cattle region round the rim,
    (c) A chain of gold and other mineral discoveries up the eastern highlands,
    (d) Evolution of a coastal sugar plantation economy worked by black (and blackbirded) labour,
    (e) Testing of numerous (often competitive) town/port sites,
    (f) Rapid growth of the capital to 1870, but low urbanisation,
    (g) Transition from unmade tracks in the 1860s to railways penetration.[1]

The taming of the land and the movement of the frontier inland and northward was well established by Separation. Indeed, by 1850 the pastoral advance from the southern settlement had absorbed the Darling Downs region and had inexorably moved towards Rockhampton. This "pastoral frontier" became a land rush, as intrepid newcomers leap-frogged over those who had preceded them, and those who were on the frontier, obsessed with what might lie ahead, moved further beyond the periphery of settlement. The land was sparsely populated, and life was simple and crude. As the majority of immigrants had little desire to go out to what they felt was the vast, virtually empty lands and preferred to stay close to major settlements, the pastoral expansion was initially dependent on convicts and freed men for labour. In the towns, import and export traders, shippers, wharf labourers, bankers, shopkeepers and so on grew in number and profited from the business resulting from these inland developments.

By 1865 the pastoral advance had reached into the north, as far as Bowen and Townsville, and by 1867 it had passed across to the Gulf country. Cattle proved their adaptability in the long haul in the hot and humid northern coastal lands; sheep were particularly successful on the Darling Downs and the Central West. The economic collapse in the late 1860s in Queensland depressed wool prices and bankrupted the pastoral industry generally, and the pastoral frontier retreated, in defeat, for more than fifteen years.

Fortunately for Queensland's economy, when the pastoral expansion was declining, salvation came with various mineral discoveries in the central and northern parts of the colony. Gold and copper were the main finds in Queensland. Also, during these decades, the opening of sugar plantations on the coast in the 1860s from Moreton Bay to Maryborough and in the 1870s from Mackay to Cairns had far-ranging effects on Queensland's prosperity. These developments stimulated the economy, increased immigration and fostered urbanisation and industrialisation. Chinese and black indentured labour came to work on the gold fields or on the sugar plantations.

The communities that evolved as a consequence of the above developments were primarily on the coastline, extending northward from Brisbane. The distance between these communities and Brisbane were immense, for example, Brisbane to Townsville being almost as far as from Brisbane to Melbourne. Cooktown was even further north again. There were no roads connecting these communities, and railways that were built at Townsville, Rockhampton and so on did not channel their goods through Brisbane. Ships often carried their wares directly from Townsville to Sydney, for example. As a result Rockhampton, in the central area, and Townsville, in the north, grew into major ports. Whereas the other colonies had one major port such as Sydney or Melbourne, Queensland had several.

Railway lines in most countries radiate from the capital or main city outward, however in Queensland, as Fitzgerald maintained, "all roads and rails did not, and were never to lead to Brisbane."[2] The beginning of Queensland's railway system was not in Brisbane, but in North Ipswich on February 25 1894 Ipswich became known as the "home of the locomotive". The railway system diffused from Ipswich, linking Toowoomba by 1867, and Dalby with Toowoomba in 1868. Brisbane was not linked with Ipswich until 1876. By 1871, 218 miles were open to rail traffic.

The first steamship built in Queensland, the "Louisa", was completed in 1872 and by 1873 Queensland was providing its own locomotives. Until Brisbane was linked with Ipswich by rail, steamers plied the river route. Ships such as the "Ipswich", "Brisbane", "Emu", "The Kite" and so on carried trade, passengers and spectators to sporting events. Linkages with northern and southern ports were also by steam; Brisbane was not linked by rail to Rockhampton until 1902 and Townsville in 1920. In the north, railway lines linked the emerging coastal towns with the major inland mineral centres. Hence the routes ran east to west. For example, the rail line between Townsville and Charters Towers was completed as early as 1882.

Brisbane was isolated in the south–east corner. The colony's pattern of growth northward along the coastline, which was reinforced by the east–west linear railway routes, resulted in a decentralisation of industry. The processing of goods tended to be located at the site of the product. Sugar mills, for example, were built near the sugar plantations along the coast. Political and social developments reflected this industrial growth pattern.

As a whole, with respect to urbanisation, Queensland "lagged behind that in other colonies."[3] In the main Queensland's urbanisation resulted primarily from immigration rather than rural migration, which had been the norm in nineteenth century European cities. In order to encourage immigration in the 1860s, the Queensland Government offered migrants an initial £18 land order and a subsequent one after being in the colony for two years.[4] By the 1870s, the colony's population had doubled and by 1889 it had tripled. Although many who came were attracted by the gold fields, most of the migrants tended to settle in the towns. The 1868 census gives an indication of the population of the electoral division of the colony and how the population had altered in four years.[5]

The migration into Queensland peaked in the 1880s, resulting in a population which had the highest proportion of foreign born of any colony in Australia.[6] Weedon analysed the birth places and religious affiliations of Queenslanders from the 1891 census. The total population at this time was 393,718 with roughly equal numbers of men and women.[7] The largest group by far (apart from Queensland–born) was born in England and Wales (77,187), with the next greatest number coming from Ireland (43,036). The majority of the latter were poor and unmarried, and occupied the lower class employment positions. The German immigrants (14,710) generally occupied the land, maintaining much of their cultural identity through the community groups that they

Table 4. 1868 Queensland census

Electorate*	No. of Members	Population 1864	1868
Brisbane, North	3	7,951	9,172
Brisbane, South	1	1,796	1,176
Burnett	2	2,689	3,276
Clermont	1	–	2,316
Downs, Eastern	1	2,225	2,867
Downs, Western	2	3,060	2,384
Drayton & Toowoomba	1	2,172	6,082
Fortitude Valley	1	2,504	3,917
Ipswich	3	4,979	5,021
Kennedy	1	–	4,955
Leichhardt	2	5,382	4,054
Maranoa	1	2,518	2,964
Maryborough	1	–	4,047
Mitchell	1	–	698
Moreton, East	2	7,806	13,921
Moreton, West	3	4,981	7,654
Port Curtis	1	6,824	4,418
Rockhampton	1	–	6,086
Warrego	1	–	1,144
Warwick	1	1,745	2,234
Wide Bay	1	2,964	7,351
Totals	31	59,616	95,737

* The Burke returns were not recorded

formed. Chinese and Polynesian or Kanaka immigrants were concentrated in the gold fields and the sugar plantations, leaving Brisbane relatively free from racial conflicts.

The religious affiliations of Queenslanders from the 1891 census provides additional understanding of the population.[8] The largest religious grouping was Church of England, followed by Roman Catholic.

The process of urbanisation and the increasing industrialism of the economy was accompanied by a transformation in the social scene. The interests, habits and pastimes of all segments of society were altered as

Table 5. Birthplace of Queenslanders: 1891 census*

	Males	Females	Total
Queensland	89,114	87,857	176,971
New South Wales	10,234	6,789	17,023
Victoria	4,907	2,555	7,462
Other Australian Colonies	2,517	1,334	3,851
England and Wales	45,781	31,406	77,187
Scotland	13,510	8,890	22,400
Ireland	22,305	20,731	43,036
Germany	8,700	6,210	14,910
China	8,513	37	8,550
Polynesian	8,557	781	9,338
Other Countries	9,641	3,349	12,990

* Aborigines do not appear to have been counted

Table 6. Religious affiliations of Queenslanders: 1891

	Males	Females	Total
Church of England	79,814	62,741	142,555
Roman Catholic	48,688	44,077	92,765
Presbyterian	25,437	20,166	45,639
Methodist	16,073	14,795	30,868
Lutheran	13,003	10,380	23,383
Baptist	5,113	5,143	10,256
Congregational and Independent	4,301	4,270	8,571
Other Protestants	3,876	3,101	6,977
Other Christians	1,784	1,458	3,242
Other Religions	18,156	1,466	19,622
No religion, unspecified, etc.	7,498	2,342	9,840

new conditions emerged, with different requirements and opportunities. Because of the geographic extensiveness of the state and the widespread nature of settlements, such changes were not uniform throughout the land. Remote communities were not as affected by the profound societal changes that occurred in the urban centres, although gradually, with progressive improvements in communications and transportation, they also underwent transformations from their traditional rural lifestyles.

In the cities, space became a decided limitation, and this was a determining factor in the nature and extent of the recreational activities of the populace. Urban living necessitated the building of specific facilities, or the establishment of areas to meet the demands for sport. For example, in Brisbane, the Breakfast Creek Sports Ground was built in the late 1880s. "The new sports ground at Breakfast Creek is being rapidly improved. The proprietors are expending £30,000. They have a grandstand that will seat 1000 persons, a ballroom lighted with electricity, a lake a quarter of a mile long, and the grounds are thirty acres in extent."[9]

Although it may appear that there were specialised grounds, such as the Woolloongabba Cricket Ground built in the mid–1890s, such facilities were generally multi–purpose. Albert Park, Victoria Park and the Exhibition Ground were frequently used by clubs, schools and others for varied sports competitions. By the 1890s the organisational developments in the sports had also effected improvements in the quality and quantity of grounds.

The construction and the increasing sophistication of sport facilities fostered spectator interest in sport. This passive involvement in sport was further encouraged by increased competition, which involved local and inter–state rivalries. Horse–racing was perhaps the most popular spectator sport of the period. However, enthusiastic crowds supported virtually all sport engagements, regattas and gatherings. Sport was one of the main social institutions which evolved, meeting the needs of entertainment and diversion, and it appealed to all segments and classes of society. Gambling on the outcome of the competitions served as an additional inducement for spectators. Wagering on sport, as well as financial and other material inducements, and gate monies cultivated the development of a "professional" athlete. By the 1890s, professional athletes were prevalent in pedestrianism, rowing, cricket and boxing. Cricket was one of the few sports that was relatively free of gambling.

Settlements exist to serve the needs of the inhabitants in their reasonably accessible locales. Small centres served very minimal needs and provided only basic services, while larger centres offered a greater variety of services to a greater number. The sports scene was understandably more profuse, varied and advanced in Brisbane, as well as in other large centres such as Ipswich, Warwick, Rockhampton, Maryborough, Gympie and so on. The proliferation and popularisation of sport that occurred manifested itself first in the larger population centres, and the interest then diffused out to more isolated areas.

This diffusion of sport in Queensland was aided by a variety of conditions. A horse–racing circuit was established; state, national and international teams appeared in Queensland; top players were brought from other states; local interest developed in a specific sport, such as rugby union in Charters Towers; and exceptional enthusiasm and leadership were shown by some individuals, as in Maryborough in cricket.

Local clubs were formed on the basis of need and interest to meet the demand for competition. Because of transportation, most competitions were local in nature and were confined to that particular geographic area. With expansion of competition there arose a need for the codification and standardisation of rules as well as for the development of a superstructure for the coordination of each major sport. First local, then regional and state bodies, were formed to legislate and administer sport. Table 7 shows the foundation dates of some sport governing bodies in Queensland from 1863 to 1904.

Table 7. Formation of Queensland governing bodies in sport

Sport	Organisation	Year Founded
Bowling	Queensland Bowling Association	1904
Yachting	Royal Queensland Yacht Club	1902
Swimming	Queensland Amateur Swimming Association	1899
Polo	Queensland Polo Association	1895
Athletics	Queensland Amateur Athletic Association	1894
Yachting	Queensland Yacht Club	1894
Cycling	Queensland Cyclist's Union	1893
Rugby Union	Queensland Referees' Association	1893
Rowing	Queensland Rowing Association	1889
Soccer	Queensland British Football Association	1889
Lawn Tennis	Queensland Lawn Tennis Association	1888
Rugby Union	Northern (Q.) Rugby Union	1882
Cricket	Queensland Cricket Association	1876
Rifle Shooting	Queensland Rifle Association	1863
Horse–racing	Queensland Turf Club	1863

Intercolonial interests sometimes spurred a sport towards the formation of a Queensland governing body. In the case of athletics, rowing, cycling, cricket and horse–racing, the governing body was established soon after that first intercolonial participation. In cricket, however, the first intercolonial cricket match was in 1864, and yet the Queensland Cricket Association was not formed until twelve years later (table 8). In the case of polo, soccer, lawn tennis and rifle shooting, the Queensland body was formed first, and intercolonial competition was arranged later. The Queensland Lawn Tennis Association, for example, was formed in 1888, and yet the first intercolonial contest was not until 1895 (Table 8).

Table 8.   Differences between the first intercolonial competition and formation of the Queensland governing body

Sport	Year of first intercolonial contest	Year of formation of governing bodies	Year differences between contest and organisation
Polo	1896	1895	– 1
Tennis	1895	1888	– 7
Athletics	1890	1894	+ 4
Soccer	1890	1889	– 1
Rowing	1885	1889	+ 4
Cycling	1884	1893	+ 9
Rugby Union	1882	1882	–
Rifle Shooting	1879	1863	– 16
Cricket	1864	1876	+ 12
Horse–racing	1861	1863	+ 2

Industrialisation provided, for many, a higher standard of living and increased leisure time. Such benefits were primarily experienced by the upper and middle classes. However, by the late 1880s and 1890s, with the rise of the union movement, conditions for the working class improved through a shortened work day and the granting of a half–day holiday, which changed the leisure patterns and habits of this group in particular.

All classes benefited from the technological developments which occurred during these decades. The electric light allowed for evening sport, and the transmission of results of competitions was accelerated by the development of the telegraph, which was particularly important in the sport of horseracing. Innovations and improvements in transportation and communication not only were commercially advantageous but also aided a community's cultural and sporting growth.

The contribution of improvements in transport technology to the rise and diffusion of organised sport in colonial Queensland in the second half of the nineteenth century was analysed through a case study of cricket by Thomas Armstrong from the period 1846 to 1896.[10]

In his outstanding contribution he outlined the use of Freeman Cobb's horse–drawn coaches, which could carry 15–16 passengers. Cobb & Co. began a regular service between Ipswich and Brisbane in 1865, but earlier cricket contact by coach had begun in 1864. Coach was the method of travel when Gympie began contests with Maryborough during the 1860s, when the Albert Cricket Club went to Warwick and Toowoomba in 1872, over 100 km, and in 1878 when a Brisbane team took nine and a half hours to get to Nerang on the Gold Coast for a match.

Visiting ships encouraged the sport as they often challenged local teams, the migrant ship "Flying Cloud" being one such in 1863. Crew from the survey ship "Salamander" played at Bowen in 1863, and the HMS "Virago" played at Gladstone in 1868. The first intercolonial match of June 1864, between NSW and Queensland, was dependent on the sea lanes. The vagaries of the sea, however, saw cricketers arriving too late for a scheduled match, or they were often seasick. Occasionally a ship would run aground. The railway, also, was utilised for sport as soon as lines were opened up. Armstrong summed up the influence of transportation.

> Isolation is a constant factor in Queensland history. Sportsmen experienced difficulties in obtaining competition just as primary producers experienced difficulties freighting their goods. Improving transportation assisted in the rise of organised cricket in Queensland through facilitating more regular contacts on a club and representative basis throughout the colony, as well as facilitating tours by intercolonial and international sides.[11]

The diffusion patterns and progressive developments from the 1850s to the 1890s will be analysed in the sports of cricket, horse–racing, rowing and pedestrianism, which were those with the greatest following in this period.

Cricket

During the latter half of the nineteenth century, the game of cricket was enthusiastically pursued in all parts of the British Empire. It was considered as "wholly an English sport and for that reason it should be encouraged in English colonies."[12] The prevailing belief was admirably expressed in the *Brisbane Courier*: "nowhere is the genius of the English people so happily and characteristically expressed as on the cricket field."[13] This "noble" game was believed to foster the development of character as well as that of the body, and was thought to exert a beneficial influence on the community. It was lauded as being a "manly" sport, and it was argued that those who played it would "grow into robust fearless men."[14] The individual who did not participate in this healthy sport invariably turned out "a timid pusillanimous weakling",[15] and besides it was argued that the game "kept young fellows together instead of allowing them to be idle in other ways."[16] Players of the game were often referred to as the "Knights of the Willow", and were heralded in verse:

> The knights of old in tournament
> would deadly combat wage
> While we who live in modern days
> find cricket all the rage
> We engage in mimic battles, our
> weapons bat and ball
> Eleven men on either side that's
> twenty–two in all
> Then here's success in cricket, boys,
> the finest game of all.[17]

Although in England cricket was a summer sport, in Queensland initially it was not specifically designated as a seasonal sport. The Moreton Bay Club, for example, advertised that its 1860 season would begin in March, however due to inclement weather its first match was delayed to May 6, when the club's 'Married' played the 'Single' members.[18] An unusual situation occurred in 1857 when William Gilbert Rees, who was living on the Darling Downs, played for NSW in an intercolonial match against Victoria. Rees was a cousin of W.G. Grace and had played for Gloucestershire.

The first intercolonial match in Queensland – 22 players from Queensland playing 11 from NSW – was contested against the southern state in June 1864 during Brisbane's winter, NSW winning easily. The climate of Queensland, of course, was considerably different to that in England, and hence the game could be played year–round. However matches were contested during the summer months, and it was even argued that "nothing was more desirable than to encourage a love for such exercise, more especially in a hot climate where habits of indulgence were especially liable to be encountered."[19] Indeed, the first century scored in Queensland was at a match played in December, during which J. Bolger "stood three hours and a half at the wicket under a hot sun"[20] to make 118.

After the intercolonial match of 1864, James ("Jemmy") Moore was hired as the State's first professional for one year, being patronised by the Brisbane Cricket Club, for the princely sum of £2 a week. He was the brother of George Moore, the grandfather of the great Charlie Macartney.

Although cricket was one of the first sports to be played in the Moreton Bay Settlement, it had not developed extensively by 1850, and was only played in Brisbane and Ipswich. However over the next three decades the standard of play improved and the number of clubs and teams increased, so that by the late 1890s the sport was described as "booming in many centres of Queensland."[21] There were even two teams on Thursday Island. Aborigines were playing the game at a high level at the Deebing Creek Reserve,[22] while Kanaka labourers had been introduced to the game by managers on sugar cane plantations near Bundaberg.[23] Also, during this era, the state organisational body, the Queensland Cricket Association (QCA), was formed, intercolonial matches were played against New South Wales, and the Brisbane Cricket Ground, the "Gabba", was officially opened in 1895.

The high point of the development of Queensland cricket occurred in 1893, when New South Wales accepted Queensland as an equal, and a Queensland Eleven played against a New South Wales Eleven. However, Queensland's inferior status was still evident, as it had to wait another three decades before the other states would accept it into Sheffield Shield competition.

The diffusion of the sport in Queensland can be seen in figure 2.[24] By 1850 games were played in Brisbane, Ipswich and Drayton, on the Darling Downs. Such matches were informal and infrequent, essentially being local challenges, single wicket matches, 'married' versus 'singles', 'squatters' versus others, and so on.

Cricket in the 1850s and early 1860s in Queensland was at a very low level. Hutcheon has described those formative years: "those were the days of extremely poor wickets, extremely poor grounds, and consequently poor scores."[25] In one advertised match, for example, one team averaged "per man only a fraction of a run."[26] The standard of play was comparatively low and this was reflected in the attitude of the players. At a match between the Brisbane and Victorian Clubs half of the Brisbane team were substitutes, and the game got underway two and a half hours after the scheduled time.[27]

By the late 1850s cricket matches were often incorporated into the program of events planned for the celebrations of a particular holiday. On Separation Day in 1957, for example, a cricket match between Brisbane and Ipswich was organised as part of the celebration of the arrival of the Governor.[28]

This inter–town match, played on Wednesday and Thursday December 7 and 8 1859, attracted an exceptionally good crowd. The

1890s	Kingaroy	1890
	Mackay	1890

	Laidley	1870
	Charters Towers	1877
	Mount Perry	1876
	Gatton	1870s
	Albion (Brisbane)	1874
	Butterflies (Brisbane)	1874
1870s	Stanley (Brisbane)	1873
	Bundaberg	1872
	Stanthorpe	1872
	Orwell (Brisbane)	1871
	Townsville	1870s
	Kangaroo Point (Brisbane)	1871

	Gympie	1868
	Roma	1864
	National (Brisbane)	1860s
	Gayndah	1864
	Victoria (Brisbane)	1863–64
	Rockhampton	1862
1860s	Albert C.C. (Brisbane)	1861
	S. Brisbane	1861
	N. Brisbane	1861
	Maryborough	1860
	Brisbane C.C.	1860
	Toowoomba	1860
	Dalby	1860

1850s	Drayton	

	Ipswich	1848
1840s	Moreton Bay Cricket Club	1847
	Local Challenges (Brisbane)	

Figure 2 Diffusion of cricket in Queensland

Moreton Bay Club was victorious, aided by the exceptional batting of Mr Bolger. Her Majesty's Birthday was another favourite occasion for cricket matches. At such celebrations in Maryborough a cricket match was arranged and the correspondent for the *Brisbane Courier* noted that it was hoped that the cricket match would help Maryborough be "a united and flourishing community."[29]

It was in the 1860s that the real expansion of the game took place. The growth was the consequence of economic development in the colony, and as towns grew in size, the competitive urge and desire for play manifested itself. Also, through immigration and migration, men who were club, and even county players in England, settled in Brisbane, and in other country areas. They were able to teach the locals as well as improving the standard of play. For example the gold rush "brought together many men from all parts of the world, many of them good cricketers."[30] In Brisbane, inter–club competitions were initiated, with teams from the Brisbane Cricket Club, North Brisbane, South Brisbane, Albert, Victoria and National clubs playing against each other. Up country, by 1860 matches were being played in Dalby and Toowoomba, by 1861 in Maryborough, 1862 in Rockhampton, 1864 in Gayndah and Roma, and 1868 in Gympie. By the late 1860s cricket was played regularly in almost all of the settled areas.

Typical of inter–town competitions would be those between Maryborough and Gympie. The two thriving gold towns, in the late 1860s, engaged in invitational inter–town matches. In 1869, for example, Maryborough issued a challenge to Gympie and even offered "to defray the hotel expenses of the Gympie team."[31] However, after due consideration, it was decided that Gympie should host Maryborough instead.

> The Maryborough cricketers arrived in Gympie by Cobb's coach and six horses, at about 5 o'clock yesterday evening, escorted into town by several Gympie cricketers and their friends on horseback; our guests put up at Farley's, where they will stay during their visit...The public of Gympie have responded to the appeals of the Match Committee for subscriptions towards defraying the expenses in a very liberal manner...The wickets, on the Commissioner's Flat, where the match will be played, have been improved as far as practicable within the past three days. There will be one refreshment booth on the ground, under the management of Mr. Lynch, of Tattersall's Hotel, who will also provide the luncheon for the cricketers and their friends...After the match, the cricketers of both teams and their friends will doubtless patronise the dramatic entertainment at the Varieties Theatre, for the benefit of the hospital, and amuse themselves in other ways.[32]

The Gympie team's captain was elected at the start of the match. The *Gympie Times* gave extensive coverage of the game and the following article presents a flavour of the times:

The most important cricket match that has taken place in Gympie was played on Thursday, and we have no hesitation in saying that it afforded a great amount of amusement and pleasurable excitement not only to the players, but also to the public, and that it was on the whole highly successful...Although the cricket ground is not so clear of trees, stumps, and other obstructions as could be wished by the local players, when inviting their antagonists to test their ability here, still it has been greatly improved. The turf is naturally good, and could be made still better in time, and the locality is in many respects an excellent one.

The match having been arranged for Thursday last, the Maryborough team arrived the day before. With cricketers, in Australia at least, want of punctuality is the fashion...the play did not commence until about 11.

...There were about 300 spectators present, including a number of ladies, for whose accommodation a booth was erected...A number of red and white flags were used to mark the ground...

...The play became very dull towards the end, the Maryborough team playing cautiously; and the spectators were continually on the move toward the scene of other attractions, such as long–jumping on horseback, foot races, etc.

At the luncheon Geo. Faircloth, Esq., President of the Gympie Cricket Club, took the chair, the vice–chair being taken by Nugent Brown, Esq., Vice–President of the same club. Mr Lynch's excellent viands were dispensed with true cricketers' appetites. There were only two toasts proposed – "The Queen", and "Success to cricket", both of which were heartily responded to. The Gympie team then gave three cheers for "Our Guests".[33]

Gympie eventually won the match, however the result was secondary to the importance of the occasion. The camaraderie and the opportunity for social interaction overshadowed the events on the pitch. Mahoney wrote: "There was no dearth of animal spirits, and most of the team landed home minus collars, ties and hats".[34] This match inaugurated a tradition of inter–town cricket competition which has perpetuated to the present day.[35] Initially Gympie dominated, with Maryborough winning for the first time in 1875.

The Maryborough district became a leading centre for cricket, and various individuals played a decisive role in its early development. Mr. N.E.N. Tooth, who had played in Sydney for the Glebe Cricket Club, migrated to Maryborough, where his knowledge and expertise in the game influenced improvements in the standard of play.[36] The Mahoney family[37] also made a remarkable contribution to cricket in the area, as they were all avid cricket enthusiasts. They strongly believed that cricket was the game of the Empire and devoted their lives to its promotion. It was through the efforts of enthusiasts like them that English teams came to the northern centre to play: "The Wide Bay and Burnett cricketers were delighted to have visits from the Hon. Ivo Bligh's English eleven in February, 1883, and from Shaw and Shrewsbury's team in February, 1885. Two years later the Shaw and Lilywhite eleven played at Maryborough and Gympie."[38]

Cricket began at Maryborough in 1860 and approximately 1868 saw the formation of the Yengarie Cricket Club, mainly through the efforts of James Mahoney, Sr., and Jotham Blanchard. James had come from Maitland, NSW, to Yengarie. "Of most powerful build, he was famous for his hitting powers, he was a fair slow bowler, and a magnificent field, in short a tower of strength to the village team before the days of concrete wickets."[39] He retired about 1898 but continued his association with the game.

His eldest son was Jas. R.D. Mahoney, who was a fine cricketer, but an outstanding organiser and promoter of the game. He became one of the leading personalities in Queensland country cricket. In 1893 he was transferred to the Central District, where he quickly established the Westwood Cricket Club, and the Leichhardt Cricket Association. The following year he was transferred to Croydon, where he rapidly established himself in cricket and football circles. He returned to Maryborough in 1899, immediately associating himself with the Yengarie C.C., the Cricket Association, the Wallaroo F.C. and the Rugby Union. He was the author–editor of *Wide Bay and Burnett Cricket*, a remarkable volume about cricket in country areas of Queensland.

Charlie Mahoney, next in point of age, died a young man in Townsville, and besides upholding the family reputation as an all–round cricketer was considered the best all–round athlete in the family. Willie Mahoney was also an outstanding all–rounder, left–handed like his father, and was good enough to be twelfth man for Queensland. Percy Mahoney was considered a stylish batsman, but Bernard preferred football to cricket, perhaps overawed by the family's accomplishments. He was, however, a fine cricketer.

J.P. (Joe) Mahoney was the best of the lot, the best all–round cricketer Maryborough produced in 1908. He first appeared seriously in senior cricket in 1890.

When we add to this list the contributions of the Mahoney's to university sport in Brisbane, and to hockey in Queensland and Australia, and also add the contribution of Sister Mahoney in writing her history of All Hallows' School, it is obvious that we are dealing with a remarkable Queensland family.

The influence of Maryborough Grammar School was also apparent, as many of the local cricketers learned the game while at school. Opened in 1881, the first match against Brisbane Boys' Grammar was in 1882, which Maryborough won by 11 runs. The headmaster, Mr Murdoch, who had played against England, scored 23 not out, and Jas. Thomson, the next headmaster, scored 9. Mahoney wrote of Thomson, who was later to become a Vice-President of the Maryborough Cricket Association for many years:

> Mr Jas. Thomson, like Mr Roe, may be claimed as one of the assets of Queensland. His twenty-five years' work in our Grammar school has already borne abundant fruitage, and there is promise of a bountiful harvest in the years to come.
>
> Mr Thomson is one of the men whose advice and assistance the author has relied upon during his close connection with Maryborough athletics, and he has been met on all occasions with unfailing courtesy and sympathy.
>
> Mr Thomson recognises the value of athletics in education, and endeavours to see the games are played according to their highest traditions.
>
> There seems to be as close a connection between the good scholar and good cricketer, as between the good cricketer and the successful citizen. This connection has been constantly borne upon me in compiling this work, for our players in their more serious hours have all been men of action in the up-building of our prosperous district.[40]

The link between sport and character, the concept of Muscular Christianity, was clearly seen in this time period. The classics master of the school, E.W.H. Fowles, was the coach of the Maryborough Grammar team in the 1890s. As well as games against Brisbane Grammar, there were games against Ipswich and Toowoomba Grammar schools. Other schools in the district playing cricket were Christian Brothers, Aldershot, Central and Newtown.

N.E. Tooth reflected on the vagaries of umpires in the country area.

> Joe Pearce, of ours, was bowling and sent in one of his shooters. Down went the wicket. "How's that, umpire?" "Well! I didn't see it. I were a-watchin' them ere billy-goats fighten', but I allus gives the batter the benefit. Not out!"...Yet another time the writer was bowling, and delivered a regular bailer, which sent two stumps and bails flying. "Hows' that, umpire?" "Well, sir, what do you think yourself?" "I think your a d——fool." "Yer do; do yer? Well, not out!"[41]

He wrote of how various players would ride in for a game from considerable distances, and afterwards they would dine at Bonarius' Southern Cross hotel, where there would be jokes and repartee, "And after dinner how we would play cribbage, swap yarns, tell of each other's prowess, not to mention the sing–songs...Then 10 p.m., a night-cap and "Auld Lang Syne", and away home and dream of the next holiday, when we would all meet again."[42] Indeed they were jolly and happy times, when there was a camaraderie of men eking out a living in isolated towns. At the time (1860s and 1870s) only rounders and cricket were played as out–door games in the area, football was being talked about, and lawn tennis, polo and golf were unheard of. "Cricket was 'the' game above all others, and this, no doubt, will account for the fact that it was played with so much more vigor and enthusiasm in bygone days than nowadays."[43] There were no Bulli or matting wickets, the games in Maryborough were on a 90–acre reserve opposite the Southern Cross Hotel and horses would cross and re–cross the wicket. It would be levelled with a hoe and smoothed with a rake. Properly turfed wickets and concrete wickets were to come later.

Outstanding Gympie cricketer, James Chapple, later to work on the *Herald* staff in Brisbane, offered 250 mining shares in Maryborough to the highest scorer on Bligh's English side:

> ...it was decided, on the suggestion of Hon. Ivo Bligh, to draw for places. I noticed Ulyett very busy folding his name up as tight as a pea. I asked, "Who is going to draw?" "Let any lad draw," said Ulyett; "here, I be a good drawer." He was certainly a slow one, and Barnes was induced to say, "What he be doing of?, to which Ulyett replied, as he produced the first paper, "Hi was feeling for the small pea." As he announced the name "Ulyett", one of the team remarked, "Thee be a bit smart." He eventually smacked up 100 in a very short time, and won the shares.[44]

This generosity of giving mining shares to the best player continued when England played Gympie. A Charley Cuffe offered 25 shares and these were won by Scotten. These shares were sold by the players, so they did well out of these unusual trophies.

The visit of the Hon. Ivo Bligh's team to play Wide Bay on 9 and 10 February 1883 was the highpoint of the north's cricketing history. Sixty committee members were responsible for the arrangements, the team being met at the wharf by the Mayor, Alderman F. Bryant, who happened to be an old Maryborough captain, and a six–in–hand was supplied so the players could enter the town in style. As was the custom at the time, the amateurs stayed at the more distinguished hotel, the Sydney, while the professionals were at the Union. In the evening some 200 aborigines gave a corroboree in their honour, and one of them, Yorkie, insisted on shaking Bligh's hand. Saddle horses were placed at the disposal of the English team so that they could visit the surrounding sugar plantations, the Amateur Dramatic Co. gave a complimentary performance, and a grand ball was held. After the match the team took part in a pigeon shooting contest, and won most of the prizes. The eighteen players of Wide Bay scored 42 and 79, their total more than Brisbane's against the eleven of England, who scored 179 in their only innings.

The next visit was Shaw and Shrewsbury's team, which played Maryborough on 6 and 7 February 1885, and Gympie on 9 and 10 February. In both cases the locals played twenty–two against eleven for the visitors. There was a controversy in the Gympie match as Power bowled a ball to the English player Scotten which dislodged one of the bails, but, becoming jammed between the wickets it never reached the ground. The umpire ruled not out, but several of the English team adjudged that it was an incorrect decision.

The next visit was Shaw and Lillywhite's team, which played Maryborough on 23 and 24 November and Gympie on 27 and 28 November 1887. The other major visit of note was Trumper's 1906 renegade visit, when they also played Bundaberg, Maryborough and Gympie. Charters Towers, Townsville, North Queensland, Rockhampton, Mount Morgan and Brisbane were also on their Queensland itinerary. Cricket in Childers experienced difficulties in the 1908 period owing to the requirements of the sugar industry necessitating work on Saturdays, and "some of the best men are averse to playing on Sunday."[45] At Gayndah a Mr Roberts managed the mine and captained the club, and at Mungar in the early days the team consisted of mill hands and a few of the bullockies.

Along the northern coastline, for many years, visiting ships provided the main source of competition. The first noteworthy match was in 1862 when a team from Bowen played against the crew from the survey vessel "Pioneer". However, it was really during the 1870s that the game was played with any regularity in the tropical north. Clubs were formed at Townsville, Gatton, Laidley, Mount Perry and Charters Towers, as well as other smaller centres. In some locales, such as Charters Towers and Townsville, inter–town competition was inaugurated in the 1880s although such was not held on a regular basis until the 1890s.[46] The standard of play was variable, although according to the Australian Cricketer's Annual for 1876–77 there were several sugar planters who had played for Oxford or Cambridge living in the Mackay area.[47]

With more teams being formed and competitions increasing in quantity, the quality of play began to improve as well. In 1875 a second intercolonial match was played against New South Wales and, to the surprise of all, victory was achieved by the northern colony, by 69 runs, though it was eighteen Queenslanders versus eleven from NSW. Alick

Bannerman and Tom Garrett were among the NSW stars. This accomplishment stimulated interest in the game, leading the *Brisbane Courier* to proclaim that "cricket is undergoing a revolution in Brisbane just now...and the game is receiving a great impetus from the extent to which the Cricket fever has spread, and the number of new clubs formed."[48] Subsequently the Queensland Cricket Association (QCA) was formed in 1876 and this step marked "the culmination of years of spadework by men who brought to Queensland the customs and the games of Britain."[49] Sir Maurice O'Connell, a grandson of Governor William Bligh, was the first President of the QCA, which at the time of its formation had seven Brisbane teams affiliated with it: Shaws, Albert, Stanley, Milton, GPO, Police and Eagle Farm. Country teams began to join the following years, and by 1884 there were some five in QCA–affiliated teams: One Mile (Gympie), West End and Limestone (Ipswich), Roma and Unsted (Toowoomba).

The formation of a state organisational body provided a stimulus for the development of the games in the colony. Brisbane teams regularly visited such centres as Ipswich, Gympie, Toowoomba, Rockhampton and Bundaberg, and these visits assisted in the promulgation of the game, particularly in the country areas. Added impetus was provided by matches against Australia in 1877 and England in 1883, 1885 and 1887.

One of the main problems that cricketers faced in all areas at this time, including Brisbane, was the poor quality of pitches. When the English team came to Brisbane it was lamented that they, the English "will find our grounds – faith that is wrong, they won't find them."[50] The New South Welshmen called on the "Bananalanders...to prepare wickets, such as will secure a bowler's immunity from a charge of manslaughter."[51] In Brisbane it was argued that the reasons for the sad condition of the grounds was that the subscription to all clubs was too low, and that members, including some very prominent individuals, never paid their dues.[52]

The 1883 English touring team, captained by Hon. Ivo Bligh, attracted considerable interest in Brisbane, as it was the first "international" team to come to Queensland. The public responded enthusiastically to the visit and a crowd of over 7,000 attended this match at Eagle Farm Racecourse.[53] Although the Queenslanders had twenty–two players they were soundly thrashed, with the English scoring 265, and the home side making only 62 and 49. Some pride, however, was salvaged in a pigeon shooting match in which the local shooters tied against eight of the English cricket team.[54] After the success of the English visit, Brisbane was included on the 1885 Shaw and Shrewsbury tour schedule, while Maryborough and Gympie were visited by the 1887 Shaw and Lillywhite team. The visits of these international teams, through example, helped to raise the level of play in Queensland.

After W.G. Grace's tour of Australia, the *Pall Mall Gazette* noted that cricket in Australia was "being assiduously cultivated and scientifically improved."[55] However, the standard of play in Queensland lagged behind that of the other states. In an attempt to raise this level, clubs started to import players from the south. One of the first was the Stanley club in Brisbane, which hired Edward "Ned" Sheridan in 1883.[56] Sheridan had played for the Warwick Club in Sydney as well as being on the New South Wales team from 1869 to 1878. After his contract with Stanleys expired he made his services available to other clubs in Brisbane.

Another club that imported players from the south was the Graziers' Club. This club was formed in the early 1890s by a Mr T.V. Francis, who was a senior partner in the Baynes Brothers Company, and his intention was to bring together an outstanding team of cricket players. He enticed a number of New South Wales players, as well as one from Victoria, to come to Brisbane, and found employment for them in the city so that they could play.[57] The extent of such recruitment practices is evident from the following advertisement in the *Brisbane Courier*: "Wanted at once, two clerks for a large butchering establishment, previous experience not necessary; must, however, be first-class bowlers."[58]

By the early 1890s interest in cricket was apparent from the number of clubs in existence as well as the regular competitive matches that were scheduled. In 1892, in Brisbane, there were 12 senior clubs involved in regular 'senior' competition (Normanby, Oakfields, South Brisbane, Stanley, Union, Woolloongabba, Albert, Coorparoo, Corinda, Graziers, Kangaroo Point and New Farm), as well as 23 in junior contests.

A similar growth pattern was evident in other centres. Ipswich, for example, by the late 1890s had four teams in local competition; namely Limestone, Southern Stars, Federals and Asylums.

In some country areas cricket was also well established by the 1890s. In Gympie, there were six teams – Excelsior, Oxford, Ranger, Monckland, Union and One Mile, while in Rockhampton there were four teams – Rockhampton, Past Grammar, Albert and Banks. Maryborough increasingly became a major centre for cricket, with seven teams formed in the town: Union, Past Grammar, Exiles, Grammar School, Waratah, Surrey Hill, United and Yengarie.

Just as Queensland cricket was achieving acceptance by the other states as being of first–class calibre, setbacks resulted as a consequence of the formation of rival organisations to the QCA. The South Queensland Cricket Association was formed, with teams such as South Brisbane, Oakfields and Toowong being aligned with it. This association was short–lived, however in 1895 another association, the National Cricket Union (NCU), was formed. Many of the top players were former QCA members and W. Welsby was the Chairman for several seasons. The main attraction of the NCU was its Wednesday competitions, as well as its annual matches against New South Wales.[59] As only QCA members were permitted on the intercolonial team Queensland, in the late 1890s, did not always have its best players on the state representative team. This was blatantly obvious in 1899, when Queensland was defeated by South Australia by an innings and 284 runs. From 1895 to 1899 the struggle for control of cricket hindered the game, but after the South Australia loss, the two bodies finally agreed to amalgamate.

INTERNATIONAL	Visit of English Teams	1880s
NATIONAL	Queensland vs Australia	1877
INTERCOLONIAL	Queensland vs NSW	1860s
REGIONAL	Ipswich vs Brisbane, etc.	1840s & 1850s
LOCAL	Local Challenges & Local Clubs	1840S

Figure 3 Cricket: Transition from local to regional to intercolonial contests

From the 1850s to the 1890s, the game of cricket underwent considerable transformation (figure 3) as it evolved from being essentially a village game, which was played informally and infrequently, to one that was structured, with regular, standardised competitions. Virtually every town of any size fielded at least one team, and competitions were conducted on an intra–town as well as an inter–

town level. The state-wide organisational structure had been established
to strengthen the links between the city and country areas, as well as to
foster the growth of the sport throughout the state. Queensland was
included on the itinerary of touring international teams and first class
cricket was played against other states and the national side.

Horse-racing

Horse-racing was the first organised sport in Queensland, and by 1880
it was well established in the Moreton Bay and Ipswich areas. However
it was in the following decades, the 1850s, 1860s, 1870s and 1880s that
it was to develop into a virile and flourishing sporting institution
throughout the state. It was understandable that, as horses were a
necessity for all segments of society, the sport of horse-racing would
come to occupy one of the foremost positions in the sporting hierarchy
of the colony.

Figure 4 demonstrates the diffusion of horse-racing throughout the
state as it became an important element in the life of practically every
town and city. Slightly more than a year after the official proclamation
of the Gympie goldfield, the first race meetings were held, on December
29 and 30 1868. A similar development was evident in Charters Towers.
The first recorded races were in 1873 and crushing equipment came to
the goldfield in 1872 after its discovery in 1871. As was to be the case
throughout the length and breadth of Australia, each town of reasonable
size was to construct its own race course and conduct regular meetings.
When the Mayor proposed that the Darling Downs races and club
should be inaugurated, he expressed the prevailing belief that races
"were of much benefit to the towns in which they were held."[60]

The first race meeting in Gympie would have been typical of such
inaugural meetings in the state. The correspondent for the *Courier*
reported that: "It is something that is not heard of every day, that in a
place which little more than a year ago was the wild bush, a very fair
course has been formed, considering the broken hilly nature of the
country in this vicinity."[61] The races were organised at Foo's Hotel.[62]

The course was on the banks of the Gympie Creek, approximately
two miles from town. As the two race days were declared public
holidays, there were some 3,000 spectators in attendance. Temporary
booths lined the road out to the course, at which the weary traveller
could imbibe soda water, lemonade, ginger beer

1880s			Beaudesert 1880s		
	Miles 1885		Chinchilla 1886	Balonne 1888	Cumberland 1889
	Hughenden 1881		Goondiwindi 1883	Isisford 1884	Emerald 1885
1870s			Gatton 1870s		
			Aramac 1877	Surat 1878	Winton 1879
	Charleville 1873	Bundaberg 1873	Ravenswood 1873		St. George 1873
	Rocky Waterholes 1873		Clermont 1872	Mount Perry 1872	Charters Towers 1873
	Port Curtis 1870		Mungindi 1871	Condamine 1871	Stanthorpe 1872
	Gilberton 1870		Cardwell 1870	Logan 1871	Pimpama 1871
			Inglewood 1870	Dalby 1870	Warrego (Cunnamulla) 1870
1860s	Maranda (Roma) 1864	Mackay 1866	Townsville 1866	Gympie 1868	
	Nanango 1860		Gladstone 1861	Peak Downs (Crinum Creek) 1864	Tambo 1864
1850s	Warwick 1850		Gayndah 1852	Rockhampton (Gracemere) 1856	Maryborough 1859
				Drayton 1856	
1840s	Ipswich 1848				
1830s		Brisbane 1830s & 1840s			

Figure 4 Diffusion of horse racing throughout Queensland

...and where, if reports be correct, those potent beverages might be diluted by admixture with certain alcoholic fluids. Arriving on the course we found a long row of publicans' booths and fruiterers' and confectioners' stall. In the centre of these was the grand Stand, on which there was room to accommodate a much larger number of spectators than there was any reason to expect. Underneath was a long oval counter, where sundry pretty barmaids and smart waiters dispensed liquid refreshments, under the superintendence of Messrs Scowen and Farley, to the thirsty public. We may remark that all the publicans appeared to be "doing a stroke!" but nevertheless there was nothing whatever in the shape of a row. Of course, on such an occasion, some few of the pleasure seekers were inclined to be argumentative over their cups, but the police acted good–humouredly as peacemakers, and prevented words from coming to blows.[63]

The program of events included the Maiden Plate, the Publicans' Purse, the Diggers' Purse, the Hack Race, the Hurdle Race, the Ladies' Purse, the Consolation Handicap and the Gympie Christmas Plate. Considerable enthusiasm was exhibited by spectators, as it was noted that "four or five hundred horsemen [were] in the habit of charging recklessly through the patches of timber and over the fallen logs during every race."[64] Before the races, two horsemen collided and were thrown, and one horse died shortly thereafter. In another accident one rider's arm was broken and a horse's shoulder dislocated.

These meetings were not organised by properly constituted clubs. Prominent citizens usually donated the purse. Eventually a club would be officially formed to administer and organise such races, making judgments with respect to such matters as handicaps and weights. There was an additional purpose related to the formation of a club, as exemplified in Warwick: "When such a club is in existence the Government will place the deed of the land in the hands of trustees, who will give authority to the members of the club to fence it in and otherwise improve it for the benefit and convenience of the public."[65]

In Gympie, the first race meeting was in December 1868, however the Gympie Turf Club was not formed until July 1870, when the Annual Race Programme was also established. In the Rockhampton area, the elapsed time was greater, as the Fitzroy Jockey Club was formed in 1863,[66] whereas the first races in the area were as early as 1856. The first races appear to have been held in the Toowoomba area before Separation, however the Turf Club was not formed until 1878.[67] The clubs were generally called either "Turf" or "Jockey", however they did not have the same standing as in England, where there was a greater aristocratic and upper class association. As Nat Gould wrote, in the 1890s, the Jockey Club in the Antipodes "is by no means the high sounding and select club it is in England."[68]

Although the honour of hosting the first race meetings in Queensland must be accorded to Brisbane, two other towns, Ipswich and Gayndah established themselves in the early 1850s as the other principal racing centres in Queensland. Considerable rivalry developed between the three areas.

Ipswich hosted the state's first Intercolonial Champion Stakes in 1861, and until 1910 the richest race ever decided in Queensland was run in that city.[69] However, the honour of instituting the Queensland Derby Stakes in 1868 falls to Gayndah, which also hosted the state's first campdraft. The wealthy squatters outside of the metropolis, reinforced by local pride, enthusiasm and a desire for change, were the mitigating factors in the shift of power in racing away from Brisbane.

Gayndah was established as the communal centre to serve the needs of the squatters in the Burnett River Valley. Some of the squatters who opened vast sheep holdings in the area were Stuart Russell, Richard Jones, the Eliot brothers, R. Wilkin, George Mocatta, Henry Herbert, J.B. Reid, and William Humphries. They

> ...were men of education, possessing the commanding influence of money and the confidence of financial institutions. For this reason Gayndah, in her period of adolescence, rapidly flourished and stepped forth in antagonism to Brisbane as the metropolis of the then confidently awaited new colony in the north...In 1849 Gayndah was declared a township.[70]

The first Gayndah Race Meeting was held on Monday, 23 June 1852, and Wednesday, 25 June. There was the Gayndah Plate worth 25 sovereigns, the Corrobbaree (*sic*) Purse for hacks or station horses, the Impromptu Stakes also for hacks, the Pigskin Plate for non-winners of previous races for owners who had been in employment in the district, the Squatter's Plate for gentlemen riders, the Burnett Stakes, the Beaten Stakes, again for non-winners, and a second Pigskin Plate.[71] The build-up to the Gayndah races was well reported by the Burnett District correspondent.

> One hundred pounds has been subscribed by the squatters of the Burnett district, and the inhabitants of Gayndah, for the first races...A good meet and much sport is anticipated; one gentleman, well known on the Northern Turf, having secured stabling for seven horses. The course is a new one, and £20 is being laid out in clearing it and fencing in the distance, etc. It is on a small plain, half a mile from Gayndah, and is oval shaped, so that a person on foot will be able to see the riders all round the course. A race dinner will be given by the stewards on the last day, at Sidney's Inn. A prize fight is also on the *tapis*, between "Billy the Cowboy", and Moffitt, the 'Exile Pet', for £50 a side. £500 is expected to change hands upon the event, the 'old uns' being determined to back Billy to the last shilling.[72]

By the early 1860s its race meetings were well established and in 1868 the Gayndah Jockey Club began the Queensland Derby Stakes. This race, of one and a half miles, was won by Mr W.E. Parry–Okeden, sometime Commissioner of the Queensland Police and President of the Brisbane Hunt Club, whose horse Hermit was ridden by Powell.[73] In 1870, the Derbies were held in Queensland, with one being at Gayndah, which was won by Mr Scott's Grafton, again ridden by Powell, and the other being at Toowoomba and which was won by the same horse and rider, and nominated under the ownership of Mr B. Powell.[74] The reason for the two derbies being held in the same year was the royal visit.

In 1871 the Derby was moved to Eagle Farm, but from 1873 to 1877 was not run. The race was revived in 1878 and was won by owner Sir Joshua Peter Bell, who also won the following three Derbies. The Derby at Eagle Farm became "one of two richest races, and the richest of the classic races associated with the Queensland Turf."[75]

In the formative years of the colony, as has been pointed out, there was considerable rivalry between Brisbane and Ipswich, and this rivalry was reflected in sport. Local pride found particular expression in horse-racing, as the two centres struggled for organisational control of the sport in the colony. A determined move was taken in 1851 when the race committee of Ipswich resolved to call their annual races the "Northern Races."[76] The following year, on July 11th of 1852, a public meeting was held with the express purpose of founding the North Australian Jockey Club (NAJC), and this was duly formed. When the second meeting, under the auspices of the NAJC, was held, eight months later, the *Moreton Bay Courier* discussed at length these developments.

> A programme in our advertising columns shows that our friends at Ipswich are determined that no efforts on their part shall be wanting, to give *eclat* to the forthcoming "North Australian Races": as those unassuming gentlemen, with characteristic modesty, designate their annual turf meeting. They are certainly worthy of much praise for the spirit with which they have set about the present preparations, and the chief prize is a very creditable amount. The course at Ipswich is an excellent one, and the position being tolerably centrical, these sports seem likely to be established on a firm and lasting basis. The great difficulty that attended the promotion of horse racing at Moreton Bay in the early days of its free settlement, arose from the exclusiveness of its rules; none but gentlemen being ostensibly permitted to ride, although in reality we have seen some of the veriest snobs in creation donning the coloured cap and jacket at those meetings. But that foolish mistake has now been remedied, and our fellow colonists in Ipswich and its vicinity, having certainly eclipsed Brisbane in racing matters, can well afford to acknowledge that there the first blow was given to the exclusive

system in racing – and a hard matter it was to strike that blow. At the
Ipswich meeting we observe that there is but one race – the Hurdle Race –
devoted to gentlemen riders. This is as it should be, and ought to be
perfectly satisfactory to all parties.[77]

From these comments it is apparent that the conflict between the
"gentlemen" and the public over the organisation of racing in Brisbane
had still not been resolved. Already, by 1848[78] the issue of whether the
town races should be open to one and all had become a matter of public
concern. Originally the Moreton Bay Races were organised by
gentlemen–squatters and they tried to run them as essentially "private"
meetings; i.e., putting up the purses, often being the jockeys themselves,
and allowing only their own horses to race. The consequence of this
struggle was that the Brisbane Races declined in popularity. The Ipswich
club – the NAJC – did not fall into the same dilemma as Brisbane, as it
reached the point earlier that it would only set aside one race for
gentlemen riders. Such was also the pattern at Gayndah, where only the
Squatters' Plate was restricted to gentlemen riders.

In spite of the moves by the NAJC to open up the races to a wider
public, that is, to democratise them, the membership of the club
committee clearly remained in the hands of the leading citizens, and
these understandably included members of the squattocracy.

The members of the NAJC read like a *Who's Who* of Ipswich
society: Francis Bigge, Esq, Member of the Legislative Council, in the
chair; Fred W. Bigge; George Fairholme; Joshua Peter Bell; Patrick
Leslie; Hannibal Macarther, Police Magistrate; Henry Hughes, and so
on.[79] When the Fitzroy Jockey Club was formed in Rockhampton,
Arthur Mackenzie was President, A. Feez, Vice President, [80] and they
were two of the leading citizens of the area. A similar pattern was
evident in Brisbane with the organisation of the Queensland Turf Club.
The power positions were in the hands of the elite. The Governor, the
Attorney General and the Chief Justice also added status to Brisbane's
race meetings with their continual presence.

The Chairman of the NAJC, Francis Bigge, recommended from the
onset that the Homebush Rules (Australia) be adopted for the running of
the Club, as they were "better adapted to the circumstances of the
colony than those of Newmarket (England), by which they are now
guided."[81] This recommendation was accepted and thereafter the races at
Ipswich were according to the rules and regulations of the NAJC. At
this time the races in Brisbane and Gayndah were according to
Newmarket rules. This step by the NAJC was a considerable departure
and an assertion of authority and colonisation.

The Rules controversy was an issue that was not readily resolved in Queensland or, indeed, elsewhere in Australia. It was not until 1912 that the Australian Rules of Racing were published, and even then uniformity of rules was not accepted, particularly at country race meetings. In Queensland, the Queensland Turf Club (QTC), in 1885, adopted the rules of the English Jockey Club, and formulated a plan for the registration of all clubs in the state. The QTC was Brisbane-based, and it had simply assumed that, representing the capital, the Club should assume the leadership of racing matters in the state. It was logical that state-wide rules and regulations should be followed and that there would be a uniformity in age rules and weight-for-age regulations. However, northern clubs resented such attempts by the QTC, as they claimed that it was "an attempt to force on them a code of rules, which were not adapted to racing conditions in the North."[82] Consequently, they formed their own association, the North Queensland Racing Association (NQRA) and, in later years, the Central Queensland Racing Association (CQRA) was established to exert control over racing matters in the Central and Centre West areas. In 1936 a fourth body, the Rockhampton Jockey Club, was proclaimed by a Government Royal Commission. Race clubs in the same vicinity could affiliate with different associations and thereby follow different rules. For example, in the 1940s in the Central and Upper Burnett River District, the Gayndah, Eidsvold and Abercorn clubs were controlled by the QTC, while the Monto and Bancroft Clubs were under the jurisdiction of the Rockhampton Jockey Club.[83]

The rise of Ipswich as a racing power was hastened by the poor state of affairs in Brisbane. The purses being offered were but one indication of the status of the races in the two centres. The Brisbane Races subscription list for the 1851 races only amounted to £150 in May,[84] while in Ipswich, for the Northern Races, the subscription in April amounted to "£250, which together with the entrance money, will, with new subscriptions, amount to at least £400."[85] Three years later, in 1854, the *Moreton Bay Courier* commented that: "we are glad to hear that an effort is being made to revive the Brisbane Races, now several years in a state of somnolency."[86]

The lack of a proper race course had been one of the major problems in Brisbane, but this was finally rectified in November 1854 when Captain Wickham, as Government Resident, instructed the survey department "to mark out a suitable piece of ground for reserve as a race-course. Accordingly a site...between Eagle Farm and the German Station"[87] was selected. Apparently the land grant included a portion of the Women's Convict Farm.[88] This was to be known as the New Farm

Course. Subsequently the Brisbane Races were successfully held at the end of May at New Farm, and the pattern was set for the following years.

> The morning of Tuesday last was as fair as the best lover of the turf could have desired for the first day of the Brisbane Annual Races for the year 1855. Notwithstanding that the Circuit Court was sitting, and that many people were thus debarred from witnessing the sports, the race course was more numerously attended, than on any former occasion. A steam boat plied between the township and New Farm Course; booths were erected on various parts of the ground, and altogether the meeting was one of the best that has ever taken place in the Northern Districts. The ground was in admirable order, and therein presented a great contrast to the last Ipswich meeting, when the heavy rain made severe labour for the horses.[89]

Ipswich, however, continued through the 1850s and early 1860s to maintain its position as the premier centre of horse-racing in Queensland. In 1863 the correspondent from Ipswich stated, with some arrogance, that "we feel a glow of pride that Ipswich takes the lead in matters of the turf far beyond all other portions of the colony, and whilst the absurdly bepraised metropolis does not venture to enter a donkey on the occasion, nor offer a plate, the Ipswichians are enabled to present to those who patronise the turf, prizes beyond £1000 value."[90]

Brisbane attempted to re-establish itself as the state's horse-racing centre, in 1863, by forming the Queensland Turf Club (QTC). The club received a grant from the government for 322 acres, and it was here where the Eagle Farm course was built. The inaugural meeting of the QTC was held two years later, on August 14 1865, and Hon Colonel M.C. O'Connell was the club's first President. Some years later Sir Joshua Peter Bell took over that office and, in the 1880s, Mr Justice Mein and John Stevenson occupied the Presidency. Then, in the 1870s, Boyd Morehead, while Premier of the state, was elected President. The leadership of the QTC was obviously in the hands of the leading citizens and membership in the highest levels of the club remained an exclusive enclave for the elite.

Although initially the QTC was secondary in importance to the NATC, it gradually usurped it from its pedestal, and the QTC races ultimately became the premier race meetings of the state. The Brisbane Cup, which was to become the leading race, was not highly regarded when it began, and for some unknown reason it was relegated to the non-holiday day of the three-day race meeting.[91] The first Brisbane Cup, run on Friday May 25 1866, was won by NSW owner J.T. Ryan's "Forrestor".

By the 1890s the QTC organised each year, at Eagle Farm, four meetings which were held over two or three days. These meetings coincided with the major public holidays: the Queen's Birthday, the Exhibition period, the Prince of Wales' Birthday and Christmas-New Year, and these were considered "red letter days in the social calendar."[92] On these occasions the Governor was normally in attendance, as were the social elite of the city. Special banquets and balls were arranged in conjunction with the races, and these were considered integral components of the annual social calendar.

Although horse-racing was considered the "Sport of Kings" and was controlled and pursued by the elite, it was also extremely popular among all classes of society. While the elite were members of the clubs, the lower socio-economic groups made up the majority of the patrons at the race meetings. All classes could identify with horses and all could gamble.

In the early 1860s half the townspeople from Rockhampton would turn out for the races, and as there was no fence there was, therefore, no charge to enter the grounds.[93]

At the 1863 Brisbane races, which were held on a Thursday and Friday, the daily attendance was considerable, although it was lamented that on Friday the attendance had dropped to fifteen hundred.[94] In the late 1880s the Queen's Birthday races, for example, drew some 12,000 people.[95] Going to the races was an inexpensive afternoon's outing for a family. Entrance to the QTC races at Eagle Farm was only one shilling. However, there were additional costs if the racegoer wished to sit in the grandstand, or go into the enclosure. The members' stand was, however, restricted to QTC members and their invited guests. By the 1990s, while the elite preferred the QTC races at Eagle Farm, the working class preferred the Breakfast Creek and other minor racecourses.[96]

The racecourse grounds were not, however, used exclusively for horse-racing. The first intercolonial Rugby Union match between New South Wales and Queensland in 1883 was held at Eagle Farm, while the inner of the Breakfast Creek course served as the launching site for the first balloon ascent in Brisbane. Other sports that were pursued at the Creek course were football, cricket, tennis, cycling, pedestrianism and even swimming and boat racing were organised.[97] Over the years Eagle Farm has served as the site for such diverse activities as pigeon shoots, croquet, polo, football, cricket, military parades, Armed Forces' Camp (1942-45), patriotic fetes, and the landing area for a world solo flight.[98]

Race courses have, unfortunately, also served as the locale for two noteworthy riots, one of which was racially inspired. In 1883, at the Mackay Boxing Day race meeting, the most significant racial disturbance between the Pacific Island Kanaka labourers and Europeans in nineteenth century Queensland occurred.[99]

The Boxing Day race meeting were the main racing event of the year in Mackay, and people from all over attended; the graziers, the planters and the leading citizens, as well as the Islanders. Although it was illegal, the Kanakas had always been supplied with ample quantities of alcohol by legitimate as well as sly-grog suppliers. At the 1883 Boxing Day race meeting Boslem, a Kanaka, who was already drunk, went to one of the liquor booths at the race course, but the publican, Mr Dimock, refused him liquor.[100] An immediate argument ensued, and in no time the Islanders started to throw bottles. Europeans around the booths, many somewhat inebriated themselves, joined in the melee. The fighting soon got out of hand and became a battle between the races, the whites versus the Islanders. The wire fence surrounding the course was cut as reinforcements came from a local hotel. One witness described the onslaught: "The white men, excited and quite without control, galloped about in all directions when ever a black head was to be seen and pounced upon the wretched kanakas, knocking them down, riding over them, and kicking, and we are sorry to say in some cases brutally ill-using them."[101] Although in the *Queensland Figaro* it was claimed that the Kanakas used spears and clubs, empty bottles were their only weapons. Although there were claims that for weeks afterwards bodies of dead Kanakas were found in surrounding sugar plantations, only two were officially recorded as being killed though many, including whites, were seriously wounded. There is conflicting evidence concerning the riot, and Moore contends that many contemporary, and later accounts, were "exaggerated and romanticised".[102] The incident was given wide publicity and fuelled racial antagonism in the state as well as in the local area. The Mackay Boxing Day race riot did, in the long haul, act as stimulus for the passage of legislation forbidding the recruitment of Pacific Islanders to Queensland.

The Brisbane Cup of 1887 was the occasion for a riot of a different type. At the start of a race there were numerous delays and then there was a false start. Some of the horses ran the complete course, although most of the heavily backed ones stayed at the post. Honest Ned, an outsider which was one of the horses that continued to run the course after the false start, was declared the winner.

> ...I have seen a few exhibitions of feeling on racecourses, but never one to equal that at Eagle Farm when this decision was given. The people rushed the Grand Stand enclosure and commenced to pull down the fencing. For a short time there was a riot...The manager of the Totalisator took the precaution to retreat with the money to a safe distance until the storm was

over. I never saw a racecourse crowd more determined to show how they felt about a race.[103]

In the early years there was very little control exercised by clubs over the methods of gambling, and games of chance, and private wagers and other legal and illegal activities proliferated at race meetings. Private wagers on challenge races were contested on race days, or on separate occasions. At the inaugural NAJC races there were several such challenge races.[104]

Although various gambling games were usually part of the race day, the NAJC adamantly proclaimed that they would not follow the English tradition of permitting such subsidiary activities.

> The people looking upon the races as a holiday, and the general prosperity of all classes of her Majesty's subjects being such that there was no necessity to resort to the low swindling games which disfigure the race-course of the old country, a sketcher of the scenes in the hackneyed style would miss the particulars for an opening description. There was no Duke of Buccleuch playing at Aunt Sally on the course – no "turn em alive oh" – or "Sixpence off the clay you win – just throw the stick, try your luck; – there, I declare, who would have thought it; better next time, try again." There was no enticing gaming board with the marked figures to deceive, and the large display of the coins of the realm both for ornaments and use if need be. No snuff–box sticking, or whirligigs, or strolling players, or thimble–riggers; but the vanguard of English amusements, as if in token that the home accompaniments would come in good time, was there, in the persons of Punch, Judy and dog Toby, which were favored with a large attendance, and disputed the honors of the day with the riders. "Cards of the races" were in request: the grand stand was the centre of attraction; and after the formulas had been gone through, the bone, blood, and sinew of the horses were put to the test.[105]

However, when the QTCs first meeting was held in 1865 "all the fun of a fair...with sideshows, three card men, an Aunt Sally and a menagerie containing monkeys, a Tasmanian Devil and a lion"[106] and a shooting gallery were part of the celebrations. While walking around the race course area, racegoers were enticed and entertained: "Three shots a penny, and a bob if break the pipe...A bob in, ten bob for the winner;...the goose'll pull the marble...A quid you can't pick it (the thimble and the pea)...Come on, put your money on the lucky 7...fifteen tickets at a bob, ten bob for the winner."[107] Such games as thimble and pea, the sweet wheel, the three–card trick, cheap jack, a duck raffle and private sweeps were all designed to get spectators to part with their money. For many years the QTC and other clubs took no notice of such gambling activities: in 1887 editorials in the press began to direct attention to such attempts to swindle, and warned spectators. Finally, in January 1888, the QTC "stewards instructed the police to prevent this type of robbery...and consequently the afternoon's racing was more enjoyable."[108]

With the proliferation of race meetings throughout the state, the amount of money gambled on horse races rose considerably. The two most popular methods for the laying of bets were the totalisator and the bookmaker. The first time the totalisator was used in Queensland was in 1875 in Ipswich, and the QTC took over its own machine betting in 1879.[109] However, numerous totalisators were run privately, though they were illegal, and these were very profitable.

Another popular form of gambling on races was the "sweeps", or consultations. For a few shillings a person was provided with an opportunity to win a fortune. In the 1890s, the biggest sweeps were those run by Tattersalls, with a "Ticket in Tatts" quickly becoming almost a national institution. The founder of Tatts was George Adams, who initially began his activities in Sydney, but was forced to take his "sweep department to Brisbane, where the Government are not so particular."[110] Adams' stay in Brisbane was, however, short–lived, as in 1895 legislation forced his move to Tasmania.

The prosperity of horse–racing was evident in the late 1870s (table 9) by the prize monies that were offered by various clubs throughout the state. However, the horse–racing industry was considerably affected by a recession in the early 1890s, as well as the 1893 bank crash and a flood. The prize monies offered in the 1890s demonstrate vividly the effects these disasters had on the QTC operation (table 10).[111]

The highpoint of Queensland racing came in the late 1870s and continued through the 1880s.[112] In 1868 the NAJC had doubled the prize money given by both Melbourne and Sydney, however the Australian Turf Register of that year did not even mention Queensland racing.[113] In spite of this oversight, there was no doubt that the standard of breeding in Queensland had reached a very high level. "It was not necessary for Queensland sportsmen to go outside the State to obtain their blood stock as brood mares were very numerous and sires of exceptional quality were available at a small fee."[114] Many of the State's horses went to the Southern States, where they were very successful in the various handicaps and classics. Much of the credit for the production of the excellent blood stock can be attributed to Sir Joshua Peter Bell. He was the first Queenslander to invest in a large way in the breeding of livestock, and his stud property, "The Grange", just outside Ipswich, became one of the leading centres in the state.

Table 9 Prize money at selected horse races, 1877–78

QTC Brisbane Cup	–	£500 & 10 sovereigns sweepstakes, & £50 trophy
Queensland Cup	–	£300 & 10 sovereigns sweepstakes
Sandgate Handicap	–	£200 & 7 sovereigns sweepstakes
Moreton Handicap	–	£100 & 5 sovereigns sweepstakes
Northern Downs Jockey Club Grand Handicap	–	£200 & 7 sovereigns sweepstakes
Ipswich Club	–	£200 & 3 sovereigns sweepstakes
Warwick Turf Club Handicap	–	£200 & 10 sovereigns sweepstakes
Maryborough Turf Club Handicap	–	£150 & 4 sovereigns sweepstakes
Townsville Turf Club Handicap	–	£100 & 2 sovereigns sweepstakes
Gympie Turf Club Handicap	–	£150 & 2 sovereigns sweepstakes
Rockhampton Jockey Club Handicap	–	£300 & 5 sovereigns sweepstakes
Toowoomba Turf Club's Darling Downs Handicap	–	£100 & 5 sovereigns sweepstakes

Table 10 QTC prize monies in principal races, 1890s to 1920s

	1891 –92	1892 –93	1893 –94	1895 –98	1900 –01	1923 –24
Hopeful Stakes*	300	300	100	100	370	1000+
Sires' Produce Stakes*	300	300	300	300	180	1200
Derby Stakes*	300	300	300	150	310	2000
St. Leger Stakes*	300	300	300	150	27	1000
Brisbane Handicap	100	100	70	60	100	800
Stradbroke Handicap	200	100	60	60	100	800
Queensland Cup	500	500	300	200	500	1400++
Brisbane Cup	500 **	300	200	200	500	2000++
Sandgate Handicap	300	300	150	100	250	1000
Moreton Handicap	300	200	100	100	250	1000
Royal Stakes	100	100	60	75	200	750

*   Prize money additional to sweepstakes
**   Additional to 100 Guinea Cup
†   This year Hopeful Stakes restricted to two year old colts and geldings and C.E. McDougall Stakes of £1000 established for two-year-old fillies
††   And £100 Cup.

Throughout Queensland the various racing centres coordinated their meetings so that horses could be taken on a circuit, from the south to the north. The 1872 race meetings, for example, that were announced were: St. George, May 6, 7; Goondiwindi, May 22, 23; Brisbane, May 23, 24; Peak Downs, May 28, 29; Rocky Waterholes, June 2; Ipswich, June 4, 5; Toowoomba, June 12, 13; Townsville, June 19, 20; Warwick, June 25, 26; Charleville, July 2, 3; Stanthorpe, July 9, 10; Ravenswood, July 17, 18; and Charters Towers, July 30, 31.[115] In the 1880s there was a boom in horse–racing which resulted in a mushrooming of clubs and race meetings. In 1880, the Queensland Racing Calendar was published, and it contains, in its first year, results from about fifty of the principal centres throughout Queensland.[116]

By the 1890s the popularity of racing in the urban areas was demonstrated by the number and extent of race courses in Brisbane and environs (figure 5).

This profusion of race courses was not unique to Brisbane, as similar developments were experienced in all major cities. However, such a proliferation was unique to Australia, as North American cities, for example, could only boast of one, or perhaps two, race courses.

This wide community involvement in horse–racing was accompanied by an extensive media coverage. In the 1850s the report of a race meeting would occupy only one or two columns of the *Moreton Bay Courier*. By the turn of the century there was a regular column, *The Turf*, in the *Brisbane Courier*, and this appeared almost daily, and additional detailed reports were given of race meetings not only in Brisbane and Queensland, but also of other major courses throughout Australia. In addition, there was coverage given in *The Referee*, as well as in other daily and weekly papers. *The Queenslander*, for example, devoted considerable space to the races. The June 25 1887 issue had two–and–a–half pages devoted to general horse–racing. Additionally, the Brisbane races were analysed in detail, and the various meetings for the rest of the season throughout the state were discussed. There were also lengthy sections on the Sandgate and Townsville races, and then shorter sections on Cunnamulla, Nanango, Cooktown and Rockhampton. Out–of–state meetings reported were Canterbury Park, Sydney Hunt Club Races, Victoria Amateur Turf Club, and the South Australia Trotting Club Jubilee Meeting. In the section "Country News", each country area included, in its report, descriptions of race meetings in its locale.

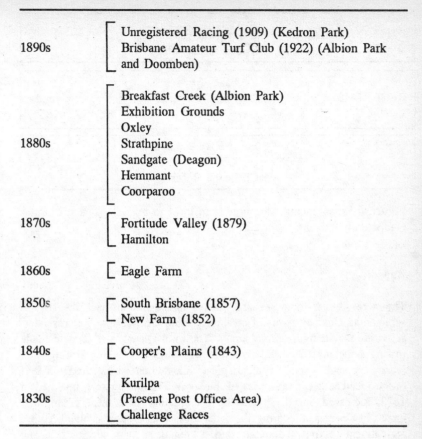

Figure 5 Diffusion of racing in Brisbane

By the turn of the century, horse-racing was a well established sport. It had become a fundamental component of the social and business life of every Queensland community. Its following was not restricted by class or sex, although certain aspects, such as members in clubs, were class and sex exclusive. By the 1890s, horse-racing was no longer solely local in nature (figure 6) as many of the best thoroughbreds were taken on a circuit throughout the State. Also, Queensland horses competed in races in the Southern States, and similarly southern horses came to Queensland meetings.

INTERCOLONIAL	Queensland Champion Sweep Stakes 1861)	1860s

⬆

REGIONAL	Brisbane, Ipswich Drayton, Warwick, Gayndah	1840s and 1850s

⬆

| LOCAL | Local Race–Courses | |
| | Challenge Races | 1840s |

Figure 6 Horse–racing transition from local to regional to intercolonial competition

Rowing

The accessibility of water and the establishment of the majority of settlements close by rivers or on the coastline ensured that water–related activities would figure prominently. The mild Queensland climate made rowing popular and essentially there was no necessity for a designated season for such a sport. Technological innovations during the latter half of the nineteenth century changed the sport. The sliding seat, invented in 1872, increased speed, as did the construction of leaner, streamlined boats. In Queensland during these decades, such a sport evolved from a recreational activity popular during regattas to a distinctive and organised sport. The popularisation of rowing in Queensland, and indeed in all of Australia, received a considerable impetus from Edward Trickett's world championship triumph in 1876. Clubs developed and a state organisation was formed to coordinate the sport. By the 1890s, rowing was considered a 'manly' sport. It was maintained that it "was sport for sport's sake and it brought forth those qualities in the young community which helped to mould their character."[117]

On holidays in the formative years of the colony, sailing and rowing regattas were held. In the 1853 Regatta, for example, there was a Waterman's Skiffs (pulling a pair of oars), a race for all Skiffs and one for "Blackfellows".[118] By 1857 a coxswain was allowed, thus moving towards present rowing.[119] Monetary prizes were acceptable as prizes.[120] These regattas were usually held on holidays.[121] By 1860 the principal event was the Queensland Championship Fours,[122] and the elite of the colony were in attendance.[123]

The first boat clubs were formed in Brisbane in the early 1860s: the Queens' Boating Club, with its shed at the Customs boat-house, the Amateur Boating Club, located at Boundary Street Wharf, the Princess Boat Club, at North Quay, and the Government Printing Office Boating Club, at Queen's Wharf.[124] Of these, the Queen's Club, formed in 1861, was applauded by the press as "an undertaking which is so universally esteemed and so beneficial in an Anglo-Saxon community...[It was]...surprising that a club of such character is not already in existence."[125] The organisers were deemed "influential gentlemen of the town",[126] and included Mr Shepherd Smith, Manager of the Bank of New South Wales, Mr J. Bramston, former Attorney-General of Queensland, and Mr W.T. Blakeney, the Registrar-General. About fifty ladies and gentlemen participated in the club's first function, a picnic and aquatic excursion that included "pulling" races.

In the 1870s more clubs were formed in Brisbane: the Commercial Rowing Club, the Regatta Club, the Brisbane Boating Club and the Mercantile Rowing Club. The opening of the Brisbane Club was most eloquently described in the *Australasian Sketcher* of September 4 1875:

> The weather was serene, a quiet balmy air only just enough to ripple the surface of the splendid reach of water on that part of the Brisbane River chosen for the occasion. The view at this part from the river is picturesque in the extreme, the high banks in parts, the green knolls reaching to the water's edge, occasionally on either side, the beautiful Botanic-gardens on the banks; the houses of Parliament as a background, whilst the city itself, with the houses forming a succession of terraces on the side, and the pretty villas on the high land opposite, were all brought out on this pleasant sunshiny afternoon. The river itself presented a rather animated scene, a number of pleasure boats of different kinds being in waiting at various points along the course to be taken by the procession. His Excellency and suite and a crowd of invited guests, amongst whom were Sir Maurice O'Connell, the Hon. W Hemmant, Mr T McIlwraith, Mr H E King, Mr A H Palmer, and other members of Parliament, proceeded on board the steamer Kate, at the Queen's wharf, shortly after 3 o'clock, the band playing the National Anthem. Seats were provided in sufficient number to accommodate the ladies present, whose presence added no little *eclat* to the affair. Champagne was on board in profusion, which was partaken of with a superior relish when coupled with the toasts that were proposed in honour of the day's event. The club's boat procession followed the wake of the steamer, but at a sufficient distance to prevent that disturbing water from her paddles being felt to any serious extent by the boats. The crews were, of course, in uniform, and presented as fine a lot of well-built young fellows as Queensland need wish to possess. At half-past 2 o'clock the crews proceeded to the 'shed', and quickly got their boats afloat, taking up a position opposite Kangaroo Point, awaiting the arrival of the Kate. This part

of the proceeding was of much interest, and the pleasant discipline of 'club law' was seen in the orderly and quiet manner in which everything and everybody found their place. The club colours are conspicuous and pretty, being composed of black, yellow and red stripes placed obliquely. The procession proceeded as far as the bridge, and returned opposite to the shed, where the Kate cast anchor, with a view to allowing His Excellency to visit that place.

Rowing, a healthy and beneficial form of exercise, was promoted as a true British activity.[127] Indicative of the desire to uphold such a British tradition was a fours with cox race, held on November 19 1863, between graduates of Cambridge and Oxford. The crews were: Cambridge:– W.P. Townson (stroke), St. John's College, A.E. Deighton, Christ's College, Rev T.B. Grosvenor, Christ's College, E. Huxtable, Christ's College, Master Walter Backhouse (cox); and Oxford;– Hon J. Bramston (stroke), Wadham College, Hon R.G.W. Herbert, All Soul's College, Rev B.E. Shaw, Lincoln College, Rev J. Tomlinson, Wadham College, Master C.S. Miles (cox).[128] The social prominence of the crews ensured considerable public patronage of the event, won by the Cambridge crew in their traditional light–blue colours.

Many of the individuals involved with rowing, both as competitors and organisers, were prominent citizens of the community. The founders of the Queen's Boating Club serve as an example. Thos. Finney, a prominent businessman and MLA, was the first Vice–President of the Commercial Rowing Club, and in 1903 the Governor, Sir Herbert Chermside, coached the club's eight–oared crew.[129] From the onset, the Governor and other government officials, if not directly involved with the races, added to such occasions by their presence as spectators. When the first eight–oared race was held in Queensland in 1885, the Governor opened the Government House Domain for the occasion. Three members of the committee for the 1880 Regatta were Hon Joshua Peter Bell (Acting Governor), Hon A.H. Palmer, and Chief Justice Lilley.[130] Three prominent Queensland rowers were Colin B.P. Bell and W.A.D. Bell, sons of Joshua Peter Bell, and J. Caddell Garrick, son of Agent–General Sir James F. Garrick. Rowing also became one of the main competitive sports in the Grammar Schools, primarily through the efforts of R.H. Roe, Chairman of the Queensland Rowing Association and Headmaster of Brisbane Boys' Grammar. The pattern was similar in other centres such as Bundaberg, where prominent figures such as J.H. Cathcart, G.T. Bell, J.W. Stewart, F. Smith and H. Burkett were the founders of the club there. Mr Rocks, the first head teacher of East State School, was the secretary of the Bundaberg Boating Club when it was formed in 1886.[131]

The regattas had a broad spectator appeal, particularly in the early years. An old-timer reminisced that, in the 1850s, "All Brisbane, about 1000 in number, used to turn out and honour the occasion."[132] At the 1875 Anniversary Regatta, the river was "enlivened with craft of all kinds, boats under sail, pulling boats, steamboats, barges, steam launches...from the trim yacht to the humble square-ended, all carrying their quota of spectators or pleasure-seekers; whilst on shore were numbers of picnic parties."[133] By the 1890s, however, with the proliferation of sports, and increased leisure opportunities, regattas and other rowing contests no longer attracted such large crowds. Only the intercolonial contests and the Grand Aquatic Carnival were well patronised and covered by the press. This was certainly evident in 1895 when Brisbane hosted the intercolonial Eights for the second time. *The Brisbane Courier* extensively reported the build-up for the event as well as the day of the contest:

> ...the banks were lined with an eager crowd of spectators, while the road was almost choked with vehicles. The open landau belonging to the city magnate, the well appointed buggy, spring carts and hawker's vans bearing the wives and families of those of humbler degree were well represented, and showed the aquatic fever pervaded all classes of the community.[134]

The Brisbane crew was most eloquently described as being "most pleasantly clad in zephers with sleeves, an amateur costume prevailing in England."[135]

Inglis, in his 1912 book of *Sport and Pastime in Australia*, stated that rowing was

> ...essentially democratic. The great public schools and the universities provide a number of our oarsmen, but the majority are men who pick up their knowledge of the game by paddling about in club boats without the thorough grounding on fixed seats which is generally considered essential. This training, no doubt, militates against style, but it does teach the men to be watermen.[136]

Some of the races were specifically for the working man. At the First Anniversary Regatta in Brisbane there was a race for 'bona fide' ferrymen, as well as races for Aborigines. The program of races for the Princess Boat Club included contests between the Civil Service and Banks' crews, and Artillery and Club crews. Only 'bona fide' ships' crews or crews of the harbour and Customs department were permitted to row in the first race at the 1872 Regatta, while the third race was a contest for farmers and trading boats under five tons.[137] At the Bundaberg Regatta, there was a separate 'farmers' race "for which a £2 prize was given."[138] In an attempt to appeal to rowing enthusiasts in the working class a meeting was called in the Tattersall's Hotel "for all those interested in the formation of a rowing club to represent the working man of Brisbane."[139] M.J. Slack, who became Australian Amateur Sculls Champion in 1892, and again in 1896 and 1900, had working class affiliations as he worked for the Baynes Brothers butchering business. The Baynes were rowing and sports enthusiasts and gave Slack time off work for practice for competitions. Although Inglis maintained that rowing was democratic, he did concede that compared with similar pastimes rowing was an expensive hobby.

By the 1880s, the issue of working men and professionals competing against amateurs became a matter of concern. Ferrymen, or watermen, whose business it was to ferry individuals from one area to another, were considered professionals. According to the 1861 Regatta program, amateurs were taken "to mean all persons employed in mercantile or public offices."[140] Interestingly, at the First Anniversary Regatta, the race for amateurs carried money prizes of £8 and £2, while no prizes were offered for the 'bona fide' ferrymen's race. Although there were specially designated races "for amateurs only", most of the others were "for all comers", and in such both amateurs and professionals competed. Even the Champion Fours race was 'open', and it was won by professionals, except for 1874. After 1880 an added distinction was made between amateurs and professionals: "The amateur rules do not debar a working man of any class in Queensland from rowing in regattas provided he does not compete for money in any race. The man who makes his living by rowing or boat–building, or receives money for training athletes, etc. is debarred."[141] However, in the 1890s the controversy over the amateur–professional ruling was again raised, the issue being over "manual labour amateurs."[142] The controversy was particularly relevant in the intercolonial Eight–oar Championships, which were dominated by Victoria. Queensland, like Victoria, had permitted manual labourers among its competitors, and its team won the Championships in 1891. New South Wales, however, had followed the English interpretation of amateur status and barred manual labourers. From 1878, its crews had only managed wins in 1885 and 1893, and hence, after its defeat again in 1896, the New South Wales Rowing Association refused to participate in the 1897 and 1898 championships.

During the 1870s and 1890s rowing experienced considerable growth, evidenced by the number of clubs formed (see figure 7).

In addition to the annual regattas during the 1880s, there were numerous events which provided impetus to the diffusion of rowing in the state. Interclub and intertown competitions became a regular feature of the club racing calendars. Some of the highlights of the era were: the

1890s	South Brisbane Rowing Club (1896) Lake's Creek Rowing Club (1894)

1880s	Toowong Rowing Club (1889) Bundaberg Boating Club (1886) Breakfast Creek Rowing Club (1885) (Later Brisbane Rowing Club) Central Queensland Rowing Club (1882) Wide Bay Rowing Club (1881) – defunct 1891 Banks Rowing Club (1881) – defunct 1885 Burnett River Boating Club (1880) – Bundaberg

1870s	Rockhampton Rowing Club (1877) Commercial Rowing Club (1877) Maryborough Rowing Club (1877) Mercantile Rowing Club (1877) (Later Kangaroo Pt. Rowing Club) Brisbane Rowing Club (1874) – defunct 1885 Regatta Club (1873)

1860s	Fitzroy Boating Club (1863) Amateur Boating Club Princess Boating Club Government Printing Boating Club Star Boating Club Queen's Boat Club

Figure 7 Proliferation of rowing clubs in Queensland

first amateur four-oared championship race in 1880; the Canadian Ned Hanlan, world champion, competing in a regatta at Indooroopilly Reach in 1884; the first eight-oared race being held in Queensland in 1885; the leading professional scullers – Searle, Beach, Kemp, Stansbury, Nielson and Matterson competing at Bulimba Reach; and Edward Trickett's race against Ned Hanlan in Rockhampton in 1888. Edward Trickett became Australia's first undisputed world champion when he defeated the world champion sculler, Joseph Sadler of England, on the River Thames in 1876. To the delight of Queensland rowing enthusiasts Trickett eventually settled in Rockhampton, becoming the host of the Oxford Hotel. A race was organised between Trickett and Ned Hanlan,

World Champion from Canada, and "people flocked from all parts of Australia"[143] to witness the spectacle. Trickett, who was completely out of form, was easily beaten by Hanlan.

With the proliferation of clubs and the increasing number of contests a need for the standardisation of rules, regulations and sizes of boats became apparent. Differing interpretations of the amateur–professional issue by various clubs frequently caused difficulties for race organisers. In 1882, representatives from the Rockhampton and Maryborough Rowing Clubs met with Brisbane officials with the expressed purpose of forming a Queensland Rowing Association. The northern delegates "were desirous that an association should be formed with its headquarters in Brisbane...and that they should be represented by delegates who would be residents of the metropolis."[144] There was no obvious resentment at Brisbane being the organisational centre for the sport, as was apparent in horseracing and athletics. Although the initial overtures to form an association were made in 1882, the state–wide Queensland Rowing Association was not formed until 1889. Although Brisbane was considered the premier centre for rowing, Rockhampton, Maryborough and Bundaberg also became strong centres. In the 1920s Queensland was considered "peculiar in that there are at least four River Championships – Brisbane, Maryborough, Bundaberg and Rockhampton – in addition to the State event."[145] Over the years, there were concerted attempts to establish the sport in Townsville and Ipswich, however these did not meet with much success.

From the 1850s to the 1890s, then, rowing developed from an event of local interest (figure 8) to the point of international competition.

By the 1890s, sailing had become a distinctly separate sport from rowing, using increasingly specialised and defined equipment and facilities. The sport appealed to a different calibre of person than that attracted to rowing. Although there were competitions, even an intercolonial Regatta in 1894, the sport was considered more of a recreational pursuit and leisure–time activity, while rowing was a physically exhausting, competitive sport. 'Yacht' clubs[146] were formed to cater to these interests, however they were primarily enclaves of the privileged. The costs associated with owning and docking and caring for a boat, in addition to the time involvement of a participant, increasingly relegated sailing to being a sport for the upper and middle classes.

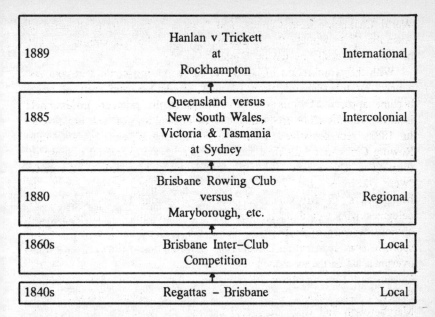

1889	Hanlan v Trickett at Rockhampton	International
1885	Queensland versus New South Wales, Victoria & Tasmania at Sydney	Intercolonial
1880	Brisbane Rowing Club versus Maryborough, etc.	Regional
1860s	Brisbane Inter–Club Competition	Local
1840s	Regattas – Brisbane	Local

Figure 8 Rowing: transition from local to international contests

Pedestrianism and Athletics

Prior to the 1850s, pedestrianism had made its appearance in the Moreton Bay Settlement and its environs,[147] though competition was spasmodic and the organisation haphazard. This was different from the British Isles, where by this time period the sport was well established and patronised.

Such activities appealed to Australians who, as in most frontier environments, highly prized physical prowess. Challenges were publicly proclaimed: "I, Edward Easton, am open to run any man in Charters Towers 200 yards for £5 or £10."[148] Added incentives included the offering of handicaps: "A foot–race has been arranged to come off on April 7th for £5 a–side between P. Kerr and H. Butler. Kerr gives Butler 15 yards in the 150."[149] Long–distance events, as well as sprint races, attracted the interest of the populace as evidenced by the large crowd at the walking match between two Brisbane residents from the city to Sandgate, with the winner completing the distance in four and a half hours.[150] A typical foot–race was described in 1872 in *The Brisbane Courier*.

The foot–race between Raleigh and Stacey, which took place on Saturday evening, on the old racecourse, attracted a very large concourse of spectators, there being fully five hundred persons present. The stakes were for £10 a side, and there was considerable speculation as to the result, the odds being generally offered in favour of the Sydney man, Stacey. The latter, we understand, is a practised runner, has taken part in several pedestrian contests in the Southern metropolis, whereas his opponent, Raleigh, is only an amateur. Considerable delay took place before the race came off. The distance (300 yards) was at length measured off and the men stripped for their work. The two were not apparently unevenly matched, both looking slight, active, and sinewy. From the start, however, it was evident that the Sydney man would have the best of it, he taking the lead and keeping it throughout. Towards the finish Raleigh put on a spurt and pulled up considerably, but his efforts were unavailing, and Stacey won easily by about three yards. The race was not timed, but the pace throughout was pretty fast. After a little jubilation over the result on the part of the winner's confreres the assemblage dispersed quietly. The utmost order prevailed on the ground."[151]

Pedestrian contests were always for a wager which ranged from drinks to large sums of money, and often challenges against the local hero enticed the greatest bets. In 1892 in Rockhampton Harry Jenkins, the local banker, competed against Tom Chamberlain from Sydney for £100 a–side, 100 yards, and Jenkins confidently backed himself, as did his friends. Chamberlain won easily and some £500 to £600 changed hands.[152] Many people considered that betting on the outcome of human competitions was, at best, as exciting as horse–racing. Occasionally 'novel' races were arranged, such as comparing the abilities of a man versus a horse. At such a race in Cooktown, the betting was slightly in favour of the man, the race being only over 20 yards. The belief was that the man would be at the finish before the horse "could get up steam."[153] Over 100 spectators witnessed a dead heat. The great Aboriginal boxer Jerry Jerome is also reputed to have competed against a horse for a wager.

The locales for these contests varied from vacant lots to race tracks and roads, although in the 1880s and 1890s special tracks were constructed in major centres. A common venue, particularly in the 1860s and 1870s in country areas, was the local pub. Publicans even organised the sweeps associated with the races. These sweeps were in addition to the prize monies. In the 1870s and 1880s, as increasingly larger purses were offered, professional 'peds' enjoyed considerable financial rewards as well as notoriety. As the number of competitions increased in the 1870s, handicapping of events became the norm. "J. McGarrigal, the

Queensland white champion, heads the list with 11 yards and is asked to give starts ranging from 4 yards up to 33 yards."[154]

Pedestrianism was a sport that was accessible to men of all socio-economic groups as it did not necessitate overly expensive and specialised equipment and facilities or a particular affiliation. The main criterion was natural talent. As material rewards for the successful were considerable, the sport functioned as a means of livelihood, and for some as an occupation. Hence, itinerant professionals emerged who travelled from town to town selling their physical talents to the highest bidders.

One such Queensland 'ped' was the remarkable Jack Wieneke, after whom the Wieneke saddle was named. He was an all-round athlete who performed outstanding feats throughout Queensland, including standing high and long jumps, sprints, hurdles, hop, step and jumps, and pole vaults. One such performance was at Roma.

At the Easter Monday sports at Roma, in 1884, he won the handicap (£20), handicap hurdles, 300 yards handicap from scratch, won the high jump, hop, step and jump, running long jump, three standing jumps, pole vault, standing high jump, and the gold medal for being the best all-round athlete. At Roma, on May 24, 1884, at the Oddfellows' Sports, he won the handicap, and handicap hurdles, standing long jump, pole vault, running high jump, and obstacle race. During that year Wieneke visited many towns in the State and won everywhere he went. At Roma, in 1885, on Easter Monday, he won the handicap (£20), handicap hurdles, running high jump, three standing jumps, pole vault, hop, step, and jump, running long jump, and gold medal for best all-round athlete. On the Roma racecourse on that day a match was ratified, 150 yards, between W.J. Gollan, Warwick, and T.J. Wieneke, Yeulba, to take place at the Oddfellows' Sports on the following May 24. The match was made quite unknown to Wieneke, by Messrs. J.E. Burrell (manager Australasia Bank), J.F. Carter, Dr. Tilson, and Mr. J.F.F. Lockett...

...Starter was "Billy" Sparks. According to Mr. Wieneke, "Billy" probably started more men and more horses than any other man...There were nine attempts to get off the mark before the gun was fired. The start eventually was a good one, and at the finish only 18 in. separated the two men, and Wieneke had won by only inches. The stakes were £150 aside, and there were many private bets of £25 each.

Mr. J.E. Burrell, manager of the Bank of Australasia, said that anything from £600 to £650 changed hands over the result of what was probably the most important foot race ever seen in Roma – or perhaps anywhere in Queensland.[155]

Wieneke was one of several successful peds to emerge during this period. It was Wieneke's daughter who married Doug McLean, thus beginning a Queensland footballing dynasty.

By far the most outstanding ped was Charlie Samuels, an Aborigine, who "at his best was unbeatable and in his prime was regarded as the greatest runner in the world."[156] Indeed Queenslanders proudly proclaimed "that Queensland while naturally enough having to give way to the superiority of the other colonies mentioned, in the combination of scientific and athletic departments of sport, can fairly hold its own against, if not beat (for Samuels belongs to us) any one of them in the new popular manly development in the athletic world of pedestrianism."[157] Numerous Aborigines were relatively successful in the sport, and most of the big meets would generally include one or two of them. Their presence was noted on the advertisements as (a), for aborigines, or (h.c.), for half–caste. After Samuels, "Australia's greatest professional sprinter"[158] was Queenslander Arthur Postle. In the early 1900s Postle electrified audiences throughout Australia with his runs.

The popularity of pedestrianism overshadowed the gradual development of amateur athletics and athletic clubs throughout Queensland. From the 1860s to the 1890s amateur athletic sports were contested intermittently, usually as part of multi–sport gatherings. According to Carmichael and Perry the first athletic sports were those conducted by the Brisbane Football Club in the early 1860s. However Old English sports such as foot racing and sack racing were indulged in "with hilarity and fun"[159] on New Year's Day, 1859.

In the 1870s the Caledonian Society became the main association organising athletic contests in Brisbane. Their meetings, held on the Queen's Birthday, naturally highlighted traditional Highland activities such as Highland dancing, piping, tossing the caber and putting the stone, but they also included foot races at various distances, jumping for height and distance, and sack races. Small monetary prizes were awarded such as 10 shillings for the sack race, £1 for member's 200 yards race and £1/10 shillings for tossing the caber.[160] Through the 1880s athletic contests were engaged in on sports days organised by cricket, football and bicycle clubs, the Brisbane Ambulance Transport Brigade, the Oddfellow's Society and other bodies. In addition they were part of celebrations on St Patrick's Days, Boxing Days and Eight–Hour Day festivities.

Participants in these multi–sport gatherings tended to be 'gentlemen' athletes. For example, the winner of the 1874 Caledonian Society Sports 120 yards and 400 yards members' races was Robt. Phillip, who years later became Premier of Queensland. Other prominent citizens who competed at such gatherings were Archibald Meston, later Protector of Aborigines, Alix H. Pritchard, manager of the Q.N. Bank in Charters Towers, Tom Welsby, Dave Scott, Edmonstone Maxwell, Tom Bond and Pring Roberts. R.H. Roe, Headmaster of Brisbane Grammar School (BGS) also had an influential role in the promulgation of the 'manly' sport of athletics, for he was instrumental in BGS becoming one of the leading breeding grounds for amateur athletes in Queensland.

As 'gentlemen' athletes wished to distance themselves from the professional 'peds' and the gambling associated with pedestrianism, steps to form an amateur athletics club were taken in the early 1870s. Similar developments had occurred in England and in the southern colonies with, for example, the Amateur Athletic Club being organised in 1864. Believing that such clubs were conducive "to the moral and physical well–being of the youth of the colonies,"[161] Brisbane gentlemen called for a meeting at the Royal Hotel on April 25 1871. The Brisbane Amateur Athletic Club was duly formed, with His Excellency the Acting–Governor becoming the patron of the Club. The newly–formed Club immediately set about to organise an athletics meeting, for which "a number of influential gentlemen"[162] volunteered to act as stewards. The meeting, held on June 17 1871, included a 100 yards flat race, throwing the cricket ball, putting the stone, 220 yards hurdle race, running high jump, throwing the hammer, 440 yards hurdle race, running long jump, 440 yards flat race, pole leaping, mile race and three–legged races. Prizes were given for each event.[163] As was the case with the amateur athletics clubs in England, the Brisbane club organised, in addition to their annual athletics meetings, such events as hare and hounds races.

In the late 1880s, the sport of pedestrianism underwent a temporary boom in the State. Occasionally amateur and professional races were run concurrently, as at the 1889 Norman Sheffield Handicaps. The popularity of pedestrianism was evident by the large crowds which came to the Exhibition Grounds to observe the twenty–five competitions from June through to November under the electric light. There were a record 145 entries for the 100 yards event, which was won by E. Allen, with H.T.S. Bell coming second.[164] However, excessive betting by both amateurs and professionals ultimately caused a decline in patronage of such events.

Charges of 'stiff' running, cheating and other discrediting practices damaged the professional sport, and these indirectly benefited the development of amateur athletics. Amateur clubs were formed in Toowoomba, Ipswich and Rockhampton, as well as Brisbane. By 1894 there were four clubs in Brisbane: Waratah Harriers, Gymnasium, Berserkers and Wanderer Harriers. The sport developed to such a degree that State championships were organised in 1894, and the Queensland champions were: 120 yards – F. Young, 13.5 sec.; 200 yards – F. Sale, no time taken as it was a walkover; 440 yards – G. Hall, 58.5 sec.; running jump – A.H. Jones, 5ft. 1in.; running long jump – C. Naseby, 18ft. 6in. Unfortunately these first Queensland Amateur Athletics Championships held on November 9 1894 were not overly successful due to "the extreme heat and counter attractions of the holidays."[165]

By the 1890s clubs in central and northern parts of the State were formed, and Rockhampton in particular became a very strong centre for the sport. As Brisbane clubs had not organised themselves sufficiently to form a central administrative body to control the sport, members of the Rockhampton clubs took the initiative and, in 1894, formed the Queensland Amateur Athletic Association, with its headquarters in Rockhampton. Brisbane athletes and administrators were understandably opposed to such a move, "contending that as they were athletically and numerically stronger than the central and northern portion of the colony the headquarters should be in the metropolis."[166]

As in the sport of horse–racing, a power struggle for the control of athletics emerged. A temporary compromise was reached in 1895 with two separate organisations being formed: the Northern Queensland Amateur Athletic Association (NQAAA), with its headquarters in Rockhampton; and the Southern Queensland Amateur Athletic Association (SQAAA), with its headquarters in Brisbane. Although the northern clubs provided the impetus for the organisation of athletics in the colony, after the foundation of the NQAAA, its members and clubs ceased to be as active. In contrast, in the southern part of the State, the formation of a properly constituted body, the SQAAA, gave the sport new direction. Additional 'harriers' clubs were formed and increasing numbers of organised meets were held. As the NQAAA became defunct, the SQAAA dropped the word 'Southern' from its title, and became the Queensland Amateur Athletic Association (QAAA). A concession was made to northern interests with the selection of Mr J.C. Tyler, a solicitor from Rockhampton, as the first President of the new body.[167] By 1900 there were 13 clubs affiliated with the QAAA: Toowong Harriers, North Brisbane Harriers, East Brisbane Harriers, South Brisbane Harriers, Gordon Harriers (Toowong), Western Suburbs AA Club, Indooroopilly Harriers, Church Institute Harriers, Toowoomba Harriers, Nundah Harriers, Ipswich Harriers, New Farm Harriers and Valley Harriers.

The QAAA quickly moved towards closer affiliation with amateur athletics associations in other States. With the underlying aim to stimulate the growth of the sport in Queensland, the honour of hosting the Fourth Australasian Amateur Athletics Championships was given to Brisbane.[169] The Exhibition Ground was chosen as the site for these championships, which attracted over 100 competitors. In the final standings Queensland came third, New Zealand (being part of Australasia in those days in athletic matters) first, New South Wales second and Victoria fourth.

In the late 1890s Charlie Campbell was one of Queensland's finest amateur athletes, and he competed successfully at numerous southern competitions, winning the 440 yards Australasian title in 1897. Other outstanding athletes were Neil Ferguson, E.J. Kellet, D. Wentworth and Peter Corrigan.[168] Although not competing for the State, several Queensland athletes competed successfully while overseas. For example, H.T.S. Bell and A. Graham Butler competed in the English championships while studying in England in the 1890s. Bell was outstanding in the sprint events, while Butler's successes were in the distance races.[169]

Figure 9 indicates the progressive evolution of the sport of athletics in the State from the 1850s to the 1890s. During that time professional athletic leagues were established in Queensland as well as New South Wales, South Australia and Western Australia.

1890s	Queenslanders at International Events	International
1899	Australasian Championships at Brisbane	National
1890	Brisbane Athletes at Australian Championships	National
1880s	Union Athletic Club Brisbane Bicycle Club Football Sports (Brisbane, Wallaroo, Excelsior)	Regional
1850s	Old English Sports Days	Local
1840s	Local Challenges	Local

Figure 9 Athletics: transition from local to regional to intercolonial to international activities

Summary

Spatial interaction and spatial organisation went hand–in–hand as Queensland evolved. Queensland was, from the 1850s to the 1890s, emerging from a pre–industrial state to an industrialised one. Primitive technology, and social controls, moved from informal to more formal structures. The value system was still basically tradition–oriented, with social status ascribed by wealth, but different norms and values were slowly beginning to emerge, influenced by the gold rush subcultures.

Expanded transportation and communications and technological innovations, coupled with accelerated urbanisation, gave rise to increased discretionary income and time. Certain sections of society, particularly the upper and middle classes, had the time and money to travel and participate in sport. However, the growth of spectator sport gave rise to a new profession, the professional sportsman, who could earn a living by attracting crowds to watch him compete.

The development of sports and games in Queensland reflected technological and communication developments, and localism, which was a feature of Queensland sport prior to Separation, slowly gave rise to regionalism in the first thirty years of the colony, and then to intercolonial, national and international competitions.

The patchwork manner of economic development was mirrored in sport. In the emerging towns some sports were still in a rudimentary stage of development, while in the major towns they achieved modernisation. Modernisation was accompanied by increased codification, spatial interaction and spatial organisation.

6

Proliferation of Sports: 1850s to 1890s

During the latter half of the nineteenth century there were remarkable transformations in the pattern of sport and leisure in Australia. Some of the most significant changes were the proliferation and popularisation of sports, the increasing time and opportunities for leisure, the growth of controlling bodies for sport, and the increasing acceptance of women in sports.

Whereas only three national sport governing bodies were organised in England by the first half of the nineteenth century – horse–racing, golf and cricket – from the 1850s onwards the need became apparent in the alpine sports, association football (soccer), athletics, swimming, rugby football, yacht racing, bicycling, skating, rowing, boxing, hockey, lawn tennis, badminton and fencing. Many of these organisations developed to preserve amateurism, and this was particularly the case in football, rugby, athletics, swimming, bicycling, boxing and rowing.[1] The growing middle classes were highly involved in these and other sports. The Great Public Schools of England and Oxford and Cambridge became the prime advocates of organised games, and the cult of athleticism and Muscular Christianity was diffused as the graduates of those institutions travelled the world. They took their games with them as part of their 'cultural baggage'. Other countries, such as Germany, the United States, Sweden and Australia followed suit with sports, and organisations controlling sport proliferated.

Although the sports pursued in Queensland were primarily of British origin they were not all adopted lock, stock and barrel, and some of them were modified because of the variant climatic and environmental conditions. The fox, for example, was not native to Australia, nor was the rabbit and hare. Cricket matches, also, were occasionally modified – single wicket, one–against–one, etc. – for at times there were not enough players and/or equipment, or many players lacked the requisite skills. The 'Sport of Kings' also changed, with 'Australian' governing rules being adopted, at least by some clubs. Various games were adopted from other countries at various times such as polo from India, baseball from the United States and lacrosse from Canada. In addition, numerous sports "unique" to the new land were developed, such as sheep shearing and wood chopping contests, camel racing in Western Australia and goat racing in Queensland. Rodeo sports were also not found in England.

The inventory of sports in Queensland in the late 1890s was markedly different from that in 1859 (table 11). Supplementing the 1890s inventory are such leisure pursuits as chess, billiards and draughts as well as hunt clubs, blood sports, fishing, goat racing, agricultural shows and various 'bush' sports.

Table 11 Inventory of sports in the 1890s

1850s	1890s		
Horse–racing	Horse–racing	Trotting	Steeplechase
Cricket	Polo	Hunting	Rifle Shooting
Foot–races	Cricket	Rowing	Boxing
Regattas	Rugby Union	Association Football	Aussie Rules
	Athletics	Cycling	Lacrosse
	Tennis	Golf	Swimming
	Sailing	Croquet	Bowling
	Wrestling	Gymnastics	Archery

Proliferation of sports and increased participatory opportunities went hand–in–hand, with differing interests and abilities being accommodated by these changes. This diversity of offerings met the needs of the population generally, but particularly those of the working class, whose leisure time had increased since the 1850s.

The limited number of sports in Queensland in the 1850s was a reflection of the general sports pattern throughout Australia, as well as other countries of the British Empire. It was during the following decades that various sports such as tennis and basketball were "invented", while others such as football and rowing were codified and transformed to emerge as modern sports. Various technological developments, such as the sliding seat in rowing and the vulcanisation of rubber for cycling, radically changed these sports and assisted in their popularisation. The electric light enabled sports such as gymnastics to be pursued indoors. With the advent of swimming pools 'bathing' became 'swimming' and competitive swimming emerged as a sport.

The organisational and administrative changes in sports during this era had far-reaching consequences and were fundamental to the developments that evolved.[2] Prior to 1850 in Australia cricket was virtually the only sport that had formalised rules and, in essence, that sport changed very little until well into the twentieth century. However, the majority of other sports were transformed from low level, informal-type 'village' games to formalised, structured modern sports. Some of the progressive steps in the developmental process entailed the standardisation of measurements for playing fields, prescribed numbers of players, specified and precise equipment, assigned positions, defined responsibilities during games and detailed conditions and rules under which the various sports could be played. The aims were to bring about conformity and uniformity to the various sports. By the turn of the century, most major sports in Australia had formed governing bodies at the local, and some at state and national, levels. Regular, organised competitions increasingly became the accepted norm by the 1890s. Most of the state governing bodies for sport in Queensland were formed from the 1850s to the 1890s, and their state championships and/or intercolonial contests were held. In some sports, such as swimming, there were no intercolonial contests as such prior to 1900.

The diversification and codification of sports internationally did not, however, progress at a uniform rate in all places. The initial developments emanated from some point of origin, which in most instances was somewhere in the British Isles. The particular sport was transported via people, newspapers, magazines and books to British colonies such as Australia. As the population base was larger and more established in New South Wales and Victoria, these progressive developments usually took hold in these states earlier than in Queensland. Brisbane, as the capital and largest centre in Queensland, was generally in the forefront when organisational changes were mooted. Occasionally, as in the sport of amateur athletics, the lead was taken by another city, in Queensland's case Rockhampton. However, in most sports the stimulus for development emanated from Brisbane outward to various towns and country areas. Sometimes, the time lapse from the point of origin was a matter of months, however more normally the rate of transmission took at least a year. Some of these transmission delays are shown in table 12. Rugby Union was organised nationally in England in 1871, in New South Wales three years later and in Queensland eleven years later.

Some sports which took hold in southern states, or other parts of Australia, did not have the same acceptance quotient in Queensland. Archery and hockey are two examples. Archery was a sport that was

Table 12 Comparison of formation of sports governing bodies

Sport	England	N.S.W.	Queensland
Horse–racing	1750	1842	1863
Cricket	1788	1858	1876
Rugby Union	1871	1874	1882
Amateur Athletics	1880	1887	1894
Rowing	1879		1894
Golf	1754		1889

acceptable for ladies' participation and there are numerous accounts and pictures of women engaging in competition in archery clubs and meets in New South Wales, Victoria and South Australia. In Adelaide, for example, Daly found that archery "had been practised since the first days of settlement and attracted upper class patronage."[3] In Brisbane and Queensland, if it were practised, it lacked chroniclers. Hockey appears to have suffered a similar fate. In contrast to tennis, which was found in Queensland almost immediately after its "invention", golf was very slow to develop.

Concurrent with organisational developments in sports was the emergence, and clear differentiation, of amateur and professional sports. Professionalism materialised in virtually all sports that had mass appeal, such as boxing, foot–racing, rowing, cricket and cycling. Although professional rugby, which was ultimately to be called Rugby League, originated in the 1890s in England, it did not appear in Queensland until after 1908. Money prizes, of variant amounts, from a few shillings to several hundred pounds, were offered at most sport competitions. Gambling, and the placing of bets, had become an integral component of the sports scene. Australians seemed to have had an incredible proclivity for gambling. Incessant gambling, accusations of 'running stiff' and cheating, and an apparent decline in standards of 'sportsmanship' and fair play, were all factors which enhanced the amateur sport movement. In an attempt to differentiate between amateurs and professionals, rules and regulations were created to allow for 'fair' competition. Although definitions of an amateur varied in different countries, and in various sports, one of the more universal definitions was that adopted for the 1896 Olympic Games, which emphasised that participation in sport should solely be for the love of it, and excluded anyone who had ever received any monetary or material gain from sport. The Olympic Games were revived specifically to preserve the amateur ethos and to allow amateur athletes an opportunity to compete against equals. Australia was represented by one competitor at these first Olympic Games in Athens in 1896, Edwin Flack, in the sport of athletics. However, it was not until 1908 that Queensland was represented by its first Olympians, F.W. ("Frank") Springfield in swimming, and W.B. Carmichael and T.J. ("Rusty") Richards in Rugby Union.

Analogous to the differentiation of amateur and professional sports was the change in meaning pertaining to the terms 'sportsman' and 'sport'. In England, over the centuries, the term 'sport' had been utilised to denote the pastimes of hunting and fishing, and a sportsman was considered to be one who indulged in such pursuits. Later, horse–racing and boxing were added to the accepted sports. However, in the latter half of the nineteenth century, the term 'sport' came to signify activities which required physical prowess, such as football, cricket, athletics, rowing, gymnastics and so on. The term 'sportsman' came to be the accepted nomenclature for a man who participated, usually competitively, in such activities. Concurrently another term came into common parlance, namely "sportsmanship", which denoted an acceptance of the rules and adherence to an acknowledged, but not necessarily written, code of ethics.

Accompanying this proliferation of sports was the emergence of 'all–round sportsmen'. Interests and abilities did not seem, generally speaking, to be confined to one sport, but rather, during one's athletic career, there would be participation in a wide range of activities. A true Queensland hero of this time period was one who played football and cricket, competed in rowing, running and cycling and, for good measure, was adept at boxing and tennis. A person might be outstanding in one particular sport, but he usually achieved a modicum of success in other sports as well. This was the 'pre–specialisation' era, during which an athlete was not known exclusively as a 'footballer', 'cricketer', or 'rower', but rather was heralded as an excellent sportsman. This 'all–round' concept was also reflected in the organisation of sport, as invariably the same individuals would be found on committees and as officers of the different sports organisations. Many of these individuals would be from the upper and middle classes, for only they had the time, and necessary educational background, for such administrative positions. Tom Hughes and J.C. Beal would be typical of such early all–rounders, competing in a wide range of sports and assisting in an administrative capacity in them as well.

Complementing, and certainly contributing to the growth of 'amateur' sports, was the Victorian obsession with the cult of 'Muscular Christianity' and the belief that sports developed character. The presumption was that values such as self–discipline, loyalty, self–control, courage, determination – all "Christian" qualities – were achieved through participation in various physical pursuits. The most favoured activities and those that were considered to be the most "manly", were cricket, football, boxing and rowing. In Australia opinions with respect to the values of manly sport were consistent with those espoused in the 'mother country'. *The Referee*, for example, heralded football as "a game which brings out the manly qualities in the players, such as physical and moral courage, unselfishness, self–restraint and resourcefulness. Everyone must admit that any sport which tends to develop these qualities must be a potent factor in the moulding of a boy's character."[4] Carmichael and Perry, in their aptly–titled book *Athletic Queensland*, are liberal in their praise of the various 'manly' sports, with boxing being considered the most meritorious. It was considered "the training ground, not alone for soldiers, but our general manhood [and also taught] good judgement...prompt thought and action...manly courage [and] self confidence."[5]

One of the salient features of sport in Australia in the latter half of the nineteenth century was the increasing number of people from all classes who became actively involved in sport and leisure activities. During this era Australian nationalism emerged as a force, and at its heart was "an equalitarian social doctrine, a belief in equality of opportunity and a conviction that in Australia men had a right to a good life."[6] Twopeny, who travelled throughout the colonies in the 1870s, stated "that no class was too poor to play."[7] By the late 1890s leisure time was no longer the prerogative of the upper class, as the middle, and particularly the working class, had acquired the opportunity to play through legislation shortening working hours and giving a Saturday half–holiday. Prior to this, Sunday was the working man's day of leisure, and yet there were laws and social pressures which either banned or discouraged the playing of sports on Sundays.

In general, the lot of the working man was far better in Australia than it was in the British Isles. There was ample opportunity to work, wages were high, there was access to land, adequate supplies of food, particularly meat, and there was a favourable climate and no established aristocracy.[8] In addition to the reduction of hours in the working day and the introduction of a half–holiday on Saturday, the common man had, by the 1890s, annual holidays over Christmas and various holidays during the year. Australians not only celebrated traditional British holidays and Her Majesty's Birthday but also created their own, such as Foundation Day, Separation Day and so on. It was not surprising that Trollope, after evaluating and comparing the working man in the colonies and at 'home', concluded that Australia was a working man's paradise.[9]

With the reduction in working hours, the working man found that he was no longer physically exhausted at the end of the day. Paralleling this development was a reduction in the amount of physical labour that a person did daily, particularly in the cities, certainly in comparison with the first settlers half a century earlier. As most early settlers were physically strong and tough – they had to be to survive – the working men of the 1880s and 1890s were from sturdy stock with high physical expectations. As jobs were no longer so physically demanding sport became an outlet for their suppressed physical energies. Proliferation of sports, and the rise of physically demanding sports such as football, helped to satisfy such needs.

Class divisions were not as apparent at sporting events as in Britain. The availability of land and the climate aided in equalising access to sports facilities, particularly in Queensland, where there was little need for indoor facilities. In country areas tennis, for example, became a popular sport, with courts being laid out at large and small stations and at private homes in towns, land being of lesser value and more available than in England. The horse was not, in Queensland, exclusively for the rich, and riding was a necessary skill soon acquired by all country people. The local publican, the blacksmith and the squatter all owned horses, and only on the race courses could the relative merits of their horses be observed. There were no restrictive game laws and hence hunting, which was a major source of class conflict in England, was not such in Queensland, where wild game, and land for hunting, was plentiful. Also, in many towns and country areas, there was a limited choice of alternatives with respect to who one could play with and where one could play, hence the various socio–economic groups were compelled to come together, and were brought into closer association with one another. Even in the cities, the various classes competed in the same sports, such as cycling, pedestrianism, football and rowing. As the Editor of *The Queensland Cricketer and Footballer* emphatically stated:

> The fittest survive in every walk of life, and those who distinguish themselves as cricketers and footballers are worthy of our admiration. Ability and pre–eminences must find their reward on the sports ground. To be the son of a duke is no recommendation to a player. The best man is the best man, even if he be the son of a labourer. Whatever we may be in politics, we are thoroughly democratic in sport.[10]

This democratic attitude in sport complemented the egalitarian ethic that permeated Australia. The middle and working classes were insistent on their rights to achieve social equality.

However, in spite of the sports field being considered a "great leveller", class differences were occasionally manifested in some sports and leisure activities. Costs of equipment confined yachting and hunt clubs to the more affluent citizenry. Dancing was popular for all classes, however different establishments were frequented by the various classes, and accepted standards of behaviour certainly varied. The upper and middle classes tended to participate in 'amateur' athletics, although they supported 'professional foot–racing', essentially a working class–participant sport, as spectators and gamblers.

The Role of the Pubs

The pubs had an important role to play. The Australian hotel "has never been a mere transplant and adaptation of an English progenitor...The pub is one of the most socially significant, historically valuable, architecturally interesting, and colourful features of Australian society."[11] In 1877 Australia boasted more hotels than it did in 1977, some one hundred years later.[12] One of the first buildings to be erected in a town was the hotel. Gold was discovered in Charters Towers in December 1871, a claim was registered in January 1872 and the first hotel was opened in March 1872. There were many more hotels to be built, for Charters Towers in its heyday offered its 2,500 inhabitants a choice of seventy – although some have claimed – ninety hotels. However, the Palmer River gold miners appeared to be even greater consumers of alcohol, as there were ninety–seven hotels on the goldfield itself with another ninety–four in nearby Cooktown.[13] Brisbane, in comparison, seemed almost to be a 'dry' town, with 'only' 102 hotels in the metropolitan area, for a population of 101,554, in 1891.[14]

Drinking was a popular pastime which was encouraged by a warm climate, the extensiveness of physical labour and, in many remote areas, by the lack of anything else to do. The most popular time for drinking was at the end of the working day, however it was possible to get a drink any time between the hours of 6.00am and 11.00pm. Although officially there was no trading on Sundays, most pubs were open. Hotels catered primarily for the working man, as the upper class patronised private clubs. In country areas and gold mining towns, however, there was apt to be a greater interaction between classes and pubs tended to be utilised by all.

A place to drink was only one function of a hotel. They provided meals and accommodation, and most had banquet halls and ballrooms. Weddings and other celebrations, particularly for the working classes, were frequently hosted at the town's local hotel. It acted as the equivalent of a modern–day community recreation centre, and provided a vital service for the surrounding community. The hotel played a major role in the popularisation and diffusion of sports in the latter half of the nineteenth century.

Hotels and the sport of horse–racing had a very close connection, and often, in the early years and in country areas, race tracks were in close proximity to them. In Roma, the race track was built so that it ran between two hotels, and the finishing line was observable from the front of both.[15] The first race course at Millmerran was along the main road from the cemetery to the hotel, and "£1/-/- bets were laid as to which jockey would finish the race actually in the bar of the hotel."[16] The benefit of the proximity of the racetrack to the hotel was the obvious increase in clientele that resulted before, during and after races. In Peak Downs the newspaper reported that the hotel made £800 in cash during race week, whereas the seven lucky owners of winning horses had to divide up only £480 between them.[17] When race courses were outside of a town, or distant from the hotel, publicans would purchase concessions to 'booths' so that they could sell their products on course.

Race meetings would invariably involve a 'Publicans' Purse' Race, which often carried the richest prize at the meeting. At the 1859 Gayndah Christmas Races, the Publicans' Purse for £90 far exceeded that of the Gayndah Plate, which was for only £25, while at the 1852 Northern Races the Squatters' Purse and the Publicans' Purse were of equal value, 30 sovereigns.[18] Financially, publican–sponsored races were at least on an equal footing with those of the elite.

The settling of bets was done at hotels, and publicans would also organise sweeps on race meetings. Hotels would rival one another with such sweeps, and these would be advertised in the newspapers. Hotel proprietors often gave considerable monies to race clubs to hold sweeps as well as club meetings in their hotels. Because of their obvious interest in sport, publicans often served in official positions in such clubs. Most sports, such as football, cricket and athletics, conducted their organisational meetings in hotels.

Hotels encouraged other sports in addition to horse–racing. The proprietor of the Enoggera Hotel, [19] for example, offered a variety of amusements for the 1871 Boxing Day celebrations and thereby hoped to draw a good response from the local community. He cleared and stumped a race course, built a dancing shed, had a target erected for shooting, and included quoit playing, swings, sack racing and climbing the greasy pole among the amusements.

Premier sites for the playing of billiards were at hotels, and advertisements by hotel proprietors highlighted the existence of such facilities. The exact size and nature of the tables were always specified, as were the brand names. Although tables were imported from England at considerable expense, proprietors viewed such tables as a drawing card for drinking customers. Challenge matches were popular and would always draw a sizeable crowd.

Quoits was another traditional English pub sport that was frequently pursued at hotels throughout Queensland. The popular nature of the sport was seen by a crowd of some 100 spectators who were attracted to a quoit match in Gympie in 1869.[20] Skittles was another regular activity associated with hotels.

Hotels were also very closely associated with virtually all gambling activities, such as card–playing, 'two–up', cock–fighting, boxing contests and foot races. The contests were organised, often in secret, by the hotel proprietor, who realised the benefits of attracting a clientele, almost for any reason.

The pub, then, has a vital place in the promulgation of sport in Queensland. It acted as a social centre for men, a place where friends could be met and one's main interests were accommodated.

The Eight–Hour Movement in Queensland

The eight–hour movement or, as it was called at the time, the "Short-time Movement", made a major contribution to the 'lot' of the working man. The major outcomes were the regulation of conditions and safety factors in factories, workers' compensation and the establishment of the Labor Party. The reduction of working hours and early closing had far-reaching consequences for the playing of sport.

The argument for shortened hours understandably preceded its attainment. In Queensland, the movement can be traced back to the Rev. Dr John Dunmore Lang, the Scottish Presbyterian clergyman who was a prominent advocate of free settlement. He encouraged industrious workers, particularly Scottish, to immigrate, initially to New South Wales and later to Moreton Bay, to establish a free society. One such mechanic who was encouraged by Lang was Andrew Petrie, who became the first white settler in Moreton Bay. Lang's migrants, called 'Langites', were industrious, and many were quite well educated. They became leaders in the working class movement in Brisbane and Ipswich.

The 'Langites' "stood up for individual freedom and rights and strongly opposed unfree labour. Their mouthpiece became the *Moreton Bay Courier*."[21] James Swan and T.W. Hill, both former Lang assistants, controlled the colony's newspaper, with Swan becoming the sole owner in 1848 and Hill being its printer and publisher. As they were sympathetic to working class aspirations, the editorials and general news reporting reflected their views.

The first movements for the reduction in working hours were made in 1855 with the *Moreton Bay Courier* announcing that "some ten specified houses of business intended to close their doors at sunset from Monday to Friday whilst the normal hours would apply to Saturdays."[22] One of the ten shops that pioneered early closing was owned by Charles Trundle, a 'Langite'. At that time the normal closing for shops on Saturdays was 11 o'clock. The following year a letter to the Editor took up the cause of the worker. The author of this letter was "Yacca", a term which was to become a colloquialism for work.[23] Such letters continued, and in the following year, 1857, three employers responded by reducing their working hours: Messrs Petrie (Stonemasons), William Pettigrew (Sawmill operator) and Thompson & Jeny's (Builders). They were all Lang colonists.[24]

The pressure for reduced working hours accelerated, with meetings, advertisements and letters. Success was finally achieved in 1858 with the foundation of Queensland's first trade union, the Stonemason's Union on January 18 1858. The first business to grant eight hours was that of Andrew Petrie & Sons.[25] Other unions were subsequently formed, the Carpenters Union on October 2 1861, and the Printer's Union on October 15 1861.[26] The same year saw the formation of the Amalgamated Society of Engineers by the workers at the Ipswich Railway Workshops. By the mid–1860s most building workers were on an eight–hour work day. These stirrings spread to unskilled workers, with railway 'navvies' calling a strike in 1865. This strike, according to Leggett, "was the first by unskilled labour in Queensland and maybe one of the earliest examples of such action in Australia."[27] The strike spread to other parts of the state but was unsuccessful.

Although the eight–hour working day had been successfully achieved by some of the working class such as the builders, carpenters and metal workers, many others, particularly shop attendants and factory workers, were still working sixty to seventy hours a week. There were a few individual exceptions, such as Thomas Finney, who was the owner of the largest retail store in Brisbane. He permitted his shop to stop trading at six o'clock weekdays and one o'clock on Saturdays.[28] In 1888 the Shop Assistants' Early Closing Association was formed for the specific purpose of reducing working hours. The struggle continued through the 1890s, and finally, in 1900, the passage of the Factories and Shops Act, and a Health Act, improved on hours, working conditions and wages for all workers. Moreover, general agreement was reached on the granting of a half–holiday for shop assistants, and that half–holiday was designated as Saturday.

The achievement of an eight–hour working day and early closing on Saturdays was not uniform throughout the various trades and businesses, nor was there consistency throughout the state. In the main Brisbane, as the capital of the state, had the most bitter strikes and continuous agitation, with the labour movement emanating out to other centres and country areas. However, there were exceptions, as the shop assistants in Charters Towers won the fight for an eight–hour working day many years ahead of Brisbane.

As Queensland lagged behind the other states in industrialisation, workers' rights and trade unions were slower to eventuate as well. The *Moreton Bay Courier* carried a letter as early as 1856, stating "eight hours per day has been considered quite enough for labour in South Australia, some 4,000 miles from here and in the fine cool province of Victoria and also in Sydney."[29] Australia preceded most industrialised countries in the reduction of working hours, and climate was advanced by some as being a major force justifying that reduction. "Most people will feel inclined to agree with the eight–hours principle who have lived for any length of time in the colonies. In such climate eight hours' hard work, more especially in summer, is enough for any man...Eight hours' manual labour, with a heat of perhaps 90° in the shade, is calculated to take the lot out of the man."[30]

The granting of the eight–hour work day was celebrated with a procession and a sports day. As early in 1865, such a demonstration occurred in Brisbane. It consisted of a procession down the main streets of Brisbane with members carrying banners, followed by a cruise on the steamship the *Settler* to Eagle Farm Flats for a sports carnival and picnic.[31] Such a demonstration became an annual tradition, so that, by the 1880s and 90s, the Eight–hours demonstration was comparable "as a spectacle, to that of the Lord Mayor's Show in London [and was] religiously observed."[32]

In Brisbane, the Eight–hour Demonstration was originally held on the first of March, but in the 1890s it was changed to the first of May. Although such events had been held since the mid–1860s, they became formally organised in 1885. The 1888 anniversary celebration in March was "observed as a general holiday...a large procession of the various Trade Unions, headed by bands and banners marched from the top of

Queen Street to the Exhibition Grounds, where sports were engaged."[33] The premier pedestrian events contested were the one mile Eight–Hour amateur championship of Queensland, the 150 yards and the mile handicap.[34] In 1895 the 'May Day' Handicap, a race of 150 yards, was inaugurated. Other organisations soon quickly met the needs associated with new working conditions.

Holidays and Multi-Sport Gatherings

Nineteenth century Australians, it seemed, clearly believed in the maxim 'all work and no play makes Jack a dull boy', and seemed to secure for themselves as much time off work as possible. By 1900 virtually all workers worked an eight–hour day, and a half day Saturday. Throughout the year there were over a dozen official public holidays which were supplemented by local celebrations. Holidays of any kind were eagerly seized upon for celebratory purposes, and colonists observed traditional British holidays as well as their own special commemorative days, such as Separation Day in Queensland. Often, if a public holiday fell on a Monday, Saturday became a holiday as well. The most extensive holiday period was over Christmas, and it was generally accepted in business that the days between Christmas Day and New Year's Day were lost.

The prevailing attitude was perhaps best summarised by Richard Twopeny: "the colonist certainly endeavours to get as much pleasure as he can out of existence. He has a full appreciation of the value of amusement. He is not himself amusing, but he thoroughly enjoys amusing himself."[35]

The holidays were typically celebrated with horse races and other sports contests, as well as regattas, picnics and 'Old English Sports'. There were Christmas Sports, Boxing Day Sports, New Year's Day Sports, Easter Monday Sports, Queen's Birthday Sports, St Patrick's Day Sports, Separation Day Sports, and so on. The primary aims of these Sports days were participation, enjoyment and social interaction. These community–sponsored events enabled the various socio–economic classes to mingle, and community spirit and cohesiveness were fostered.

Boxing Day was one of the most joyous days of the year, and holidaymakers indulged in pleasurable activities from early morning until late at night. Horse–racing, cricket, sailing and sundry other amusements were organised in all centres throughout the state. After horse–racing, the favourite pastimes were 'old English sports', which reminded many colonists of 'home' and served to reinforce their heritage. The activities included various running–jumping–walking races, as well as novelty races such as walking backwards, three–legged races and sack races, which encouraged the average person to participate. Throwing events often involved putting the stone, throwing the hammer, and throwing the cricket ball. Most enjoyment came from such old–time favourites as, in the 1858 Drayton Boxing Day celebrations: "climbing a greasy pole...catching a greasy pig by the tail...running in sacks...wheeling a barrow blind–folded and several other amusements."[36]

For Queenslanders, the special day of the year was Separation Day. Great care was taken in the planning of the first celebrations in 1859, with the day beginning with the hoisting of the flag of Queensland, accompanied by a 21–gun salute. In the Botanical Gardens a pavilion and tents were set up to sell fruits and drinks (though no alcohol) and a Band played throughout the day. Although the highlight was the Anniversary Regatta, cricket matches, quoits and other amusements were arranged "and as a finale to the day's rejoicing, the Gardens will be illuminated as far as practicable in the evening and a display exhibited at night."[37] In Charters Towers there was a magnificent procession featuring bands, the major associations such as the Oddfellows, the Caledonian Society and the Miners, variety minstrels, billy–goat carts and so on. Festivities included "a grand old English fair at the Show Ground with the accompanying merry–go–rounds, Aunt Sally's tents, gypsies and all...In the evening there will be a Fancy Dress Ball."[38]

Any excuse for a holiday was taken so as to engage in local celebrations. On Thursday Island, two public holidays were granted so the community could properly entertain a visiting Australian Squadron. The special sports program included rifle shooting, cricket and lawn tennis matches, rowing races and athletic sports.[39]

In addition to multi–sport gatherings being contested on general holidays, associations and clubs organised days which primarily featured athletic events. The Caledonian gatherings incorporated some traditional Scottish events such as tossing the caber, putting the stone and Highland dances. Often gatherings were restricted to members of that association, however at times there were 'open' events and separate prizes for 'all–comers'. The Brisbane Football Club and the Caledonian Society, beginning in the mid–1860s, were two of the first groups to conduct such meetings. They proved to be so successful that, by the 1880s, virtually every group or association was running such functions, of the multi– or uni–sport variety. Table 13 demonstrates the proliferation of these meetings in the Brisbane area. Some were organised by ethnic clubs, such as the Caledonian Society, and the Hibernian Society; some

Table 13 Some early sports days

Intercolonial Cycling Carnival Sports	1897
Combined Amateur Cycling Carnival Sports	1896
Oddfellows' Sports (Toowoomba)	1896
Protestant Alliance Sports	1896
Toowoomba Bicycle Club Sports	1895
A.O.F. Gala Sports	1894
Brisbane Ambulance Transport Brigade Sports	1894
Brisbane Hospital Sports Carnivals	1893
Australian Natives Association Sports	1893
West End Sports Committee Sports	1892
Brisbane Safety Bicycle Club Sports	1891
Queensland Scottish Association Sports	1891
Druids Sports	1891
Temperance Society Sports	1890
Breakfast Creek Sports	1890
Norman Sheffield Handicap	1889
Oddfellows' Society Sports (Brisbane)	1889
Brisbane Sports Club Sports	1889
Sandgate Football Club Sports	1888
Coorparoo Cricket Club Sports	1888
Centennial Sports Committee Sports	1888
New Farm Cricket Club Sports	1888
Western Star Lodge Sports (Ipswich)	1888
Nundah Sports	1887
St. Patrick's Day Sports	1887
Kedron Park Sports	1886
Hibernian Grand Handicap	1885
Eight–Hour Day Demonstration Sports	1885
Brisbane Amateur Cycling Club Sports	1885
Union Athletic Club Sports (Toowong)	1883
Brisbane Bicycle Club Sports (Toowong)	1883
Hibernian Sports (Townsville)	1881
Highland Society Gathering	1876
Brisbane Grammar School Sports	1871
Caledonian Society Sports	1864
Brisbane Football Club Sports	1860s

were religious, such as the Protestant Alliance; some were political, like the Eight–Hour Demonstration Society and the Australian Natives' Association; some were very specific, such as the Brisbane Football Club; and some were local committees, such as the Kedron Park Sports.

Some of the larger business enterprises and unions organised picnics, river excursions and sports gatherings as well and miners, butchers, bakers and so on participated in work–related leisure outings. Such gatherings involved extensive socialisation between the workers, employers and bosses, and were instrumental in improving employer–employee relationships.

Ploughing, Digging and Draining Contests

The country areas were not left behind when it came to having sports days. The competitive urge and the desire to see who was the best led to various work activities emerging as 'sports'. Agricultural competitions were a regular feature in the country areas in Britain, and they were encouraged by the agricultural societies and community leaders as a means of improving farmers' work habits and performances. As agriculture developed in Australia the British precedent was followed, so that by the 1850s ploughing contests were conducted in South Australia, which by that time had become one of the centres for wheat in Australia.[40] Queensland lagged behind the southern colonies in the development of farming and agriculture, and such contests did not emerge until the late 1860s. Prior to the final exhibition of the Ipswich Agricultural and Horticultural Society on December 17 1868, there were ploughing competitions for horses and for bullocks. George Beulah won the ploughing and John Haswell the bullock team contests in front of the Governor, Colonel Blackall. During the 1870s and 1880s the agricultural contests flourished, with each community and association regularly organising competitive matches. Their popularity was evident from the extensive newspaper coverage devoted to such events and the extensive detail in which they were described.

A typical contest was that organised by the East Moreton Farmers' Association near Breakfast Creek on Mr Child's Farm in 1870, and included ploughing matches for horse and bullock teams, the details being announced in the *Brisbane Courier* on June 7. The proliferation of such contests was characterised by similar matches being held at Eight Mile Plains by the Eight Mile Plains Agricultural Society in 1870, at New Farm in 1871 and in 1872 at Macaulay's Farm, Indooroopilly, New Farm and Oxley.[41] Agricultural contests were particularly prevalent in country areas, and in 1882 the press highlighted the Allora Ploughing Match sponsored by the Central Downs Agricultural and Horticultural Society.

The contests were highly organised and featured clearly delineated regulations regarding the equipment to be used and the exact nature of the work to be completed. As such contests involved subjective evaluations, judges were invariably criticised for making poor and/or biased decisions. The competition was fierce as winners were awarded cash, and other substantial prizes, such as plough harnesses, corn shellers, shovels, bridles and so on. Personal and local pride were also at stake, and a champion 'ploughman' was lauded and feted by his local community.

Agricultural contests were frequented by His Excellency the Governor, thereby according status to such events. Although competitive matches were the highlight, the luncheons and/or dinners contributed to the social dimension of such occasions. The formality was enhanced by the numerous toasts that were proposed: "Health of His Excellency the Governor", "Judges", "Agricultural Interest" and so on. These contests served a very important role for the agricultural community, as they encouraged the development of excellence in the necessary work skills, and provided an opportunity for social interaction and relaxation.

Newspapers

In the decades prior to the turn of the century there was a considerable increase in coverage of sport by the media, who assisted in the popularisation of sport. In Brisbane the leading daily papers, the *Brisbane Courier*, the *Telegraph* and the *Daily Mail* had regular sports sections by the 1890s. However sports received coverage in numerous other sources such as the *Queenslander*, the *Queensland Figaro* (which emphasised the social side), the *Town & Country*, the *Boomerang* and *Brisbane Evening Observer*, to name but a few. Then there were special sports publications such as the *Referee* (although this was published in Sydney), the *Queensland Cricketer & Footballer*, the *Queensland Racing Calendar* and the *Queensland Sportsman*. All these helped to increase public awareness and stimulate interest in sport.

Sports

By 1900 opportunities for sport and leisure, then, had expanded enormously from those available in 1850. The sports of cricket, horse-racing, rowing and athletics were developed in the previous chapter, as examples of the diffusion of sport. Polo and yachting are also covered in other chapters. In this chapter a variety of other sports will be discussed: cycling, football, boxing, swimming, rifle shooting, wrestling, hunting and fishing, tennis, golf, croquet, billiards and various other leisure activities. Some were major participant activities, some minor, but all were part of the Queensland sports pattern.

Cycling

In the 1850s and 60s there were a few enthusiasts utilising cycle machines in France, England and the east coast of the United States, though the word 'bicycle' did not even come into common parlance until 1868.[42] It was not until the early 1880s that cycling could be considered a sport in Queensland. However, a decade later, with the introduction of the safety bicycle, a cycling craze swept Australia. In Brisbane, as in most urban centres in Australia, it become the 'boom' sport, with numerous amateur and professional clubs and regular competitive meets, informal bicycle excursions and even magazines devoted exclusively to the sport.

Bicycling did not begin in Australia until 1867, when W.A. George built a 'velocipede' in Goulburn, and it was introduced to Melbourne in 1868. The following July Australia's first bicycle race was held at the Melbourne Cricket Ground, though a Joseph Pearson has claimed that the sport began at the Albert Ground in Sydney in 1867.[43]

BICYCLES! BICYCLES! BICYCLES!!!

FOR SALE, an invoice of best FRENCH BICYCLES, Polished, Steel, Patent Bushes, Lamps, &c., now landing, ex Artimenia. Apply at WITTY's Hotel, Queen Street.

(Advertisement for Bicycles in the *Brisbane Courier* of 1870)

The first newspaper advertisements for bicycles in Queensland appeared in 1870, and soon thereafter there is record of a cyclist racing a Cobb and Co. coach to Sandgate.[44] Gradually, during the 1870s, the number of owners of 'velocipedes' and tricycles increased, and impromptu challenge races were held on any available stretch of road. The first officially organised race was in 1881 in the Botanic Gardens. However, it was another two years before the first bicycle clubs came into existence. The year 1883 saw the formation of the Brisbane Bicycle Club, as well as the Rockhampton Cycling Club and another club in Brisbane, the Queensland Bicycle Club. Warwick formed a club in 1884, while Ipswich did not organise one until 1886, the same year one was formed in Townsville.

The officers of the Brisbane Bicycle Club (BCC) were: Messrs E. Markwell, captain; T. Coutts, sub-captain,; G. Stombuco, hon. secretary and treasurer; and T. Welsby, W. Johnson and A.F.G. Dye as committeemen. W. Johnson was also captain of the second club, the Queensland Bicycle Club (QBC), whose other officers were Mr T.E. White, president; Mr. J.G. Vidgen, vice-president; T.B. Aird, vice-captain, T. Jones, hon. secretary and A.R. Bennett, bugler. Mr R.H. Roe of Brisbane Grammar became active in 1885.[45] During the 1880s a 'healthy' rivalry existed between the two clubs, with each club running its own meetings and only occasionally organising combined fixtures.

The BCC's first annual sports was on September 8 1883, at the Sports Ground in Toowong, and twenty-two cyclists took part in the opening parade. The events contested were: ¼ mile children's tricycle race; 2 mile race; 1 mile handicap for boys; 100 yards race and novelty events, such as riding without holding on to the handle-bars. Indicative of the rapid acceptance of the sport by the general public was the presence of two thousand spectators including the Governor, Sir Anthony Musgrave, and his vice-regal party, at the 1883 Boxing Day Meet.[46] The following year a crowd of four thousand was attracted to the main meet.

Road races also began to attract interest, with the first such ride, from Brisbane to Southport, being completed in 1883, in 8 hours, by G. Stombuco. Nine months later the same distance was covered by H. Isles in 5½ hours, and, by 1938, the time had dropped to 2 hours, 6 minutes and 32 seconds. In 1886, the first one-day ride from Brisbane to Toowoomba was accomplished in 16 hours, a considerable feat considering the condition of the roads. Although the first overland ride by ordinary bicycle from Sydney to Brisbane (and on to Rockhampton) was completed in 1885, the first Brisbane to Sydney ride was not until 1891, being executed by Queensland's first long-distance cyclist, Lou Isles, in 7 days.[47]

In addition to road races the other highlights in the early years were Queensland Championship races, and visitations by cyclists from other colonies. The first intercolonial competitors appeared at the 1884 meet sponsored by the Brisbane Bicycle Club, and that year G.H. Perry and W. Morse represented Queensland at the first Intercolonial meet in Sydney. In 1885, the Five Mile Intercolonial Championship was hosted by the Brisbane Club, with J.E. Harris of Sydney winning the main event. At this same meet the first Championship of Queensland was held, with F.W. Belbridge, of the Brisbane Bicycle Club, taking the honours. This 1885 Meet was particularly significant, for the 'Safety Handicap' served as the introduction of the safety bicycle into competitions in Queensland.[48]

As in the other states, this initial curiosity with the bicycle waned in the late 1880s, and the Centennial Championship Meeting of the BCC, at the Exhibition Ground, in 1887, only attracted some one thousand spectators.[49] The major reason was that the 'Penny Farthing', which was the major type of bicycle in use at the time, was both expensive and difficult to ride. When the safety bicycle was first introduced it was ridiculed as having 'dainty' wheels. The first pneumatic tyres reached Australia in 1890, and were sarcastically referred to as 'sausage rolls', 'balloons' and 'steam rollers'.[50] However, the benefits of the safety bicycle and pneumatic tyres were quickly realised. These were safety, increased speed, ease of riding and reduced cost. The BCC, at first, fought against the safety bicycle as an 'acceptable' vehicle and refused membership to such advocates. However, the Club membership declined to the point that, in mid–year 1892, the Club reluctantly succumbed to the change.[51]

During the early 1890s Brisbane experienced a sudden upsurge of interest in bicycling, perhaps unmatched by any other sport.[52] New clubs were formed, with the main one being the Brisbane Safety Bicycle Club (BSBC) in 1892. Coverage of the sport increased in the newspapers. The *Queensland Cricketer & Footballer*, for example, expanded its coverage from one small column to a full page in 1893. Even a separate magazine, *Brisbane Cyclist*, was published in 1890, and although it was short–lived, another specialist magazine, *Queensland Wheel*, came out in 1896. Later a rival *Queensland Wheelman* appeared, but both were merged and became the *Queensland Sportsman*.

A new era in amateur cycling began with the formation of the Queensland Amateur Cyclist's Union (QACU) in 1893. The first officers of the club were: the hon. H.J. Thynne, president; Sir Henry Norman, patron; vice–presidents, Messrs E.J. Stevens, MLA, C.W. Lavarach, J.J. Kingsbury and J.C. Beal; hon. secretary, Mr J.R.P. Adams; hon. treasurer, Mr George Driver; and Mr J. Naylor and Mr C.A. Hawkins.[53] Affiliated with this Union were the BCC, the BSBC, the South Brisbane Cycling Club and the Rockhampton Bicycle Club. The Union held its opening venture on Saturday April 22 1893, and approximately one hundred cyclists appeared at the starting point at Parliament House. His Excellency the Governor, accompanied by Lady and Miss Norman, greeted the cyclists with a brief speech and concluded that he "was pleased to see so many ladies amongst the riders and wished them all an enjoyable trip to Sandgate."[54]

The mid–1890s were significant years for amateur cycling in Queensland. Two Australasian Championships were contested in Brisbane on the Exhibition track, and both meetings were well patronised by the public. In 1895, Carl Swensson became the first Queenslander to capture an Australian Championship, when he won the 1 Mile race. He also came second in the 10 Mile Championship race. 1895 also saw the commencement of Ben Goodsen's championship career, when he won the State 5 Mile title. The following year, Goodsen was selected for the Australasian squad to compete in the English Championships. Because of a transfer at work, he went to compete in Sydney, where he was selected for the 1899 World Championships,[55] at which he gained a second place.

By the turn of the century, amateur cycling was flourishing, and the numerical strength of the various clubs affiliated with the QACU was an indication of its popularity: BCC – 240 members; BSBC – 160; South Brisbane Cycling Club – 90; St Mary's Gordon Club, Kangaroo Point – 40; St Andrew's Gordon Club, South Brisbane – 25; Redfern Gordon Club, South Brisbane – 30; Queensland Cyclists Touring Club – 75. In addition to these, there were the Commercial Travellers' Cycling Club and the Ladies' Clubs, while external to the Brisbane area were the Rockhampton Bicycle Club, the Rockhampton Touring Club and other clubs not affiliated to the QACU.[56]

The rapid transition from local to intercolonial to national and international status was realised in only sixteen years.

The cycling craze was such that, by the early 1890s, professional cycle clubs arose and professionals competed in cycle carnivals for prize monies. The League of Queensland Wheelmen was organised to control and coordinate the extensive number of races that were being held, and most of the country clubs, except for Rockhampton, affiliated with the League.[57] In 1897 the main locale for the League's Meets became the newly–opened Brisbane Cricket Ground (Woolloongabba), and over eight thousand spectators patronised the 1898 meet, at which prize monies totalling 110 sovereigns were contested.[58] One of the most eminent Queensland riders was Bob Walne, who later became one of Australia's top professional riders.[59]

The passion for cycling was not only manifested in competitive cycling, but in the utilisation of bicycles for recreational and leisure purposes. Sundays and, for some, Saturday afternoons, were occasions for pleasure rides, and gentlemen and ladies pedalled away to nearby

Queenslander (Ken Gordon) competes for Australia at English Championships 1897	INTERNATIONAL
First Australian Champion from Queensland (Carl Swensson) 1895	NATIONAL
Australian Championships in Brisbane 1892	
Formation of Queensland Cyclists Union 1893	STATE
Queensland competes at Intercolonial Championship Meeting 1884	INTERCOLONIAL
New South Wales visit Queensland for Intercolonial races 1884	INTERCOLONIAL
Brisbane Amateur Cycling Club 1884	
Brisbane Bicycle Club	LOCAL AND REGIONAL
Rockhampton Cycling Club 1883	
Bicycle Races at Sports Gathering in Botanic Gardens 1881	LOCAL

Figure 10 Cycling: transition from local to regional to intercolonial to national to international contests

parks and picnic areas. For ladies, the bicycle offered one of the very few available opportunities for invigorating physical exercise. The following that bicycling had at the turn of the century was unmatched by any sport on a mass participation basis. Moreover, the Queensland climate permitted year–round participation.

Football

Of all the grand old English games, football was thought to engender those sterling qualities that made the British rulers of the world.[60]

By the late 1890s football, that is rugby union, was the major 'manly' sport competed in, and crowds to games usually far out–numbered those at cricket matches. Although the other codes of football, Association Football and Australian Rules, attracted some adherents, the premier code and winter sport was, by this time, rugby union. In football preference, then, Queensland followed the New South Wales pattern, whereas Victoria and South Australia chose the 'Victorian' or Australian Rules version of the 'football' game.

The earliest form of football played in Queensland appeared to be that of Association Football, or soccer. Such was indicated by the advertisement for the 'Christmas Sports' to be held on Boxing Day 1861, when 'foot–ball' was one of the 'Old English Sports' to be played.[61] When the Brisbane Football Club was formed in May 1866,[62] it adopted the Victorian football rules of play. Some of the rules that corroborate this conclusion were:

> ...Two posts...shall be erected at a distance of twenty yards on each side of the goal–posts and in a straight line with them
> ...In case the ball is kicked behind goal...any player catching the ball directly from the foot or leg may call 'mark'. ·
> ...Tripping and hacking are strictly prohibited
> ...The ball may be taken in hand at any time, but not carried further than is necessary for a kick;
> ...The ball while in play may under no circumstances be thrown.[63]

However, Rule 3 stated that in "case of a ball being forced (except with the hands or arms) between the goal–posts in a scrimmage a goal shall be awarded,"[64] and this was more indicative of the Rugby style of game. It was difficult at times to discern, from newspaper accounts, and to state with absolute certainty, what form of football was being played. In England in the same period, there were essentially two forms of football, the Rugby School running type and the kicking game. As codification of these games was in its formative stages, there was no uniformity of play in Queensland nor in England. Since Australian Rules, or 'Victorian' Rules as it was then called, was "invented" in 1858, a third form of football became a possibility for a player. Possibly all three forms were played, depending on who was playing, how many players were present, and what equipment and size of playing facility were available. Indeed, at times, there probably was little appreciable difference between the codes.

By the 1868–69 season there were four clubs in operation in Brisbane, the Brisbane Football Club, the Volunteer Artillery, Brisbane Grammar School and the Civil Service, and eight first class games were played during that season. Indication of public interest in the game was the presence of some three hundred spectators, including females, at an inter–club match.[65] When a team was formed in Ipswich, in 1870, inter-town rivalry stimulated ensuring competitions, and those present saw the Brisbane team emerge victorious in the first three encounters.[66] The Ipswich club wore red caps, while the uniform of the Brisbane club consisted "of a blue cap, white flannel jersey and white trousers."[67] The wearing of white was quite surprising, and impractical, considering the contact nature of the game.

By the 1860s, inter–school football matches were regular events at English Public Schools. As the Grammar Schools in Australia generally emulated the practices of English schools and embraced the concepts of Muscular Christianity and athleticism, it was understandable that football soon became an accepted game in these schools. The football matches played between Ipswich and Brisbane Grammar School, from 1869 onward,[68] were customarily covered in considerable detail by the newspapers. In 1870, the first game was played in Queen's Park, Brisbane, according to "Victorian Rules".[69] The return match was in Ipswich, necessitating an over–night journey on the steamer. Such a journey emphasised the need for a railway link between the two cities. About forty schoolboys left on the 'Nowra', at 3.30pm on May 24, sleeping "as best they could until daybreak, soon after which coffee was provided on board, and all made a hearty breakfast."[70] The steamer reached Ipswich at 8 o'clock in the morning. During the day the boys played two games, one which lasted an hour and three quarters, the other one hour and a half. The games were played fourteen aside, and in the first game "Master F. Kent by a good long kick"[71] won the game for Brisbane Grammar, and the second game was similarly won on a kick by the Brisbane school. Right after the second game the Brisbane boys left Ipswich at 4 o'clock, arriving back at Harris Wharf at 9.30pm.

Due to the sparsity of teams, the schoolboys played against senior teams. In order to compensate for their youth, they were permitted extra players. For example, on June 18 1870, fifteen of the Brisbane Club competed against twenty–two of the Grammar School. About the same time, a Brisbane senior team played an Ipswich club, seventeen–a–side. This particular game was terminated after two and a half hours of play, when a goal was scored by Brisbane.[72] Meanwhile these teams met the following month, and this time the game was played fifteen–a–side.[73] There were, obviously, changes in player composition due to variant circumstances.

Beginning in the mid–1860s, there were annual 'Football Sports' which were held at the end of the football season and were considered as "a grand finale".[74] The Sports, however, did not consist of football matches, but were rather pedestrian competitions, with only one event as a concession to the game, 'Kicking the Football' for distance. J.R. Coutt won the event in 1873 with a kick of 51 yards, while Pring Roberts took the event the following year with a kick of 149ft 3in.[75] Footballers, as well as professional 'peds', competed at these gatherings, which always drew a good crowd. The 'Football Sports', under the auspices of the Brisbane Football Club, were held annually until 1880, when a combined committee from the Brisbane, Wallaroo and Excelsior Clubs took over the organisation. They continued regularly until 1888, and then were revived in 1891 by the Northern Rugby Union. However, this meeting was sparsely attended and the tradition was discontinued.

In 1878 Fred Lea, who has been called the 'Father of Rugby' in Queensland,[76] arrived in Brisbane. Lea, born but eight miles from Rugby School in England, was an avid player of the rugby code. He joined the Brisbane Football Club in 1879 and was introduced to the Australian Rules game. "It was while engaged in a match in an enclosure where the Botanic Gardens now stand, that he induced the players to 'try their hand' at rugby."[77] Lea's suggestion was accepted and, during the 1881 season, three matches of rugby were played in Brisbane. The 1882 schedule[78] still indicated the dominance of Australian Rules, as nineteen of the twenty–two games were of that code, however that year proved to be the turning point for the establishment of the rugby game.

Negotiations, initiated during the 1881 season between Sydney and Brisbane, were finalised for the 1882 season. Although the Brisbanites wished to play both Australian Rules and rugby matches while in Sydney they agreed to play only rugby, as the Southern Rugby Union offered to totally cover their expenses while the Australian Rules Association was only willing to meet half the costs.[79] Finances, then, determined the choice of football to be played, and this decision changed the emphasis of football in Brisbane. A team of Brisbane players was selected to travel to Sydney to play what was to be the first intercolonial match between New South Wales and Queensland in rugby union.[80] This is developed in detail in the intercolonial competition chapter. When the Brisbanites returned, they were full of enthusiasm for the game and over the reception they had received. They had become firm advocates of the rugby code and were resolved to induce other footballers to convert. The following year, the prominence of rugby union was firmly established by the return visit of the New South Wales Rugby team to southern Queensland. Matches were played against the Brisbane Football Club, the Wallaroo and Roma clubs, as well as two intercolonial matches. Although New South Wales won the second intercolonial game with a score of 13–0, Queensland won the first 12–11. This historic event took place at Eagle Farm Race Course before a crowd of 3,500.[81]

From that game onward rugby union quickly gathered in strength and Australian Rules declined in interest. The year 1882 has been accepted as the official beginning of rugby union in the state, with the centenary game being played in 1982. The formation of the Northern Rugby Union has, however, been a subject of controversy. Tom Welsby, the first secretary of the Union, has maintained it was formed in 1882.[82] Mr J.R. Forbes, after researching the subject, stated that the Union "was formally incorporated at a meeting in the Exchange Hotel, Edward Street, Brisbane on November 2 1883."[83] Regardless of whether the actual year was 1882 or 1883, the name remained the Northern Rugby Union until 1893, when it was changed to the Queensland Rugby Union.

Fred Lea and Thomas Welsby were two of the key figures in the establishment of the game in the state. Lea, as well as introducing the rugby game to the Brisbane Football Club, later held the positions of President of the Union, Chairman of the Executive and Selector. Thomas Welsby was one of the players in the first intercolonial game and became the Union's first secretary. His contribution is commemorated today with the Welsby Cup.[84]

During the late 1860s the Union game continued to gain acceptance. A major development was the conversion to the game of Brisbane Grammar School. The other Grammar schools, notably Ipswich Grammar, did not originally change away from the 'Victorian' game, and hence Brisbane Grammar School team was compelled initially to play in the Brisbane senior league.

A further impetus to the game was the 1888 visit by the British team. An indication of the interest in the game was the team's reception by some three hundred people when they arrived by train from Sydney at 6 o'clock in the morning.[85] The British players were far superior to the local side, winning all four matches against the Queensland team the Queensland Junior team and Ipswich. Harry Speakman, who was a member of the British team, later returned to Queensland and captained the state side form 1889 to 1891. He went to Charters Towers, where he was influential in making Charters Towers one of the powerhouses of rugby in the 1890s and early 1900s. Another 'foreign' player to adopt Queensland as his home was William Warbrick, a star on the New Zealand 'Natives' team which toured Australia in 1889. Warbrick played for Queensland from 1891 to 1893, and in 1892 successfully captained the state side to victory over New South Wales.

The 1890s were 'boom' years for rugby union and Brisbane. In 1893 there were forty teams, a total which included junior and Grammar school teams.[86] The *Brisbane Courier* reported that it was being "played throughout the length and breadth of the colony,"[87] with teams at Toowoomba, Maryborough, Rockhampton, Ravenswood, Charters Towers, Warwick, Townsville, Gladstone, Longreach, Gympie and Barcaldine. Typical of the widespread acceptance of rugby was the formation in 1892 of two clubs, the Artisans and the Barcoo Rangers, in Barcaldine, a small outback town in Central Western Queensland.[88] This led to the first inter-town competition between representatives of properly organised clubs in the Central West. On Saturday June 11 1892, Longreach came to Barcaldine and a game was played on the black soil flats over Lagoon Creek. Longreach won the game 2 nil, and after the game the players were "led back to town by the Barcaldine Town Band...[and] the visitors were taken to dinner at the Shakespeare Hotel."[89] A return match was played on July 3, but this game was marred by a dispute over a try awarded to the home team. After the captains conferred, a gentleman from among the spectators was appointed the referee, but the Longreach team protested the appointment and walked off, thereby ending the game. Through the 1890s and until World War I the sport flourished in Barcaldine as well as at many other country areas.

The visit by the 1893 New Zealand team was eagerly awaited by players and officials, who planned an extensive social itinerary: a trip down the bay in a Government steamer, a Sunday trip to Humpybong, an all-day picnic to White's Hill, an all-day picnic to Enoggera, three theatre nights, smoke concerts and suppers.[90] Perhaps the locals should have spent more time in training, as the New Zealanders "utterly routed the Queenslanders...thrashed them so unmercifully...until then Queensland had rather good opinion of its football prowess."[91] In spite of the defeats public attendance was very good. Two weeks later, a crowd of over three thousand turned out on a rainy day to watch an interstate game.

The first Queensland team to tour overseas was in 1896 to New Zealand, but unfortunately the team did not win a match. The following year a New Zealand team returned to Queensland and again soundly beat the home side. However, both games drew a considerable crowd, six thousand being at the Union Ground, Bowen Bridge Road, and a record eleven thousand to the second game at the Exhibition Ground.[92]

International success finally came to the state team when, in 1899, Queensland defeated a touring overseas team, Great Britain and Ireland, 11 to 3, at the Exhibition Ground. This accomplishment was witnessed by some ten thousand spectators. Three weeks later the first "Test" was played in Brisbane, Australia versus this team, and Bob McCowan of Queensland was the captain. On this occasion some fifteen thousand supporters were on hand.[93] Obviously, from the size of crowds attending these international as well as inter–state matches, the rugby union code had captivated the public's interest. The game attracted players and spectators from all socio–economic groups. This spectator interest could certainly not be attributed to Queensland's dominance of the game as, by 1900, Queensland had only won fifteen of forty–five intercolonial matches. The physical and aggressive nature of the game appealed to the populace, as was apparent by the 'delightful' recounting of the 1891 match between New South Wales and Queensland.

> It must have been a merry game, for, in addition to one collar–bone, happily belonging to different individuals, being broken, another player was carried off, knocked out, three times and subsequently returned to the field of battle. Now, when a boxer is knocked out he never faces the music again, so I have just been wondering whether the footballer has more heart in him the fighter, or puts on more 'side'. I think the latter; it is a magnificent thing to be carried off the football field eyes shut, a little blood judiciously smeared over the left eyebrow and the body generally limp, past the grandstand where sit a host of sympathising ladies and followed by a host of awe–stricken boys and barrackers...[94]

Figure 11 shows the development of the game from local to intercolonial to international competitions. Figure 12 shows the rapid diffusion of the game throughout Queensland. Each town would generally field several clubs.

Australian Rules football, which was *the* game in the 1870s, declined in popularity in the late 1880s and virtually disappeared in the 1890s. In 1882 it was the dominant code in Brisbane, while in 1883 only two clubs played the game. It was also the preferred game in the Grammar Schools. Brisbane Grammar was the first to switch allegiance in 1887, and soon thereafter the other schools followed suit. The fate of the game was sealed with a disastrous game at Albion Park in 1890. Queensland played against the South Melbourne Club, and although "the official scores disappeared...one of the visitors kicked 30 goals."[95] Although a

1899	First Test played in Queensland	First Test played in Queensland
1897	New Zealand All Blacks in Queensland	Third International visit to Queensland
1896	Queensland tour New Zealand	Queensland makes first International visit
1889	New Zealand Maoris in Queensland	Second International visit to Queensland
1888	British Lions in Queensland	First International visit to Queensland
1883	First Intercolonial Game in Brisbane	Intercolonial
1882	First Intercolonial Game in Sydney	Intercolonial
1872	First Game of Rugby Union	Local

Figure 11 Rugby: progression from local to intercolonial to international game

1899	Mount Morgan, Bundaberg
1893	Maryborough, Gladstone, Longreach, Barcaldine, Gympie, Warwick, Rockhampton
1890s	Charters Towers, Townsville, Ravenswood
1887	Ipswich
1886	Toowoomba
1883	Roma
1882	Regular Competition (Brisbane Football Club v Wallaroos)
1870s	First Rugby Games (Brisbane)

Figure 12 Diffusion of rugby in Queensland

Queensland team took part in the first Australian Championships in 1908, the game was not really revived until after the First World War.

By the 1890s the second strongest code was Association Football (soccer). It is possible that the game was played in the early years particularly at festivals and sports days which emphasised English sports. In 1884 the Anglo–Queensland Football Association was formed and regular competitions were played between three clubs, the Rangers, Queen's Park and St Andrew's.[96] Three years later, two teams were organised in Ipswich, which was to become a stronghold for the game. By the mid–1890s Rockhampton and Maryborough also fielded teams.

The governing body for the sport was renamed in 1889, becoming the Queensland British Football Association, and one of its first organisational ventures was dispatching a state side to New South Wales in 1890. This first Queensland team won all of its four games in Sydney and Newcastle, including two against the New South Wales state side. At that time Queensland was being beaten by the southern states in rugby union, cricket and Australian Rules, and this performance was well received. However, the sport for some reason never attracted the public support that the rugby union code managed. Association Football matches only drew a couple of hundred spectators, while rugby drew thousands.

Bathing–Swimming

Although the art of swimming was known to the ancient Greeks and Egyptians, swimming did not develop as a 'sport' until the latter half of the nineteenth century. In Queensland competitive races do not appear to have been held on an organised club basis until the 1880s, however informal challenge races probably occurred much earlier. Swimming, or 'bathing' as it was generally referred to, was indulged in by the first settlers, the tropical climate and the extent of water encouraging such pleasures. However, natural dangers such as sharks and crocodiles discouraged swimmers in many areas. Far greater deterrents were Victorian attitudes surrounding bathing and the moral issues associated with such activities. Laws were passed regarding 'public' swimming, and some, such as the banning of swimming on beaches in daylight hours, were in effect as late as 1900.

In the late 1840s a 'fixed' bath had been constructed in the Brisbane River, however, due to vandalism, the settlers were without a bath in 1853.[97] They had to wait three years before another was established, although Ipswich had one in operation from 1852.

FLOWER BANK BATHING HOUSE,
IPSWICH

The above Bathing House being now completed, and rented to several of the most respectable families of Ipswich, by the quarter; the Proprietor begs to inform the public generally, that it is his intention to erect immediately another apartment for the accommodation of gentlemen arriving from the interior; one apartment being insufficient for the present demand.

Parties desirous of renting the Bathing House by the quarter, will please apply without delay.

OWEN CONNOR

Flower Bank, Ipswich
December 1, 1852[98]

The authorities finally granted permission for the construction of a Floating Bath in Brisbane in 1856.[99] In order to encourage bathers, Mr. Winship, the builder of the baths, offered hot coffee to morning bathers. These Baths, similar to the later River Baths, would periodically submerge and/or be damaged by storms. In 1861, the baths "experienced the misfortune of a total instead of a partial submersion...several attempts have since been made to bring the baths back to their proper position, but as yet without avail...as a natural consequence, the patrons both male and female are deprived of their usual bathing luxury."[100]

Another Public Baths was opened on January 1 1863. The swimming hours were for gentlemen from 6am to 9am and noon to 8pm daily, except on Sundays. For ladies, the hours were 9am to noon daily, except Sunday.[101] The announcement also indicated that instruction would be offered and that swimming races would be conducted. A month after the opening, the Baths sunk, but fortunately they were raised a few days later.[102] Obviously there were problems with such River Baths as the 'Military Baths' also deserted its moorings, floating "away bravely, and were last seen below Breakfast Creek."[103]

In country areas creeks, rivers and water holes served as swimming areas, and were readily utilised throughout the hot, humid summers. Regulations did not extend to such country areas. In Brisbane, however, swimmers could not indulge at will in the Brisbane River. There were sharks to contend with, but there were also moral standards. Mr W.E. Hillier of Creek Cottage, Breakfast Creek, made his complaints public, objecting to the dressing and undressing on a public road by men, women and children.[104] Such objections were frequently made in newspapers, however at the same time they reinforced the basic need that people wanted to swim.

The Baths both properly controlled swimmers, as well as offering them a relatively safe area where they could indulge in their exercise. Drownings throughout the colony were frequent as people swam in unknown waters, and usually with limited skills. A drowning in 1872 in Brisbane provoked a reaction from a citizen, who informed all and sundry that the life might have been saved through 'artificial respiration'. It was noted that such information that could have saved the person was actually circulated by the Royal National Life Boat Association, and such methods were used in Her Majesty's fleets and armies, at Coast Guard stations and in New South Wales by the police. The method recommended was Dr Hall's method, but if this was not successful it was recommended that Dr Silvester's method was to be followed. The writer proceeded to describe, in detail, the two methods. Dr Hall's method was to place the patient face downwards and to immediately clear the throat. If there was slight breathing, or if breathing failed after starting, "excite the nostrils with snuff, hartshorn, etc., or tickle the throat with a feather, etc., if they are at hand."[105] Essentially the method necessitated the moving of the person from the face down position to the side position about fifteen times a minute. The Silvester method was to place the person on his back, to raise the arms above the head, and then take them back towards the side of the chest. This latter method was adopted later by the Australian Surf Lifesaving Movement.

The first swimming club to be formed in Queensland was 'The Old Brisbane Amateurs' in 1885. The decision to form this club was made in a small wine shop on Queen Street by Messrs J. Dent, E. Beattie and Mr. Leo.[106] Shortly thereafter the club conducted a carnival at its headquarters at the Metropolitan Baths on Edward Street, and it was such a success that "hundreds of people were turned away".[107] The following year another club was formed in Toowong, and its headquarters became the Spring Hill Municipal Baths, which was opened in December 1886, after intense public pressure.

With the formation of these clubs, and following the construction of the Spring Hill Baths, the popularity of swimming increased. This led to the building of a facility in South Brisbane, which became known as the 'Old Imperial Baths'. Some floating and tidal baths were still in existence in the Brisbane River in the early 1890s, however most of these disappeared as a result of the 1893 flood.[108] In the late 1890s a number of clubs were formed: the Valley Club – 1897; the City Club – 1897; the St Mary's Gordon Club – 1898. These clubs, which totalled some one hundred swimmers, came together to form the Queensland Amateur Swimming Association on February 23 1898.[109] Mr R.H. Roe was elected the first President of the Association, a position he held until 1901. Under Roe's direction, swimming sports had been introduced to the Brisbane Grammar School in 1889.

By the turn of the century the sport of swimming was just beginning to be organised properly. In this sport Queensland lagged behind the southern states, and this was, on the surface, surprising, considering the more favourable climate in Queensland. Population differences and urban density were factors that mitigated against the growth of the sport in the north. Queensland's first representative to the Australasian Championships was J. Hogan, in 1900–1901.

Boxing

Throughout Queensland, and indeed Australia, boxing was popular from the first days of settlement. Though frequently condemned and considered a sport of the lower class, it was at the same time patronised by the upper class, who often put up the money for the contests. Many publicans also sponsored bouts, with boxing saloons being a feature at some hotels. After the Marquis of Queensberry Rules were officially introduced in 1884, and gloves were utilised, the sport became more respectable. However, bare-knuckle fighting was still practised until the turn of the century, particularly in country areas and gold-mining centres. Beginning in the 1880s there was a differentiation between the 'manly' exercise of boxing for gentlemen and the professional sport in the prize ring. By 1900 there were two forms of boxing practised, 'amateur' boxing, essentially for the middle and upper classes, and professional boxing, mainly for the lower classes.

Early prize fights were rarely reported in the press, though occasionally there would be references, such as in the *Moreton Bay Courier*, 21 December 1850: "Perry, the prize fighter, who claims the title 'Champion of the fistic ring'...arrived in Brisbane" ready to challenge the locals. Fights were usually arranged in remote areas or on vacant lots, and word of a fight was often by word-of-mouth. "Many of Brisbane's early fights were held in the bush at Kangaroo Point, where in addition to landward 'guards', a watchman in a boat 'kept nit' against police crossing the river from the city...many knuckle-ups were held with 'cockatoos' keeping watch for police who tried to break up the contests."[110] Although spectators and/or participants were in actuality charged, the sport was not officially illegal as no laws were ever passed "and all prohibition depended upon the old laws of breach of the peace and riotous assembly."[111]

Harry Perry, a champion featherweight in Queensland prior to the turn of the century, criticised the standard of boxing of the 1860s and 70s, stating that it "had not then been placed on its current scientific footing, strength and courage, counting more than any amount of neatness or display."[112] The first instructional facility for the sport was established in the early 1870s when two professional fighters, Fred Shaw and 'Soldier' Knight, set up a bare–knuckle academy in Brisbane.[113] Their efforts apparently met with little success. However, the next venture, in 1875, by Jack Dowridge, quickly gained acceptance, and his boxing saloon at the corner of Turbot and George Streets became the main centre for the sport in Brisbane. Dowridge, born in Barbados, had been a competent fighter in England and was known as the 'Black Diamond'.[114] Several of Dowridge's pupils became outstanding amateur fighters: 'Did' Harris, G. Cowlishaw, and Ambrose Taylor (the 'Game Chicken'). The most famous pupil of Dowridge's was 'Starlight' Rollins, who was born in British Guinea. Rollins was 30 years of age when he took up the sport, and 57 when he retired after fighting in Australia, Great Britain, the United States and New Zealand. He held the European middleweight title and claimed the 'coloured middleweight championship of Australia'.[115] One of the fights in which he met his superior was against the professional 'Billy' Smith, a middleweight from Sydney.

> Starlight asked "Who is the Johnny?" and for reply got, "A stockman of a well–known squatter," his reply being "poor devil", but on the fourth round Starlight played poor devil, and was carried out of the ring. It was one of the hardest fights seen in Brisbane.[116]

The sport of boxing, in the mid–1870s, was encouraged by the visit of Larry Foley, Champion of Australia. While touring around Queensland giving lessons and exhibitions, Foley discovered Frank P. Slavin, who under his tutelage became a champion fighter. Slavin won the Australian heavyweight title in 1889, and then went overseas, never to return. He had an illustrious career, defeating the English champion Jem Smith and Jake Kilrain of the United States. In 1892 he fought for the British Empire title against Peter Jackson, who also had been trained by Foley and had held the Australian heavyweight title. The fight, held at the National Sporting Club of London, was won by Jackson by a knock–out in the tenth round. Jackson eventually returned to Queensland, dying of tuberculosis in Roma.

During the 1880s, amateur boxing grew to be popular among the gentlemen of Brisbane. It was hoped that the opening of the Brisbane Gymnasium in 1882 would provide a proper facility for the sport, however it was not until 1887 that "those desirous of practising boxing...were allowed Monday nights in each week for the exercise of the polite art, to the exclusion of all other branches of athletics."[117] It was not until 1892 that the committee of the Gymnasium permitted the teaching of the sport and the holding of contests. Some of the outstanding amateur boxers of the era were Frank Baynes and George Dawson. Baynes defeated Arthur Scott, who had fought in Sydney, and "was declared the winner of the 10 stone amateur championship of Queensland"[118] in 1886. In the 1890s, F. Bell, L.H. Nathan, A.E.J. Austin and J. Ross were some of the top participants.

During the 1880s and 1890s both amateur and professional boxing received considerable patronage. Numerous facilities were utilised to host the fights such as the Albert Hall, the Gaiety Theatre, Columbia Skating Rink, the Australian Gardens and the Town Hall. Boxing had many advocates as there was still enough of the frontier society in Brisbane and Queensland, and they extolled the virtue of being able to handle oneself in a fight. Endurance sports, and those requiring courage, always operate as important elements in such societies.

Tennis

"Royal" tennis had been played since the twelfth century in England and France. By the nineteenth century there were very few advocates of this indoor racquet game. The courts on which the game was played can be found in Hampton Court, Lord's Cricket Ground and various aristocratic country homes. In Australia two 'Royal' courts were built, one in Tasmania and the other in Melbourne. These courts are still in existence and are the only places where 'Royal' or 'Court' tennis is still played in Australia.

The modern sport of tennis evolved from a game invented by Major Wingfield in 1874. Wingfield chose to call his game 'Sphairistike' which was a term derived from the ancient Greeks, referring to ball games played on a court. The game was played on an "hour–glass shaped court, with a net over five feet in height, using a racquet midway in size between a modern tennis racquet and a racquets bat, a method of scoring similar to that of racquets by single points up to fifteen."[119] He patented the game and sold sets consisting of "a court, four racquets and a supply of balls from French and Co. for the sum of five guineas."[120] The All-England Croquet Club, situated at Wimbledon, changed some of the rules, the shape of the court and the height of the nets, thus breaking the patent and in 1877 organised the first Wimbledon Lawn Tennis Championship.

Major Wingfield's 'Sphairistike' quickly spread to other countries, as interested individuals purchased complete sets of the game and then brought the 'package' with them. Miss Outerbridge introduced the game to the United States in the spring of 1874, after purchasing a set while on holidays; Reginald Roe, who became Headmaster of Brisbane Grammar School, brought a set of the game 'Sphairistike' from Oxford with him to Brisbane in 1876. Roe has, traditionally, been credited with introducing lawn tennis to Queensland, however, in actuality the game he introduced, as Dr Wilton Love has stated, "[was] known as Sphairistike and was played in an oblong court pinched in at the level of the net. The rackets were weird structures, with the head bent over laterally from the handle, and the points counted from 1 to 15, which was game – 14 all being deuce."[121] So strictly speaking Roe did not introduce tennis, but 'Sphairistike', an earlier form of the game, but a different one.

The exact beginning of the sport of lawn tennis in Queensland is unclear. The *Illustrated Sydney News* of 17 August 1864, noted that "A racquet ground is about to be established at Green Hills." However, as this was before Major Wingfield's invention of Sphairistike, and the term 'racquet' is used, the game that would have been played on such a court would probably have been 'racquets'. This was another of the various racquet ballgames that were played in England. The first mention of a 'tennis court' in Queensland was in 1876 on an outback property. William Hill recounted that when George Hodgkinson explored the country from Cloncurry to the South Australian boundary in 1876, a month out of Cloncurry he arrived at a station which had a piano and tennis court.[122] It would be assumed that if there were a tennis court at an outback station, then surely there would have been tennis elsewhere in Queensland.

By the 1880s the game had spread sufficiently in southern Queensland that clubs were formed in Brisbane, Ipswich, Goodna and Woogaroo. Inter–club competitions evolved for both men's and women's events. In 1882, for example, an inter–club tournament involving one men's doubles, two mixed doubles and one women's doubles matches was conducted between the Ipswich and Woogaroo clubs. The tournament was played on a Saturday afternoon on the asylum grounds.[123] During this decade the sport continued to spread through the state. In Townsville, a club, although it had been in existence for several years, was not placed on a permanent footing until 1886, when three courts – one grass and two antbed clay – were constructed.[124] As a consequence the membership increased rapidly.

The major impetus to the game came in 1888 when the Queensland Lawn Tennis Association (QLTA) was formed. The first President of the Association was Mr Reginald Roe. Roe played a most significant role in the growth of the game, and it was primarily through his efforts that it developed into an organised, competitive sport in the 1890s. At his instigation interschool competition, Brisbane Grammar against Toowoomba Grammar, was established in 1883, and an annual school tournament was started in 1885. Dr William Moore, who was a pupil at the school in the 1870s, recalled: "Mr Roe brought out from England a set of tennis things and gave them to us and we played tennis on a gravel pitch alongside the school building."[125]

In the early 1890s the game was played competitively at Maryborough, Bundaberg, Charters Towers, Ipswich, Gladstone, Townsville, Warwick and Toowoomba, and inter-town tournaments such as those between Bundaberg and Maryborough, and Charters Towers and Townsville, were regularly held. In Brisbane there were numerous clubs, with Coorparoo, Indooroopilly, Corinda, Brisbane, Wanderers, South Brisbane, Milton and Enoggera being the main ones.[126] The number of clubs and participants necessitated that fixtures would be played in two divisions.

One of the first initiatives of the QLTA was the organisation of state championships. These began in 1889, although women's competitions were not inaugurated until 1892. Mr Hudson was the first Queensland Men's Singles Champion. Queensland titles in the early years were dominated "by Sydney men, who took their holidays in August, and came to Brisbane to play in the tournaments."[127] Mr A. Taylor and Mr O.S. Poidevin were two Sydney-ites who won various Queensland titles in the 1890s. Intercolonial contests between Queensland and New South Wales began in 1895, but southern players dominated these contests. Queensland's first victory came in 1902.

After the Woolloongabba Cricket Ground was opened in the mid-1890s, the state tournament and the intercolonial contests were held on the lawn courts laid out on the cricket field. Other locales for public courts were the Botanic Gardens, Albert Park and the Exhibition Ground, as well as at private homes. Although it is generally stated that tennis was an upper class sport, this was not the case in Queensland. Perhaps it was the tropical climate and the availability of land that enabled the sport to be played by the middle class. Tennis courts became a common feature on most stations, and in many country towns. Interestingly, McIntosh has maintained that in England tennis was a sport invented by the middle class for the middle class.[128]

Tennis was one of the few sports that were acceptable, and available, for women to play. Most clubs had lady members, and they competed in inter-club and inter-town tournaments. Mixed doubles were a regular feature at tournaments, and it was the only sport in which men and women competed together.

By the turn of the century, tennis was established in the sport pattern of the state. However, it was not until the 1920s that the sport began to emerge as a major sport.

Golf

Golf was slow to develop in Queensland, behind all the other states (except for the Northern Territory) in the building of golf courses and the establishment of golf clubs in capital cities.[129] Even Western Australia, which developed economically later than Queensland, established the Perth Golf Club in 1895. While golf was first played in Australia in the 1820s near Hobart, an official golf club was not formed there until 25 April 1896. The Brisbane Golf Course was not formed until November 1896.

Golf, in the nineteenth century, was considered a healthy form of exercise, "involving as it does a great amount of muscular exercise and plenty of walking, without at the same time calling for those spasmodic outbursts of violent energy which render several outdoor games simply 'forbidden fruit' to hundreds of boys and young men."[130] As it was not such a vigorous sport, it is surprising that it was not played more extensively prior to the turn of the century. Queensland's hot, humid tropical climate should have been ideal for the sport.

The availability of land was another factor that should have encouraged the early adoption of the game. Particularly in the country areas, and on the stations, there was more than ample space for the setting up of courses. The traditionally accepted beginning of golf in Queensland has been by two brothers, Frank and Alexander Ivory, from Scotland. They laid out a few holes on their Eidsvold Station which they had purchased from the Archer brothers in 1856. The dating of this occurrence has been variously reported as being "in 1880", "as early as 1880" and even "1886".[131] If the early 1880s is the accepted date, then it is possible that there was an earlier course in the Stanthorpe area, as there was a golf course on the McGregor Estate and players "drove off from a tee in Bridge Street just N-> E-> of the hospital also part of the racecourse".[132] The race course that is referred to is one that was utilised in the mid–1870s.

Difficulties also exist in ascertaining the "first" golf club in the state. It has been normally represented that the first golf club in Queensland was the Brisbane Golf Club. However, Townsville, Charters Towers and Toowoomba have also claimed this honour. When Brigadier–General Jim Cannan became the President of the Queensland Golf Association, it was reported that he came "from Townsville, which disputes with Charters Towers, the honour of having harbored the first Queensland golf club."[133] Townsville claims to have established a club in 1893, called the North Queensland Golf Club, and then in 1924 it changed its name to the Townsville Golf Club.[134]

The first Brisbane club, appropriately called the Brisbane Golf Club (BGC), was founded on November 4 1896 "by a dozen addicts who started a nine hole course at Chelmer, some way out of Brisbane on the Ipswich railway."[135] The early office bearers of the club were indicative of the upper class nature of the club, and the sport: Lord Lamington, the State Governor, was the first President; Mr A. McIntosh, General Manager of the Royal Bank of Queensland, was the first Vice-President; Archdeacon Evan David, a founding member of the club, was a vice-president; and Sir Samuel Griffith, Lieutenant-Governor of Queensland and Premier of the State, was President of the BGC from 1901–1902.[136] Lord Lamington was a zealous golfer, and on 12 December 1896 he drove off from the first tee, thereby officially opening the Brisbane Golf Club.[137] His contribution to the club has been carried on by the Lamington Cup, which he initiated in 1899 and, with Gilbert Wilson, won in 1900.

The cost of equipment, as well as the entrance and annual fees to clubs, were economic factors which put golf beyond the means of the working class, at least in Brisbane. Also membership to a club was through nomination which, in essence, was a means of screening out the lower classes. Phillips, in his analysis of the membership of the Brisbane Golf Club found that during "...the club's first decade over half of the golfers possessed dual membership with the elite Queensland Club."[138] Women were permitted, after 1898, to become 'associate' members of the BGC, although their playing times were restricted.

Due to the financial and other restrictive aspects of the sport, golf could not be considered a 'popular' sport in Brisbane by the turn of the century. The first public course opened in Brisbane in 1931. However, it was well established by 1900, and state amateur championships were even inaugurated by that year. The championship was conducted on the Brisbane Golf Club course and was won by A. Carvosso of Brisbane.

Hunting

Although hunting generally was not the exclusive domain of the elite, the Hunt Club and its activities most certainly were. As the meetings of the Club until the 1890s in Brisbane were on weekdays, the participants could only be from the upper class. Extensive newspaper coverage was devoted to the Hunt Club and its activities, with the sport even being accorded the privilege of a regular column in all local newspapers. Normally, over half of a column would be taken up by listing the names of the participants. The membership lists read like the social register of the city. Despite the improvisations and limitations imposed by organising a hunt in the Australian countryside, the elite were adamant in pursuing this "most manly of all field pastimes."[139] Moreover, there were many of the supposed elite who were not of aristocratic heritage nor could they be considered 'landed', but these aspired to replicate the social life of the English gentleman and gentlewoman, which included 'riding to the hounds'. Daly, after analysing the South Australian gentry, concluded that the Hunt was "truly symbolic of the Anglo–Australian attempt at gentility."[140]

The honour of forming the first hunt club in Queensland rests with Gayndah. The Burnett Hunt Club was officially formed on 29 August 1867, and its first meet was run on September 17 from the Barambah Hotel. The Master of the Hunt was W.E. Parry–Okeden (winner of the first Queensland Derby) and the club "hunted a fine pack of kangaroo dogs, trained to rally to work by the sound of the horn...the club was a huge success from the start, all the members turning out in 'pink'."[141] Actually the Gayndah club only preceded the Brisbane Club by a few weeks.

It is possible, however, that the Gayndah Club was preceded by the Kangaroo Hunt Club in Rockhampton, which Bird claimed in *The early History of Queensland*[142] was formed in 1865. However Pattison described the activities of another club, the Criterion Hunt Club, in 1865. As Tom Nobbs, the publican of the Criterion Hotel was the Master of the Hounds, this was probably the same club as Bird referred to. The club's 1868 Meet was an overnight affair, with all the huntsmen appearing in approved outfits: "red shirt, corduroy breeches, riding boots and cabbage tree hats, a sheath knife hung at each belt."[143]

> A spring cart had been loaded with blankets, cooking gear, rounds of beef, a loaf of cheese, and other good things, to which was added liquid refreshments in the shape of Hennessy's brandy, West Indian rum, and for the temperate ones there was a case of drinks on the dray. The cart was driven out to the Archer Bros' Wells Station, near the Agriculture Reserve...Camp was formed and the huntsmen...settled down to a night of conviviality.[144]

At dawn the men, with the hounds, set out for a day's hunt, during which they made twenty–one kills, the kangaroo being the prey. The Hunt finished back at the Criterion Hotel, where a supper was provided by the 'Master' of the Hunt.

In the early 1870s other clubs were formed, with one in South Brisbane and another one in Toowoomba in 1874. In Roma a Hunt Club was formed in 1877 by David Benjamin and R.W. Stuart, with J.B.

Nutting as the Master of the Hounds, and their activities were noted in the Brisbane press: "They hunted a very good pack of hounds, ten couple or so being purchased in Melbourne for the club, and from the social point of view the meets were most popular."[145] Charters Towers, in its heyday, formed a Hunt Club as well, and their approved uniform was similar to that elsewhere: scarlet coat, top boots or garters and breeches.[146]

A case study of the Brisbane Hunt Club will be presented. The first Brisbane Hunt Club was formed in September 1867, when Captain Creagh, who was in charge of the 50th Foot Regiment in Brisbane, with a few friends, procured some hounds and hunted kangaroos and dingoes. The other main supporters of the Club were Judge Pring and D.T. Seymour, Queensland's First Commissioner of Police. Several meets were held at Rocklea, Cooper's Plains and Eagle Farm, and one particularly good run is described as "from Byrne's paddock, Bowen Bridge, to the Albion Hotel, over a stiff country."[147] Although initially the Club was highly successful, in the 1870s it ceased to exist.

In 1888, paralleling the general economic prosperity of the state, the Club was revived, and was often referred to as the Brisbane Hounds. Gawne Echlin, a former British Army officer, was the first Master of Hounds and was "generally mounted on 'Pilot', a clever little bay with docked tail, quite in the English hunter style."[148] When Echlin returned to England, Adolph Feez took over the mastership. The club was a properly organised Hunt Club, "with a 'Master' and a 'Whip', a pack of English foxhounds, pink–coated huntsmen and all the paraphernalia that goes with such an institution."[149]

The Club became so successful that it was announced in the newspaper that "hunting has now become recognised in sporting circles, and the numerous assemblages which weekly flock to the 'meet' would lead one to the conclusion that the sport will, at no distant date, rank foremost amongst the field sports in the colony."[150] The most popular sites for the meets were Rocklea, Oxley, Coorparoo and Hamilton, as well as Goodna and Ipswich. The usual runs were from five to seven miles, jumping some 30 to 40 fences en route, then came a "check", followed by another five to seven miles, with a similar number of jumps. These runs would be described in detail in the daily newspaper.

One run with the hounds was humorously described in doggerel in *The Queensland Punch*, July 1892. Some of the names mentioned were deputy–master Adolph Feez, on "Pilot", Miss Mabel Newton on "Bolivar", George Baynes on "Fairfax", F.L. Barker on "Demon", Dr Scholes on "The Tucker", Dr Griffin on "Common", F.W. McGill on "Problem" and Gordon Harding on "Blue Peter".

The meets, which were originally held on Thursdays were, during the 1890s, conducted mostly on Saturday afternoons. With this change, the meetings drew large crowds, such as one in 1889, when some three to four hundred people came to watch the assemblage of the Hunt Club at the Hamilton Hotel.[151] Of these, only forty actually started with the hounds. The presence of such a sizeable crowd indicated the underlying curiosity of the general populace in activities of the elite, and the overt attraction of their imposing and brilliant assemblages.

The social gathering at the conclusion of the Hunt was almost as important as the Meet itself;

> ...a large party of ladies and gentlemen were entertained at dinner by Mr and Mrs F.G. Coe at their residence, Moolabin, Oxley Creek. The house was gaily decorated for the occasion...Conspicuous among the decorations surrounding the veranda on which the dinner was served...the words "Welcome to the Hunt Club" cleverly worked in white cotton wool...on a scarlet ground, the whole surrounded by a tastefully arranged border of evergreens and flowers...after the dinner, dancing and singing were indulged in till well on in the evening.[152]

Ladies, although they were in a minority, actively engaged in both riding to the hounds and the associated social activities. Those who rode were "all great horsewomen...and were generally to be seen, like Uriah the Hittite, right in the forefront of the battle."[153] Among the regular riders were Miss Mabel Newton, Mrs Adolph Feez, Miss Yaldwyn, Miss Eileen Persse, Miss North, Mrs Paxton and Miss F. Harding.

In addition to the regular Hunts, members of the Hunt Club were also active participants in jumping events at the Brisbane Show, at which they competed in the club costume. Also, in 1892, the Brisbane Hunt Club Sports were initiated which included such events as a Maiden Hunter's Plate, a Ladies' Hack race, a High Jumping Contest for horses and a Hunter's Plate. At the inaugural meet 'Spondulix' set an Australian record by clearing 6 feet 6 inches.

The Brisbane Hunt Club boasted a membership that included many of the finest families and the social elite of the city. In the detailed newspaper accounts of the meets, every person who participated was listed, as were their horses. Frequently mentioned names were: Ernest Baynes, F.W. Thurlow, Ernest Winter, George Baynes, J. Alexander, J.W. White, M.B. and Henry Goggs, G. Hanbury, S.R. Watson, B.E. Fenwick, J.E. Trude, F.W. McGill, Silas and Gordon Harding, U.E. Parry–Okeden, Fred and "Rowdy" Barker, Dr Scholes, Alex Rule, F. Newton, Spencer Browne, J. Prentice, George and Jack Graham, C.H.E. Lambart, O.M.D. Bell, J. Harrap, Eric Molle, E. Barter, Pat Moylan,

J.C. Higginson (General Manager of the Australian Pastoral Company) and Archibald Dowall, the Surveyor–General.

At the Annual General meeting of 1892 the Annual Report showed three Honorary Members, John Bell, De Burgh Persse and Andrew Scott. De Burgh Persse, for example, was a BA and an MLA, and was President of the Queensland Club in 1889. He came to Australia from Ireland in 1864 and was qualified as a doctor but did not practise, preferring instead to control his properties from Tabragalba, which be bought in 1865. He owned properties at Eidsvold, Galway Downs, Connemara, Hawkwood, Buckingham Downs and Palparara. Much of his time was spent in Ireland, where he was Master of the Galway Blazers. There were 29 full members of the club, nine members of whom were also members of the exclusive Queensland Club. Some of these were William Allan, MLA (grazier), Auriol Barker (merchant), Ernest and George Baynes (meat–works), Adolph Feez (solicitor), B.E. Fenwick (grazier), Dr Griffin (medicine), A. McDowell (surveyor), Richard Newton (planter), John Stevenson, MLA (grazier) and J. Trude (merchant), another President of the Queensland Club.

There were, in addition, some forty ordinary members, including grazier John Little, solicitor Walter Heath, Queensland Premier Sir S.W. Griffith, grazier J.F. Carter, solicitor P.L. Cardew, headmaster F.S.N. Bousfeld, and so on. The Club obviously represented many of the social lions of the city, but the increasing Australianisation of migrants and changing economic and social conditions eventually resulted in the Club's demise. The mimicking of British customs did not have a lasting impact in Queensland. The hounds were from England, but the prey was the dingo, the kangaroo and the wallaby, so that the hunt had a different meaning, even an unreal quality, in this new land. The sight of traditionally uniformed fox hunters pursuing disinterested dingoes had an element of humour in it, and in the long haul it lacked public acceptance. It was doomed to extinction. The Brisbane Hunt Club was disbanded in the late 1890s, but a few of the old followers and many of the horses continued to compete in the jumping events at the Shows in the early 1900s.

Fishing

Coastal waters, estuaries, rivers and streams were well stocked with fish of numerous varieties which provided ample sport for the angler. Fishing was good, varied and inexpensive. The availability of fish and the relative ease with which one could indulge in the sport was exemplified by a fishing excursion to Flat Rock from Brisbane in 1871.

There were 27 in the party, and in just over two hours 513 schnappers, some weighing 70 pounds, were caught.[154]

One of the best accounts of the fishing in the state is found in William R.O. Hill's *Forty-Five Years Experiences in North Queensland*. Hill was a devoted fisherman, and as he travelled around the state he would describe the quantity and quality of fishing in the various centres. According to Hill the choicest spot was Mackay, which even surpassed Caloundra.[155]

Nat Gould, however, extolled the excellent fishing and porpoise-shooting at Redcliffe.[156]

Rifle Shooting

Rifle shooting, in the nineteenth century, was considered a major sport that attracted participants from a wide cross-section of the population. The ability to shoot was another activity considered essential in a frontier society. A gun was considered as vital as a horse to the pioneers of this state. Proficiency with a rifle was also intrinsic to the defence of the community and, subsequently, the sport of rifle shooting was encouraged by the Government, which viewed it as a para-military activity. In the twentieth century, although the sport still has its loyal adherents, it in no way approximates the high status that it was accorded in the early years. It is no longer patronised by a large section of the elite of the community, and the associated costs for rifles and ammunition have taken the sport well beyond the means of the working class.

In the 1850s gun-related activities were prominent in the daily lives of settlers, for defence, and for hunting food. The understandable desire to determine the most accurate shooter led to challenge matches and eventually to the formation of clubs. Often such competitions were held in conjunction with other sports meetings and gatherings. Normally the elite were involved in such activities. In 1859, for example, a meeting was held at the Downs Hotel, Drayton, whereby "about 30 of the most influential inhabitants assembled to make arrangements for the formation of a cricket and rifle club."[157]

The Governor, Sir George Ferguson Bowen, formed the first Queensland Volunteer Force in 1860. The government provided uniforms and artillery for the volunteers, and what could be regarded as an inducement was the Land Order "granting 50 acres of land in country areas, or 10 acres of suburban land was issued to every member who qualified by five consecutive years of service."[158] The Queensland Volunteer Rifle Corps was formed the same year, with its principal objective being to promote rifle shooting in the colony.[159] Customarily the Corps would muster early in the morning, go through the usual parade, and then practise target shooting. The Volunteers were required to attend eight drills if they wished to partake in the competitions.[160] The Queensland Free Rifles also arranged competitive shooting matches.

Queensland Free Rifles

The arrangements for the Rifle Match with No. 1 Company having been concluded, the Free Rifles will parade at half–past 7 sharp, on the Morning of BOXING DAY, at the Armoury.

New undress uniform, with white trousers and cap covers.

No member who has not fallen in when the firing commences will be permitted to take part in the match.

Luncheon will be provided on the ground.

EDWARD R. DRURY,
Captain

N.B. – Ball practice on TUESDAY AFTERNOON, at half–past 4.[161]

The formation of a state governing body for this sport was relatively early in comparison with other sports, as it became, in 1863, the first sport, along with horse–racing, to form a coordinating structure. The generally acknowledged data for the formation of the Queensland Rifle Association (QRA) is 1877,[162] however, the present research has established the actual date as being 1863. The *Courier*, on 11 July 1863, carried the relevant announcement, citing that the newly–formed Association was under the patronage of Governor Bowen and the Presidency of Sir Maurice O'Connell, Commandant of the Queensland Rifle Brigade, and then continued on about the regulations of the Association. The Association conducted nine different meetings in its formative year, as well as competitive inter–town matches against the Ipswich corps.[169]

Although the Association was noted as conducting an international match against an Irish team in 1871,[164] the Association appears to have been re–organised in 1877. At a meeting in the Brisbane Town Hall on 1 October 1877, with Sir Maurice O'Connell, a member of the Queensland Parliament and President of the Legislative Council, presiding as President, the rules of the Association were formally adopted.[165] The office bearers of the Association were: President: Sir Maurice C. O'Connell; Vice–Presidents: Majors J. McDonnell, E.R. Drury and W.H. Snelling; His Honour Mr Justice Lutwyche and the Hon. John Douglas; Council: Captains G.H. Newman and E.H. Well, Lieutenants A.J. Thynne, J.B. Stanley, J.O. Bourne, J. Mills, and A.

McFarlane; Messrs J.B. Ellis, G. Cowlishaw, T. Finney, E.W. Walker and J. Lennon. The Premier, the Hon. John Douglas, who was also a Vice-President of the Rifle Association, was immediately approached for funds for a proposed rifle range, and Parliament subsequently granted £600 to construct the Metropolitan Rifle Range in Victoria Park.[166] The following year, the Government granted another £100 for prizes at the First Prize Meeting, which was held Tuesday 20 August to Saturday 24 August 1878. The opening match at this inaugural meeting was a Cadets' Match, contested by forty-five Cadets from the Brisbane and Toowoomba Corps, and was won by Brisbane Grammar School.[167]

In Grammar Schools the Cadets were an integral part of the total school program. At Brisbane Grammar School (BGS) the first rifle shooting matches were organised by the rifle company that was formed in 1870.[168] This company lasted only three years, but in 1878 a volunteer cadet corps was constituted. Thereafter, shooting matches were a regular feature in the Cadets' program, and the school cadets competed in the QRA Prize Meetings. An Intercolonial Schools competition was inaugurated in 1887 involving the following schools: Melbourne Church of England Grammar School, Scotch College, Melbourne, Geelong Grammar School, Sydney Grammar School, Dunedin High School and BGS. In the initial years shooters from BGS dominated the meets, and in 1890 were permanently awarded the Sargood Shield, as they won the Intercolonial meet four consecutive years.[169]

The Defence Act of 1884 specifically provided "for the encouragement of rifle shooting throughout the Colony"[170] and thereby legislative recognition, and approval, was given to rifle clubs. Within a year clubs were formed in Rockhampton, Townsville, Maryborough, Mackay, Gympie, Mitchell and Herberton. These clubs subsequently received Government monies to assist in the building of facilities, and were able to purchase Army rifles and ammunition at less than cost price. Moreover, some of the prize monies for matches were donated by the Government. At the 1879 QRA Meeting, for example, the Queen's Prize Match was £150 "which was donated by the Queensland Government."[171] Such expenditures were occasionally criticised in the press, it being claimed that rifle clubs were of very limited military value and that the Prize Meetings only encouraged the development of elite shooters.

The state organisation of the sport was affected by the 1885 decision of the Queensland Government to divide the state into two military districts. Subsequently a separate North Queensland Rifle Association was formed in 1887 to coordinate all the rifle clubs north of Rockhampton, and its headquarters was designated as Townsville. In

1894, through a further military division, a Central Queensland Rifle Association was formed. Although the initial Association retained the right to select all intercolonial and international teams, all three Associations received separate Government grants for their Prize Meetings.[172] After Federation, the North Queensland Association was designated as a 'State' Association and given "equal status to the other Rifle Associations of the Commonwealth."[173]

Although intercolonial competitions were first held in 1873, Queensland did not compete until 1879. Throughout the 1880s and early 1890s the southern shooters were too strong for the Queenslanders, however success was finally achieved at the 1895 Match. On their home turf at the Toowong Rifle Range, Queensland won the coveted "Federal Challenge Cup", which they proceeded to dominate for the four succeeding years. In 1899, the Cup was presented permanently to Queensland, as they had the greatest number of wins over a twelve year period.

The first Queenslanders to compete overseas were Colour–Sergeant W.S. Barron and Sergeant T. Grimes, who were selected as members of the 1886 Australian Military Rifle team to England. In Queen Victoria's Jubilee year, 1877, Queensland sent a full team to the Bisley, which was the highest competitive match for shooters in the British Commonwealth. At the 1903 Bisley Queensland became the proud holders of the Kalopore Cup.

The popularity of the sport was evident by the proliferation of clubs and the number of matches that were held throughout the State. In Brisbane alone, by the mid–1890s, there were twenty affiliated clubs. Newspapers devoted extensive coverage to matches, giving full details of the various shooters, the total scores and the names of the competitors. The Governor customarily attended the Annual Meetings in Brisbane, which were considered to be among the major social events of the year. At the 1894 Meeting it was noted that there "was a brilliant gathering of about 300 ladies and gentlemen...The Headquarters Band rendered a selection of music during the afternoon and the invited guests were served with afternoon tea."[174]

Pigeon Shooting

The English tradition of pigeon shooting was copied by the colonists, even though, with the diversity of birds in Australia, other types of shooting could have resulted. Pigeon shooting became an organised 'sport' in the 1870s, with the formation of clubs in Brisbane, Ipswich, Toowoomba and Gympie, and the commencement of inter–town competitions. At the Ipswich match of 1873, three traps were used, with one pigeon under each, and to increase the difficulty of the shoot, competitors were unaware which trap would be released. The distance from the trap was twenty–five yards.[175] As was the custom at most sports matches of the era, money prizes were awarded. The popularity of the sport continued throughout the following decades, with clubs being formed in most established centres, such as Charters Towers and Rockhampton.

Other Sports and Leisure Activities

There were a wide variety of other sports and leisure activities that were part of the total sport picture in nineteenth century Queensland. The majority of these did not attract a major following, nor were they accorded substantial coverage by the press. However, this lack of media coverage could simply have been a reflection of the interests of the writers. There is no attempt to develop comprehensively the following sports, as the documentary evidence is far too limited. However, they are briefly developed, to point out the range of available activities.

Lacrosse

Lacrosse was introduced to Australia in the 1870s, and it acquired a popular following in Victoria, Sydney and particularly South Australia where, by the turn of the century, it was considered one of the major sports. Queenslanders also took up the game and, by the 1890s, a Queensland Lacrosse Union was formed. In Brisbane three clubs, Toowong, Mochican and Brisbane, were formed by 1893.[176] However, the Union generally conceded that the game was too difficult to learn to become as popular as football. "It is within the scope of all...to play football somehow, but in the case of lacrosse, every player must pass through a state of tuition. To handle a crosse for the first time is as difficult to attempt as to eat soup with a fork."[177] In an attempt to popularise the sport, the Union endeavoured to introduce it to the schools.

Although there were some enthusiasts, probably those who had played the game in Canada, the United States, or in the southern states, the sport never did gain much acceptance. Thus, it was surprising that Brisbane was chosen as the site for the first game of the touring 1907 Canadian team. The Australian team that played in this international match was composed entirely of South Australians and Victorians.[178]

Lawn Bowls

The first form of bowling that was practised was indoor bowling. As early as 1858, "Bowling Saloons" were to be found in Brisbane. The *Moreton Bay Courier* carried an advertisement on 25 December 1858, inviting "Gentlemen of Brisbane and its vicinity [to a] Bowling Saloon in Charlotte Street, near the Prince of Wales Hotel."[179] However, it was the 'lawn' form of the game that became the popular and accepted game.

Prior to the turn of the century, the sport of lawn bowls presented no indication of the 'boom' sport that it was to become in the latter half of the twentieth century. The first green in Queensland was reportedly laid down by James Fairlie at his Maryborough home in the 1870s.[180] The next club to be formed was the Brisbane Bowling Club in September 1878, under the sponsorship of Sir Thomas McIlwraith. The club laid its greens in the Botanic Gardens, but within two years they were required to move. The site selected for new greens was at Roma Street, however, in 1893, that land was taken over by the Railway Department to build the Roma Street Railway Station.[181] The club was again forced to move, and this time they amalgamated with Booroodabin Club, that was formed in 1888. The sport attracted the older age group, with the membership being primarily from the upper classes.[182] Only men were permitted as members, women having to wait until the 1920s before they were allowed to play.

Interest in the sport increased during the 1890s, with clubs being formed in country areas such as Maryborough (1898) and Toowoomba (1900). Intercolonial matches against New South Wales started in 1899, however the Queensland Bowling Association was not formed until 1903.

Croquet

Croquet, which bears obvious affinities with golf, was a leisure pursuit popular among the upper classes. It was played by children and adults, and was considered a 'genteel' enough activity for proper ladies to play. Croquet lawns were laid in front of most homesteads on large stations, and around the homes of the elite in the cities. Mary Macleod Banks recounts her family's home at Cressbrook: "From the gravelled walk at the entrance front of the house, a croquet-lawn lay on the station side;...My parents, our governess and various visitors played when the day had grown cool; crinolines swept the lawn, balls rolled briskly from the mallets, contending voices argued points of the game, but gaiety was supreme for the most part."[183] Great care was taken to keep lawns properly manicured, and even special seed was used for their maintenance. In the 1870s The *Brisbane Courier* would carry advertisements for: "Fine Bright Green Grass, for Croquet Grounds and Lawns, New Seed, Just Arrived."[184] Expensive mallets and balls would also be imported from England.

What was both a first and last occurrence was when the men's Bowling Club gave up their land, in the Botanic Gardens, for the ladies' croquet lawn.[185] Some years later the ladies established the South Brisbane Croquet Club at Musgrave Park, and then another club was formed at Eagle Farm.

Coursing

Coursing, a traditional 'field' sport of the English gentry, did not emerge in Australia as an organised sport until the 1870s. Hares were not native to Australia, nor were greyhounds, however the latter were brought out on the First Fleet in 1788. As there were no hares to hunt, greyhounds were used to hunt kangaroos, and hence, came to be called 'kangaroo dogs'. The resultant sport of 'kangarooing' came to be organised in a similar manner to coursing, and can be considered the Antipodean version of the English sport.

Kangarooing

THE LOGAN CUP, a Sweepstake of Ten Shillings each, with £5 added, will be run for about next Christmas, near the Logan. Points will be given for pace, killing, &c., &c. Those desirous of entering dogs will oblige by at once sending their names to the advertiser, NORMAN D'ARCY, Homemead, Eight–mile Plains.[186]

English methods of training greyhounds were copied in the colonies and, generally, English dogs were considered superior to the local product. Mr D'Arcy, the leading proponent of the sport in Queensland, imported Bengal Light, the champion winner of over twenty cups, plates and prizes in England, including one at Crystal Palace in 1871, and immediately offered him "for Kangaroo sluts...for a stud fee of £6/6."[187] A race in 1873 matched Myrtle, a recently imported dog, against another English import, Belle of Queensland, as well as dogs imported from Melbourne.[188]

By the 1870s rabbits, which had been introduced into Australia were being used for greyhound races. The *Brisbane Courier* of 11 November 1892 announced there was to be a race on the flats behind South Brisbane, between Bengal Light and Scalper, "the best of three events to be run on wild rabbits, which have been sent for from Sydney." The utilisation of wild rabbits, however, did not always meet with success.

Attempts were made to import hares, however initially they did not survive very well in the Australian environment. They were classified as protected game and could not be hunted, or 'coursed'.[189] In 1873, coursing was legalised and enthusiasts quickly formed clubs. The first coursing club in Australia was in Victoria, but others throughout the country followed very quickly. By 1900 coursing was an established sport in Queensland, although it did not rival the patronage of horse-racing.

Hurling

Occasionally there would be references to hurling. One was from the *Brisbane Courier*, 24 March 1874, of St Patrick's Day celebrations at Gatton.

> Amongst other things the playing of a hurling match was introduced, for the first time, we believe, in Queensland. This game is thoroughly Irish, and bears about the same relation to the national sports of the Emerald Isle that cricket does to those of England. Usually the picked athletes of one parish or county are matched against those of some neighbouring district, and as the number of men playing is frequently very large, and thousands of persons throng to the scene of contest, and take almost as active an interest in the proceedings as the players themselves, an Irish hurling match is about as lively an affair as anyone could wish to see...it would seem that the attempts to introduce the sport there was very successful...Mr William Sullivan of Helidon, and Mr P. O'Sullivan, of Ipswich, were chosen as captains.

Summary

The 1850s to the 1890s witnessed a rapid diffusion of sports, changes in sport generally paralleling sweeping technological and societal changes. The English influence was paramount, not only in the sports engaged in but the attitudes towards sport relating to Muscular Christianity and athleticism. Welsh immigrants had little influence on sport, but the Scots did, in athletics and golf in particular, and the Irish were largely confined in their impact in athletics as well, though they were vociferous in their arguments for lesser working hours and thus had a marked indirect influence on sport. Unique Australian sports were participated in, such as Australian Rules, dingo and kangaroo hunting, rodeo sports and so on. Women slowly emerged in roles other than as spectators. The major story from the 1850s to the 1890s was that of the sheer proliferation of sports. Professionalism became more rampant, and amateur organisations evolved to combat trends thought at the time to be insidious. Sport became a vital force in Queensland from the 1850s to the 1890s.

7

Intercolonial Competition

During the latter half of the nineteenth century sports became "one of the characteristics of Australian life,"[1] and one of the strongest vehicles for the expression of national identity and national pride. Mandle[2] has argued that Australian sport successes have demonstrated the strength and vitality of Australia, and have helped to negate the colonial inferiority complex. A similar argument can be advanced for the colony of Queensland. Sport became one of the few means by which northerners could display their strength and manly qualities. A victory in the sporting arena was seen as an indication of the progress and development that the colony was able to achieve.

Sport functioned as a catalyst for creating a sense of community and of group identification, both in urban centres and in isolated farspread communities. The choice of cultural and recreational activities was not extensive, even though in towns there was greater variety than in rural areas. Nevertheless, sports and other leisure pursuits were among the first forms of entertainment to evolve, and they provided a necessary respite for those whose normal working day was long and physically demanding. The natural urge to play and compete ensured that various sports would be pursued. Sports participation and gatherings served as avenues for social and spatial interaction between communities. Isolation was overcome by sports contests as participants and spectators mingled together. Intercolonial contests served an additional purpose in breaking down Queensland's insularity.

Diverse members of the community came together on the sports field, on which they played as equals, competing for the same goals. A sense of commitment and belonging was developed on the field of play. Being able to represent a club, a town, or the state was considered an honour, such aspirations helping solidify community spirit.

Initially competitions were local, however with transportation and communication developments, the desire to test one's skills, and prove one's superiorities, naturally led to regional and inter–town contests and competitions. The ongoing enthusiasm for sports competitions ultimately manifested itself in the initiation of intercolonial contests. In the early years, these contests were in the form of challenges, issued by one colony to another. Often different rules were utilised in each of the colonies, and hence disagreements arose as to methods of scoring, officiating and playing. As sports governing bodies were formed uniformity and standardisation in rules and conduct eventuated.

Horse–racing was, organisationally, more advanced than other sports and hence was the first sport in which an intercolonial contest was promoted.

> INTERCOLONIAL CHAMPION RACE – The movement of establishing an intercolonial champion race, whereby to test the blood and breeding of horses in the several colonies, has at length assumed something like a position of significance in the colony of Queensland. The matter has at length been taken up by an active and influential organisation of our fellow-colonists, and the large sum of £850 has already been subscribed.[3]

The date of this auspicious event was, therefore, fixed for 29 May 1861. "The stakes are £100 each, with one thousand guineas added, and are open to all horses in the Australian, New Zealand, and Tasmanian colonies...The bait is certainly attractive."[4] This champion race, to be held in the then centre of horse–racing in Queensland, Ipswich, captured the imagination of the new state residents. "'The Queen of the South', 'Zoe', was sent with Ben Bolt to show the Queenslanders a thing or two."[5] Excitement mounted as Queensland's greatest sporting day approached.

THE CHAMPION RACE

(PER ELECTRIC TELEGRAPH)

Ipswich, 9 pm

(from our own correspondent)

The Governor arrived here at a quarter past three o'clock, and was very quietly received by an assemblage of seven hundred people. His Excellency was escorted from the wharf by a detachment of the mounted volunteers.

Tattersall's opened at eight o'clock this evening, when there was a very crowded meeting. The state of the betting is as follows:

    100 to 10 agst Fisherman
    100 to 25   "   Eclipse
    100 to 30   "   Van Tromp

The above were offered and refused, but I heard a bet of 50 to 10 against both Eclipse and Van Tromp being taken.

Zoe and Ben Bolt against each other even.

Five to 3 is offered against the Queensland horses.

I have just been told, positively, that Fisherman will not start.

Betting is still going briskly on.

The town is full of people.[6]

The great day occasioned a general holiday in Brisbane and Ipswich. Spectators came by the steamers *Ipswich* and *Nimrod* to Ipswich, while others came by road "from the aristocratic drag to the colonial bullock dray."[7] It was a day to savour in the new colony.

These Queensland Champion Sweepstakes, which were the third Australian Champion Sweepstakes, were run over a distance of three miles. Although initially there were five horses entered, Fisherman was a late scratching. Eclipse was indeed "eclipsed", coming in a poor fourth. The two New South Wales horses, Zoe and Ben Bolt, took the honours, placing first and second. The other Queensland horse, Van Tromp, came third, finishing eight lengths behind the winner. Queenslanders were understandably disappointed, however there was general consensus that it was "as good a race as we have ever seen in the colonies."[8]

This event, which mesmerised the fledgling colony, was the beginning of numerous encounters that would occur over the following thirty year period. Cricket was the next sport to arrange an intercolonial contest in 1864, then rifle shooting in 1879, rugby union in 1882, cycling in 1884, rowing in 1885, soccer in 1890, athletics in 1890, sailing in 1894, tennis in 1895 and polo in 1896 (see figure 13).

There were, then, significant developments in the growth of sports and their organisation from basically the 1850s to the 1890s. Local competition naturally continued and expanded, as did regional competition, but superior athletes were finally given the opportunity to compete with those of other colonies, NSW in particular, and for Australian championships. The need for intercolonial competition and the codification of rules caused the formation of Queensland sport governing bodies. These were natural evolutionary processes.

Four sports have been selected for a more extensive coverage: cricket, rowing, athletics and rugby union.

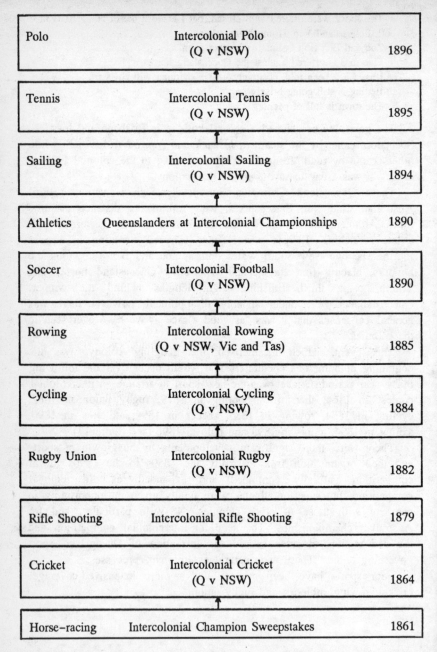

Figure 13 Intercolonial competitions in the various sports

Cricket

By the 1850s cricket had developed considerably in the southern colonies, particularly in NSW and Victoria. Intercolonial competition commenced in 1851, with Tasmania competing against Victoria in Launceston, and then, five years later, the first intercolonial competition on the mainland was held in 1856 between Victoria and NSW. In Queensland at the time the game was still in its infancy with the players' standards being quite low, particularly in comparison with the southern players. In 1864 Queensland made its first venture into intercolonial competition, competing against NSW in Brisbane.

Before the Queensland team was selected, practice matches between Brisbane and Ipswich teams were held. Some of the members of this first Queensland representative team were: the Hon G.W. Gray, who was very active in the promotion of the game and was a trustee of the Brisbane Cricket Ground, T. Cowlishaw, who became a MLC, Bryant, a manager of the South Australian Land and Mortgage Company and T. Fowles, the Registrar of the Supreme Court.[9]

The "grand match" was played on June 3 on Green's Hill wicket at Countess Street in Brisbane. The ground was considered inferior to the well-grassed Domain in Sydney, and it was made even worse by the rain which had caused the match to be delayed by two days. On some parts of the field there "were two or three inches of water; but seeing very few hits were made very far away from the wicket, no very inconsiderable inconvenience was caused thereby."[10] The match, played over four days, was won by the NSW Eleven.

The following year Queensland travelled to Sydney for "a friendly game with knights of the willow in New South Wales."[11] However, the Queensland twenty-two were again overwhelmed by the NSW Eleven. Ten years were to pass before another interstate match was scheduled, and then to everyone's amazement Queensland won the match. The standard of play was gradually improving in Queensland, and this was indicated by the number on the Queensland team. In the 1864 and 1865 matches Queensland had fielded twenty-two players, in 1875 they had fielded eighteen, in 1889 it was fifteen, and finally, in 1893, Queensland's Eleven competed against NSW's Eleven.

Numerous attempts were made to compete against the other states, but these were not met with success for several years. The first interstate match against South Australia was in 1889, against Victoria in 1903, against Western Australia in 1948 and against Tasmania in 1978. Queensland was, for many years, not accepted into Sheffield Shield competition, which began in 1892. Indeed, their request for admission was not successful until 1926.

Rowing

Although the first intercolonial eights race was held in 1878 between a Sydney and a Melbourne club, Queensland did not venture into this competition until 1885. It was not until that year that an eight-oared boat was possessed in Brisbane, and hence the first eight-oared race was held in Queensland as part of the Commercial Rowing Club's regatta.[12] Obviously this race was not sufficient preparation for the Intercolonial in Sydney, as the Queensland crew came last, with NSW first, Victoria second and Tasmania third. Queensland's second venture, in 1889, was not met with any more success, although this time it was in the four-oars championship. The crew from the Commercial Rowing Club competed in the Four-oar Championship of Victoria, and although they got a good start, they came last in the race.

The fortunes of Queensland changed radically in 1890, and the high point of Queensland rowing came in that year and 1891 with two wins in the intercolonial competitions. Both of these successes could be attributed to the skill, expertise and coaching of the Bell brothers, who returned to Brisbane from their studies in England. The Bell brothers joined the Breakfast Creek Rowing Club, and with two others entered the NSW Four-oar Championship, which they won. "Queensland was jubilant"[13] and this victory spurred the preparation for the 1890 intercolonial eight-oar race. This championship was rowed on the Parramatta River against Victoria and NSW. Queensland took an early lead and were a certainty for first, however a quarter of a mile from the finish the wash of a steamer caused an oar to break.[14] As a result, Queensland was beaten by the Victorian boat.

The 1890 loss made the Queensland even more determined to win the Championship. The Bell brothers coached the crew that went to Melbourne in 1891 and "the boys from the tropics rowing with a nice even swing, good length, and hard leg drive, steadying down to 32, won the first and only intercolonial eight-oar race for Queensland by over 100 yards from New South Wales, the Victorians being last."[15]

In recognition of Queensland's feat, the hosting of the 1892 Intercolonial Eight Championship was granted to Brisbane, to be held on the Bulimba Reach. Normally, the championships had been held in November, but considering Queensland's climate they were held this time in May. The Queensland crew did not live up to expectations, and even the home town crowd could not keep them from coming last. During the next decade, the best that a Queensland crew could achieve was a second place in 1898. In the twentieth century, up to the 1980s, Queensland achieved only two victories in the King's Cup, the Eight–Oared Championship of Australia, and these were in 1924 and 1939.

In the amateur sculls competitions Queensland colours were dominant in the 1890s. Prior to 1892, the Amateur Champion Sculls of Australia had only been contested twice, in 1868 when it was won by A. Nicholls of Victoria and in 1884 when it was won by W.G. Brett of NSW.[16] Primarily under the initiative of the Queensland scullers, the intercolonial championships came to be held on an annual basis after 1895. The two outstanding scullers, and Australian champions from Queensland, were M.J. Slack and J.B. Johnston of Bundaberg. Slack won the 1894 race by three lengths. However as there had not been any Victorians in this race, Slack went to Melbourne to compete in that colony's championships. Slack easily won the race, and hence the Australian Sculls title.[17]

The next intercolonial sculls race was contested in Brisbane in 1895. Slack performed poorly and was defeated by the Victorian E. Powell. However, Slack regained his title the following year in Sydney. The 1898 championships were hosted by Brisbane, however, no southern scullers competed. Alick Dennis became the second Queenslander to win the Australian Championships by defeating Slack, the two–time champion. Two years later Slack again made a comeback to capture the title in 1900. Not until the 1920s did Queensland produce another champion sculler when A.A. Baynes captured the title in 1920 and 1926.

Athletics

In amateur athletics, a small team of Queenslanders competed at an intercolonial championship in Sydney in 1890. Neil Ferguson captured the half–mile title, while E.J. Kellett won the high jump event with a height of 5ft 5in. These are not considered official Australian titles, as it was not until 1893 that the Australasian Championships were first held. As the Queensland AAA was not formed until 1895, Queensland did not compete in the first Australasian Championships in 1893, but did send a small team to the second Championships in 1896. However, it was not until the third Championships in 1897 that a Queenslander won a title. Charles Campbell dominated his opposition, winning the 440 yards race by three yards and the 880 yards by two yards.[18]

The fourth Australasian Championships were hosted by Brisbane on Thursday 9 November, 1899 at the Exhibition Grounds. There were twenty–three events contested (six being cycling races) by a total of 112 competitors.[19] Queensland athletes put in creditable performances, winning four events, and in two of these set new Australasian records. D. Wentworth, from Mt Morgan, won the 880 yards and the mile championship events. Peter Corrigan captured the 3–mile walking championship, and came second in the one–mile event. George Hawkes set a new record in the shot put with a throw of 43ft 2in, and his record lasted until 1914.[20]

These championships were the highpoint for Queensland amateur athletics, as only D. Wentworth was able to win a title at the next championships in 1901.

Rugby Union

The major football game in Queensland in 1882 was Australian Rules. The teams for this season in Brisbane were Brisbane, Wallaroo, Excelsior and Ipswich. Other teams that were in existence in Queensland were at Toowoomba, Maryborough, Rockhampton and Gympie.

The itinerary for the 1882 football season in Brisbane included three rugby games, nineteen Australian Rules games and a sports day. The kick–off for the opening match of the season, for example, "did not take place until some time after 3 o'clock",[21] and the sides were captained by Messrs T. Welsby and F. Ransome, who were also the secretaries of the Brisbane and Wallaroo clubs, respectively.[22] "Towards the close of the game a suggestion to engage in a 'little Rugby' was accepted, and, as the game closed, one or two good 'sketches' were made by T. Welsby, Roberts, and Stokes."[23]

There were attempts during the season to arrange an intercolonial football match. Correspondence had been undertaken without result in 1881 "between Mr Roberts, of the Brisbane Football Club, and some prominent footballers in Sydney,"[24] and the issue was reopened in 1882 between Messrs Roberts and Welsby on behalf of the Brisbane and Ipswich clubs.[25]

The original plan was for the Brisbane team to go to Sydney and play a game of Australian Rules football as well as rugby. Two offers for games were received in Brisbane in 1882; one from the rugby union in Sydney offering to pay all expenses of a team from Brisbane providing that only rugby was played; and the other from the Australian Rules authorities offering to pay half the expenses if the team played

Australian Rules. The Brisbane group did not concede easily, as they really wanted to play both codes.

The Southern Rugby Club did not accede to the Brisbane request, and a special meeting of the committees of the different football clubs of the city was informed that Mr Roberts finally agreed to the eventual generous rugby offer to pay all expenses provided rugby only was played.

Not everyone agreed with the decision to send a team to Sydney. James M. Stafford, in particular, used the column of The *Brisbane Courier* to voice his displeasure.[26] It was noted that there were forty-eight active clubs in Sydney, and that the Brisbane team would be overmatched. His main point, however, was that a team representing the colony should be Australian Rules players, as it was the main game in the colony, and that the people selecting the team were mainly interested in the free trip and excursions offered by the Union. It was also inferred that the original negotiations in Sydney were solely done by biased rugby people. This accusation appears to be valid, as Pring Roberts, who did much of the preliminary work, was an avid rugby proponent.

The team left by the *Leichhardt* on Monday, August 7. It was delayed by adverse winds, and consequently did not arrive in Sydney until Wednesday, August 9, at 7pm, to be welcomed at the wharf by prominent members of the Southern Rugby Union. The historic encounter, the first intercolonial rugby match, was on the Association Ground on Saturday, 12 August 1882. The players are shown in table 14.

There were two games against NSW on the itinerary (the second one was added at the request of the visitors), and matches against the University Club, the County of Cumberland, a Combined Suburbs team, and the Wallaroos. The record was a surprising two wins and four losses, the wins coming against the County of Cumberland and the Wallaroos. The social itinerary was considerable, with a trip to the Blue Mountains, a harbour excursion, a banquet, free passes were given all players on any of the railways, and free tickets were also available to the Garden Palace and the theatres.

The first intercolonial match, played at the Association Ground, was won by NSW by 28 to 4. The Queensland team was warmly received, and the Sydney captain said it was the best game seen in the city that year.[27] The spirit in which the game was played was of the highest order. A complete description of the intercolonial tour, including all the matches, is in the 1983 *Journal of the Royal Historical Society of Queensland* by Howell and Howell.[28]

Table 14 The 1882 Qld team to play NSW

Name	Position
A.H. Pritchard	Three–Quarter
A.J. Hickson	Three–Quarter (Captain)
P. Roberts	Full–Back
J. Burrell	Forward
T.A. Bond	Forward
T. Welsby	Half–Back (Manager)
F.L. Hardgrave	Forward
H. Stokes	Forward
J. Blake	Forward
J.C. Boyd	Forward
F. Baynes	Forward
A.H. Feez	Three–Quarter
Dr D.R. Cutfield	Forward
E. Markwell	Half–Back
H. Macintosh	Forward
J. Townson	Forward
C. Tully	Forward

The first intercolonial rugby tour can only be judged an outstanding success. The schedule was horrendous by present–day standards, particularly considering that only seventeen players were sent. Six games in ten days, two of them interstate games, was a backbreaking assignment. That two games could be won in such circumstances and with such an inexperienced complement is a credit to the players' dedication and courage. The social side was also of the highest order, the Southern Rugby Union doing everything possible to establish the importance of the visit. It is easy to understand, considering the lack of rugby expertise among the Brisbanites, that they were somewhat astonished at the excellent reception they got from the Sydneyites. The experience was one that did much to establish the rugby union game in Brisbane.

A banquet was held to welcome the intercolonial team back, at the Cafe de Paris, on Friday evening August 25. Some sixty to seventy people attended, with Mr J. Hardgrave in the chair. "The Queen" was toasted, followed by the Chairman toasting "The Queensland Team". Mr. Hixson [sic] replied as captain and concluded by proposing a toast to the "Southern Rugby Union". Mr. Sheridan, an old player from

Sydney University, responded. Mr George Markwell then proposed "Success to Football". Other toasts followed, such as "Our Visitors" by Mr F. Lea, responded to by Mr T.H. Burrell, and the "Ladies", proposed by Mr Feez. MLA Hickson, the captain, summed up the sentiment:

> The members of the team were all very much astonished that such a reception should have been accorded to them...He [Hickson] spoke very highly of the way in which they had been treated, both by players and the public, stating that the latter had greatly encouraged them by their warm applause; and hoped that an opportunity would be given, by a visit to Brisbane of a Southern team, to return the compliment.[29]

The old Sydney player who spoke, Mr Sheridan, rightly observed that if a Southern team ever came north, "they would find men worthy of their steel." History has demonstrated how prophetic that statement was. A great sporting tradition had begun as a result of the first intercolonial visit in 1882.

Summary

Intercolonial matches mirrored societal changes. As the land opened up and changes wrought by industrialisation were brought to Queensland, local competition progressed normally in a logical fashion from local to regional and finally to intercolonial competition. Steamer links with NSW, in particular, were utilised to allow Queensland's athletes to compete against their counterparts from the south. Such matches not only afforded healthy competition, but they developed pride in the state that could not be achieved by economic or political considerations. Sport also offered an instance where representatives of the state could vent many of their grievances in a reasonably friendly manner. Feelings of inferiority, isolation and insularity proved to be strong allies in the importance attached to the state's sporting successes.

8

The Country Elite

The Squatters

The term 'squatter' came to Australia via the United States,[1] though there it had the connotation of a small land–owner, a homesteader. When the word was first used in Van Diemen's Land it referred to poor farmers, bushrangers and ex–convicts who engaged in various nefarious activities on small holdings, and who acquired sheep and cattle by both legal and illegal methods.[2] The first mention of the term on this continent was on an order from the Chief Secretary's Office, in February 1828.[3] In New South Wales the terms 'squatters' and 'runs' were very quickly adopted into common parlance, but there they came to denote individuals who occupied land in an unauthorised manner.

Gradually, however, it came to be assumed that a squatter had certain rights and, in 1836, Bourke's Squatting Act was brought into effect to legalise and regulate the practice, whereby each squatter could occupy any amount of land, from one acre to 10,000, for an annual payment of ten pounds.[4]

By 1839 this Act had been modified so that the squatter faced a fixed licence fee and a tax which varied according to the number of his stock. The only stipulation placed on the squatters was the maintenance of adequate stock for the amount of land acquired. Under such benevolent conditions, particularly in contrast to regulations in the home countries, men rushed to acquire lands. Usually on horseback, but sometimes even on foot, men eagerly set out to push out beyond the settlement boundaries to lay claim to their own land. By 1840 in the Colony there were 718 squatting stations which contained a population of 7,800 people and 1,250,000 sheep.[5]

Although Allan Cunningham's expedition had proclaimed the richness of the Darling Downs in 1827, it was not until 1840 that squatters moved into these lush and green pasture lands. As the convict settlement at Moreton Bay did not allow for free settlement within a fifty mile radius, the squatters came in via a long migration from the south. By 1850 most of the land stretching from the coast to the inland mountains and on the Darling Downs had been claimed.

Many of the squatters were Scots, such as Patrick Leslie from Aberdeen. His was the first stock movement into Queensland, and he was accompanied by his brother, a friend and "400 breeding ewes, 100 ewe hoggets, 1,000 wedder hoggets, 100 rams and 500 wedders 3 and 4 years old. We had two teams of bullocks (24 in all) and 2 drays, a team of horses and a dray, and 10 saddle-horses. We had 22 men, all ticket-of-leave or convicts, as good and game a lot of men as ever existed, and who never gave us a moment's trouble – worth any 40 men I have ever seen since."[6] Leslie established his first station at Canning Downs, where the land claimed consisted of one hundred thousand acres, from the bottom of Toolburra to the head of the Condamine. He eventually had to give Glengallan to the Campbells and Rosenthel to others.

Sir Arthur Hodgson[7] took up Eton Downs, Dalrymple, Goomburra, the Gammies, Talgai; Campbell, Westbrooke; the Gores, Yandilla and Tummaville; the Kents and Wienholts, Jondaryn; H.S. Russell, Cecil Plains; and so on until the Downs was occupied. Russell and Glover went on to Burnett in 1843, Mitchell to the Fitzroy; the Archer brothers to Rockhampton; and Ernest Henry to the Burke district. On and on they moved, restless and rapacious.

Many of the large properties, such as Glengallan, Yandilla, Jimbour and Jondaryn, were actually self-contained villages, with schools, post offices, stores, chapels, stables and cottages, and the owners often adopted a *noblesse oblige* towards their workers.

Resentment over the vast domain claimed by these early squatters led to the passage, in the early sixties, of the Free Selection Act, which limited the amount of land any one person could hold. The Government also moved to 'free' up land when the pastoral leases expired. The large land-owning squatters immediately contrived so that they could still maintain their holdings. One common practice was the establishment of 'dummy' selections, whereby brothers, sisters, wives or managers were nominally put to be owners of portions of the properties, and thereby control of the land remained in the hands of a select few.

The taming and cultivating of the land in the Antipodes has at times been compared to that in the United States. However, there were many fundamental differences and these have most aptly expounded by Mary Durack, who contended that the Australian mateship developed out of a need for collective security, compared with the competitive individualism of the United States.[8]

The first pastoralists to Queensland, particularly in the eastern Darling Downs area, were "men of good birth, education and capital."[9] Some had aristocratic connections such as the Wienholts and Ramsays in England and Gore in Ireland, while others such as the Leslies were backed by Scottish financiers as well as having aristocratic roots. Whatever, these influential squatters formed "a privileged, closely knit and self-interested group,"[10] and they became known as the "Pure Merinos".[11] Many of the 'Pure Merinos' attempted to recreate the lifestyle and society of Britain. They considered themselves as British, not Australian, and some, such as John Watts and Sir Arthur Hodgson, returned 'home' after succeeding economically. William Archer, travelling through Queensland 1876–77, commented that on a "station, even though it be a hundred miles away from any town, one could live all the year and from year to year as luxuriously as in the heart of London."[12] Governor Bowen wrote of the squatter's lifestyle: "These gentlemen live in a patriarchal style among their immense flocks and herds, amusing themselves with hunting, shooting and fishing."[13]

The 'Pure Merino', however, was in actuality in a minority. As French and Waterson put it:

> The majority of squatters, more particularly those on the Western Downs, were shrewd and hardworking men of Scots origin. Some of them had even risen from the ranks of pastoral managers and employees to become individual owners. By contrast with the Downs elite, they were rough diamonds such as the ex–stockman James Taylor, successor to Russell at Cecil Plains, William Miles of Dulacca or, much later, Australia's reticent pastoralist–millionaire, James Tyson, whose empire included Felton and Beauaraba. They lived, by choice, in more utilitarian dwellings of wood and brick. With success, however, most readily adopted behavioural patterns of the Pure Merino whom they had largely replaced by the 1870s.[14]

These gentlemen squatters exhibited a general sameness in their ways and habits. Roberts said they even looked alike, with whiskers, beards and moustaches, resembling brothers, cabbage–tree hats, Hessian riding boots and spurs, strapped trousers and blue Crimean shirts.[15]

There were, however, exceptions to this basic similarity. Some, such as the Archers, did not consider themselves transplanted Britishers, and instead endeavoured to adapt to the new environment. Though many of the 'Pure Merinos' had upper class backgrounds, some such as 'Cocky' Rogers and 'Tinker' Campbell, and later the Duracks, had lower class origins. La Meslee described, in *L'Australie Novelle*, a young gentleman returning to Brisbane after having spent three years studying at Oxford. He was the son of a wealthy Downs squatter who had started as a shepherd and his mother had been a cook at a station. The ex–shepherd had sent his son to Brisbane Grammar School, where the boy had won a scholarship to Oxford, and the son was returning to Brisbane "to take his place among the intellectual elite."[16]

The pastoralisation of Queensland was effected through the efforts of both large and small land owners. The 'average' squatter was "more likely to be an educated member of the middle class,"[17] and his life was not as enticing as generally pictured, being quite dissimilar to that of the gentleman squatter, reeking of "mutton fat and smoke."[18]

The possession of land and stock was only the beginning for a squatter, as Aboriginal attacks, stock diseases, loneliness and obscurity, and natural disasters such as fires, floods and drought were but a few of the many hardships that had to be faced. The daily life on the stations in the early years left little time, or energy, for leisure pursuits and sport. However, as the pattern of life became more established, varied recreational activities were incorporated into the lifestyles of the squatters. Many of these pursuits were patterned after those practised in the British Isles, but some unique leisure activities were also fashioned. Case studies of selected squatters are presented in order to provide an anecdotal picture of the leisure habits and sports among the squatters.

The Squattocracy

The aristocrats of the country were the large land–owning squatters, who came to be called the "Squattocracy". Many of them endeavoured to set up the lifestyle of the English gentry, mimicking their manners and habits. In the Squattocracy, leisure pursuits and sports were integral components of their lifestyle.

The Archers

David Archer, in 1834, was the first of his family to come to Australia, going to his cousins' – the Walkers' – station in NSW to work. Eventually nine of the children[19] of a timber merchant from Perth, Scotland, came to the Antipodes, and several were among the pioneers of Queensland. In 1841 David, with his brothers Thomas and John, and five thousand sheep, went northward, and eventually took up the Durundur and Cooyar stations in the Brisbane River Valley. One of their guests in the early years was Ludwig Leichhardt, who stayed for some months at Durundur in 1843–44. Thomas, in particular, played an important role in the opening up of central Queensland, and with his brother Charles took up the Eidsvold run. The name of Eidsvold was taken from the name of the town in which the Constitution of Norway as an independent nation was signed in 1814, and Norway was the home of the Archer family from the mid–1820s. David and William took up the adjoining Coonambula run, and then the brothers went further north and established Faris station. This was ultimately named 'Gracemere' after Thomas' wife Grace, the first white woman to travel that far north. Both cattle and sheep were originally stocked at Gracemere although, after the 1870s, the station was switched solely to cattle.

The Archer family was close–knit, and the children kept the parents regularly informed of their exploits. William's general cheerfulness and his acceptance of the Australian conditions are clearly evident in a letter written four years after his arrival in Australia.

> I have been leading the usual routine of an Australian bush life, travelling in company with my black boy from station to station; gathering, branding, weaning and driving sheep and cattle; and with the exception of a month's stay at Wallerowang from whence I have just returned here...I have seldom been two nights in one place...When spreading my opossum cloak for the night by a blazing bush fire, under our beautiful climate I often reflect with thankfulness that I am engaged in a pursuit so congenial to my taste and conducive to my health.[20]

Perhaps it was their Scottish upbringing, but the Archers seemed to possess the ability to endure the hardships, as well as to appreciate the beauties, and benefits, of the new land. They adapted to the Queensland environment better than most, as they did not attempt to overly recreate or transplant the British lifestyle and values. They lived in harmony with their environs, and this included the Aborigines. While many squatters had continual trouble with the Aborigines, this was not the case with the Archers, who developed an "excellent understanding"[21] with them.

The Archers would have led a typical life of the 1840s and 1850s in the Queensland bush. As William Archer stated in his *Australian Journey*, in Queensland, the opposite of 'the town' was not 'the country' but 'the bush'.[22] Depending on the area, there was even the opportunity to fish.[23] As they were hundreds of miles from shops, their recreational pursuits were dependent on their ingenuity, consisting of a hand–made chessboard and stalking kangaroos and other game.[24] The visitations by neighbours were a welcome relief to the general isolation. These were special times, impromptu occasions, when

> several of our neighbours happened to come in and we had a good *Spektakel*. The table was moved to one end of the room; a three legged stool stuck upon Mr Mossman's perch, from where he discoursed most elegant music. Mackenzie's superintendent – a Highlander – footed sundry national dances, such as Highland Fling, Jacky Tar, the Sword Dance etc. Gradually the mirth increased. The Accordion joined apparently in the

excitement, and at it we all went in a sort of medley, something between a *Holling* and a Quadrille.[25]

William Archer, son of Thomas, who was one of the original Archer brothers, journeyed to Australia in 1876–77. Aged nineteen, he had just received his MA from Edinburgh University, was a trained but non-practising lawyer, electing instead to be a drama critic and playwright. His letters and writings provide us with an insight of Australian life in the 1870s,[26] particularly that in Central Queensland.

Although Archer considered Rockhampton as "one of the least beautiful places it has been my fortune to visit,"[27] he very accurately analysed the social structure of the town. There were four grades of society: the squatters; the aristocrats of the town, being the government officers, bankers, lawyers and doctors; the successful, prosperous shopkeepers, and lastly the small shopkeepers, mechanics and manual labourers. Archer recounts how class divisions were reflected in the attendance at social events such as balls. Individuals of the top classes were at first reticent to attend balls organised, for example, by the Volunteer Corps, as it was possible that the lower classes, such as butchers and their wives, and so on, could also be in attendance. However, as balls provided temporary relief from the isolation and monotony of Rockhampton life, class consciousness was put aside and most attended such events. One ball that Archer described was held on a sailing vessel, for some two hundred people. The dancing was vigorous and was proclaimed by both the Celts and Saxons as "the vinest barty that coom to a het that year."[28]

When the Premier of Queensland, the Hon George Thorne, visited Rockhampton, many festivities were organised, including a ball and a picnic. The Premier hosted the picnic for over 400 invited people and it was held twelve miles out of town. Archer expressed surprise that the Premier had appropriated £350 out of public money to pay for this festivity.[29]

Gracemere was more to young Archer's liking. The station life had obviously changed considerably from that described by John Archer in 1842, when the homestead was a single-roomed bark hut, and the diet consisted of damper, mutton and tea, and forks were considered "an unnecessary refinement."[30] In the 1870s William Archer maintained that one could live at Gracemere as comfortably as in London.[31] William was further impressed by the bathing house that was at the foot of the lake at Gracemere, and the pelicans, swans and wildfowl which abounded in the lake. In front of the house an oval croquet lawn had been set up.

During his visit he went with his father on a tour round Peak Downs to Port Mackay, accompanied by two riding horses and a pack horse. William found riding considerably different to that in England and "not quite so easy work."[32] The Cooroora station and surrounding areas were affected at the time by a marsupial plague, which William asserted was the result of the declining Aboriginal population. There were "more kangaroos than sheep and the squatters are literally being eaten out of house and home...At several of the stations...from thirty to fifty thousand marsupials had been slaughtered within the last two years."[33] In many instances blacks were hired to slaughter the marsupials – kangaroos, wallabies and paddymelon – and many became relatively wealthy as a consequence.

Kangaroos were run down by dogs and horsemen, some fifty kangaroo–dogs and greyhounds being kept for that purpose at Peak Downs station. This led Archer to state that "kangaroo hunting is the principal national sport in Australia."[34] While at Peak Downs he experienced a unique Australian blood sport, in which wallabies would be driven into traps and then dispatched with clubs.[35]

Archer's experiences in Australian bush sports were rounded off by his participation in wild duck and possum shooting. William's lively narrative affords an invaluable record of town and country life in Central Queensland.

The Archer's Durundur station was taken up by the McConnels in the 1860s. Although the life of A.J. McConnel will not be developed, one passage of his diary in particular needs to be mentioned. The arrival of a 'new chum' is detailed, a Mr Wood, who arrived at Durundur by horse, wearing his "M.C.C. cap of which cricket club he was a member."[36]

Sir Joshua Peter Bell[37]

The history of Dalby is inextricably linked with the Bell family and Jimbour station. Artesian water was first discovered and used in the Downs District at Jimbour, and it was there that modern water harvesting was pioneered for the region.

Thomas Bell, the father, was born in Northern Ireland, and came to Australia in charge of convicts. He brought his three sons – Joshua Peter being the youngest – and two daughters with him when he arrived in 1829. In 1843 he bought Gimba [Jimbour] for 3200 pounds, and at this time the property extended "from the Bunya Mountains on the east to the Condamine River, and from about where Jandowae now stands in the north to the present site of Dalby."[38] There was a reapportionment of the property in 1844, it being reduced to some 211,000 acres, being 22 miles by 15 miles and containing 12,000 sheep. It become one of the most valuable sheep properties in Queensland, its wool being highly prized. The Jimbour homestead became one of the finest and grandest squatter's mansions in Queensland. It was built at a cost of £30,000, with over 200 men cutting the stone, and, as well as 10 stone masons, 9 carpenters and numerous manual workers worked just on the main building.[39]

Thomas Bell died in 1874, leaving Joshua Peter as the sole owner. Joshua had been educated at King's College in Sydney and became a solicitor. He had an illustrious career in politics, which began in 1863, and in 1879 he was appointed president of the Legislative Council. Of his six children the eldest, Joshua Thomas, followed in his father's political footsteps. The Bell family contributed immensely to the sporting life of the state, particularly in horse–racing and rowing, and to a lesser degree in cricket. Sir Joshua Peter Bell was very active in the organisational sense, being President of the Queensland Turf Club and the Queensland Cricket Association, and Vice President of the Queensland Rowing Association, while his sons Willie A.D. and Colin P. were outstanding rowers. Also, two of Queensland's most outstanding athletes prior to the turn of the century, Charlie Samuels, a pedestrian, and Jerry Jerome, a boxer – both Aborigines – were born on Jimbour station.

Horse–racing in Queensland is indebted to Sir Joshua, as he established the first breeding stud for thoroughbred horses in the state.[40] There were not a dozen thoroughbreds in Queensland when he began his breeding program, the next largest number being those owned by Chief Justice Lutwyche at Kedron Brook. His breeding was initiated at Jimbour, but it was transferred to a property near Ipswich, which he named 'The Grange'. Ipswich was designated 'Limestone' by the locals, and Sir Joshua, when he moved his stud there, fittingly had his fences made of pure limestone rock.[41] His pre–eminence in racing was exhibited by his successes in most of the premier races in the Queensland Turf Club's calendar. The most important wins were the Queensland Derby Stakes (four times successively), the Brisbane Cup, the Brisbane Handicap (three times), the Sandgate Handicap and the Queensland Cup (twice). Although he patronised the big race meetings he also "attended regularly the local race meetings to which he would drive his own carriage."[42]

Sir Joshua sent his sons to Great Britain for their education, and two of the sons, W.A.D. and C.P.B., were particularly outstanding in rowing, both rowing for Cambridge and being members of the victorious Grand Challenge Eights at Henley, W.A.D. in 1886 and Colin in 1887.[43]

When the brothers returned to Australia they first went to Sydney, where they won the New South Wales Rowing Championship. In Brisbane they joined the Breakfast Creek Club, where their "rowing was a revelation to Brisbane oarsmen, as their style was totally different to anything seen here...There had really been no distinct style in Brisbane at all up to this time."[44] Utilising the Cambridge style of rowing, the Breakfast Creek Club fours – two of the crew being the Bell brothers – won the Queensland Fours Championships in 1890. Colin was considered the best rower of the Bell brothers.[45]

As a result of the rowing skills of the Bell brothers, and their coaching, Queensland almost won the Intercolonial Eights Championship in 1890. Unfortunately a broken oar, just before the finish line, deprived them of the title. Although the Bells retired from rowing they turned to coaching, and with their assistance Queensland won its first Eights Championship in 1891. They continued to assist in the development and promotion of the sport of rowing in Brisbane, and Willie even coached young ladies in the sport in the mid–1890s.

The eldest son, Joshua Thomas, although also participating in the sport of rowing while at Cambridge, was more renowned as a superb horseman and rifle shot. Like his father, Joshua Turner turned to politics, and he became the member in the Legislative Assembly representing Dalby. As a politician, Joshua Turner was described as representing "an increasingly anachronistic group – the independent Australian Briton: he combined in his person the manners and education of an English gentleman and the earthly political skills of the native– born."[46] He had a superior air, displaying at times a pompous bearing which was parodied by Smith of the *Worker* in 1901.[47]

Although of Irish descent, the Bells were models of English sportsmen and their baronial home and elite lifestyle epitomised that of the English aristocracy. The sons served as fine examples for sports– minded youth and were ever willing to offer themselves for public service. The Bells were among the true aristocrats of the new state.

Patrick Durack

The lifestyle pursued by another Irish squatter, Patsy Durack, and his family, was quite different to that of the Bells, and it is brilliantly narrated[48] by Mary Durack in *Kings in Grass Castles*. By no means wealthy, Darby Durack arrived in New South Wales from Ireland in 1849. He was followed by Michael Durack in 1853, who knew he had to leave his beloved country or see his family starve to death. Michael was nominated as a farm labourer, and the children were listed as farm servants. One of the children was Patsy Durack, then 18 years of age,

Mary's grandfather. The family luck changed very dramatically when Patsy made £1000 in eighteen months digging for gold. It was on the goldfields that he met two other Irishmen, Dinnie Skehan and Pat Tully, who were ultimately to become his brothers–in–law.

Darby and Patsy Durack bought land in New South Wales at Dixon's Creek, near Goulburn, in 1855. This was the beginning of the fantastic land acquisition of the Duracks. The restless disposition of Patsy had the family moving north in 1867, settling at Thylungra at Kyabra Creek. Patsy's holdings at this time amounted to 3,800 sq. miles, quite an advancement for the son of a poor Irish immigrant. However, he was not satisfied, and for the next several years continued to move north-west into the unknown country in outback Queensland, and to acquire new lands. By 1873 Patsy's holdings had increased to two and a half million acres, while his friend John Costello claimed eight and a half million acres. Patsy divided the land adjoining his property into runs of one hundred thousand acres each, the land being allotted to various members of his family and relatives. The Irish influence is apparent in the early naming of the blocks of land: "Clare, Scariff, Galway, Lough Derg, Lough Isle, Lough Neagh, Shannon View, Limerick, Yass, Whees, Grabben Gullen, Goulburn."[49]

Isolation did not appear to be a concern to the family, as they readily adapted to their bush environment. Even when a tutor was hired he could not compete with the wonder of the natural environment, with children's toys "of their own and the blacks devising."[50]

To squatters such as Patsy and his family the horse was central to their lives, and riding was a skill that had to be mastered by all. Although a horse was a practical necessity, it also provided the environs for recreation and sport, and one of Patsy's obsessions became horse-racing. He gradually acquired thoroughbred stock for breeding purposes, and his horses competed with distinction. One of his sons, "Galway Jerry", was responsible for the first organised races on the Cooper, and "before Windorah was established there were picnic meetings on Galway Downs."[51]

The race meetings were the main entertainment in the bush, and they attracted people from diverse stations, often hundreds of miles apart. One such meeting followed the discovery of opals less than 75 miles from Thylungra, and it was organised by Patsy and Galway Jerry. Shelters and stalls were hurriedly set up, and traders brought ladies' materials for sale, plus riding apparel – and of course liquor. Some four hundred people turned up for the merriment, with various races including the Cooper Cup the main attraction.[52] The spectators at times got overly enthusiastic, with fights being the order of the day. There were few regulations to restrict the conviviality, which usually lasted five days, and consisted of gambling games of various kinds, acrobatics – probably influenced by alcohol, dancing and drinking.[53]

Holidays such as Christmas and St Patrick's Day were particularly special occasions at Thylungra, as family and friends would come from far and near for the festivities.

> We'd start early in the morning and carry right on through 'til late at night, horse races, foot races, jumping, boxing, tap dancing and stunts. Everyone had a special stunt of some sort, walking on his hands, balancing knives on his nose, lifting weights...turning handsprings, or maybe just singing or reciting or giving a tune on a tin whistle or a gum leaf. Your Grandpa played the fiddle and the flute by ear and Stumpy Michael's wife was a first–rate pianist.[54]

One gets the impression that, among these Irish squatters from the labouring classes who became successful, unlike Sir Joshua Bell from Northern Ireland, there was no attempt to imitate the English country squire. Their humour was more down–to–earth, and the activities they engaged in were more improvised, boisterous and rugged.

Fanny Durack, incidentally, Australia's first female gold medallist at the Olympic Games, came from a branch of this pioneering family.

The Tullys of Ray Station[55]

The Duracks, the Tullys and the Costellos and Scanlans, for that matter, were all related by marriage. Patsy Durack's sister Sarah married Patrick Tully, and at the urging of Patsy, they came north to Queensland, settling at Ray station in 1874. The property originally covered approximately 270 square miles. In the first land resumption of 1925 some 20,000 acres of the Conaway Downs were lost, and another 45,000 acres of Grammar Downs were resumed in 1955. Thus, only 100,000 acres of the original property survived.

Life on the station was a rugged existence and, as on other such stations, not all children reached adulthood. Seven of the Tully children died during Sarah's lifetime: four died in infancy; one daughter, Anne, died after wandering off in the bush; Jack was killed while kangarooing; and Patrick died from drowning. Again and again drought struck the property, causing severe privation. In 1900, for example, the Tully boys worked and lived some twelve or so miles away from the main house, in the scrub, to feed and care for the cattle. Often "the girls rode the twelve miles to the camp on pushbikes, carefully balancing the food and extras they so painstakingly gathered and prepared."[56] There were, however, happy and joyous occasions, particularly when it was shearing time: "The shearing's end was celebrated by "cut–out" races – the shearer's horses versus station steeds, after which the station entertained the shearers to dinner – a festivity for which the Tully girls always made and iced a five tier cake."[57]

Hunting was done on the property, plus fishing and swimming in the creek. As the property developed it had its own tennis court, polo field and even a race course. The horse races and polo matches attracted people from considerable distances, as they were considered 'the' social occasions for the region. The horse assumed an important role, and riding, horse–breaking, breeding and racing were considered 'natural' activities to be pursued by all.

Patrick and Sarah were both from Ireland and, understandably, they sent their sons to Nudgee College for their Catholic schooling. Two sons in particular, Frank and Jim, were excellent athletes, excelling in athletics and football at Nudgee College in the early 1880s. The Nudgee College Annual recorded the sensational performance of Frank in athletics.

Who at the College at the time does not remember the night that Frank Tully won the first Queensland £100 Sheffield run at Woolloongabba? The great Postle ran second to Frank that night. Postle about five years afterwards won the world's championship over 130 yards from Donaldson. Frank, who was only a schoolboy at the time, was on 16 yards, and Postle was on seven. The distance was 130 yards. We received the news about mid–night in the big "dorm". What a "scourge" there was that night in the big "dorm". About a week later Frank gave a "spread". The "spread" (lemonade, cakes, and too many speeches) was always a wonderful occasion in those days of the College.[58]

Like the Duracks, the Tullys worked the land with respect and diligence, endeavouring to tame a land that bestowed favours grudgingly. They laboured hard to leave their Irish imprints on this harsh, unforgiving and relentless land. They were markedly different to squatters such as the Bells, as they did not assume pretentious airs or aristocratic lifestyles. To them their station was their home, not their country residence. However, they were part of the Queensland squattocracy by virtue of ownership of extensive land properties. Patrick Durack may have reached the soul of the land, when he remarked of his cattle empire: "If this is a kingdom, we're kings in grass castles. We can be blown away by a puff of wind."[59]

The Non-squatter Elite

In addition to the squattocracy, there were others who were adjudged to be members of the elite in the country areas. These were individuals who held influential and prominent positions in various towns, such as bank managers, police commissioners, owners of shops and businesses, solicitors and doctors, as well as those with political and public service appointments. Some were well-educated, and had upper class connections. Perhaps most could not be classified as being upper class, but in their respective towns and areas, they were recognised as important members of the community and were accorded high status. The two 'Protectors' of the Aborigines, Dr Walter Roth and Archibald Meston, were two such individuals. Meston, in particular, was actively involved in sport and made significant contributions to its development. One individual, W.E. Parry-Okeden, has been selected as a case study of the non-squatter elite.

W.E. Parry-Okeden

William E. Parry-Okeden was born in Australia "of ancient English stock"[60] and was educated at Melbourne Diocesan Grammar School. This was followed by some years of legal training, and grazier work, after which he embarked on a career as a Public Servant. In 1870, the Queensland Government, under Sir Arthur Palmer, formed the Border Patrol to prevent smuggling, with Mr Parry-Okeden being placed in charge. In later years he was Police Magistrate at Cunnamulla, Police Magistrate and Land Commissioner at Charleville, and Police Magistrate, Land Commissioner and Gold Warden at Gayndah. He held the position of Immigration Agent in Brisbane, and in 1889 became Under-Colonial Secretary and then Principal Under-Secretary. In 1895 he was appointed Commissioner of Police and held this position until he retired in 1905. Because of the positions that he held Parry-Okeden, then, operated in the highest circles, and was well-known throughout the length and breadth of Queensland. He was described as "Lean, active, and standing 6 ft 4 in. in height, he was a typical bushman, a perfect horseman, splendid boxer, runner and cricketer."[61]

Parry-Okeden's cousin, J.W. Haygarth, played cricket for Oxford in 1864 and came to Queensland with his brother Graham Haygarth. J.W. went to Maroon Station and Coochin Coochin, and settled down at Boonah, marrying the daughter of the owner of Dugandan Station. J.W. was President for many years of the Fassifern Cricket Association and the Boonah Cricket Club. He became the race handicapper at Charters

Towers, but was shot to death by a gambler who objected to his handicapping.

Parry–Okeden was, similarly, a keen advocate of the sport of cricket. Whenever he was assigned to a town in the Queensland outback, he would invariably become the president of the local club, or if none existed, he would organise one. His athletic talents were aptly summarised in the *Sydney Bulletin*.

> Mr Parry–Okeden is one of the most accomplished of men and one of the best fellows in Queensland. He can sit a buckjumper, bowl an over "dead on", and with no end of pace, knock together a score in slashing style, throw a boomerang as well as any blackfellow, sing a good song, playing his own accompaniments on the piano, throw off a set of verse, sketch a prospect, take a turn with the gloves, administer real justice from the bench, and play a game of billiards – all with equal excellence.[62]

Mount Debatable Station, four miles from Gayndah, was purchased by Parry–Okeden and his friend Dick Stuart in 1867. Since the early 1850s, Gayndah had been one of the premier centres for horse–racing in Queensland, and in those days Gayndah could not be rivalled as a pastoral centre. At the 1867 June meeting of the Jockey Club at Gayndah, Parry–Okeden, who had a love of the horse engrained since childhood, entered four of his own horses: Trumpeter, Blue Jacket, The Young Gentleman and Cashbox. A fifth horse he rode to victory in the Hurdle Race. The 1868 race meeting was of particular significance, as Queensland's first Derby was run at Gayndah. 'The Hermit', owned by his friend Mr Scott of Taromeo Station and entered by Parry–Okeden, was the winner of this first Derby. Parry–Okeden had another winner, 'The Baronet', in the Hurdle Race, ridden by his friend Dick Stuart.

He also hunted wild horses in the Bunya Mountain area, and when on a visit to Brisbane in 1866 he hunted the kangaroo with Captain Creagh, who had procured some dogs.[63]

Their Brisbane experience with the Hunt Club encouraged Parry–Okeden and Stuart to form such a club in Gayndah. They had the horses and the dogs, and had even brought red coats for themselves back from Brisbane. The leading citizens – police magistrate, banker, and so on – agreed with the idea, and the Burnett Hunt Club was formed, with Parry–Okeden its first Master. Orders were sent to Brisbane for the correct costumes, which all felt were essential. Herbert Wilson published his account of that first chase in the Burnett *Argus* in 1867.[64]

Parry–Okeden typified the well–educated and reasonably rich squatter–gentleman who was a muscular Christian in every sense of the word. He had a considerable sense of public duty and service, and yet knew that happiness lay in balancing his work with his leisure pursuits.

Polo and the Feez's

Polo, an aristocratic sport that was introduced to Australia by army officers from India, was first played in Melbourne in 1875, and in Queensland in 1889 at Toowoomba.[65] The sport did not diffuse throughout the state to any extent, but remained localised in the Darling Downs and the southwest corner of Queensland. The main centres became Clifton, Pilton, Spring Creek, Greenmount, Toowoomba and Warwick, where the sport had an extremely high profile among the elite. Indeed, polo originally was a sport played virtually exclusively by the country elite.

Polo has been selected as a case study of an exclusive country elite sport. The development of the sport is closely tied to the Feez family, in particular Adolph Feez, and hence an in-depth analysis of the Feez's will be presented.

Toowoomba, then, served as the inaugural locale for polo in the state, where it was played

> in Robinson's Paddock situated at the corner of Holberton and Wombyra Streets. Those remembered at the time were Cam Turner, Willie Robinson and Bromley. After them came Tom Brown and his son Stewart, and sons-in-law Jack, Bob and Ernest Edols of Hambledon near Wellcamp. Later at Hambledon were the Barclay Brothers supported by Jack Jennings and Herbert Mardon both of Westbrook Station where Sunday Polo was a feature of entertainment besides Poker and Billiards at night. The first meeting to form the Downs Amateur Race Club was held on the polo ground at Westbrook.[66]

Subsequently the polo ground was moved to the Toowoomba Racecourse at Clifford Park, and matches were arranged between the Toowoomba Club and the Toowoomba Half Holiday Club. Soon other clubs were organised in Brisbane, Ipswich and Gatton, leading to interclub and intertown competitions. The need for an organisational structure to coordinate the activities led to the formation of the Queensland Polo Association in 1895. One of the founding members of this Association was Adolph Feez, and he organised the first interstate match in 1895 against a team from New South Wales. Members of the Queensland team were Adolph Feez, Willie Peak, Eddie Philp and Norman Caswell, with Feez paying the expenses for himself as well as one of the other players. The Feez family was certainly one of the most influential in the development of polo in the state, and after the turn of the century a cup in their name, the Feez Cup, was competed for.

Adolph Feez was the son of a prominent merchant in Rockhampton. His father, Albrecht, was from Bavaria, where he had served in the

German Army, and he had been attracted to Queensland by the Canoona gold rush. He eventually settled in Rockhampton, where he opened a business, became one of the prominent citizens in the town and then was elected Alderman and Mayor.[67] He sent both his sons, Adolph and Arthur, to be educated at King's College in Sydney. Arthur, after graduating in law from the University of Sydney, settled in Brisbane and, after the turn of the century, was considered one of the leading barristers in the colony. He later became President of the Queensland Bar Association. although not as keen a sportsman as his brother, Arthur played rugby union for Queensland, and, indeed, even scored in that historic first intercolonial game.

Adolph was an all-round athlete and a lover of the outdoor life. Professionally he first joined his father in business, but abandoned it in favour of surveying. He worked in the far West of Queensland for several years, but due to illness had to return to Brisbane. He subsequently became a solicitor and was partner of a prominent firm in the city.[68] Adolph was an enthusiastic angler and tennis player, and became one of the founding members of the Queensland Lawn Tennis Association. However it was in the sports of hunting and polo that he made his greatest contributions. He was an excellent horseman, competing regularly in jumping events. He helped found the Brisbane Hunt Club, which he virtually single-handedly kept alive for some eight years.

> *Adolph Feez* was always well mounted, either on "Nemo" or on a brown house called "Gladstone". When the Brisbane Hunt Club struck hard times in 1893, Adolph Feez replaced Gawn Ecklin, taking the hounds to his Yeronga home. As Honorary Master, he carried the club along for three years, when it was finally disbanded. The hounds were then distributed among members and other dog lovers.[69]

When the Hunt Club folded, Adolph turned to polo for his recreation and sport. He captained the 1895 Queensland team which won all its matches on its New South Wales visit, against Sydney, Camden, and Sydney and Camden combined. Adolph's only son, D.R. ('Billy') Feez, took over the family property 'Pilton Paddock' via Clifton, and in the early and middle 1920s was probably Queensland's leading polo player.

After the inaugural interstate match, the Sydney Association sent a representative combined team to Queensland in 1896. Three matches were played, one in Toowomba and two in Brisbane, and Queensland decisively won all three. Adolph Feez again captained the team, with the other members being W.G. Peak, N. Caswell and S. Harding. Although interstate matches were the highlight of the year, the main activity

centred around intraclub and interclub competitions. Married versus singles were popular competitive events.

Some of the earliest players on the Downs were Willie Peak, E. Godsall, W. Trevethan, Cam Robertson, Alex McPhee, Charlie Cook, Jack Allan, Jim Taylor, Jack McQuade, Lucas, Dr Woodward, Jack White (Police Inspector), Cecil Roberts, Norman Caswell, Herbert Mardon, William Best and Kit Warner.

Summary

Roberts has been oversimplistic in generalising about the sameness of the squatters. They were not all English, but Scots and Irish, occasionally even German. Their background was not always upper or upper middle class, some could be classified as self-made men of humble origins, like the Tullys and the Duracks. Some such as these were likely anti-English, as they had been involved in the Eureka uprising protecting Crown demands on the miners. There is, indeed, a marked difference between the Tullys and Duracks, on the one hand, and the Bells and the Parry-Okedens, on the other. The former scratched out their living in parched and difficult areas, their incessant toil in dedication to their adopted country. They lacked the mansion at Jimbour, and the leisure style that accompanied such wealth. This is not to say that one group made a greater contribution in Queensland. Each left his mark in opening up the vast lands, but in different ways. They were, indeed, all unique individuals, and to assume a sameness when describing them is incorrect.

Bolton has argued that it was "in Queensland that the myth of the gentleman-squatter was strongest [and that there were] a conspicuous number of settlers who seemed to have regarded Queensland as the last outpost of the gentlemanly ideal."[70] The attraction of Queensland in the latter half of the nineteenth century was that it offered suitable opportunities for some of British aristocratic families, and only minimal capital outlays were necessary. The Leslie brothers Patrick, Walter and George, were "the first of a flood of the sons of Scottish lairds and English gentlemen."[71] Arthur Hodgson, a graduate of Eton and Cambridge, and Gilbert Elliott, the son of an admiral and aide-de-camp to the Governor, established Eton Vale, which they named after their old school. Allan Macpherson, on his way to Mount Abundance, emphasised the requisite requirements for a gentleman. "I'm not going into the bush like a savage. I have a good cellar here, a piano, cigars, eau de cologne, scented soap."[72] Robert Herbert, an Oxford graduate and cousin of the

Earl of Carnarvon, was a member of Sir George Bowen's first Ministry. He was imbued with the ideal of a gentleman and the contribution that such could make in Queensland. Similar to the formation of the 'Family Compact' in Canada, Herbert, with fellow Oxonian Arthur Scott, founded the "Valley of Lagoons, a North Queensland property where they helped systematically to attract young Englishmen of family and fortune to learn the skills of a pastoralist and found estates in the bush."[73] The pastoral decline ended this aristocratic concept which embraced the control of vast lands by the scions of the wealthy. By the 1890s the rewards, both financial and social, that were thought to have been available in Australia, had lost their attraction. The outcome of the aristocratic migration had not been, according to Bolton, the establishment of a powerful colonial gentry in Queensland. Bolton further argued that "although some Englishmen of aristocratic origin established families in Queensland, they merged before long undistinguishably into the communal background."[74]

In the early 1850s Gayndah was one of the centres for the squattocracy in Queensland. Through the eyes of Dick Stuart we can gain an insight into the life of the gentleman squatter.

> In Gayndah, and on all the stations around the squatters were genuine sportsmen, and what with races, cricket, hunting, balls, picnics, and the usual attractions for healthy youngsters we passed the time right pleasantly. We kept a pack of goodly kangaroo dogs with which we hunted the wily kangaroo, and on a Saturday afternoon sometimes accounted for six or eight big fellows. The dances once or twice a week were something to remember. It was a matter of honour that every man under 30 years of age had to dance every dance, and we never finished before sunrise. Faith, they were merry times...sometimes we organised a picnic to some neighbouring station, and one of these was held at Tenningering where lived a splendid lot of fellows...there was a famous waterhole at this place where we swam every morning...A strong plank had been fixed to act as a springboard.[75]

The sports of the squattocracy and the elite in the country reflected the background of the individuals. The environment placed various limitations on that prior experience.

The most important sports were those involving the horse. The horse was essential for survival and life on the stations could not exist without it. Riding skills were learned by all from an early age, and horse and rider developed a rare understanding and indeed love and respect for each other. There was pride in one's horse, as well as in the accoutrements that went with riding. At race meetings, particularly in the early years, the squatters rode their own horses as gentlemen jockeys, and organised their own races 'for gentlemen riders'. Good horses were eagerly sought after, the ultimate for the horse lover being the possession of a thoroughbred. The breeding industry in Queensland developed under the leadership of such individuals as Sir Joshua Bell.

As the horse was central to the lives of the country elite, horse-racing was naturally one of their favourite recreational preoccupations. Informal challenge races, matching the best from one's station against those of another were common occurrences, and considerable monies were apt to change hands. Some of the stations even organised their own race meetings on private race courses. Race meetings, whether private or organised by town clubs, were premier social occasions, which involved not only horse races, but also luncheons, dinners and balls.

The country elite were the pivotal forces behind the formation of racing clubs, and subsequently occupied the organisational positions in such clubs' administration. When the 216 acre race course reserved in Ipswich, for example, was created by the government in 1861, the Trustees were Thomas De Lacy Moffatt, John Panton, Francis Bigge of Little Liverpool Station, Arnold Wienholt of Maryvale Station and Joshua Peter Bell of Jimbour Station.[76]

Hunt clubs were the province of the elite, and their status was reinforced by the purchase of the correct hunting habits. The ownership of a hunting dog and a pack of kangaroo dogs was considered a status symbol. The dingo and the kangaroo were the main pursuits, as the fox and deer were not native to Australia and had to be introduced. Six red deer were given to the Queensland Government in 1873 and they were taken to Durundur. They were released at Cresswick between the property and Kilcoy, and many still live in the area. The hunting of the kangaroos and the dingo served a purpose for the owners of stations as they were considered pests and were, in some areas, of epidemic proportions. David Murray described one such hunt at a squatter's property on the Downs. "Before the heat of the day had set in we started, with our mounted beaters riding easily in front of us – a sturdy handful of centaurs who looked born to the saddle. The cartridges we carried were marked "K" and "H", the letters standing respectively for kangaroo and hare."[77] Good horses were essential for the sport of hunting, as well as for the sport of polo.

Cricket was a game that required both equipment and players within reasonable reach of one another, and hence there is little evidence of it being played on stations to any extent. However, individuals from the stations often played on town teams, and assisted in the organisation of that sport. Although not the first cricket game in Ipswich, there was a game on 22 June 1850, between the Squatters and the Ipswich Cricket

Club. The Squatters team consisted of H. Thewell, Fairholme, F. Bigge, Burgoyne, Collins, Bell, Davidson, Horton, Bowerman, Thelwell and Walker. The squatters were narrowly beaten.[78]

David Christie Murray, visiting an unnamed squatter on the Darling Downs in 1889, gave his initial impressions:

> At the end of our drive we reach a handsome house of freestone in the midst of well–kept gardens, with a raised lawn of very English–looking turf for tennis and cricket practice. In a paddock not far removed is the cricketing ground, on which the station hands practice and play their matches. The employer is an enthusiastic votary of the game, and trains his men assiduously, though they confess that last year the neighbouring station beat them.[79]

Tennis and croquet were also leisure pastimes indulged in by the elite, and many built facilities for such on their stations. Picnics and balls were eagerly organised and awaited, as they provided opportunities for social interaction. Although the sport of rowing could not obviously be practised on a station, the Bell family in particular was influential in the development of the sport in the capital.

In the early years there was a 'sport' that was occasionally indulged in by white settlers. It is rarely mentioned in the literature, however Holthouse, in his book on the squatter, described one such occurrence. An early migrant, James Demarr wrote, in 1843, that there was a certain type of squatter who hunted blacks for sport.[80] There was also an instance when some fifty Aborigines were poisoned by placing arsenic in the flour at Kilcoy Station in 1842. But the murderers were never apprehended "for lack of legal evidence."[81]

Such murders were not one–sided. The squatter Horatio Wills, for example, arrived in Queensland in 1861 and started to establish a homestead at Cullen–la–Ringo with some ten thousand sheep to graze. Everyone at the station was slain by a group of Aborigines. His son, T.W. Wills, was away from the homestead collecting stores and therefore survived the massacre, which outraged white settlers and caused quick retribution. T.W. Wills was a graduate of Rugby School, and on his return to Victoria became one of the state's leading cricketers, and a prime agent in the organisation of the Aboriginal team from Victoria which toured New South Wales and ultimately went to England in 1868. It is the same Wills who endeavoured to get cricketers to continue their conditioning in the off season, and thereby originated the game now generally known as Australian Rules football. He later became an alcoholic and committed suicide.

The elite of the country, then, influenced the early sport patterns of Queensland. Though not all gentlemen–squatters were descended from the aristocracy or upper classes, in the main they encouraged those activities that were expected of them: horse riding and racing, horse breeding, polo, rowing, hunting and cricket. The Irish among them liked their sport with a dash more vigour and boisterousness, but even they came to the realisation that they indeed were the aristocrats of the seemingly never-ending bush and accepted leadership because of the status of ownership of vast properties. They were generally hard riders and tough men. The new land was not for the faint-hearted, but was there for the taking only for men of spirit, courage, adventure and resolve.

Those who were public school men were imbued with the ideals of muscular Christianity and excessive nationalism, and though they had been subjected to a classical education that had little meaning in the bush, the very athleticism on which the schools were founded assisted their adaptations. They were reasonably fit and muscular through the games they had played, and their boarding school experiences, by no means cocoon environments, assisted their survival in the wilderness.

Gentlemen's havens arose like the Queensland Club, where like souls could meet, and the influence of the squattocracy was felt in social and cultural matters. As the years went on, however, there was an 'Australianisation' of the emigrant. He and she became less British and more Australian. The 'cultural baggage' they brought with them was modified by the sun and the heat, the flies and the mosquitoes, by the variant weather and the geography. The land itself changed the emigrant, and this affected a change in sport patterns. Though early on many of the sports that were pursued were those of the upper class, increasingly that participation reflected the activities of the new land. Adherence to previously learned experiences slowly disappeared under the Queensland sun.

9

The Stockmen, Drovers, Selectors and Townspeople

During the latter half of the nineteenth century the inland frontiers were expanded westward and northward and the emphasis turned to the taming and utilisation of the land. In 1859 the State's population was concentrated in four major towns: Brisbane, Ipswich, Drayton and Toowoomba. In the following decades Queensland experienced considerable growth and development, and there was gradually increasing settlement of the inland and northern sections of the state. The population pattern was from the major centres outward, towards 'rural', often virgin territories. This growth pattern in Queensland, as in the rest of Australia, was the reverse of that which had occurred in the British Isles and Europe, where the population was drawn inward from the rural areas to the cities as a consequence of industrialisation. Although Brisbane, and the other already established centres, continued to grow, it was in the 'country' areas where the major growth was evident. The discovery of gold and minerals, the inauguration of the sugar industry and the availability of 'unoccupied' land were all factors which induced settlers to Queensland's open spaces and ultimately led to the establishment of large and small communities throughout the length and breadth of the state.

One of the initial problems faced by the Government of the new colony was the ownership and utilisation of land under its purview. In 1860, the Legislature, which was dominated by pastoralists, passed a Land Bill which essentially protected the interests of the Darling Downs squattocracy. However the Bill also made available vast unsettled lands and, more important for the future of the colony, began to "experiment with agricultural lands and smaller farming allotments."[1] The Government encouraged immigration, particularly by experienced farmers, offering them free passage and forty acres of land. Such an amount of land was considerable inducement, as in the 'Old World' most farmers were restricted to from four to six acres. Many Scots and Irish, attracted by the various possibilities, subsequently came to establish farms in Queensland. German settlers were, in particular, "appreciated by the Government for their love of the land which expressed itself in their sturdiness, self–reliance, working ability and drive to make the farms successful. The Germans tended to settle in groups"[2] and did so around Meringandan, Glencoe and Goombungee.

As well as the newly–arrived migrants there were also ambitious newcomers who generally came from the south and who already possessed pastoral experience. They came in search of land, but they were considerably different from the 'Pure Merinos'. They came to be known as 'selectors'. Many bought key land areas and forced the squatters to buy them out. They were called "cockatoos", or "cockies". The owners retaliated by buying key areas themselves, and putting dummy selectors on them. This was called "peacocking".[3]

Many of the first selectors had an extremely difficult time, not only in making their property productive, but also in meeting the terms of their licence for occupation of the land. They were required to maintain continuous residence, make annual payments of one–fortieth of the purchase price and to enclose and fence the land within five years. One of the few means of acquiring cash was by hiring themselves out as labourers to large landowners and working at stock work, droving, fencing and other station jobs.

The squatters had principally occupied the land in order to use it for grazing, and they made minimal changes, or improvements, to their holdings. The farmers, on the other hand, had to completely clean their tracts before they could be worked, and this was painstakingly difficult. In addition to the hardships associated with clearing the land, the farmer faced other problems, such as limited capital, lack of adequate markets and difficulty in transporting produce to potential purchasers. The construction of railroads and the subsequent linkage with coastal communities significantly accelerated the expansion of agriculture in the state. Another hindrance to the early success of agriculture was the importation of European and American farming methods and techniques without adjustments necessitated by a differing Queensland environment. Gradually such adaptations and modifications appeared. When a plan for free selection of land was initiated in New South Wales and Queensland in the early 1860s, many of the large land owners chose to move further out. Encouraged by favourable reports relating to land in Western Queensland, many migrated north and west in search of havens. As lack of rainfall was a perennial problem, many of the first 'runs' were taken along water sources, and this left large sections of unoccupied land with insufficient water. It was, however, the discoveries of various mineral fields that finally led to viable settlements in central, western and northern Queensland.

Although often romanticised, the life of the early settlers in the country areas of Queensland was not an easy one. For families to move their belongings, and often a year's supplies into 'no man's land' entailed great sacrifice, courage and physical stamina. These journeys by horse and bullock–drawn carts occupied weeks or even months. Edward Palmer, who in the 1860s took up and developed a station in Northern Queensland, halfway between Normanton and Cloncurry, described the life of the early settlers.

> there was little or nothing of comfort or relaxation; there was always hardship and exposure; there was no Sunday for rest, no holiday, no Eight Hour Day, nothing but constant moving and watching. The duties were shared by all alike; each had to take a turn at anything and everything, cooking one time, driving a team another, shepherding sheep occasionally, herding cattle sometimes, cutting timber, making bough–yards for sheep, lambing down a flock of ewes, shifting hurdles, and poisoning dingoes, killing and salting beef, ear–marking, washing and shearing sheep, looking for stragglers, yoking bullocks, building huts, tracking and hunting stock, all little duties that made up the routine life of the outside grazier.
>
> They all took their turn, and generally there was one dish and one table. Where the ways and customs consequent on the life brought all on a partial level, the man who could turn his hand to anything from shoeing a horse to weighing out a dose of quinine or driving a bullock team, was the most valuable.[4]

It was through the efforts and dedication of the selectors, farmers, miners, plantation workers, shopkeepers, and butchers as well as the graziers, that the country areas of Queensland were settled and cultivated. Gradually towns emerged to meet the needs of the settlers, and essential services such as banks, stores, schools, churches, hotels, hospitals and sporting facilities were established. In spite of the hardships of life in the country, there always seemed to be time for some form of sport, and it was deemed a matter of course "that every young man shall be able to swim, to ride a horse and to handle a gun or a rifle."[5]

Impromptu challenges were perhaps the most common way of engaging in sport, a buck–jumping contest, for example, being arranged to determine the best rider in the district.[6]

Horse–racing was by far the most popular sport in country regions, by virtue of the fact that virtually everyone owned a horse, and if they did not then they would bet on the races in the hope of purchasing one. Big race meetings were the main entertainment in many country areas, particularly in the early years and in isolated areas in the west. Special days such as Her Majesty's Birthday, Boxing Day, St. Patrick's Day and so on served as occasions for organised race meetings. For example, the first race meeting at Peak Downs was on Boxing Day, 26 December 1864, and four races were held: a Bushman's Purse for £20, a Second Race for a saddle and bridle, a Third Race for a Good English Lever Watch, and a Fourth Race for a Silver Hunting Watch. In addition, a first class dinner was provided free on Christmas and Boxing Day at Mr Solomon's Water Hole Hotel.[7] Often such races would be followed by events such as pigeon shoots, and billiard contests in the evening.

These country races were boisterous affairs, with the inevitable consumption of prodigious amounts of alcohol. The Boxing Day Races at Logan in 1872 were "a great improvement on former race meetings. It was not disgraced by drunkenness, no quarrelling."[8] This would have been an exception, for excessive drinking seemed to be standard fare.[9]

Lack of proper facilities was never a concern, with the main streets often doubling as race tracks. Many towns were like Ayr, where in the 1880s the sports were held on Queen Street with the adjacent Queen's Hotel verandah serving as the grandstand.

Next to horse–racing, fighting was "the chief amusement. Some fought for the fun and love of the thing, and perhaps some rubbed out old scores...At the time Roma was formed, the order of the day was racing, fighting and drinking."[10] Whenever there was a fight, whether between two individuals, or even stray dog fights or domestic quarrels, crowds would gather and bets would be laid. Gambling on fights, horses and cards and, indeed, on any other type of contest, was enthusiastically indulged in by all classes, and by men and women. Some made fortunes, but many more lost.

The traditional urban team sports of cricket and football had their devotees, and occasional games were played. However, the numbers required to indulge in such activities, the equipment needed and the distances that often had to be covered for adequate competition were hindrances that affected their diffusion and popularisation. An example of a football match, at the turn of the century in the northern bush, was that engaged in during the building of the Bowen–Collinsville Railway.

Again the camp moved along the line, this time stopping at the 38 Mile, Little Blue Rock, and here the first football match was held between the men on the gangs, bridge teams, carters and miners. The Referee, Mr. Curley Pye (Bowen man doing plumbing work at the State Mine) used a small horse bell because there was no whistle.[11]

It was not until well into the twentieth century, however, that these two sports were organised and came to play a significant role in the sporting scene for country people. Holidays, in particular, all served as occasions for sports, similar in format to those in Brisbane. One such occasion was in Durham on 1 January 1889, when some three hundred people gathered to picnic and watch athletics. The athletes competed for the total prize money of £75 in such events as: a Maiden Plate – 100 yards, the hop, step and jump, putting the heavy weight, a Durham Handicap – 150 yards, throwing the hammer, the running long jump, a walking handicap – 1 mile, a hurdle race handicap, a consolation handicap, tug–of–war and the Durham Championship race – half a mile. The last race was restricted to employees of the Durham and Lord Byron mines.[12]

In many outback areas no sports day program was complete without a goat race. Occasionally even separate 'Goat Derbies' would be held and these would attract thousands of spectators. The 'Phar Lap' of the goat fraternity would pull specially designed carts, or jockeys would ride them bareback.[13] Goat racing appears to be a sport that was unique to the central and northern areas of Queensland.

In country areas various other 'bush' sports developed, such as sheep shearing contests, ploughing matches, and wood chopping competitions. In Kingaroy, for example, the regular Saturday afternoon pastime was woodchopping competitions. On one occasion Bob Otto, the Queensland champion, defeated Amos Murrel, New South Wales Champion, for a £50 match, during which Otto chopped a log of 47 inches girth in 54 seconds.[14]

The sports of tennis and golf did not appear on the competitive scene until well after the turn of the century. Golf, in particular, was very slow to develop in country areas, in spite of the obvious availability of land. Tennis courts were reasonably common–place on stations, large and small, and also in towns. However, the sport at this time was primarily seen as a 'social' activity, being played regularly by both men and women solely for 'fun'.

Hunting was obviously a popular sport in country areas. However, such hunts were rarely formally organised, as clubs were not formed, except at a few centres such as Gayndah and Rockhampton. Only at such exclusive clubs were special hunting costumes worn. The hunting of kangaroos, wallabies and rabbits provided the average person with a few hours of 'sport', as well as supplying food for the table. In Cooktown, until a Sunday School was founded, the favourite Sunday pastime for children was "shootin' roos."[15] Because of the prolific marsupial population and the damage they inflicted on the crops and grasslands, 'blood sports' were avidly pursued, and even encouraged, by station owners.[16]

Games played in the country were generally more informal, less organised, more boisterous and spontaneous than those in the metropolis or among the squattocracy. Their leisure activities, often self-devised, tended to be more variable, combining traditional urban sports with unique 'bush' contests. Life, of necessity, was simple, as were the pleasures which often grew out of, and were part of, the ordinary life of the community.

The Station Hand, Stockman and/or Stockrider

The station hand and the life he led are part of the enduring legend of the bush, immortalised by the *Bulletin* at the height of its glory. He was usually depicted in the saddle with a well-worn hat and riding outfit, with cigarette in mouth, shy, tough, the master of understatement; at other times he would be seen branding cattle, buckjumping, tending to the fences, mustering, droving, chasing the brumbies; and he would also be depicted expressing bewilderment about "new chums" and "city slickers", both of whom caused him much consternation. These were the bush stereotypes.

In point of fact the station hand is difficult to stereotype, just as the squatter is. There were Chinese who worked mainly as cooks; there were the Aborigines, many of whom adapted well to station life and rode with the best; there were the selectors, many of whom went bankrupt in the depression and yet wanted to stay in the country, working for someone else; and then there were the genuine "bushies", born to station life and committed to the freedom, the mateship and the masculinity ethos that went along with it.

The latter was typified by a poem in Palmer's *Early Days in North Queensland*.

> He was a native to the soil and bred,
> Merely a cowboy he;
> A nomad's life was what he led
> And all he wished to be[17]

Palmer endeavoured to sum up life in the early years for those individuals who worked at the stations.

> His work is not by any means easy; there are long hours, in fact all hours, hard fare, and often no lodging but the bare ground; he must endure hunger and thirst, cold, heat, and wet, and often has to take a watch at night. When

at work in the yard branding and drafting, he either has to endure tremendous dust, or else he is covered with mud. But the trained stockrider makes light of all these discomforts, in fact he looks on them as all in the bill of fare, and belonging to the day's work. He is hardy, wiry, as well as possessed of a good deal of endurance and pluck, and like all men who ride much, is nearly always lean in condition. He is generally the owner of a couple of horses and an outfit of saddle, swag, stock whip, and spurs, and takes an interest in all racing and sporting matters. As a rule, he is not a saving man, although some may lay up enough money to start a small store...To draft on horseback in the cattle yard, or in the yard on foot, to castrate and brand horses and calves, to ride a young horse, to make a leg or head rope out of green hide, or a pair of hobbles, to counterline a saddle, to cook a damper, all comes within the province of the stockman.[18]

Out of deference to the stockman, local race meetings invariably had a 'Stockman's Purse', sometimes called the 'Helter Skelter'. Only *bona fide* stock horses were eligible to run in these contests, and usually the stockman would ride his own horse. Other races that stockmen would participate in were the novelty events, for example where a man on foot would race a man on horseback, fifty yards, around a post.[19] Such race meetings would last up to five days, and during that time there would be gambling at the race track and away from it. Liquor was avidly consumed and there were the expected resultant brawls. Most stockmen returned to work after the festivities with empty pockets and sore heads.

The drovers did not have a bunk-house for their retreat, as did station hands. They generally lived a nomadic life moving cattle and sheep from one area to another, sometimes from Queensland to Victoria or South Australia, covering incredible distances in all kinds of weather. Their way of life had a certain fascination, and even 'Banjo' Paterson was captivated:

In my wild, erratic fancy, visions come to me of Clancy,
  Gone a droving down the Cooper, where the western drovers go;
As the stock are slowly stringing, Clancy rides behind them singing,
  For the drover's life has pleasures that the townsfolk never know.

Although their life was rarely recorded, and even less rarely lauded, the bullock-drivers also made a lasting contribution to country life. In the early days when roads, if there were any, were in a poor state, bullock-drivers were of considerable importance as they would drive teams of ten to twenty bullocks up mountains, down steep inclines and through creeks, bringing vital supplies to far-distant settlements. Bullock drivers had to possess brute strength, great experience and unrelenting energy in order to carry out their duties, which would often entail weeks, and even months, en route. Bullock races naturally occurred when the "bullockies" got together.

Shearers were another breed, as they were basically itinerant workers who would travel from station to station, sometimes by horse, later by bicycle and then by car and truck. Their work was such that in a few months they could earn enough to sustain them for a year. The shearer in the early days was described by Palmer as being "a flash man, given to gambling, dicing, and other sports, and a good deal of his money is spent at roadside shanties."[20] Shearing contests emerged out of the work performed by these men.

Numerous Queenslanders have won acclaim in shearing competitions, and of these the most prominent has been Jackie Howe. Born on the Leslie station on the Downs, he did most of his shearing in Central Queensland. He revolutionised shearing, the average number of sheep being shorn daily before his time being about one hundred. Jackie Howe was described as being 5 feet 10 inches, 15 stone in weight, with a chest of 50 inches, biceps of 17 inches and a thigh of 27 inches. His hands were reputed to be like small tennis racquets. He became a folk hero, being lauded throughout the country. Warwick, for example, commemorated his feat with a public plaque.[21]

JACKIE HOWE

John Robert Howe, better known as Jackie Howe, was born on Canning Downs near Warwick on 26th July, 1861.

He learned the art of blade shearing in the woolsheds of this district before moving to Central Queensland in the 1880's.

At "Alice Downs", Blackall, on 10th October, 1892, he shore a total of 321 sheep in a standard working day of eight hours and thereby established a record that was never equalled by blade shearers.

By adopting a sleeveless shirt which facilitated the action of the blade shearer, he gave his name to its modern counterpart; the 'Jackie Howe' singlet.

Jackie Howe died at Blackall on 21st July, 1920.

Numerous sports developed out of the work habits of the "bushies" and workers in the country. There were the rodeos, bareback riding, shearing contests, roping contests, bronco riding, camp drafting, sheep dog trials, and buck jumping. Farmers competed in ploughing matches and axemen in woodchopping contests. In most of these sports local and even state competitions evolved, and eventually there were Australian Championships. In various rodeo sports there are now World Championships, and Queenslanders have been eminently successful.

Beginning in small towns and diffusing to larger centres were agricultural shows. These annual shows became a tradition in Australia, and were eagerly awaited by children and adults alike. At these shows, as well as agricultural displays and the judging of various livestock, there were sports competitions of the rodeo variety, and equestrian activities included horse showing, horse–racing and jumping, wood chopping contests, sheep dog trials, hay tossing and so on. Some of the competitors became so proficient in these specialities that, as prize monies increased, they followed, on a circuit, such shows around the state. Some of the competitions were for the country elite, but there were also those for the average country stock hand, drover or shearer. Ribbons and prizes that have been won at shows proudly adorn thousands of Queensland country homes.

In recognition of the contributions of stockmen and other outback workers, the Australian Stockman's Hall of Fame and Outback Heritage Centre was established in 1977 in Longreach. The location of this national centre in a central–western Queensland town is an acknowledgement of this state's contributions in the development of the outback. The aim of the Centre is to bring to life the history of the collective culture of the Australian hinterland, with art galleries, a library, museum and archives.

Some Country Towns

When Buley wrote of Australian life in the town and country at the turn of the century he highlighted the significance of sport in country towns. "It has been said that when an Australian settlement is planned, the first care of the pioneers is to mark out the site of the cemetery, the second to plan a race course."[22] Indeed, sport came to play an important role in the social life of townspeople. Sporting events were primary sources of entertainment, offering a welcome respite from the daily hardships and monotony of a bush existence. They were occasions for people to come together to socialise and relax. Although occasionally class divisions were apparent, in most instances this was not the case. The sports field served as a demonstration of the importance of physical skill and endurance in the country, and these characteristics were unrelated to class. Achievements by individuals, or by town teams, became a source of pride and strengthened community identification. Indeed, pleasure over victories on the sports field was a common bond shared by all in a town.

In order to better appreciate the role of sport in the country, selected towns are presented herein as case studies. The extensiveness of the material does not permit a complete analysis of any town's sporting heritage and hence only the beginnings of sporting contests and significant events will be discussed in the main.

The following towns and shires have been chosen for analysis: Gayndah, Cooktown, Stanthorpe, Winton, Hughenden, St. George, Dalby, Gatton, Beaudesert and Monto. These towns cannot be considered 'typical' in any sense, for each area is unique, with its social life being determined by the particular composition of its inhabitants and its environment.

Gayndah

It is appropriate to open this review of some country towns with Gayndah, as it was one of the premier centres for horse-racing in the formative years of the state.[23] The town takes its name from the aboriginal word meaning 'thunder', and is located on the Burnett River. It was founded in the late 1840s by Thomas Archer. Because of the wealthy squatters who settled in the area, the town quickly flourished and, by 1851, was rivalling Brisbane as the home of the 'Sport of Kings'. Its status was acknowledged with the running of the first Queensland Derby there in 1868.

Gayndah has a further distinction in the domain of equestrian sports, because the State's first campdraft took place there in July 1889, on the Gayndah race course. Mr A.P. Maltby was the principal organiser, calling a meeting of district cattlemen. Subsequently a committee was set up to draw up the rules, have the course in order and to appoint the first judge, Mr G.H. Jones. Prize monies were set at £100 for first place, £25 for second and £15 for third. The honour of becoming the first Queensland campdraft champion went to Mr W. Hampson on the chestnut mare 'Minnie'. The meeting was a success, with "all the booths [reporting] a roaring trade,"[24] and a concert in the School of Arts rounded off the meeting.

Campdrafting is a unique Australian sport and it had its genesis in the cattle stations of the outback, where fences were few and far between. Highly skilled musterers would keep a herd of cattle together, while other stockmen would "cut out" some of the cattle, in ones or twos. The purpose originally may have been to brand the cattle in turn. The skill of the horses in "cutting out" became a matter of personal rivalry, and slowly but surely competitions developed.

Gayndah is also in possession of one of the oldest cricket club books in Queensland. The entries are in lead pencil, with the first game being recorded in 1881, between Gayndah and Wide Bay. A.P. Maltby and W.E.P.-Okeden were among the home team players.

Cooktown

After the discovery of gold in 1873 in the Palmer River, almost overnight the port town of Cooktown emerged. It became for a time the major port in Northern Queensland, and traded directly with Hong Kong, Shanghai and Europe. The population boomed as miners, gamblers, shop keepers and tradespeople, as well as Chinese, flocked to the area. Throughout the 1870s and 1880s trade burgeoned, and life in this boom town was wild and vigorous. However Cooktown's prosperity was shortlived and now, in the twentieth century, the town is but a skeleton of its former glorious years.

Cooktown was proclaimed a municipality in 1876, and by that time there were some ninety-four pubs, as well as numerous dance halls, gambling dens and brothels to service the miners and relieve them of their hard-earned monies. Fighting seemed to be one of the most prevalent preoccupations, with brawls after almost every horse race. One of the most famous boxers in the area was Dr Jack Hamilton, and many stories were told of this "tall, dark and handsome"[25] doctor. The "fighting Medico", as he was known, was a miner, expert horseman, strong swimmer, crack pistol and rifle shot, and was extremely competent with his fists. Hamilton was later elected to Parliament and for some twenty years represented the district.

Horse-racing was understandably a popular activity for the miners. A Jockey Club was formed and race meetings were held regularly. The biggest event was the Boxing Day races, these being part of the total Christmas celebrations.

Although, in the main, the sports and amusements of Cooktown reflected the wild nature of a typical mining town, there were some more sedate pastimes. The elite of the town amused themselves with such refined activities as piano recitals and formal balls.

Stanthorpe

Although Stanthorpe did not become a leading centre for any sport in particular, the extensive developments in various sports in the early years singles out this town in the Granite Belt area. Tin was successfully mined in 1872 and almost immediately a Race Meeting was held. The first day's activities were followed by a banquet and ball, which was attended by some 118 people. The following year, 1873, Christmas Race meetings were held not only in Stanthorpe, but also in nearby Sugarleaf and Herding Yard Creek. The popularity of the sport was evident by the crowd of five to six hundred which attended these two-day race meetings, where the prizes were from thirty to fifty sovereigns. Usually at least one of the events on the program was a Chinaman's Race, with Fook Sang Long being a frequent winner.[26]

By 1875 the Stanthorpe Jockey Club had held eight race meetings in its three years of existence. In search of a better appointment, the race course was shifted several times in these early years. The first one was near Mt. Marlay, the second near Lynch's Hotel, the third on the McGregor estate in front of the hospital, and the fourth was in Sheadon's Paddock near the slaughter yards.[27]

Cricket was played in the early 1870s, and the enthusiasm for the sport resulted in several teams being formed. Regular matches were held throughout the mineral fields, and intertown competitions against Warwick were conducted even before the coming of the railway, the arrival of which made intertown travel considerably easier. The *Border Post* regularly reported on the activities of the 'Knights of the Willow', and even a Fancy Dress match against Warwick received extensive coverage.

Due to the prevalence of the animal population in this area, which is just north of the New South Wales border, kangaroo and koala shoots and dingo drives were organised for 'sport'. In 1875, the *Border Post* carried an invitation for a "Good Day's Sport". Over ten thousand kangaroos were yarded in the Kangaroo Hunt and Drive, and afterwards dinner was provided for three hundred shooters at Gillman's Hotel.[28]

One of the town's most popular leisure pastimes were picnics, which were organised and hosted by Church and Temperance Groups as well as private individuals. Some of these attracted hundreds of people, and games and footraces were invariably a part of a day's outings. A unique picnic event, which has remained as one of the town's highlights, was a balloon ascent, originally held on January 27 1873 to mark the anniversary of Captain Cook's landing in the colony. Mr Jenner's Half Way House was the site for the balloon launch.

Winton

Winton is located 178km north-west of Longreach, in central western Queensland. Two significant events in Queensland and Australian history occurred in this remote area: 'Banjo' Paterson wrote "Waltzing Matilda" at the Macpherson Station at Dagsworth, some eighty-four miles from Winton in 1895, and in 1920 the first registered head office of QANTAS was in Winton.

Paterson was visiting the Macpherson Station when he heard Christina Macpherson playing the Scottish tune 'Craiglea', which she had heard at the Warrnambool Race Meeting in Victoria.[29] Later, while riding on Macpherson Station, Paterson was told the story of a 'tragic drowning' that had occurred at the Combo Waterhole. According to Macpherson, police had come to the waterhole to capture a stockman, Harry Wood, who had killed a black boy, 'Charlie', because he had fled with his horse while he was playing cards. Intrigued with the story Paterson composed his famous poem. The poem, set to the tune of 'Craiglea', was first sung at Oondoroo, and then at Ayrshire Downs en route to the Winton Amateur Race Meeting in 1895. During that race meeting at the North Gregory Hotel, the song was sung in public for the first time.

By the time Paterson wrote 'Waltzing Matilda', horse–racing had been an established sport for many years. As soon as there were "a few huts established on the site of the town...about the year 1878 [there] were races up and down the main street."[30] However, the first authenticated meeting was that organised by the Never Never Jockey Club on 25 and 26 June 1879. It was a two–day race meeting with six races on the first day and five on the second, with the longest race being twenty–one miles. This was the Great Western Steeplechase. One of the races was for the Corinthian Cup (housed today in the Winton Museum), and only horses owned and ridden by members of the club were eligible to race.

By the 1880s the popularity of horse–racing was such that there were two clubs, the North Gregory Turf Club and the Winton Jockey Club, both of which were formed in 1883. They raced on the same days, though on different courses. One of the features of these race meetings was a Chinaman's Race, "when all the Chinamen brought their horses to the course – piebald included – and rode them themselves. It was the event of the day, as many of them could just about hold on, their pigtails soaring in the air."[31]

Hughenden

Hughenden and District's history of white settlement goes back to 1841, when the Flinders River was discovered by Lt. Stokes of the 'Bligh'. The first white people known to have trod the land were Frederick Walker and his party in 1861, and William Landsborough and his party in 1862, searching for the ill–fated Burke and Wills expedition. Squatters were soon on their heels, with Ernest Henry laying claim to Hughenden Station in 1863, followed by Sheaffe, Walpole and Walter Hayes taking up selections at Teleman, Marathon and Richmond Downs, and Oxley and Betts at Fairlight, all in 1863. In 1864 James Gibson took up Cargoon, the McDonald Brothers Cambridge Downs, Ernest Henry Burleigh, Kirk and Sutherland Afton Downs and Anning Reedy Springs. The Palmer Gold Rush was in 1873, and the Cloncurry Copper

Rush not long thereafter, and these changed the nature of the town, as it became an artery to get to and from the fields.

As in most country areas horse–racing became the main sport in Hughenden and the Flinders district. When the first race meetings were held is not known, however the *Charters Towers Times* of 14 April 1881 carried an announcement for the Annual Meeting of the Hughenden Jockey Club. The site for the first meetings "was on the northern side of the river on the Rosevale property, which was then owned by Mr. J.D. O'Leary. Later the course was shifted to the claypan...when the grandstand was the buggies, it was easy to shift."[32]

For those on the stations, a race meeting was viewed as the main social event of the year. There was considerable excitement as four–in–hand drags, buggies, cane carts, wagonettes and horse riders made their way to the course.[33] The prosperity of racing was evident from the prizes. The 1889 Hughenden Handicap, for example, was worth 100 sovereigns, at the time when a weekly wage of £2 was considerable remuneration. Fights were staged regular from the 1880s onward.[34] The masculinity ethos, as well as the country environs, also ensured that rifle shooting would become a prominent sport. Although the sport was actively pursued prior to the turn of the century, the first recorded club was the Flinders Target Club. Formed in 1901, it utilised two target machines.

St. George

St. George, in the south–west corner of the state, has had a sporting history typical of that of most country towns, with horse–racing being most prominent prior to the turn of the century, and then other sports were gradually introduced as the town increased in size.

The first races in the St. George environs were contested on the Willowthall Plain, and the earliest records of the Balonne Jockey Club show a race meeting on 18–19 April 1888. The seriousness of racing men in the area was demonstrated by many of the squatters importing high quality stallions from England. An example of the quality of the horses from the area was 'Buttons', from Bullaman Station. Buttons won the 1890 Brisbane Cup in spite of trotting behind a sulky all the way to Brisbane. One of the finest racing men of the area was Fisher, whom "the coveted C.B. Fisher plate [is named], a weight–for–age event competed for by Australia's best middle–distance horses and stayers each year in Melbourne."[35]

Dalby

Dalby, in the Darling Downs, has a heritage of sporting prowess that extends from the mid-nineteenth century. Two of Queensland's finest and most renowned athletes, Charlie Samuels and Jerry Jerome, came from the area. Both were Aborigines and were born on the Jimbour Plains. Another important sporting claim from the Dalby area is that "the first [Queensland] breeding stud for thoroughbred horses"[36] was located at Jimbour. In the latter part of the nineteenth century many of the state's top race horses came from Jimbour, which was built by Sir Joshua Peter Bell.

Gatton

Gatton, one of the oldest towns in Queensland, began as a centre for several large station properties and a changing point for horses of the Royal Mail Coaches. As the first railway line was from Ipswich inland, Gatton had a railway station and was serviced by the railway many years before Brisbane. Over the years the train provided an invaluable service to the townspeople, and was often used for sporting and leisure pursuits. Annual train excursions to the seaside, for example, were organised for school children.

As there were many large stations around Gatton, the 'Sport of Kings' had many proponents. Most of the stations imported thoroughbreds, with Sir Joshua Peter Bell of Buaraba and James Williams of Trent Hill showing the most leadership. Race meetings, followed by balls, were held on various stations. Some of the squatters owned teams of horses which travelled the Queensland racing circuit. In the 1870s, races at Gatton were at both registered and unregistered clubs, and were "over the sticks and on the flat."[37]

Beaudesert

Beaudesert, founded in 1874, is situated sixty-four kilometres south of Brisbane and is surrounded by rich farm land. Its sporting heritage dates from the early 1880s when the Logan and Albert Jockey Club was formed.

Beaudesert's first race course was at Kagorum, the property of John Maxwell, who was also one of the foundation members of the Jockey Club. The Maxwell family has continued to be active in horse-racing and other equestrian sports in the area.

After 1899, there were annual picnic races organised by the Logan and Albert Amateur Picnic Race Club as well as the race meetings organised by the Jockey Club. Virtually everyone in the district came into town for the two days of festivities. The Race Ball was the highlight of the year. The premier races were the Ladies' Bracelet of six furlongs and the Squatter's Cup of a mile and a quarter.[38] Although these meetings were successful, they were not resumed after the war.

As is the case in many other towns, the presence of one interested, keen devotee of sport is essential for its establishment and continuation. Monty Selwyn-Smith is considered the 'father' of sport in Beaudesert and was responsible for the sports of tennis and cricket, among others, as well as his abiding interest, rugby union. Monty, a former outstanding player, introduced the game to the town in 1889. The game was enthusiastically adopted, and competitive matches were soon arranged. The early games were relatively informal, as evidenced by the fact that the referee, Mr Morell, had to leave one game when it was only three-quarters completed. Morell was the local station master, and he had to be on duty for the 4.45pm train.[39]

Monto

It is fitting that this analysis of sport in Queensland towns concludes with Monto, a small Queensland country town which has produced outstanding athletes far in excess of its population and the available facilities.   It is extraordinary that so many state, national and international athletes have come from this centre. In the twentieth century the sports of boxing, tennis and rodeo have benefited immensely by Monto-bred athletes, such as Daphne and 'Chilla' Seeney, Rusty and Ernie Cook, Jackie O'Brien, Harry Cain, Darryl Norwood, Philip Hampson and the Fancutts.

Activities related to the horse made their appearance early in the Monto area. Thomas Bailey, one of the first squatters, who in 1874 took over the Old Cannindah Station, some sixty-six square miles in total,

> gave his attention almost exclusively to the breeding of horses running neither sheep or cattle on the estate. Considerable success attended his operations and his beautiful Clydesdale colts sold from £18 to £25 per head. Two of his best sires were Lock End and Knight of the Thistle; these horses were led up from Brisbane after winning first prize at the Brisbane Exhibition. It would take three weeks to do the trip in those days, sometimes a month as the horses had to be led very steadily.[40]

When he died his eldest son took over the station, and started breeding bloodstock, as well as draught horses and horses for the Indian market. The blood horses raced successfully in Brisbane and Sydney.

The old race days at Old Cannindah were recalled: "The stations used to bring their best race horses there about once a year, and held a picnic meeting among themselves, the prizes being a case of whisky, a jar of rum, or six stubs of derby tobacco...Only last year an 1856 shilling lost by some old punter was picked up there."[41]

The races were held once or twice a year, and a dance would follow. Each family had a tent at the race course, and everyone brought food, which was served from the pub.[42]

Life for the Womenfolk

Life in the Queensland outback was a harsh one for men and women alike with drought, flood and other setbacks testing their spirits. Subsisting on meagre provisions, the pioneer womenfolk shared the spartan existence with her husbands. They reared their families, with minimal medical assistance, in tents, humpies, slab huts, or if they were lucky, in houses with wooden floors. Though household chores were their primary occupations they were expected to help work the land whenever necessary. Theirs was not an easy life!

On the smaller and less well-to-do properties the work of the drover and shearer, as well as the breaking in of the horses, had to be accomplished by the owners themselves. For many women, the carrying out of these physically demanding chores – though considered to be men's jobs – were accepted by them as simply being part of their daily life. Some became very adept, and renowned for their abilities, such as Miss S.E. Gallagher, the daughter of a hotel owner in the Kilkivan district. She was known as an equestrienne 'par excellence' and as a young girl broke in horses with "all stout heart and bridle hand of any male breaker."[43] Then, there were the daughters of Tim Alexander, one of the best jackeroos at Dunmore Station near Dalby.

> The Alexander girls were all rough-riders too and went out mustering after their father died. They became famous in the Kogan district and were often referred to as "The Kogan Girls". They were noted as the best of bushwomen who could put the head rope on, throw the cattle and brand them, and break in some of the horses too.[44]

The word "jillaroo", the feminine equivalent of "jackeroo", was later coined to describe the women on cattle properties who did the same work as the men.

Indoors was the realm of the station mistress. Much of the housework was done on the large, shaded verandah, storing peaches for jam, peeling oranges for marmalade and paring and coring quinces for jelly. The kerosene lamps had to be washed and trimmed each morning, and there was the continual sewing; these were a women's duties. For those who could afford it there were maid–servants aplenty in those days, willing young girls straight off the ships from England. But the mistress was always in charge and was expected to solve all household dilemmas and be ready for emergencies.

It was a pleasant life for the upper middle class: croquet, tennis, entertaining visitors with walks and rides, picnicking, and planning for festive events such as those on Boxing Day, where the surrounding populace would disport themselves to Middle Plain for a picnic and horse races.[45] The women and children would vie with each other with their beautiful new prints and muslin gowns. The day always ended with a dance in the school–house and for the children, who retired to bed early, "the throbbing of the accordion and the sound of time–beating feet on the floor were soon part of their dreams."[46] Such affairs were egalitarian, the shearer and stockmen mixing freely with the aristocracy of the bush. At a picnic in the Ayr district, unmarred by social class and distinctions, everyone would be invited, including the itinerant traveller on the track searching for work.

Such occasions allowed for community competitive expressions, not only between the men, but also between the sexes.

> The ladies actually challenged the men to tug–o–war – and did they win? Certainly – but to quote one of the original competitors – the men used to give way. Chivalrous men in those days. And of the greasy pig, treacle bun and Maypole dancing, sticky, though none the less sweet, recollections remain in many minds.[47]

It took strength of character to endure the harshness and hard work of living in the outback. However, for most, the hardest to overcome was the physical and mental loneliness. Some understanding of the desolateness experienced can be garnered from the recollection of one woman who was so lonely that she found amusement "in surreptitiously taking the horse saddle to the pig–sty, putting it on the pig and riding round and round the sty."[48]

Pioneers in Country Sport

The following are but two examples of Queenslanders who have made various contributions to Queensland sporting, and indeed social, history. There are countless thousands more, who could have been mentioned and who have made similar contributions in small towns throughout the state. Most have been given little acknowledgement, their efforts passing virtually unnoticed as time moves inexorably on. Their main legacy is left in the memories of those they helped, and in the communities that have prospered by their presence. Perhaps they were like many of the squatters, who moved into the next world unnoticed, unacknowledged, though their sacrifices and impact on their local community were major. Halls of fame could not possibly be built large enough to contain the unsung heroes and heroines who left their mark on the land in sport.

W.R.O. Hill

"Willie" Hill has written a simple but unpretentious narrative of his first-hand experiences in North Queensland, from 1861 to 1905. For the first seven years in Queensland he was a member of the Native Mounted Police and then, in 1868, he commenced his civil service career, in which he remained until retirement. His appointments took him to most parts of the state. Some of the towns and areas in which he was stationed, sometimes for as short a period as one year, were the Cape River Gold Field, Ravenswood, Georgetown, Byerstown (halfway between Cooktown and Maytown), Cairns, Springsure, Gayndah, Clermont and Mackay. His principal appointment was that of Police Magistrate, however, as was evident in Gayndah, he occasionally held a variety of positions, from gold warden to church warden.[49]

"Willie" Hill was born in 1844 in St. Helier's, Jersey, where his father held a commission in the regiment. In 1860 his father heard glowing reports of Queensland and advised Willie and his brothers to seek their fortunes in the new land. Coming from modest financial circumstances they were not able to afford first-class passage, however good connections enabled them to have the use of superior facilities while on board. These connections were of immense benefit when they arrived in Brisbane. Willie's appointed custodian was Colonel O'Connell, who immediately introduced him "to all leading families, who were very few in those days."[50] He was soon actively involved in the social life and attended numerous musical evenings. As he was a keen athlete, he participated in an athletics competition organised in 1861 by a detachment of the 50th Regiment. At the meeting, he "annexed the high jump, five feet four inches, the flat jump, eighteen feet six inches, and pole high jump, nine feet seven inches, in All-comers' events – fairly creditable performances by a lad of seventeen years of age".[51]

The highlight of Willie's tenure with the Native Mounted Police was his appointment as second in command of the Aboriginal escort for the Duke of Edinburgh when he visited Brisbane in 1868. The twelve Aboriginal troopers, specially selected, were "all grand looking men averaging nearly six feet, while some were over, and all matchless horsemen. We did our best to outvie the white escort, and succeeded too, for the duke himself told me he had never seen cavalry anywhere with such splendid seats in the saddle."[52]

In his travels around Queensland he had the opportunity to view life on some of the large stations. He described a well-appointed station in 1876 between Cloncurry and the South Australian boundary, its requirements including "a comfortable house, piano, tennis court, and plenty of bottled beer."[53] In the early 1860s he was billeted with the Archers at Gracemere. During the day everyone worked hard, and there was "no loafing...during working hours, but evenings were enlivened by music and boxing which were the favourite pastimes."[54] Occasionally, for fun, they would turn somersaults over hay stacks on the front lawn. While staying with the Archers, Willie was invited to a dance at Rockhampton, and he relates how the butler readied his clothes and horse for the occasion. Then "off I went, a ride of eight miles, dancing all night, another eight-mile ride home about five am, a plunge in the lagoon, and to work feeling fit for anything."[55]

Willie was not over-descriptive of life in the towns he visited and/or worked in, but those comments he did make were at times not very complimentary. Dalby, in his opinion, was "the dullest and most uninteresting place (bar Adavale) I ever saw, the inhabitants' one and only excitement being a daily visit to the passing trains."[56] Gayndah, on the other hand, was "one of the oldest in Queensland and a truly rural spot, with a perfect climate, and situated on the banks of the Burnett River, a fine running stream of pure fresh water."[57] His evaluations of towns may have been coloured by his personal interests. Fishing was his main hobby, and around Gayndah there was "exceptionally good fishing, including fresh water mullet averaging from two to four pounds caught in the season in thousands on hooks baited with green moss."[58] It was perhaps the reason also why he enjoyed his stay at Charleville. He maintained that there was splendid fishing in the Warrego and he related how, with two friends, they caught, in one night, eight cod which "weighed three hundred and four pounds. I won a good sweepstake by securing the biggest fish, which turned the scale, cleaned and without head, at sixty one and a half pounds."[59]

The only 'traditional' urban sport that Willie described was cricket, and that only sparingly. Although one of the games took place in Bourke, NSW, his comments are worthy of quoting, as he mentioned single wicket cricket

> While at Bourke I met that splendid athlete, Vessey Brown, and witnessed a unique cricket match.
> Brown challenged the Bourke Eleven at single wicket, provided they allowed him his two nephews, the Walkers, to field for him. Brown was to

use a pick handle. He won the toss and went in to bat, but as it was an afternoon match and they could not bowl Brown out, he retired, and the Eleven gave him best.[60]

While at Roma he was involved with arranging a fancy dress cricket match for the benefit of the hospital. At Clermont, there was interest in the game, there being three or four active teams. At a concert given in honour of the cricketers, Willie's musical talents were demonstrated with the composition and performance of a cricket song.[61]

Willie once displayed his athletic talents to win a wager. At Charters Towers, he bet £5 that he, weighing nine stone, could carry the Warden, who weighed nineteen stone, on his shoulders around the Town Square, a distance of some 150 yards. He performed the feat and won the wager.[62]

Interestingly Willie did not refer to hunting, other blood sports or horse-racing, all of which were prevalent in the country areas. His personal interests understandably determined the events and episodes described, and hence fishing is mentioned on numerous occasions throughout the book. The absence of references to horse-racing perhaps demonstrates that not everyone was captivated by the sport. Regardless, Willie Hill's reminiscences are an invaluable record of the daily life of a man travelling around Queensland during the latter half of the nineteenth century.

Richard Symes Alford

The diary of Richard Alford provides a first-hand description of life in southern Queensland in the latter half of the nineteenth century. When his family came to the Darling Downs in 1842, his mother, along with Mrs Arthur Hodgson, were the first white women on the Downs. His sister was probably the first white child born there. From 1842 to 1852, the Alford family lived at Drayton, which was then called "The Springs", prior to moving to present-day Toowoomba, then called "The Swamp". When the family arrived at Toowoomba, there was only one other building in the area, and his brother was the first white child born in the town. The Alford family was certainly among the early pioneers of the state. In 1853 the family moved to Brisbane, where Richard and another brother were born. The family finally returned to Toowoomba, where his father ran an auctioneering business until his death in 1864. At the age of fifteen Richard went to work on a station, but very quickly left for the city, where he accepted a bank position. He was basically a restless person, and during his lifetime worked at several different jobs: as manager of a station, a drover, a miner, and finally he took over his brother's business as a Stock and Station Agent. In his diary, Richard vividly recalled many interesting episodes as he travelled around the state in these various positions.

Horse–racing was one of his major interests, and wherever he lived or travelled he regularly attended the races. Races were held annually at Brisbane, Ipswich, Toowoomba and Warwick, with the same horses often competing at these meetings. Richard wrote that there was a bellman hired at Toowoomba to clear dogs off the course between the races. In addition to the meetings at the four main centres, racing was the 'King of Sports' wherever there were settlements.

> Up to the year 1870 private race meetings were held on the Logan, each station owner taking it in turn to give the entertainment. In 1869, together with my brother Tom, I attended a gathering of this kind at Tambourine where Captain Williams presided. Representatives were there from all the surrounding stations. There was a day's racing. Both my brother and I had mounts on horses which we had brought with us from Coochin, but our horses suffered defeat...
>
> There was also a paper chase, but the fences were too high, nearly all the horses got stuck up at a three rail fence near the homestead...
>
> ...Next year (1870) the races were held at Nindooimbah, De Burgh Persse of Tabragalba being the host. He was then a bachelor and had borrowed the Nindooimbah head station for the occasion. Two day's racing were held and dancing at night, till the small hours of the morning. It was an expensive entertainment, so much so that no one else cared to emulate Mr Persse and it turned out to be the last private race meeting held on the Logan.[63]

Supplementing the organised meetings there were informal ones as well, as when two drovers arrived at Nanango ahead of the stock and "the spare time was put in...by matching their droving horses against local animals...The races were run from one public house to another, a distance of a quarter of a mile."[64]

In his travels around the state Richard frequently witnessed various "blood sports". He wrote of the kangaroo and wallaby problems on the Taabinga Station, near Nanango, in 1875. Various methods were practised to rid the area of what were considered pests, and one way was the use of kangaroo dogs, which would occasionally engage in a death struggle with the 'roo, who was particularly dangerous when "bailed up", or when he would take to deep water.[65]

Shooting *battues* were also held, using double–barrelled breach–loading guns. Men were placed behind trees about one hundred yards apart, and horsemen spread out to drive the kangaroos towards the guns. This was not overly satisfactory at Taabinga, as "the excitement of the men was so intense that the shooting was very faulty."[66]

A third method, described in another section, consisted of the building of yards and the driving of the kangaroos towards these yards, where Aborigines with nulla nullas awaited them. On one occasion some four hundred kangaroos suddenly declined to enter the yards and turned back, and mayhem resulted.[67]

In Warwick, an inducement for the 'hunter sportsman' was the offering of a bonus of a penny for each animal's scalp and thus hunters would not only get money from the selling of skins but a bonus as well. This "method" was adopted at Taabinga and some twenty thousand marsupials were subsequently killed.

From the number of detailed accounts, Richard Alford seems to have been unduly intrigued and fascinated by 'blood sports'. Although a lover of horses, he also described the 'sport' of shooting wild horses (brumbies) at Burrandowan.[68]

Although Richard was not considered an athlete, and indeed he said that he had not "even been out of a walk," he entered a foot-race competition in the Botanical Gardens, in Brisbane, in 1873, and won against the best runner in Brisbane, the professional Stacey, though Richard ran with his trousers tucked into his socks.[69]

In his diary he also described the occasional fight and a high jump competition between a black and white man. There were also numerous accounts of winning and losing at race courses. Richard Alford's diary affords us with a unique insight into the interests of an average man living in the formative years of this state.

Summary

Sport in the country areas, then, has undergone profound changes over the course of time. The main organised sports in the early days were those by the squattocracy. This group dominated the organisation of sport, and some sociologists may possibly see something sinister in that organisation. They had hegemonic control, to be certain, but there is also the viewpoint that many of the squatters had a deep social commitment and were endeavouring to put that resolve into practice. In other words, it can be postulated that the purpose of the squattocracy in establishing and controlling sport was not so much for financial and/or personal goals but because they, too, were simply endeavouring to break the monotony of life in the country and wanted to have 'fun'. It is too easy to criticise in hindsight. If the squatters had not organised horse-racing and other ventures, would others have taken their places?

The squatters organised the early sports, gave the participants time off if they were at their stations to participate, and bred or bought the horses that improved the quality of the races. Because of their wealth and influence, they also offered a bulwark against the 'sharpies' and entrepreneurs who infiltrated the courses.

There were limited social and sporting experiences in those early years in the country, and unmarred by social class and distinctions everyone took advantage of the few opportunities that there were to gain release from a rugged and demanding existence.

Some of the squatters were instrumental, to be sure, in promoting what we think of as elite sports, such as polo, hunting with hounds, and hunting kangaroos with kangaroo dogs. Sport for others in the country – the selectors, the station hands, the town workers, the axemen, the railway men – is rarely dealt with in depth by the chroniclers of the past. It is generally only sport for the elite that is recorded. This chapter is a modest attempt to correct that failing, and to reconstruct a picture of leisure patterns in the country that does justice to those honest toilers who carved out the wilderness to make Queensland what it is today. The pity is, however, that too few individuals are developed, two few towns, too few events. There is a type of person who has a deep love of sport and will not be denied in searching out his/her limits of physical ability. There are men and women, boys and girls, who will not be persuaded away from that physical and social experience.

What has impressed us is the way individuals banded together and voluntarily constructed the various race courses, football fields, and cricket pitches, through personal and community devotion. People would come in by foot, bicycle or horse, not only to play, but to assist in the building of facilities. Slowly but surely that personal initiative and commitment have all but disappeared – local, state and/or federal governments are expected to do all things in the twentieth century.

Indeed, there were problems associated with country living, but there was a sense of community involvement, of people caring, of the feeling that everyone was building something new, and these motivations spurred people on. Sport, then was basically a part–time involvement, and was viewed as a welcome leisure pursuit.

Each town analysed herein has demonstrated a similar trend towards a continuous diversification of leisure pursuits, as we moved into the twentieth century. Whereas there was only horse–racing, cricket, football, athletics and shooting in the early years, at the present time there is sky–diving, climbing, orienteering, table tennis, hockey, basketball and netball, indoor cricket, and so on. This expansion of sporting interests is the reality of the present day, and represents a marked shift away from the narrow interests of the 1900s. Sport is reflecting the availability of diverse activities, which are no longer constrained by difficulties in transportation and communication. The sport pattern is much more complex than it was a hundred years ago, changed forever by technology and industrialisation.

The traditional sports have also undergone change. Now there are professional coaches even in the country regions, itinerant professionals without the same local commitment. It can be argued that cricket, for example, is no longer a major sport in the country areas – that is, from the participant viewpoint. Cricket may still be eagerly followed as a spectator in a national or state sense, but it is slowly losing its status as a major participant sport in the country. The television set brings the state's, and the nation's finest athletes directly into an airconditioned living room, diminishing greatly any desire to go outside and watch the local team or play oneself.

Not enough acknowledgement has been accorded the lonely station hand who became part of the Australian sporting ethic. Sports such as campdrafting, the rodeo, sheepdog trials, shearing and woodchopping contests, goat racing and so on developed around the exploits of the Australian cowboys and the "bushies".

Country people have made immeasurable contribution to the Queensland and Australian sporting heritage.

Among the Miners: Charters Towers

The first recorded find of gold in Australia was by a shepherd in 1823.[1] However, it was the discovery at Ophir in New South Wales by Edmund Hammond Hargraves in February 1851 that launched the gold rush in Australia. In the following decade the Australian population virtually trebled, and this increase was primarily attributed to the gold discoveries. Some eighteen thousand Americans flocked to Australia after the news of the 1851 find. Gold seekers also came from England, Scotland, Ireland and China. Some forty thousand Chinese immigrated into this country in the 1850s and this rapid influx of a culture so alien to that of the white European gave rise to racial prejudice.[2] The hardworking Chinese were discriminated against and persecuted on the gold fields and elsewhere. The Chinese influx, and later the Kanaka labourers brought to work the sugar fields in Queensland were instrumental in the subsequent formation of the "White Australia" policy.

Life on the gold fields was rugged and primitive, with gambling, drunkenness and disorder being the norm. Very few became wealthy from their discoveries, and it was primarily the shopkeepers, bankers and publicans who benefited the most from the new gold towns. However, it has been claimed that gold "made society more democratic and optimistic"[3] and that the gold rush was instrumental in "the growth of a distinctly Australian national feeling."[4] Gold wealth expanded the oligarchy. Miners would say, "We be the aristocracy now...and the aristocracy now be we."

The discovery of gold in Queensland had the same economic and social effects as it had on the southern, more established, colonies. Goldmining and the subsequent industries that evolved helped to firmly establish the economic stability[5] of Queensland as well as to serve the purpose of opening up "the north". Population statistics dramatically demonstrate the very significant effect of the gold discoveries; 23,520 was the population of the colony in 1859; ten years later, it was 109,161.[6]

The beginning of many Queensland coastal and inland towns can be traced to the gold discoveries. The ports of Rockhampton, Townsville, Cooktown and Port Douglas were outlets and receiving centres for the gold and the resultant trade, while the towns of Gympie, Mayfield, Palmerville, Croydon, Ravenswood, Mount Morgan and Charters Towers came into existence with such finds. Some of these centres disappeared almost as fast as they appeared. Cooktown, Mayfield, Palmerville and Croydon were thriving towns in the heyday of the gold rushes, but today they are virtually ghost-towns. For example Cooktown, in the late 1800s, boasted a population of thirty thousand, while today it is three hundred. Charters Towers and Gympie have survived but they are not as prosperous as they once were – Rockhampton, Townsville and Cairns, however, have steadily continued to grow and prosper.

Although Queensland experienced, fundamentally, the same economic and social ramifications as did the southern colonies, there was one very significant difference in Queensland, particularly in the north. In the southern colonies, gold was discovered in previously settled areas, while in Queensland "with two exceptions, gold brought the first entry of the white man into rough and difficult terrain: the frontier was a mining frontier. Even in the two exceptions, Charters Towers and Ravenswood, conditions were extremely primitive."[7]

The pastoral industry developed hand-in-hand with the mining industry. Gold followed the incursions of the squatters, and as interior towns developed there arose a need for agricultural products and cattle. The ports that emerged and the railway lines and other transportation improvements allowed for the movement of such goods from one area to another in a manner that was obviously not possible beforehand. The gold period was an agricultural, cattle and sheep bonanza.

By 1871 Queensland had more overseas ports than any of the other colonies, and by 1891 there was "more shipping (mainly exports) than the extra-metropolitan ports of other colonies."[8]

Queensland's first discovery of gold was in 1858 at Canoona, near Rockhampton. Although the Canoona find was disappointing, within six weeks some eight thousand gold seekers, brought by seventy-three ships, had arrived in the north.[9] As a consequence the town of Rockhampton began to develop as a shipping and commercial centre.

In the early 1860s small finds were made at Peak Downs in 1861, Calliope near Gladstone in 1863, and then Nanango and Eidsvold. The first major find was that by James Nash in 1867 on the Mary River, and immediately the rush was on. The town of Gympie quickly arose around the site with pubs, banks, houses, theatres and even a library being built almost immediately. This find was a boon for Queensland's sagging economy, as the colony had become virtually bankrupt the previous year.[10]

The gold fever continued northward and, in the late 1870s, various discoveries were made at the Cape River, the Gilbert River, Woolgar, Etheridge, Ravenswood and the Hodgkinson. Of these, the find at Ravenswood was the most significant. This was subsequently overshadowed by a nearby find, the area later to be known as Charters Towers. Gold was also found at the Palmer River near Cooktown, and south at Cania, Kroombit, Rosewood, Croydon and Mount Morgan. Of all these discoveries the largest yielding and the most enduring were those at Charters Towers and Mount Morgan. At these sites stable communities evolved and roads, railways and communication networks, as well as nearby ports, were quickly established to link the gold centres with Brisbane and other parts of Australia.

Although there was a ten-year lag between the finds at Charters Towers and Mount Morgan, both of these isolated centres exhibited a rapid development, where sport was to play an important role in their social life. Sport offered a welcome respite to the confinements experienced by the miners in particular, and an opportunity for them to display their physical prowess. Sport also served as a vehicle for the mining towns to demonstrate to the outside world their strength as well as their superiority. Competitions in all forms of sport provided opportunities for social interaction and served as the main avenues of entertainment for these isolated communities. Russel Ward, in *The Australian Legend*, claimed that on the gold fields there was an "obliteration of class barriers,"[11] and certainly the sports field afforded an opportunity for the workers to mingle with their bosses.

Gold was discovered in what was later called Charters Towers in December 1871, but the claim was not registered until late January 1872. The name originally given to the field was "Charters Tors": "Charters" for the first Gold Commissioner, and "Tors" for the tower like hills surrounding the site.[12] However, the "name was quickly bastardized"[13] and the town soon became known as Charters Towers. The influx of gold seekers was rapid, as by the end of the first year three thousand were digging in the area. They arrived overland by bullock teams from Townsville, with many walking the distance, some 135 kilometres, over very rugged, uninhabited terrain.[14]

Charters Towers became one of Australia's greatest gold producers and was rivalled in gold production only by Mount Morgan and much later, Kalgoorlie, in Western Australia. Although it was not until the

1880s that it achieved worldwide recognition, the settlement was declared a town in 1877 when its population reached ten thousand. In 1909, the city of Charters Towers was proclaimed, the population at that time reaching thirty thousand. It had, in this short period, become Queensland's second largest city. The boom years lasted until 1916, and today, it is a quiet inland town with a population of approximately 8,500.

In its heyday, Charters Towers was simply referred to as "The World."[15] The residents claimed that their town was "superior in wealth, equal in commerce, culture and refinement to any European city of the same population."[16] North Queenslanders would say that: "If you haven't been to Charters Towers you haven't been anywhere.:[17]

By the 1880s "Charters Towers was a vigorous self–confident community, a model for lesser centres...With several schools instructing about 2,500 children, eight churches, three newspapers, two iron foundries, a hospital, fire brigade, jockey club and gasworks, it was a thriving city, never more lively than on Saturday evenings. Then Gill and Mosman Streets were crammed with so many people that the roads were closed to wheeled traffic."[18]

As on all goldfields, drinking was a favourite pastime. The first pub was opened on 12 March 1872, Joe Woodbum's "Reefer's Arms". It preceded, by almost three months, the first issue of a newspaper, the *Charters Towers Miner*, on 2 June 1872.[19] In its boom years, Charters Towers boasted of seventy – there are claims of ninety – hotels, and the Excelsior Hotel alone employed some thirty barmaids. The finest hotel was considered to be the Collins "Exchange Hotel".

> There was true democracy at Collins', and wealthy men, managing directors of big mining companies, sat at the same long tables as the truckers in their mines, lawyers, bankers, doctors, woodcutters, engine drivers and all classes talked freely of the dip in the reef, or the likelihood of a shaft "bottoming" or "going through a blank".[20]

The hotels at the time were far more than places to drink. They were the social centres of the community and the sites for various sports events. Sports such as cock–fighting, boxing and later "two–up" were popular "pub sports", but also other activities such as foot racing, wrestling, quoit competitions, billiard matches and even horse–racing were organised in and around the hotels.

Raper, the owner of the "Diamantina Hotel", was one of the more entrepreneurial hotel owners, laying a racing track beside his hotel as well as making his ground suitable for all kinds of sport.[21] He organised regular Thursday afternoon sports which commenced at three o'clock.

He offered monetary prizes as well as material prizes such as "a silk racing suit valued at £3 3s, a first–class lady's bridle etc."[22] In order to further entice his customers he offered music and dancing for the evening. Billiard tables were one of the drawcards used by various hotels to attract patrons, and were always highlighted in their advertisements. Tables, such as "Alcock's Duke of Edinburgh Table", announced in the *Charters Towers Times*, were imported at considerable expense from England. By the 1870s billiard challenge matches were regularly advertised in the newspapers[23] such as on 14 July 1877 in the *Northern Miner*.

The sport that the publicans were most involved with was horse–racing. Most local race meetings would have one event called the "Publican's Purse", and of course an essential component of all race meetings was the publican's booths, at which they could sell their products. Occasionally the publicans were involved in the organisation of racing in the city. Thomas Coyle, the owner of the "Excelsior Hotel" in the 1860s, and a keen sporting man, served on the Turf Club Committee.[24]

Gambling

The general environment and lifestyle of goldmining towns were conducive to the promulgation of gambling activities. Wagers were placed on virtually anything and everything, and bookies appeared at rugby games, athletic contests, goat derbies, "dog fights, cock–fights, man–fights and women–fights (the latter did not abide by Queensberry rules!)."[25] The extent of gambling at the Towers was evident from the numerous sweeps that were advertised throughout the year in the newspaper. Leyshon and Francis were the most prominent sweep–organisers, their motto being "Fair & Square". On one five shilling sweep, there were prizes totalling one thousand pounds. It was the Christmas Gift Handicap of 1890 at the Towers.[26]

Sweeps were held not only for local races but also for those in other parts of Australia and as far away as England. The Melbourne Cup created the greatest interest, with five different sweeps being organised, for example, in 1889.[27] The 1890 sweep by the Feroch Fortior Company was for £10,000.

By the mid–1890s the weekly cash sweeps and the magnitude of the monies involved became a community concern. Gambling at the Towers was even reported in the Sydney press: "a disease...and men, women, and children idolatrously worshipped the God of Luck."[28] In an attempt to curb the evils of gambling that appeared to be sweeping the community, fines were levied on the sweeps' promoters. But it was to no avail.

All sports competitions, but particularly horse–racing, provided the main incentive for betting. Even on Sundays, bookmakers would be around the hotels calling out their odds, which caused religious citizens to complain that betting men "should not be allowed to desecrate the Sabbath."[29] However, such protestations were in vain, as betting was part of the daily life of the gold mining town.

The most popular of the illegal gambling activities was "two–up". "Two–up" games were held at such isolated venues as "behind the mullock heaps – round the hills or down in some isolated shack" and "ever keeping watch was cocky."[30]

Blood Sports

Although officially cock–fighting was illegal, as it was in all parts of Australia, the sport flourished, particularly in the 1870s. One popular site for a "main" was behind Towers Hill; and the results would be avidly discussed by the men at the Collins Hotel[31] and other pubs. That birds were bred especially for cock fights was exposed in a court case when a neighbour was accused of killing the complainant's "game cock of rare breed valued at £4 10s."[32]

Cock–fighting was only one of the several "blood sports" which were popular among the mining community. Rat killing, or "ratting", was another all–time favourite indulgence that had been exported from the mother country to the new colony. However, in Charters Towers the sport of ratting, which normally utilised dogs, was performed in a unique manner.

> Occasionally Mr J.H. Walker entertains his friends with an exhibition of rat–killing. He has a snake in his possession about eight feet in length which manipulates rats and mice in an amazingly quick manner. The snake doesn't mind numbers. The more the merrier, and he negotiates each faster than an old pioneer can get outside long–sleevers. Here's a chance for St Leon.[33]

Another form of blood–sport was dog–fighting, and gambling was always involved in these contests. As such activities were not condoned by the community, very little official acknowledgment was made of them. Only occasionally would it be noted in the *Charters Towers*

Times, in the 16 June 1890 edition, that "a couple of hundred" congregated to watch a dog–fight on a Saturday evening.

Although gambling of all types was rampant and widely practised both legally and illegally, it was against the law to erect a house specifically for gambling purposes. Police, for example, charged a Chinese man, Ah Poo, as keeper of a gambling den, and arrested fourteen other Chinese in a raid at Queenton. Whether there was a racial bias in the arrest was not acknowledged, however, statements were made in the press that the Chinese were "childlike and bland" and that Europeans "may countenance gambling but they do not make a livelihood by such means."[34]

Sports in Charters Towers

As no copies of the early newspapers exist, there has been difficulty in ascertaining the precise dates of the first sports and sports events in Charters Towers. Various secondary sources, giving no reference, have indicated that foot racing and boxing began in 1874, and cock–fighting and dog–fighting appeared in the 1870s.[35] From later references to the "Annual" Towers Races it has been possible to ascertain that organised horse–racing began in 1874. However, the 1905 *Pugh's Almanac* gives 1877 as the first date for the Towers Jockey Club.

In the 3 February 1877 issue of the *Northern Miner*, the first available newspaper issue, mention is made of an adjourned meeting of the Charters Towers Jockey Club. The discussion had centred around the site of the course, which was to be "known as Hurley's course."

In this overview of sports and their significance in Charters Towers, the various sports will be dealt with in turn.

Horse–racing

The first organised sport in the Towers was horse–racing, and over the years it retained its high profile and popular appeal. If one is to judge by column space devoted to sport in the newspapers, the conclusion would have to be that it was 'the' major sport in this mining town.

In 1892, there were three or more full pages devoted solely to "The Turf" in each issue of the *Northern Miner*. The coverage extended not only to a detailed analysis of each race at the recent, or forthcoming meetings, but also included training observations, weights, notices of sweeps and bookmakers' odds, as well as a special section called "Turf Gossip". Races in nearby towns, in other parts of the state as well as in Sydney and Melbourne also received detailed coverage. The Caulfield and Melbourne Cup races were discussed in detail in the papers for weeks.

Although the Towers Jockey Club was the most influential and most active club, other clubs such as the Towers' Queen's Birthday Club and the Towers Hibernian Racing Club were formed. Moreover, organisations such as the Miner's Association, and Friendly Societies, conducted their own races. In its boom years, the Towers races attracted horses from the south and the prize monies offered in the Towers Jockey Club and Millchester Handicap, £500 and £400, respectively, were "the highest in Queensland."[36] In the 1897 *Handbook for the Colonies and India* it was claimed that the "town possesses one of the finest racecourses in Queensland and few communities are better patrons of sport than the Towers people." The popularity of the sport, as well as the gambling aspect, led to races being held at Christmas, though it was the hottest time of the year.

By 1877 the Annual Towers Races, which were inaugurated in 1874, were held over a two-day period, on July 18 and 19, which was a Wednesday and Thursday. There were eleven races in all, with the highest purse being 200 sovereigns for the Towers' Handicap. The success of the meeting was detailed in the Saturday paper. It was also noted that although there had been "a fair attendance...there was no one drunk and no fighting."[37] Any unruly action would have been thwarted by the police who were well prepared to handle the "hawks" and "rascaldom" that travelled around attending colonial race meetings.

Although of a less serious nature, another disruptive influence, dogs, was dealt with severely. In order to solve the canine problem, the Towers Jockey Club decided to post signs that poison had been laid on the course for the dogs. However, "the ignorant quadrupeds failed to interpret the posters. Result: speedy despatch of their souls to another world. A repetition will occur tomorrow should the dunces favour the races with their presence. That poison is fatal to dogs who cannot read."[38]

Throughout the 1870s and 1880s there were continuous accusations of shady deals, cheating, devious behaviour, and so on, by committee members. Horse owners, jockeys and newspaper writers repeatedly criticised the various fraudulent actions and argued for improvement and reform in the organisation and administration of the sport of racing. Expose seemed to follow expose, charge followed charge. However, it was not until 1890, following the adoption of the North Queensland Racing Association rules and regulations, that some order and respectability were established within the racing fraternity of the north.

When the sale of booths for the Annual Towers Races in 1877 brought in less money than the previous year, the editorial in the 19 December 1877 *Northern Miner* blamed the committee, stating that "the members of the Committee do not stand high in public estimation...the management is not in good hands, and the sooner there is a change the better for the respectability and honesty of racing in Charters Towers." Over a decade later similar complaints were still being laid. When it came to the 1889 election of the Towers Jockey Club executive, past members were not highly recommended by the paper, as many "were anything but creditable."[39] Even jockeys joined in the criticism. One addressed the stewards after the running of a race and stated bluntly: "You are a lot of bush–whackers. Decent jockeys have no business up here, you blooming bush–whacking lot."[40]

In fairness to the Charters Towers' racing fraternity, their shady and dubious dealings were not unique. As early as 1877 the general opinion of race committees throughout Queensland was that the majority of the committee members were "scoundrels...black leg gamblers, seedy horsey men and gambling publicans."[41] A decade later, when the need came to elect a new executive for the North Queensland Association, the *Charters Towers Times* on 17 November 1888 argued that it "should comprise of men of the highest integrity in addition to a knowledge qualification."

Other complaints were addressed to the bookmakers for not paying up, and then there were problems associated with handicapping. Moves were even made in November 1888 to remove the handicapper, and the *Charters Towers Times* kept up a continuous campaign for the club to have a paid handicapper. It was argued that an amateur could be more susceptible to bribes, while a paid person would be more professional in his decisions. In addition, it was held that such a move would aid in the standardisation of racing in the north. However, the North Queensland Racing Association rejected such a proposal. This raised the ire of the *Times* writer, who called the decision "humbug" and parochial, as "Townsville is the lock, stock and barrel of the Executive." It was further argued that Charters Towers should proceed on its own, as local handicapping was "so disgusting."[42] The state of affairs was considered to be in such a bad way that a member of the public took matters into his own hands and threw a bucket of water over the handicapper in Gill Street.[43]

During the early years of organised horse–racing in the north, Brisbane horses invariably would win the main races including, for example, in the Towers, the Town Plate. By 1889, however, the Towers Jockey Club was proud to announce that the calibre of local horses had improved so that "the North can hold its own."[44] In spite of this claim, the depth of racing talent in the north was open to question when one horse could win three races in one day.[45]

By 1890 racing in the north was an extensive industry, with twenty-two approved meetings. An organisational pattern was evident, for horses could be taken on a circuit from one town to the next from March through November.

As the racing industry expanded it became increasingly obvious that uniform rules and regulations had to be enforced. Steps had to be taken "to prevent a continuance of the evils which have so long prevailed and whereby the public have so long been victimised."[46] Measures, long overdue, were undertaken in early 1890.

At the April meeting of the Towers Jockey Club it was approved, as previously mentioned, that all race meetings were to be run under North Queensland Racing Association (NQRA) rules, that all race meetings were to be registered with the NQRA, that all horses were to be registered with the NQRA and, if unregistered horses were run, then they would be disqualified unless the NQRA saw "just and sufficient reason to remove such disqualification."[47] It was hoped that the registering of clubs and horses would protect the public from shady, entrepreneurial practices.

The 1890 Annual Towers Jockey Club Races were held under the new rules and were highly successful. Over three thousand were in attendance.[48] The reverie following this successful meeting was unfortunately shortlived and was interrupted by another scandal. Accusations were made after the suspicious running of a favourite. This led the editor of the *Charters Towers Times* to write a scathing editorial published on 15 July 1890.

> In our opinion there are four classes of men who own and run racehorses. The first is the rich man to whom a thousand, ten or even twenty thousand pounds is only a trifle, and who races his horses, for the pure love of the sport. Persons of this class are very few and far between. The next is the breeder who trains and starts out his youngsters to make the name of his stud famous throughout the length and breadth of the land. This class are honourable men almost without exception. The third class are the men who race to make money by it, and the fourth class are – fools, men who buy a horse with the intention of running him straight, and making a living out of him at the same time. The latter class are gradually dying out.

The editor argued for an end to the swindling. The paper's turf reporter "Carbine" agreed, but warned, on 28 January 1891 that those who were about to elect new members of the Towers Jockey Club should "bear in mind that they are not electing a church committee, but a committee of practical racing men." Perhaps a few church men would have been beneficial to the organisation. Horse-racing appeared to be "identical with roguery and swindling"[49] during these early years, virtually at all levels.

From the very beginning the miners were actively involved in horse-racing. At the Towers Jockey Club Annual Races there was a race for the "Miner's Purse". In the 1877 race, the purse was for 25 sovereigns, and was open "for all horses the bona fide property of miners 3 months, residents of Charters Towers or Ravenswood gold field for a like period of time."[50]

Beginning in 1887 the Miners' Association conducted their own race meetings. They would be held on Miners' Demonstration Day, which was a public holiday, and all the stores were closed. The announcement for their second annual meeting had the accompanying slogan: "United we stand, divided we fall."[51] For their meetings the Miners' Association rented the Towers Jockey Club race course for £10. Such races were beneficial to the Miners' Union, as a percentage of the amount taken by the totalisator would go into union funds.

Various other race meetings were organised by associations, such as the Friendly Societies and the Hibernian Society, the latter meetings being held, appropriately, on St Patrick's Day. In order to add to the festivities of race meetings there were often times parades and bands. For example, in 1891 the St Patrick's Day Race Meeting started at nine o'clock, with the Defence Force Band leading a procession of members of the Hibernian Society. Shops closed at eleven o'clock so that all could get to the first race at twelve o'clock.[52] Over two thousand attended these races.

In addition to the officially organised horse-racing meetings by the Jockey Club, and other associations, challenge races were extremely popular over the years. The newspapers would carry announcements before and after such events, and the odds and/or stakes would be announced: "Tomorrow morning a race meeting will come off between the horses Deception and Professor for £20 aside. The event will be run on the racecourse at 9 a.m."[53]

Trotting, although not as popular as horse-racing, was occasionally organised, as was seen by the announcement in the *Charters Towers Times* of 13 August 1888: "A trotting match between Mr Hutton's Bones and Mr Warner's Maid of the Vale for £20 aside has been arranged to come off on the 25th August, distance two miles. Bones concedes 500 yds."

Cricket

As the majority of those who flocked to the Charters Towers goldfields were of British descent, it was understandable that traditional British sports would soon be contested. Cricket was probably the first participant sport to be organised, as was the case in many other towns throughout Australia. Although foot racing, boxing, cock–fighting and of course, horse–racing were other early sports that were played, cricket was "free from all taint of betting," while still being "a fine manly game calculated to develop the body."[54]

By 1877, not only was there a cricket team in existence, but also a specific area had been set aside for that sport and matches had already been held against other towns. However, the Towers Club appeared to be sub–standard and "to be in a frightful state of coma [and] we would recommend the secretary to try the electro–galvanite battery."[55] In the hope of reviving the Towers team, a match against Queenton, in Queenton, was scheduled for Thursday 14 June 1877. The scheduling of the match for June indicated that the sport was being played as both a winter and summer sport.

The disorganised state of the Towers Club was reflected in the lack of planning and preparation for this match. The club met only one week prior to the game, at which time they elected a captain, Mr Doherty. The captain was then asked to select a team and to hold a practice. At the same time, the secretary noted that he had telegraphed to Brisbane "for bats and two balls."[56] No mention was made of these items arriving on time, though it would be doubtful due to the lateness of the request. Regardless, the Towers players went to Queenton, arriving a few minutes after the match was scheduled to start, 10 a.m., and then, in their haste, "jumped out of the coach, forgetting all their cricketing implements, while the coachman, without a moment's grace hurried away."[57] It is not surprising that Towers was thoroughly beaten, scoring only 77 runs to Queenton's 182.

The next day further humiliation was accorded the Towers team by a public challenge: "Eleven of the Boys Cricket Club, C.T. will play fifteen of the C.T. Cricket Club Men. Apply to Sec. C.T. Boys Cricket Club."[58]

It appeared that the players had improved their standard of play by the end of the year. The editor of the *Northern Miner* on 5 December 1877 praised the team going to play against Townsville on Boxing Day as being "representative of the bone and muscle of Charters Towers and of its manly and sturdy independence." After such a build–up, the Towers team fortunately won handily.

In the late 1880s the cricket club seemed again to be experiencing the same problems as it did in the late 1870s. The editor of the *Charters Towers Times*, 11 June 1888, asked: "Is it [the Cricket Club] comatose or actually dead." Their lack of commitment was evident with their subsequent thrashing by Townsville. A writer, using the *nom-de-plume*, 'Wilson', summed up the state of affairs, a few months later, 12 January 1889: "The Charters Towers crickets arc not worthy of the finest of all England games. They don't practice, are indifferent to victory or defeat and generally speaking deserve no encouragement whatever at the hands of the public." Perhaps the cricket club was devoting too much of its time to organising such novelty events as a cricket match "in fancy costume", a match between "Muffs and Duffers", or annual concerts featuring violinists and dramatists.[59] It almost appeared as if the club were trying to attract a different "social" clientele, rather than simply good cricket players.

The Hughenden Cricket Club suffered from the same malaise of disorganisation and disinterest. Such was not, however, the situation in Townsville, as its team soundly defeated the Towers team in April 1889. The captain of the Towers observed that in Townsville "cricketers obtained more practice in a week than they on the Towers did in a month."[60]

In 1890, in an attempt to raise interest and support for the Towers Cricket Club, a game between "Britishers" and "Australians" was organised. All who wished to see the sport "played in its perfection"[61] were invited to the Athletic Reserve on Richmond Hill on Sunday 11 June 1890. Enthusiasm for the match was built up during the week preceding the game by publishing in extensive detail, the "pedigrees" of the team members. A few examples follow.

> Britishers: J. Clancy (captain) wicket-keeper. An old veteran at the game, but owing to galloping consumption, and the advice of his physicians (Clifton and Co.) he has not been seen in the cricket field for some time. He intends, however, to don the pads and show Blackham that he has a worthy rival. E. Swords (longstop), good old professional, formerly coached for a University, six miles south of Ireland. H.S. Stockham (bowler). This year's colt for the Union C.C., a demon bowler when on the wicket. J. Fisher (short-leg). Formerly played for Bedfordshire Club and Ground, but his services were dispensed with, as the Club were not sufficiently wealth enough to keep him supplied with bats. J. Willey (point) has played for his county (Somerset); splendid trundler and daisy cutter and in every respect a cricketer. M. Hannon (slip), as good with the bat and ball as with the knife and fork, and promises the natives a treat if he once gets set.[62]

Some 250 spectators attended this match, at which the "Australian" team introduced an innovation into the game, whereby all the players retired at the end of each over "for a long sleever," that is, a beer. After the match the conviviality of the day continued at the Picnic Hotel, where the evening ended "with a short bible class and knee drills."[63] For the townspeople the game had been an excuse for a good social afternoon and evening.

Although the Towers Cricket Club was the oldest and most established club, other clubs, sometimes catering to a different clientele, were soon formed. For example, the Union Cricket Club was formed in March 1889. Fred Pfeiffer, a company director in Charters Towers, became its Patron, a Dr Browne was elected as its President and a banker, Mr A.L. Gardiner, called the meeting.[64] These individuals, obviously from the upper or wealthy classes, were part of the organisational committee of a club whose membership appeared actually to be drawn from the miners themselves.

In 1890 a match between the Quills and the Trades was played, with Joe Carroll, manager of the Brilliant and St George Mines, captain of the Trades. One writer described the game as "understandably the most interesting and exciting game ever witnessed on the Towers [and] many unknowns were brought out as full blown cricketers."[65] Over three hundred spectators, including a fair number of ladies, attended the game.

It was the agitation for a half holiday by the shop assistants in the mid-1890s that accelerated the popularisation of the game. This half-holiday permitted workers to play the game on a day other than Sunday, with the first Thursday half-holiday being celebrated by a cricket match between teams representing Mosman and Gill Streets.[66] It was such a success that it was decided to form a Mercantile Club, with players coming from the ranks of shop employees. Also, at the mine Rising Star, a club was organised called the Queenton Rising Star Club, and its players were made up of some of the mining fraternity. Teams were subsequently formed by the railway men and the printers' union. At the same time, informal games were played between the Muffs and the Aldermen.[67]

With the formation of these various clubs a need for an overall coordinating and controlling body was evident. In September 1891, a meeting of the representatives of six clubs met at the Collins' Exchange Hotel to form the Charters Towers Cricket Association. The executive of this association was chosen, with Mr A.H. Pritchard, a banker, as President, and Mr T. Millican, a company director and Mr R. Craven, also a company director of the King of the Brilliant Mine, as two of the vice-presidents. Although the game had spread and was being actively competed in by the working classes, leadership was still in the hands of the elite.

The ground used by the cricketers was the Athletic Reserve, which was used by the footballers as well. A concrete wicket was built in early 1892. By the early 1890s it appeared that cricket games, which were originally played year round, were being held in the summer months only, and this was probably a consequence of the rise of rugby union as *the* sport of the winter months. The 1892 cricket schedule was printed in the *North Queensland Registrar*, 12 October, and its extensiveness was indicative of the quantitative spread of the game.

Cricket in Charters Towers, however, never achieved the prominence and status that the sport of rugby union enjoyed. The English, gentlemanly game was perhaps too tame, too slow and not physically demanding enough for the tough, rugged mining community. Only a few from Charters Towers were ever selected for representative teams, and then only for North Queensland teams.

Football

Football, and more specifically rugby union football, was the sport in which Charters Towers etched its name into Queensland and Australian sport and record books. Outstanding state and national players emerged from this northern goldmining town, including "Rusty" Richards, who is still today "rated among the greatest loose forwards Rugby has seen."[68] For a twenty–year period, 1890 to 1910, Charters Towers was considered a rugby stronghold in Queensland. The prowess exhibited on the football field even brought claims that Charters Towers should be "proclaimed the capital of the new colony."[69]

The exact beginning of football in Charters Towers has not been possible to ascertain. The most authoritative source on sport in Charters Towers, Robert Davies (Merlin) has stated unequivocally in *Sporting Flashbacks* that rugby union "was introduced in the Towers with the arrival of the celebrated English footballer, Henry Speakman." However, Speakman did not arrive until 1892 and by that time the game was already well established, with club and intertown matches occurring on a regular basis. Also, *Pugh's Almanac* of 1905 does not list any football clubs prior to 1894, however there definitely were clubs in existence from at least 1892. It would appear that a form of football was played in the Towers area from 1885 onwards.

In the early years, there is difficulty ascertaining which code of football was being reported; association football (soccer), rugby union or even Australian Rules. It was not until 1890 that the two codes were clearly differentiated in the press. There even appeared to be confusion on the field of play. In May 1888 teams from Millchester and Ravenswood State Schools played a match in which it was apparent that the two teams were accustomed to playing two different sets of rules, and it was suggested that in the future "it would be well to come to an understanding beforehand as to what rules will be observed."[70] Millchester won the match with "6 goals and 6 behinds", from which it is inferred the game was Australian Rules.

Other football matches reported in the local press in 1888 were between Queenton and Towers Clubs, played on Plant's Ridge on May 26 and on June 2, and between the Cadets and Boys' State School on Richmond Hill. The playing field was very inadequate, in fact, it was considered "a disgrace to a goldfield like Charters Towers."[71] Some of the matches were played away from the town, as it was not until 1890 that a proper ground was laid out and surveyed by Mr Sellheim, an avid football player himself.[72]

Although rugby union football was gaining ascendancy in the area, association football did not completely die out. Regular competitive soccer matches in 1889 and 1890 were played between the Charters Rovers and Queenton Rangers teams. The games were played on a Saturday afternoon and drew a large number of spectators. The game was also a popular pastime for Towers soldiers when they attended a military camp. In 1891, the Queenton team played against Townsville, and many of the spectators laughed and applauded "the head play and the various clever tricks of hooking and twisting the ball peculiar to the Association game."[73] By 1892 the Queenton club had over thirty players and competed for the Drummond Trophy.[74]

By the beginning of the 1890 season the Charters Towers Rugby Football Club was sufficiently established to form a "second" team. Two teams were selected to play a scratch match on Saturday May 3 on the Athletic Reserve. On the basis of their performance in this trial, a team was selected to play against Townsville. In preparation for this upcoming intertown match a scratch match "against all comers"[75] was called for, which was in sharp contrast to the disorganised state of the town's cricket team, which only selected its players a week prior to such games.

The Charters Towers versus Townsville match, the first for 1890, was played in Townsville on Saturday May 29. The enthusiastic reception accorded the team attested to the status of the game in both locales.

On arriving at Townsville the visitors were met by several of the local players, and were escorted to a row of hansoms all drawn up in a line. At the sound of "all aboard" the procession started down Flinders Street. Cheers for the visitors were given on all sides, and their large hats (3 feet wide) with the colours flying were much admired. All the team with their supporters put up at Buchanan's Imperial Hotel where they were well treated by the landlord.

In the evening the visitors spent an hour at the Rink, at the invitation of Mr Byrne, and then went to a smoke concert at Long's Hotel. Mr J.M. Parkes made a most efficient chairman and added considerably to the evening's amusement. At 11.30 the company joined hands in Auld Lang Syne and so concluded a most enjoyable evening.[76]

A crowd of approximately fifteen hundred witnessed the game, which was won by the Towers men two points to nil.

The return match was played on Saturday July 5 on the Athletic Reserve on Richmond Hill. Although this was the fourth encounter between the two towns it was the first such to be played in Charters Towers. The Towers men again proved their superiority by winning four points to nil. They thus won the Dundee Whiskey Trophy, which had been presented by Samuel Allen and Sons Ltd. for intertown rugby union.[77]

Although the Townsville–Charters Towers competition was firmly established by 1890, intertown competition was only in its formative stages. When the Central Queensland Rugby Football Club issued its invitation to Charters Towers to come to Rockhampton it offered to pay "railage and steam fare."[78] It was obvious that the Central Queensland enthusiasts did not know the calibre of play in the Towers, for they suggested including Townsville men to strengthen the Towers team.

The standard of play in the Towers was maintained by various matches arranged during the season. Indeed, in mid–season the rugby reporter for the *Times* stated on 16 June: "I am pleased to see the play improves each Saturday." However, he felt that the game was "not fast enough yet owing the heavy scrums indulged in by the forwards." Obviously the players had not completely heeded the advice given earlier in the season, for the writer went on to say that they hung on to the ball too long, and should pass more and back up.[79]

One well–contested match was between teams selected from the Tradesmen and Inkslingers, which resulted in a tie. The competitive aggressive nature of the play was evident as two of the Tradesmen were "stripped of their guernseys and one player lost his knicks."[80]

The Charters Towers Rugby Football Club also organised an Athletic Carnival on Thursday October 9 at the Show Grounds. The program included: 120 yards handicap (open); 120 yards handicap (members only); 440 yards handicap; one mile handicap; place kick and drop kick. A variety evening, complete with opera arias, clog dancing and Christy

Minstrels was also organised at the School of Arts.[81] Such activities were symptomatic of sporting clubs of the era, which catered to the diverse, as well as specialised interests, of its clientele.

Advertisers using athletes and sports to help market and sell their product is a common feature today, however, such an association was only in its embryonic stage in the 1890s. Beer companies were among the first to recognise the value of such an association.

> Footballers, cricketers, and other athletes, who make themselves hot and exhausted in the field adopt various means of quenching their thirst at intervals, but many of the drinks they take only tend to increase it. They will find nothing so effective in giving them an increase of vigor and a renewal of wind as West End Beer – ADVT.[82]

The amber fluid was evidently appreciated by the footballers, and in their boom years it was claimed that the Towers boys used to train on beer. They were "as full as frogs on Saturday night and then played the game of their lives on Sunday."[83] On their away trips they carried their own "Towers Brew" with them, refrigerating the casks with onion skins.

The 1891 season saw the game of rugby football become more firmly established in Charters Towers, with crowds of over four hundred attending intertown matches. The organisation of the sport improved with the formation of two separate clubs, Rangers and Imperials, at the start of the season. At the inaugural meeting of the Towers footballers two suggestions were made to raise the level of play and to ensure a successful season. One was to publish a pamphlet titled "Hints to football players", and the other was to arrange exercise sessions on Tuesday, Wednesday and Friday nights.[84] An extra inducement for the players was the announcement by Messrs Clifton and Co. of the Towers Brewery to award "silver medals to each, and a gold one for the captain of the most successful team whether in Townsville or Charters Towers during the present season."[85]

The Charters Towers team continued its dominance of the intertown competition with Townsville. Its superiority was such that not only did it win all of its games, but the Townsville team did not even manage to score any points. Their lack of success was explained in a letter stating that it was "a moral impossibility to get a team to visit Charters Towers as the Townsville men will not play on the Charters Towers ground under any consideration."[86] Although during the previous season there were indications that the ground was not of the highest standard as the team winning the toss could choose to play up or down hill, the ground had in the interim been levelled and thus had improved considerably. In future years complaints of the hardness of the Towers ground were also reported, but usually these were after a visiting team had lost.

The strength of the Towers team was augmented by the arrival of Mr Skeen from Mount Morgan. Skeen had captained the Mount Morgan Rovers to being the champion club in the central Queensland district.[87] Skeen was the first of several football players to move to Charters Towers, of whom Harry Speakman, arriving in 1892, was the most well known. This led to resentment and accusations of professionalism from other towns. The following open letter from Rockhampton stated the issue bluntly:

> For the purpose of winning efforts are made to get players of skill from other towns, and thus clubs which did not descend to such tactics are placed at a disadvantage. One had only to note the many famous players who have migrated to Charters Towers during the past twelve months to see if professionalism does not exist, these appearances are exceedingly deceptive.[88]

Whatever the motives for moving to Charters Towers were, it was for certain that the calibre of play was high and the support in the town was excellent. Over one thousand attended the first interclub match of the 1892 season between the Wanderers and the Rangers. Money was raised for the club by charging five shillings for ground memberships, ladies being admitted free. Some prominent citizens donated the "Kirkbride" trophy (Mr R. Kirkbride was Mayor of the City and the President of the rugby club) and a ten guinea prize for the winning team in the interclub competition.[89] Such, then, was the status of rugby football in 1892, when Harry Speakman, supposedly the founder of Charters Towers football, arrived.

Harry Speakman was on the 1888 British Rugby Tour of Australia and obviously enjoyed his playing experience in the colonies as he migrated to Australia after the tour. He contributed immensely to Queensland's rugby, captaining the state side in 1889, 1890 and 1891. Speakman was revered by his fellow players such as Thomas Welsby, who referred to him as "my hero...He was a real daisy! I can still hear him on the football field calling, 'Coom, lads, coom!'"[90]

The arrival of Harry Speakman in Charters Towers in February 1892 was, surprisingly, not greeted with any fanfare, with the *Northern Mining Register* simply stating on February 3 that: "Mr Speakman, a well-known football player, both in New Zealand and Brisbane, has taken up residence in Charters Towers, and should be a valuable addition to the ranks of footballers here." However, Bickley, who wrote the *Highlights of One Hundred Years of Rugby in Queensland*, called

Speakman "The Father of Football at the Towers," and his arrival has been acknowledged as heralding the start of the "golden age" of Towers rugby. He remained in the city until 1900 and, during his residence, "he imparted a lot of his genius to local players and raised the game to a high standard."[91]

Speakman's playing and coaching were tested shortly after his arrival by Brisbane Past Grammars, the strongest Brisbane team. Some of the visitors who played in this first Charters Towers–Brisbane series were: E. Lord, G. Pratten, H. Scale, G. Hensler, F. Baynes, E. Scott, F. O'Rourke and H. Luya, while the locals relied on Speakman, the old Maori A.S. Anderson, W. Tregear and C. Mellamby.[92]

The contrast between the city players and the mining town men was apparent as the men lined up for their match: "The visitors played in Cambridge blue jerseys and Oxford blue knickers and stockings, and presented a good tan, wiry and neat appearance. The Charters Towers men were in all white and looked much heavier and stronger than their opponents."[93]

Although the Towers men appeared the stronger, the Brisbane team dominated the play for the first three quarters of the game. Then the Towers men began to stage a brilliant comeback, and the wild cheering of the crowd was heard over a mile away at the race course. The character of the Towers men, who won by a score of 14 to 9, was lauded.[94]

The success of this initial encounter ensured a good crowd for the second game. Over three thousand spectators[95] came to cheer their local men to another victory, this time the score being 5 to 0. The Brisbane team had fielded nine players on the state team that had defeated NSW twice in Sydney, and hence these unexpected victories gave a considerable boost to the confidence of the local team. It was, also, a fine inauguration for Speakman.

During the eight years (1892–1900) that Speakman resided in the Towers, the record for their representative games was 14 victories, 11 losses and 3 draws. This certainly could not be claimed as an overly imposing record.

In the decade after Speakman's departure (1900–1910) the results were considerably different. Out of 38 representative games played, there were 34 victories, 3 losses, and 1 draw, a much more impressive record.

These figures are not intended to denigrate Harry Speakman's contribution, but rather to emphasise that he was but one of the many factors that were instrumental in the rise of Towers football. Speakman's presence at the Towers doubtless gave the team and the area a certain degree of status in rugby circles. His expertise and experience in the game would have provided invaluable assistance to the local men, who had the drive, determination and enthusiasm for the playing of the game.

The Towers players were essentially all miners, or came from mining backgrounds. The state of their playing field exemplified their rugged character. The ground has been described as being "the world's worst. A reef outcropped on the field, protruding in places like chisel edges."[96]

Although the players were from the working class, support for the game came from all classes. For example, in 1892 the Mayor, Mr R. Kirkbride, was also the President of the Rugby Club. In 1900, the President was John Marsland, a leading lawyer in the city. Also, the owners and directors of the mines were advocates of the game, and they were determined that the best team would always be able to represent their city. Thus, the owners and managers gave representative players "leave" to play the game. The miners were not paid while they were playing, or when they represented their city, however they received the necessary time−off and their jobs remained secure.[97]

At the turn of the century a major problem arose which threatened the very existence of the game at the Towers. Although in the early 1890s games had been played on Saturday afternoons, they were later switched to Sundays as this was the miners' day off. Sunday sport became a controversial issue which divided the town. An injunction was passed by the municipal council banning the playing of sport on Sundays. John Marsland, the President of the rugby club, came up with an ingenious method of thwarting the injunction.

> He displayed rare comprehension of possibilities by lodging an application on a Friday before the date for an important match for a gold mining lease on the Athletic Reserve. So, until the application was heard by the Warden's Court, which would take 30 days, he was virtually the owner of the ground.
>
> Thus, to all intents and purposes, the Athletic Reserve was, temporarily at least, private property, and the court's jurisdiction to prevent Sunday play was circumvented.[98]

Thus, rugby union in Charters Towers was saved.

The decline of interest in association football (soccer) is somewhat of an enigma, as association football is generally thought of as the working man's game and it is clear that rugby union football became the game of the working class at Charters Towers. It is felt by the authors that the main reason appears to be that the miners were simply more attracted by the rough and tumble nature of the rugby game. Additionally, the success of the rugby team gave the city status, not only locally but also regionally and nationally. Players, followers and townspeople all gloried in the prowess of the rugby team. For the players, the game brought them public idolation, social acceptance, and possibly social mobility, as well as providing them with opportunities to prove their physical skill and prowess.

Boxing

The pugnacious nature of many of the miners and the physical nature of their work occasioned a natural admiration of the individual who could survive in the ring through the ability of his fists. Boxing was both a legal and illegal sport and it drew supporters from all walks of life.

The first recorded boxing match was in 1874 when a local, Sam Shepherd, defeated Englishman William Perry in the third round with a punch that "stove in three of Perry's ribs." Sam, nicknamed "Sam the Shepherd," became a local hero, and the proprietor of the All National Hotel offered to back Shepherd for £50 against any man in the North. There were no takers of this challenge, however, quite accidentally, a fight came about over an issue related to fair play. A match between Sam and Ted Easton, who had recently arrived on the goldfields from Bendigo, was hastily organised in front of the Royal Hotel. After four rounds, the police interrupted the fight, which then had to be moved to the bush flat at the end of Mosman Street. After another ten rounds the Victorian emerged victorious. The two policemen who had initially stopped the fight actually assisted in keeping "a good ring, and declared for fair play."[99]

One of the most notable fights that old Towersites reminisced about was the one in early 1875 between Ted Easton and William Brown, a Cornishman and veteran of over one hundred fights. A properly staked and roped ring was set up and seconds, umpires, referees, timekeepers and bottleholders were all organised. By the third round, Brown's face was so bunged up that his second cut open his cheek with a blunt knife and the cut bled freely. However, the veteran did not admit defeat until the fifty-second round. The fight lasted a total of two hours and five minutes, and was fought according to the London prize-ring rules.

A year later Brown and Easton met again, but this time it was "with the gloves." The fight was held at George Cooper's boxing booth on the race course. The result was the same as the previous year, although the fight was much shorter. Brown, however, was very well liked and his early death, at age 29 in 1880, was mourned by the sporting community. His funeral was one of the largest held up to that time in Charters Towers.[100]

One of the most famous boxers who toured around Australia and fought in mining, and other towns, was Frank "Paddy" Slavin. Slavin was taught by the incomparable Larry Foley, who was also the mentor of Peter Jackson and "Young Griffo". In 1884, Slavin arrived in the Towers and fought a "spectacular bout"[101] against Martin Power, defeating him in the fifth round. The following year, he overcame Burke. These two fights by Slavin were considered by boxing enthusiasts to be the finest ever seen in the Towers. Slavin went on to become heavyweight champion of Australia in 1889, and then went overseas and defeated several of the top boxers of the time.

Many of the fights that occurred in the late 1880s in the Towers were informal matches, which were the norm in most mining towns in those days. These were often arranged by word-of-mouth and held in such places as "the rising ground to the north-east of the town [and] Chuck's paddock."[102] Invariably they were interrupted by the police.

However, legal fights could be arranged and these were held at places such as Athenaeum Hall, the Pioneer Hall and the Prince of Wales Theatre. Such fights were advertised in the newspaper and the stakes would be announced, for example: on 13 November 1889, in the *Charters Towers Times:* "Boxing Contest: Jones versus West: for £25 a side, To A Finish, Saturday, November 30th."[103]

The itinerant glove men who toured around the countryside and made their living from their victories in the ring were more often than not engaged in fixes. Locals were not, however, impressed at being "taken", as was evident in the public announcement in the *Charters Towers Times* on 9 December 1889 against one Brown, who was told he would get the "reception he deserves" if he would "again appear in a public ring" at the Towers.

As such itinerant professionals became increasingly suspect, the way was opened for the development of amateur participation and clubs. The Amateur Boxing Association of Charters Towers was formed in 1888, based on the Pelican and other clubs in England, and run by "lovers of sport...men whose actions are above suspicion."[104]

One man who did a great deal to encourage the sport as it should be was "Professor" St Clair, champion of Queensland. He was considered without doubt "the most terrific fighter we have seen here and he excited the admiration of the audience by his display of science, coolness and hitting prowess."[105]

Another development at the Towers was an interest in learning the proper techniques and training in the manly art. Hence, Mr W.D.H. Walker opened an Athletic Club and Training School, where he taught boxing as well as club swinging and dumb bell exercising.[106]

The interest and enthusiasm for the sport in Charters Towers was readily apparent from the quantity of space allocated to it in the newspapers. Local fights were covered in detail, with round–by–round descriptions. Similar coverage was also given to any fights of relevance that were held in surrounding towns, as well as the rest of Australia and overseas.[107]

Wrestling

Wrestling attracted a considerable amount of interest, which was doubtless related to the value placed on strength and endurance by the locals and their country of origin in Great Britain. Wrestling events were included in the Sports Day programs as early as 1877. The most popular types were Cumberland and Westmoreland, collar and elbow (Irish) and Cornish, and obviously miner migrants from the particular areas of the British Isles would be keen supporters and practitioners of a particular style. In the 1870s the best wrestlers in the Towers were Jack Pernaul in the Cornish style, Tom Featherston, the Cumberland style and Jack Dempsey in the collar and elbow style. In 1892, Mr T. Davies offered "a handsome gold medal...value seven sovs"[108] for competition amongst Cornish wrestlers.

Athletics

Athletics was one of the first sports in which competitions were held. By 1874, two years after the establishment of the goldfield, Ted Honey was considered to be the fastest sprinter in the Towers, although he was challenged by a "black boy" who was "owned" by Mr Charters, the first Warden of the goldfields.[109] Although races were obviously held from 1872 or 1873 onwards, the first formal athletics meeting is generally maintained to have been held in 1876.[110] The site for this meeting was where the 'Just in Time' goldfield later operated, and all events were won by Tom Roberts. He apparently easily defeated the other 'peds', including Warden Charters' 'black boy'.

Foot races over various distances for stakes from £5 to £200 became a regular feature in the Towers. One of the first major foot races was that between Tom Roberts and a newcomer "Honest" George Cronk, in the late 1870s. About 1500 witnessed the race and £4000 changed hands when the favourite (Roberts) was beaten.[111]

In the 1880s, as in other parts of Australia, pedestrianism became one of the major sporting pastimes at Charters Towers. The Grand Federation Handicap, in October 1888, attracted seventy–two competitors, which required eighteen heats to be run as well as semi–finals and finals. The handicaps for the 'peds' ranged from four yards for W. Moore to twenty–five yards for W. Hearn, and the prize money was £100, which was "with the exception of Brisbane, the only one of such amount ever run for in this colony."[112] There were three Aborigines entered: C. Mitchell eight yards, E. Stewart nine yards and A. Wicker fourteen yards. Wicker, "the darkie coming like a steam engine [won this] greatest athletic event"[113] that had ever taken place in the Towers.

Footracing, or pedestrianism as it was called, served as a means of livelihood for many men. Considerable sums of money could be earned by those who were successful, as not only were there the official prize monies for the races, but also the winners could receive a portion of the sweeps. For example, the North Queensland Athletic Club (NQAC) Handicap in December 1888 had a £100 prize, but in addition Leyshon Brothers organised a £1,000 sweep, with £500 going to the winner. Hence the peds approached such races with considerable seriousness, training intensely to improve their chances. Prior to the NQAC Handicap the local daily noted on 21 December 1888 there were "peds training all over the place. Hillyard's track, Jones' grounds, Rainbow, Queenton, Mowbray Park, Milchester and elsewhere [and some were even] training at night or on a private track."

Pedestrianism incurred similar problems to the sport of horse–racing. There were frequent accusations that runners were not running fairly and that races were fixed. Newspapers often carried allegations such as the peds were "running stiff" or were "dead birds". The Grand Federation Handicap of 1888 was typical, with T. Madsen, the favourite for the race, being disqualified for life.[114]

"Stiff" running, and other controversial episodes, were reportedly the reasons for the collapse of the first controlling body for the Athletics Club, which was formed in 1882. One major achievement of this club was the selection, and subsequently the permanent reservation of, the Athletic Reserve on Richmond Hill, which was to figure prominently in Towers sport. It was not until late 1891 that a new controlling body for athletics, called the Charters Towers Athletic Association, was finally formed. The first President of the Association was Mr Millican, the Mayor. With the formation of this association the sport of pedestrianism was subjected to more scrutiny and definite attempts were made to stamp out "stiff" running.[115]

Professional foot racing continued to boom in the 1890s and, in 1895, the "Towers Hundred" race was inaugurated. This race, which was actually 130 yards in length, became one of the premier foot races in the colony, and attracted some of the top peds from other parts of the country.

Although pedestrianism attracted a considerable following in the town, particularly among the gambling fraternity, the sport was not confined to these specific, highly organised races at which only the best 'peds' competed. The less skilled, and the average person desirous of testing their skill, could compete at the various Sports Days that were organised during the year. Such Sports Days, as well as providing an essential avenue for competition, also provided for social interaction for community members. In 1877, for example, one of the major hotels in town, the "Live and Let Live", organised an end–of–the–year Sports Day, with wrestling (collar and elbow in Cumberland style), a quoit match, a sack race and various running and jumping contests.[116]

In 1890, Good Friday, a holiday for workers, provided the excuse for an extensive Sports Day, arranged by private entrepreneurs, for money prizes. There were horse races, foot races for boys, girls and old buffers, a quoit match, "tilting at ring" and "devil's ride to market".[117]

Various societies, such as the Oddfellows and Hibernian, as well as organisations such as the miners, butchers, bankers, infantry and so on, organised special gatherings for their members and/or workers on holidays or on other special occasions. Usually horse–racing served as the main attraction, however various athletic events filled out the program for the remainder of the day. Such gatherings also provided an opportunity for local athletes to show, and test, their talents.

As early as 1877 various athletic events were included in the Charters Towers St Patrick's Day Celebrations. At the Odd Fellow's Anniversary Meeting, held on the Queen's Birthday, after the specific athletic events were contested, the ball which followed ended at six o'clock the next morning.[118]

In 1881, the Charters Towers Anniversary Sports were held at the race course, with a grand procession of members of the International Order of Oddfellows and the miners' union being the curtain raiser. An extensive fifteen event athletics program was held.[119]

The Miners' Association in 1887 initiated the tradition of organising an annual sports day for its workers. The program was divided into two sections: horse–racing and athletics. Events were open to all contestants, with the exception of a "members' handicap, a race of 150 yards, which was only for members of at least three months' standing."[120] The various events contested in the 1888 Anniversary Meeting were: Boys' Race, Miners' Association Handicap, Old Buffers' Handicap, Members' Handicap, Bicycle Race Handicap, Wrestling (Cornish style), Wrestling (Cumberland style), Amateur Boxing (Queensberry Rules), heavy weights, Amateur Boxing (Queensberry Rules), light weights, Handicap Walking Race, Obstacle Race and Tug–of–War. Prior to the start of the program there was a procession of several hundreds of miners down the main street to the race course. For the third anniversary in 1889, the bicycle and boxing events were dropped but a handicap quoit contest was added.[121]

The Hibernian Societies' St Patrick's Day Celebrations were primarily devoted to horse races, and only three athletics events: a juvenile members' race, putting the heavy stone – Irish style, and putting the light stone – Irish style.[122] It appeared that athletics competitions on St Patrick's Day were organised by private entrepreneurs and were held at the same time as the horse races.[123]

Athletics became very popular among the banking fraternity, and they even organised their own races and sports days. At the Bankers' Sports held on the Athletic Ground in December 1890, the most important event was the Managers' Race, in which all the local bank managers competed, and the 1890 race was won by Mr Phillips, paying "his admirers a dividend on nine shillings."[124] Even the bankers were involved with gambling, sometimes backing themselves, as occurred in the Bankers' 440 yards Handicap. Also, Harry Cupples, a banker, was accused of running "stiff" in the 150 yards Bank Handicap.[125]

Included in the general category of athletics was "tug-of-war", which was a popular event in Sports Day programs. For the infantry, the tug-of-war was the feature event of their Sports Day, and a Challenge Shield was offered annually after 1886. In the early 1890s a "tug-of-war epidemic"[126] swept Charters Towers. Over three hundred spectators witnessed the tug-of-war contest between the boarders of Day Dawn Hotel and those of the Brilliant Hotel.

Bicycling

Bicycling and pedestrianism were closely aligned in the early years, and most cycling club carnivals included foot races. These foot races provided additional interest for spectators, and helped broaden the program. In 1888, the Charters Towers Invincible Bicycle Club organised a "Bicycle Athletic Carnival", which included such foot races.[127] Although the £10 Bicycle Races for one, five and ten miles were for the professional championships of North Queensland, the foot race, with a £100 prize, was obviously the drawcard.

The sport of bicycling continued to grow in popularity and, by the late 1890s, cycling had become "a popular exercise and hundreds of machines are used by residents of the district."[128] On Saturday afternoons road races from the Park Hotel to the Squash Shop and back drew many participants and big crowds.

The most outstanding cyclist to come from Charters Towers was Billy Beasley. Beasley's most important accomplishment was winning the Queensland Test Road Race of sixty miles from Charters Towers to

Liontown and return. The time for the sixty miles was three hours, three minutes.

Shooting, Hunting and Fishing

The gun was an essential implement for anyone living in a frontier society. Although most men owned a gun, the use of it for sporting purposes was mainly favoured by the middle and upper classes and military personnel.

The first competitions consisted of informal challenges, and these usually involved stakes of varying amounts. For example, the local paper announced that on July 14, a Sunday morning, a match was arranged "between Messrs Hutton, Ayton, Craven and Cavey...for a stake of £5 aside, seven birds each." Another shooting contest was for only one pound, but it was noted that there would "be no charge made for looking on. Refreshments not provided on this occasion."[129] It was surprising that the time chosen for these contests was Sunday mornings. On one occasion a scheduled rifle match for one pound failed to materialise, as one of the parties preferred "to attend divine services."[130]

Organised shooting competitions appear to have been initiated in 1881, which would make it the first sport to hold organised competitions in Charters Towers. At the seventh annual competition in 1888 for the Mills Trophy, fourteen prominent shooters competed at distances of 200, 400 and 600 yards, and Mr A. Millican was the winner with a total score of 87.[131]

By 1888 rifle shooting competitions were firmly established in the north, and the North Queensland Rifle Association was formed to oversee and organise regular competitions. The highlight of the competitive schedule in 1888 was the First Meeting on May 29 and 30 in Townsville, where for the first time the Queen's Prize was shot for in North Queensland. Only two events were open to "all-comers", with other events being restricted to members of the Defence Force of North Queensland, the Volunteers, Cadets, Police and Members of the Association.[132]

Interest in competitive shooting remained high, with regular shooting matches organised by the Rifle Club and the Charters Towers Defence Force. Initially, the Mills Trophy was the sole trophy, but by 1890 the West End Beer Trophy was also included. At all matches there were cash prizes.

After 1888 intertown challenge matches became a regular feature, with competitions against Townsville, Ravenswood, and Mackay. In 1891 Rockhampton was included. These matches consisted of teams of ten men a side, and were usually conducted on a home-and-away basis.

The most intense rivalry was with Townsville, and each year there would be several intertown matches. Charters Towers consistently defeated Townsville, and hence gained the reputation for being "phenomenal"[133] in shooting.

Such success obviously generated interest and enthusiasm in the town. As a consequence there was extensive coverage of the sport in the newspaper, with lengthy and detailed descriptions of all the matches. The calibre of the Charters Towers marksmen was acknowledged by an invitation to send a team to compete in Brisbane at the Queensland National Rifle Association Matches in 1891. The men did particularly well, leading in several of the events, even the Queen's Prize, during the first few days. The Towers team victories in the Battalion match, the Ladies' Bracelet (tied) and the Rifle Club match demonstrated to the Southerners that there was considerable talent in the North.[134]

Enthusiasm for shooting sports was not restricted to rifle shooting, and hence the Charters Towers Gun Club was officially formed on 16 July 1888. The first meeting was held at the White Horse Hotel and the club membership fee was set at two guineas. The club immediately set about building a pigeon hatch and procured some two hundred pigeons from Townsville.[135] Interest in the sport increased, and regular club competitions were organised for club members and individual challenge matches, for stakes, became common.

Even though Charters Towers was essentially a mining town, some of the traditional sports for gentlemen were not entirely forgotten. On 17 January 1888 a group of gentlemen met at Pat Ryan's Hotel and formed the Charters Towers Hunt Club. The subscription fee was set at five shillings per quarter, and it "was also decided that the uniform consist of scarlet coat, top boots or gaiters and breeches."[136] Two weeks after the formation of the club, the first hunt was organised. The hunting party, which consisted of some twenty gentlemen, included the President, Mr J.C. Hutton, Mr Thomas Edwards, Master of the Hounds and Mr Walsh, the whipper. The hunt was subsequently described in the local newspaper:

> They reached the camp at the Ana Branch at 2.30 am and found a substantial supper or early breakfast produced. Owing to the musical proclivities of several of the members sleep was impossible. Camp was left at daybreak and hunting started, but when the party returned to camp at 8.30 they had, so far, been unsuccessful. After dinner fishing, shooting, bathing, singing, etc., was indulged in up to 3.30, when the company started hunting homewards. Much more success was met with as five kangaroos, three kangaroo rats and one dingo came to a violent death. Town was reached

about 8.30, and the health of the officers was drank at Pat Downey's, also success to the next meet which will come off in a fortnight.[137]

Charters Towers hunters believed that they lived in "a sportsman's paradise."[138] The Burdekin and Fletcher Rivers and the Powlathanga Lakes were nearby, where game such as turkeys, ducks, pigeons and even flying foxes and wild pigs were plentiful. In 1888 there was some lament expressed by hunters when the government passed an Act which prohibited the hunting of native birds between October 1 and March 1.[139]

Hunting of bigger game appeared to be restricted to kangaroo hunting. It was proudly noted in the local newspaper, that "Messrs Hutton, Edwards, Fisher and party had a very successful kangaroo run...and succeeded in bagging three fine specimens."[140]

The nearby rivers and lakes also provided ample opportunities for the sport of fishing, and by the late 1890s a Charters Towers Angling Club had been formed. As early as 1888, the "unsportsmanlike practice of dynamiting fish in the Burdekin River"[141] was deplored by genuine sportsmen of the field.

Roller Skating

Roller skating was one of the most popular participant recreation sports in the late 1880s and 1890s. The numbers "rinking" would vary from as few as fifty to over one hundred and fifty. One of the main factors that contributed to the sport's popularity was that it was "a really healthy means of recreation for the winter."[142] Moreover, it was a physical activity, a sport that could be engaged in by a wide age range, and more important, by both sexes. The prices were kept "well within the limit of public means...so that everyone may participate in the healthful pastime of Rinking."[143]

The sport of roller skating was inaugurated in 1888, the same year that it was in Brisbane. When the rink in Charters Towers was opened at the Athenaeum Hall, it was modestly described as being "The Largest and Most Perfect Rink in Queensland."[144]

For the 1891 season, the management went to considerable expense to provide the finest musical accompaniment for the skaters. The music, "consisting of piano, cornet, and first and second violins is spirited and suitable, and forms a most enjoyable feature of the rinking season."[145] Friday evenings became the most popular for the skaters. The highpoints of the season were the skating carnivals, which were ever so eloquently described in the press. One in 1890 was called "a treat as has never before been witnessed in the Towers."[146]

Only a month after this carnival another "gorgeous, brilliant, indescribably grand" skating carnival was held, and the *Times* proclaimed that the "fairyland of our childhood's dream was reproduced in all its dazzling splendour."[147]

In addition to the carnivals, several other special events were organised to add variety to the regular rinking season, which extended from April through to October. For example, during the 1890 season, the special events were: A Mile Handicap for a prize of £2, and a Half-mile Hurdle Handicap over hurdles and toboggan slides for a Ladies' Bracelet. Later on "Tilting in the Ring" for ladies only was added,[148] and still later separate competitions for "juveniles".

For women, skating was one of the few socially acceptable physical activities, the "movement of ladies over a perfect floor...being the poetry of motion."[149]

The highpoint for roller skating enthusiasts in Charters Towers was the appearance of Miss Mabel Sylvester, champion lady skater of the world. Miss Sylvester gave several performances during the 1890 season for which she drew rave reviews for her skating expertise and beautiful presentations. She was simply "a perfect wonder,"[150] and Towerites flocked to her shows.

Skating had, indeed, become very fashionable in Charters Towers in the 1890s. Its significance was perhaps best summed up by the *Times* writer: Skating "[has] convinced [us] that there is something worth living for...and that there is joy not only in heaven, but also on earth."[151]

Tennis

Tennis had its adherents principally among the social set. By 1889 a local tennis club was formed, indicating that there was considerable interest in the sport. Handicap matches for ladies and gentlemen for prizes were then organised,[152] and a tennis pavilion was built.

Beginning in 1889 intertown competition between the Townsville and Charters Towers clubs added additional interest to the local competitions. The Townsville players proved to be superior, particularly in the men's competitions. In 1891, for example, the Charters Towers ladies were only beaten by one game, while the men were repeatedly soundly trounced by the Townsville gentlemen.[153]

There was very little coverage of tennis by the local press, although the club continued to flourish. It can be assumed that tennis was a low-profile sport as its leisurely manner of play did not appeal to the general populace of the mining town.

Swimming

During the summer months the weather in Charters Towers was extremely hot and it was understandable that residents were desirous of indulging in bathing. The closest place for sea bathing was at the Townsville beaches, 135 kilometres away, and hence was not readily accessible to the majority. As early as 1877 a small swimming bath was constructed in a local creek,[154] however the more popular places in the 1880s became the nearby Planter's Dam and, further afield, the Burdekin River.

After the exceptionally hot months of November and December of 1890, there arose a public clamour for a proper swimming baths in the town. However the municipal council appeared lax, and Alderman Ben, in particular, was openly criticised in the local newspaper for not making "one practical stride towards ensuring the erection of baths"[155] in the city. At the end of 1890, the demand for a city baths was raised again. As the municipal council continued to drag its feet an initiative was undertaken by a private firm. The enterprising proprietors of the skating rink offered to convert the successful rink into a public bathing place. In order to accomplish this expensive undertaking they appealed to the Water Board for special water rates, which were later granted. A public Swimming Baths Company was formed, and fifteen thousand shares, at three shillings per share, were made available to the Charters Towers residents. It was maintained that buying a share was a contribution for a most worthy cause, as well as being a profitable investment. The company presented its case publicly in the *Charters Towers Times*, where it was argued that the pool would be open nine months a year and to be profitable would require an average daily attendance of two hundred.[156]

Although the majority of the people participated in bathing for purposes of recreation and enjoyment, there were competitive opportunities for those interested. Initially, these were in the form of challenge matches, and usually involved money stakes. For example, T.H. Smith, a local, competed against F. Saunders, a touring professional, who had swum against English champions.[157] This match took place at Planter's Dam at five o'clock in the morning for £20 aside, and over a distance of one thousand yards, which was twelve times the length of the course. In February 1890, Mr MacDonald was matched against Mr W. Thompson for a swimming contest of one hundred and fifty yards on the Burdekin.

The Swimming Club's first public competitions were not held until 1891. They were organised at Planter's Dam on December 16, and over six hundred spectators, including women, were attracted to the event. This maiden competition consisted of nine events, five handicap races (two for boys and one for novices, two open), walking the greasy pole, a tub race, a long diving competition and a one hundred yards champion race.[158]

After the turn of the century the Elizabeth Street swimming baths were constructed and this helped to increase interest and numbers participating in the sport. Swimming lessons, with separate sessions for ladies and gentlemen, were initiated, and regular competitions were scheduled.[159]

Handball

At the height of Charters Towers' prosperity, even the sport of handball was indulged in. There was a handball court, Hayles' Court, built at Queenton and in December 1890 a Grand Handball Handicap was organised with prizes of £8, £5 and £3. There was another court at the Waverly Hotel where Messrs Healy and Brophy played a challenge match for £50 a side. The match was easily won by Mr Healy with a score of 41 to 12.[160]

Goat Racing

Although horse-racing was the premier animal racing sport on the goldfield, according to old timers, a close rival was goat racing. Indeed, goats were so plentiful in the region that they would parade down the main streets and through the shops. Goats were useful not only for the milk and meat they provided, but also for their racing potential. Owners would vie with one another in selecting future champions, and then would build carts which the goats would pull in the races.

Goat derbies became annual occurrences and thousands would come from surrounding areas to watch these "nannies" race for valuable prizes. The popularity of these goat races continued throughout the 1900s.[161]

Class

It is impossible to state with complete certainty the role that class played in the participation, organisation and evolution of various sports. Precise data is simply not available on the class affiliation of the majority of participants in such sports. Indeed, the ethnic and social class make-up of the Charters Towers population has escaped authoritative analysis to this point by historians.

In the late 1880s and early 1890s Charters Towers was the centre of the union movement in Queensland. Class action, through the formation of unions, improved working class participation and the democratisation of sport. The instigation of the half–holiday for shop assistants in the mid–1890s, and various other union demands with respect to hours and conditions, gave the average working person opportunities for the playing of sport on days other than Sundays. The formation of the Mercantile Club (shop employees), Queenton Rising Star Club (miners), and the Railway Men's Club and Printer's Union Clubs, in cricket, were examples of the spread of this one sport after the change in working hours.

The Miner's Union was the first union to be formed in 1886 and they had their own horse races, and sports and athletics meets. Also, there were miners' teams in cricket (1888) and rugby football. On the anniversary of the Miner's Union, a public holiday was declared in the town, and sports and horse meetings dominated.

Summary

The following model developed by the authors endeavours to explain the uniqueness of Charters Towers as a mining community and how sport was affected (see figure 14).

There were certain imperatives in a mining community that were evident in Charters Towers: there was an isolated and unsettled area where the discoveries were made, the class makeup was heterogeneous rather than homogeneous, with differing ethnic groups, and there were conflicts with the indigenous population, that is the Aborigines, who saw the area as their own territory.

These imperatives gave rise to what may be described as a frontier or mining mentality. Some of the elements were: male dominance, with qualities such as aggression, strength and physical endurance lauded; an egalitarian value system, where social niceties and graces were at a minimum, individuality was highly prized and rigidity of class lines was resisted; a lack of concern with tradition; a concern for the present; class lines for women, in which barmaids were part of the frontier mentality with a similar value system, whereas wives were part of a conservative social order; and a high risk and adventure component had general acceptance in the society.

The sports scene, in turn, was a reflection of that frontier society, and gave rise to the following: sports which stressed frontier aspects such as strength, physical endurance and toughness, such as rugby,

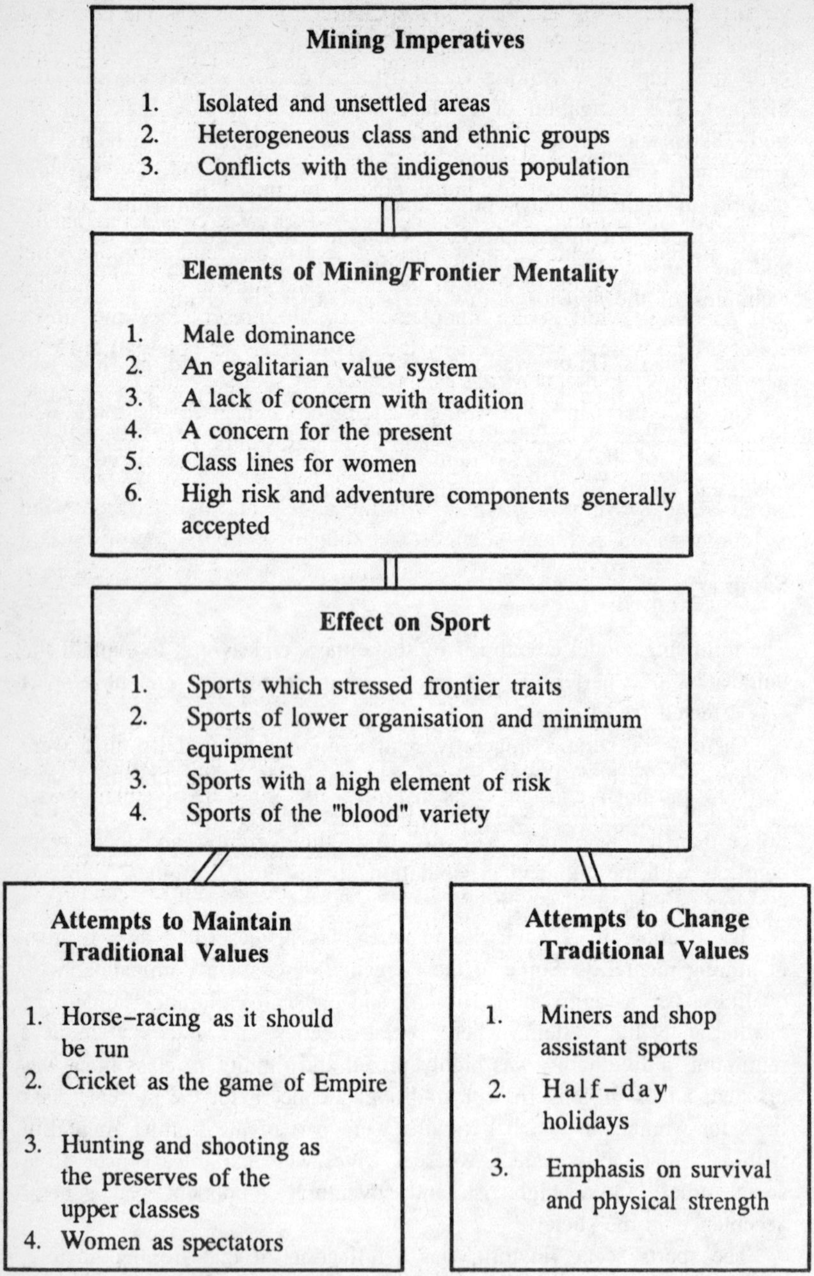

Mining Imperatives

1. Isolated and unsettled areas
2. Heterogeneous class and ethnic groups
3. Conflicts with the indigenous population

Elements of Mining/Frontier Mentality

1. Male dominance
2. An egalitarian value system
3. A lack of concern with tradition
4. A concern for the present
5. Class lines for women
6. High risk and adventure components generally accepted

Effect on Sport

1. Sports which stressed frontier traits
2. Sports of lower organisation and minimum equipment
3. Sports with a high element of risk
4. Sports of the "blood" variety

Attempts to Maintain Traditional Values

1. Horse-racing as it should be run
2. Cricket as the game of Empire
3. Hunting and shooting as the preserves of the upper classes
4. Women as spectators

Attempts to Change Traditional Values

1. Miners and shop assistant sports
2. Half-day holidays
3. Emphasis on survival and physical strength

Figure 14 Model depicting sport in a mining town

boxing and wrestling; sports which were of low organisation and minimum equipment, such as boxing and goat racing; sports of the "blood" variety, with cruelty elements, such as ratting and cockfighting.

There were owners, professional people, managers and so on in the society, who attempted to uphold traditional societal values in the sports they fostered, evidenced by: horse–racing, organised in such a manner to exclude undesirable elements; cricket, which was considered as the sport of Empire which taught "proper" behaviour and attitudes, and passed on the meaning system of the upper and middle classes; hunting and shooting, which were maintained as the preserve of the upper classes. And women were seen by these individuals as non–participants, as adornments, their main role as spectators at sports events.

On the other hand, the workers attempted to change the traditional value orientation, by: mine and shop assistants sports, organised by the workers themselves; their argument for half–day holidays, so that workers had the time to compete with the middle and upper classes; and an emphasis on physical strength and toughness in the activities that were stressed, as these were the qualities that it was felt would prove their superiority.

Based on the historical analysis of the data that is available, several generalisations are advanced.

1. Sport appeared to become more egalitarian from the 1870s to 1910. Participation by the working classes, in particular the miners, underwent considerable change in these years. Such participation was a variable and not a constant, demonstrating that class involvement was a changing process over the years rather than an absolute.

2. The power and control positions in the organisational structure of sports were primarily located in the hands of the upper and upper middle classes from 1870 to 1910. The mayors, aldermen, mine owners and managers, leading business men, doctors and lawyers appeared to have hegemonic control over sport. Although it is fashionable among Marxist historians and sociologists to conclude that such organisational control included domination, and that such a hegemonic process would include the subordination of the interests of the lower working classes, there is no actual evidence to substantiate this in this case study of Charters Towers with the facts that are available. Indeed, it can equally be argued from the evidence that the participation of the elite in the organisational domain of sport in Charters Towers was effected for altruistic and service motives. The sparse evidence that exists tends to lean towards the fact that Charters Towers society was generally egalitarian. For example, it was a feature that the owner and miner would drink, and even talk together, at the Collins Hotel. It would

appear that, in Charters Towers, life and society revolved around the mine and its fortunes, and as such class barriers tended to be obliterated.

3. The Charters Towers Jockey Club was *the* horse-racing organisational body and it was primarily controlled by the elite of the town. The working classes held their own races, for example the Miners' Union Races, as did certain ethnic groups, such as the Irish, who held a separate Race Carnival. Yet even with the Towers Jockey Club there was considerable evidence of infiltration, into control positions, of those who had other than the grandiose aims of racing at heart. In other words, there was either infiltration of members of other classes, or infiltration of individuals with a different meaning system or value system to the 'ruling' class. Perhaps this was due to a different ethnic mix of the total society in comparison with other large Australian cities at the time. Perhaps this differing ethnic make-up sought a different meaning system and this affected the hegemonic process. Perhaps there was a different mentality in mining towns such as Charters Towers – a frontier mentality with a new meaning system.

4. Certain sports in particular appealed to the mining fraternity: rugby union football, boxing, wrestling and athletics, as well as horse-racing, cockfighting, ratting and gambling in general. The main participant sports that attracted miners were those in which physical strength and endurance were highly prized, and were essential features. All of the sports that they were engaged in involved betting, even in rugby union.

5. Certain activities and sports remained as the pastimes of, but were not exclusive to, the upper and upper middle classes: cricket, tennis, rifle and pigeon shooting, roller skating and hunting. These all required specialised equipment, as well as time and financial commitments which would generally not be available, or be out of the reach of, the average worker. Cricket was, however, played by all classes but this sport never achieved the prominence and status that the sport of rugby union enjoyed. The English, gentlemanly game was perhaps too tame, too slow, and not physically demanding enough for this tough, rugged, mining community.

6. The active participation of women in any sports was extremely limited, as only a restricted number of sports were available to them. There was only roller skating, dancing and later tennis; at least it was only in these sports that female participation was noted in the press. The chief role of women lay in the support system and encouragement they offered male participants. They were spectators at horse races and cricket and rugby matches, but did not appear to be present at cockfighting or boxing. It appears that women's active participation in

competitive sports in the goldfields lagged behind that in the cities. In Charters Towers the society was male–dominant, a male frontier society, and women's role in sport was a reflection of that society and its value system.

In summary, sport came to play an important and integral role in the social life of this isolated mining town in Northern Queensland. Sport offered a welcome respite to the confinements of the miners and an opportunity for them to display their physical prowess. Sport also served as a vehicle for the mining town to demonstrate its strength and superiority. It brought status and recognition to the town. To the players, there was, at the least, public acknowledgement of their feats and possibly social mobility in a few cases. For spectators as well as participants sport served as one of the main avenues of entertainment and provided opportunities for social interaction.

Notes

Abbreviations

AS	*Australasian Sketcher*
B	*The Bulletin*
BA	*Burnett Argus*
BC	*Brisbane Courier*
C	*The Courier*
CM	*Courier–Mail*
CTT	*Charters Towers Times*
GT	*Gympie Times*
JRHSQ	*Journal of Royal Historical Society of Queensland*
MBC	*Moreton Bay Courier*
MM&EG	*Mundie Miner & Etheridge Gazette*
MS	*Mackay Standard*
NM	*Northern Miner*
NMR	*Northern Mining Register*
Q	*The Queenslander*
QCF	*Queensland Cricketer & Footballer*
QF	*Queensland Figaro*
R	*The Referee*
SM	*Sydney Mail*
SMH	*Sydney Morning Herald*
TC	*Town & Country*
TH	*Townsville Herald*
WT	*Weekly Times*

Chapter 1. Games in Queensland

1   Constance Campbell Petrie, *Tom Petrie's Reminiscences of Early Queensland*, (Victoria: Lloyd O'Neill, 1981), see Chapters II, III, VI and VIII.

2   Ibid., p.46.

3   See W.E. Roth, "Games, sports and amusements", *North Queensland Ethnography, Bulletin No. 4*, (Brisbane: Government Printing Office, 1902); W.E. Roth, *Ethnological Studies among the North–Western Central Queensland Aborigines*, (Brisbane: Government Printing Office, 1897); W.E. Roth, "Games, Sports and Amusements of the Northern Queensland Aboriginals", *Report of the Australian Advancement of Science* 9 (1903):516.

4   Michael Albert Salter, "Games and Pastimes of the Australian Aboriginal", M.A. Thesis, University of Alberta, 1967.

5   Ibid., pp.191–192.

6   Alan Moorehead, *The Fatal Impact*, (London: Reprint Society, 1966).

7   Ross Fitzgerald, *From the Dreaming to 1915: A History of Queensland*, (St. Lucia: University of Queensland Press, 1982), p.215.

8   *MBC*, August 16 1858, as quoted by H. Reynolds, "Racial Thought in Early Australia", *Australian Journal*

of Politics and History, 20:1 (April 1974):51.

Chapter 2. Early Settlers and Their Cultural Baggage

1   Ross Fitzgerald, *From the Dreaming to 1915: A History of Queensland*, (University of Queensland Press, 1982), p.65.
2   Ibid., p.74.
3   Hector Holthouse, *Illustrated History of Queensland*, (Brisbane: Rigby Ltd., 1978), p.27.
4   The census for the Darling Downs was not included. The population of that district was 658. The Stanley district included North and South Brisbane, Ipswich, the Brisbane River squatting stations and Military and Government establishments.
5   Holthouse, *Illustrated History of Queensland*, pp.105–106.
6   P. Bailey, *Leisure and Class in Victorian England*, (London: Routledge & Kegan Paul, 1978), p.2.
7   Scott A.G.M. Crawford, "A History of Recreation and Sport in Nineteenth Century Colonial Otago", PhD. thesis, University of Queensland, 1984, p.15.
8   Ibid., pp.15–16.
9   John Robertson, *Uppies & Doonies*, (Aberdeen: Aberdeen University Press, 1967).
10 Eric Dunning & Kenneth Sheard, *Barbarians, Gentlemen & Players*, (Oxford: Oxford University Press, 1979), pp.33–34.
11 A.G. Ingham and R. Beamish, "The Maturation of Industrial Capitalism and the Bourgeoisification of America's Ludic Interests", Unpublished Paper, 1982.
12 P.C. McIntosh, *Sport in Society*, (London: C.A.Watts & Co. Ltd., 1968).
13 H.A. Harris, *Sport in Britain: Its Origins and Developments,* (London: Stanley Paul, 1975).
14 see J. Strutt.
15 Reet Howell and Max Howell, *Foundations of Physical Education*, (Brisbane: William Brooks, 1984), p.34.

Chapter 3. Queensland's First Sporting Industry

1   Keith Dunstan, *Sports*, (Melbourne: Cassell Australia Ltd., 1973), p.47.
2   Jack Pollard, *The Pictorial History of Australian Horseracing*, (Sydney: Lansdowne Press, 1982), p.11.
3   Jas L. Collins ("Orion") and Geo. H. Thompson, *"Harking Back": The Turf: Its Men and Memories*, (Brisbane: Standard Press, 1924), Preface.
4   *S.W. Jack's Cutting Book*, No. 37, Oxley Library, p.1.
5   C.C. Petrie, *Tom Petrie's Reminiscences of Early Queensland*, (Victoria: Currey O'Neill, 1981), p.277. They also added, "They were well-born, these squatters, and they were also gentlemen who enjoyed a piece of fun and mischief."
6   *SMH*, February 22 1843. Our thanks to John Smith for alerting the authors to these pre–1846 references. He came across them while doing research on Evan Mackenzie.
7   *SMH*, April 19 1843.
8   Ibid.
9   *SMH*, July 25 1843.
10 *SMH*, October 12 1843.
11 *SMH*, March 19 1844.
12 *SMH*, June 3 1844.
13 *SMH*, May 7 1845.
14 *SMH*, May 27 1845.
15 *SMH*, June 26 1843.
16 *MBC*, Saturday, June 20 1846. The reference here is to David Bow, the host at the hotel.
17 Ibid.
18 Ibid. Ropes were utilised as "hurdles" for these races. In spite of being made from rope, the horses still baulked at the jumps.
19 Ibid
20 J.J. Knight, *In the Early Days: History and Incident of Pioneer Queensland*, (Brisbane: Sapsford and Co., 1898), pp.166–167.

21 *MBC*, June 20 1846.
22 Ibid.
23 Ibid.
24 Ibid.
25 Knight, *In the Early Days*, p.167.
26 Ibid., p. 165.
27 Ibid.
28 Ibid.
29 *MBC*, March 27 1847.
30 *MBC*, May 22 1847.
31 *MBC*, May 29 1847.
32 Peter Smith, "Evan Mackenzie". Paper presented at the Brisbane Historical Society, Kilcoy Homestead, October 1986.
33 Knight, *In the Early Days*, p. 212.
34 *MBC*, April 29 1848.
35 *MBC*, June 3 1848.
36 *MBC*, March 24 1849.
37 *MBC*, June 9 1849.
38 Ibid.
39 Ibid.
40 Knight, *In the Early Days*, p.167.
41 The steamer *Experiment* had established a regular boat link with Ipswich in 1846, the journey taking less than seven hours, depending on the tide. Such a linkage enabled sportsmen, teams, turf enthusiasts, and even horses to travel in relative comfort between Brisbane and Ipswich.
42 *MBC*, May 11 1847.
43 *MBC*, May 27 1848.
44 Knight, *In the Early Days*, p. 167.
45 *MBC*, June 9 1849.
46 *MBC*, May 12 1848.
47 *MBC*, May 20, 1848. These races were duly reported on June 24 1848 and July 1 1848.
48 *MBC*, July 1 1848.
49 *MBC*, February 16 1850.
50 *MBC*, April 27 1850.
51 *MBC*, June 22 1850.
52 Ibid.
53 *MBC*, May 29 1847.
54 *MBC*, August 14 1847.
55 *MBC*, July 11 1846. The "small Australian horse is the best for India, say 14½ to 15 hands high", stated Sir

Charles Burdett in the *Courier* of July 31 1847.
56 Ibid.
57 Ibid.
58 *MBC*, June 3 1848.
59 *MBC*, August 7 1847.
60 *MBC*, December 11 1847.
61 *MBC*, May 20 1848.
62 *MBC*, May 13 1848.
63 *MBC*, March 17 1849.
64 *MBC*, May 22 1847.
65 *MBC*, June 2 1847.
66 *MBC* as quoted in Knight, *In the Early Days*, p.212.
67 *MBC*, June 20 1846.
68 *MBC*, September 26 1846. This continued in later years, for example, January 23 1847 and July 3 1847.
69 *MBC*, October 10 1846; October 24 1846; January 23 1847, and April 3 1847.

Chapter 4. Sports of the Early Colonists to 1850

1 Thomas Dowse, "Old Times", *BC*, September 18 1869. This reference was kindly forwarded to the authors by John Smith.
2 E.H. Hutcheon, *A History of Queensland Cricket*, (Brisbane: Queensland Cricket Association, 1948), p. 4.
3 *SMH*, April 19 1844. The authors are indebted to John Smith for alerting us to the early references in this newspaper.
4 *MBC*, Saturday, June 27 1846.
5 Hutcheon, *A History of Queensland Cricket*, p. 13.
6 *MBC*, October 28 1848.
7 *MBC*, May 25 1850.
8 *MBC*, June 29 1850.
9 W.B. Carmichael and H.C. Perry, *Athletic Queensland*, (Brisbane: Diddams, 1900).
10 *SMH*, January 25 1844.
11 *SMH*, December 4 1843.
12 *MBC*, December 26 1846.
13 Ibid.
14 *MBC*, January 2 1847.

15   Ibid.
16   *MBC*, February 6 1847.
17   *MBC*, January 29 1848.
18   Ibid.
19   J.J. Knight, *In the Early Days: History and Incident of Pioneer Queensland*, (Brisbane: Sapsford & Co., 1898), pp.231–233.
20   Constance Campbell Petrie, *Tom Petrie's Reminiscences of Early Queensland*, (Victoria: Currey O'Neil, 1981), pp.302–303.
21   Knight, *In the Early Days*, n.p.
22   *MBC*, January 20 1849.
23   *SMH*, December 4 1843.
24   *SMH*, January 25 1844.
25   *MBC*, July 11 1846. Another was available at a public auction announced in the paper on July 10 1847.
26   *MBC*, January 26 1850.
27   *MBC*, February 22 1850.
28   *MBC*, April 24 1847.
29   *MBC*, January 12 1850. Another report from Ipswich, February 2 1850, detailed a drowning in the Bremer River. Another was noted on December 21 1850.
30   *MBC*, February 26 1846.
31   *MBC*, January 6 1849.
32   *MBC*, January 20 1848.
33   *MBC*, March 10 1849.
34   *MBC*, December 14 1847.
35   *MBC*, March 18 1848.
36   *MBC*, December 19 1846. Another fight in front of spectators was reported on December 18 1847.
37   *MBC*, March 4 1848.
38   *MBC*, May 27 1848.
39   *MBC*, February 26 1848.
40   Ibid.
41   *MBC*, June 10 1848.
42   Carmichael and Perry, *Athletic Queensland*, p.217.
43   *MBC*, August 7 1847.
44   *MBC*, August 14 1847.
45   Petrie, *Tom Petrie's Reminiscences*, p.263.
46   Ibid., pp.137–138.
47   *MBC*, October 4 1847.

48   *MBC*, September 16 1848.
49   *MBC*, September 23 1848.
50   Ibid.
51   *MBC*, September 30 1848.
52   *MBC*, October 14 1848.
53   *MBC*, October 24, 1848.
54   Knight, *In the Early Days*, pp.252–253.
55   Ibid.
56   *MBC*, July 7 1846.
57   *MBC*, September 16 1848.
58   *MBC*, July 7 1847.
59   *MBC*, April 24 1847.
60   *MBC*, April 10 1847.
61   *MBC*, December 9 1848.
62   *MBC*, December 30 1848.
63   *MBC*, December 29 1849.
64   *MBC*, December 7 1850.
65   *MBC*, January 10 1849.
66   *MBC*, May 26 1849.
67   *MBC*, May 1 1847.
68   *MBC*, May 29 1847.
69   *MBC*, June 12 1847.
70   *MBC*, July 1 1848.
71   *MBC*, January 29 1848.
72   *MBC*, June 9 1849.
73   *MBC*, January 29 1848.
74   *MBC*, November 11 1848.
75   *MBC*, May 29 1847.
76   *MBC*, January 26 1850.
77   *MBC*, December 18 1847.
78   *MBC*, June 12 1847.
79   *MBC*, May 25 1850.
80   *MBC*, June 8 1850.
81   *MBC*, January 29 1848.
82   *MBC*, February 2 1850.
83   *MBC*, May 27 1847.
84   *MBC*, May 29 1847.
85   *MBC*, November 13 1847. This was repeated on January 8 1848.
86   *MBC*, June 9 1849.
87   *MBC*, May 29 1847.
88   *MBC*, January 26 1850.

Chapter 5. The Diffusion of Major Sports

1   R.K. Wilson, *Australia's Resources and Their Development*, (Sydney: Department of Education, University of Sydney, 1980), p.45.

2 Ross Fitzgerald, *From the Dreaming to 1915: A History of Queensland*, (St. Lucia: University of Queensland Press, 1982),p.266.

3 Wilson, *Australia's Resources and Their Development*, p.47.

4 Hector Hothouse, *Illustrated History of Queensland*, (Sydney: Rigby Ltd., 1978), pp.109–110.

5 *WT*, June 24 1868.

6 Ronald Lawson, *Brisbane in the 1890s*, (St. Lucia: University of Queensland Press, 1973), p.19.

7 T. Weedon, *Queensland Past and Present*, (Brisbane: Government Printer, 1897), p.80.

8 Ibid.

9 *CTT*, February 23 1889.

10 The information presented is a summary of the work of Thomas Armstrong. This paper was originally presented at the IV History of Sporting Traditions Conference, held at the Melbourne Cricket Ground 17–19 August 1983.

11 Ibid.

12 *BC*, January 6 1884, as quoted in Armstrong, p.7.

13 *BC*, December 23 1863.

14 *QCF*, September 15 1894, p.14.

15 Ibid.

16 *BC*, December 23, as quoted in Armstrong, p.8.

17 *QCF*, August 21 1894, p.4.

18 Ernest H. Hutcheon, *A History of Queensland Cricket*, (Brisbane: U.E. Martin, n.d.), p.5. Ernest played for Queensland in the 1920s and was also a State selector. He came from a cricket family where his brother John also played for Queensland in the early 1900s, and his father gave great service to cricket in Warwick. His book is the most authoritative history of Queensland cricket.

19 *BC*, January 20 1862.

20 Hutcheon, *A History of Queensland Cricket*, p.5.

21 Ibid., p.69.

22 See Max Howell and Reet Howell. "Sports Among the Queensland Aborigines", Unpublished paper, University of Queensland, 1988.

23 *QFC*, February 4 1893.

24 Hundreds of references are involved in compiling this figure. Some dates may be disputed, but generally these arguments will centre on when the first cricket was played in an area, rather than when a club was actually formed. The later clubs were often subsequent developments. The authors would appreciate hearing from local historians, etc., if additional information can be provided.

25 Hutcheon, *A History of Queensland Cricket*, p.4.

26 Ibid., p.5.

27 Ibid., p.12.

28 *MBC*, October 26 1859.

29 *C*, May 27 1861.

30 J.R.D. Mahoney, *Wide Bay and Burnett Cricket, 1864–1908*, (Maryborough: Alston, 1908), p.30.

31 *GT*, February 6 1869.

32 *GT*, February 11 1869.

33 *GT*, February 13 1869.

34 Mahoney, *Wide Bay and Burnett Cricket*, p.31.

35 Murray Phillips, "The Development of Sport in Gympie during its First Decade, 1867–1877", Unpublished paper, University of Queensland, 1984, p.12.

36 Hutcheon, *A History of Queensland Cricket*, p.35.

37 Mahoney's enthusiasm for cricket resulted in the writing of his most informative book, *Wide Bay and Burnett Cricket*.

38 Hutcheon, *A History of Queensland Cricket*, p.56.

39 Mahoney, *Wide Bay and Burnett Cricket*, p.13.

40 Ibid., p.17.

41 Ibid., pp.24–25.

42 Ibid., p.25.

43 Ibid.

44 Ibid., p.50.

45 Ibid., p.87.

46 For a comprehensive analysis of these intertown matches see Chapter:

"Sport Among the Miners: Charters Towers".

47 Jack Pollard, *Australian Cricket: The Game and the Players*, (Sydney: Hodder and Stoughton, 1982), p.816.

48 *BC*, February 26, 1876.

49 Hutcheon, *A History of Queensland Cricket*, p.1.

50 *QF*, January 6 1883.

51 *QF*, March 24 1883.

52 *QF*, January 6, 1883.

53 Hutcheon, *A History of Queensland Cricket*, p.222.

54 Ibid., p.223.

55 *BC*, July 18 1874.

56 Hutcheon, *A History of Queensland Cricket*, p.55.

57 *QCF*, January 15 1894.

58 *QCF*, October 8 1892, p.5.

59 Hutcheon, *A History of Queensland Cricket*, p.56.

60 *C*, April 21 1863.

61 *BC*, December 20 1868.

62 Phillips, "The Development of Sport in Gympie", p.8.

63 *A Golden Past: A Golden Future*, (Gympie: S.N., 1976), n.p.

64 Ibid.

65 *WT*, February 24 1866.

66 Phillips, "The Development of Sport in Gympie", p.10.

67 Jas L. Collins and Geo. H. Thompson, *"Harking Back": The Turf, Its Men and Memories*, (Brisbane: The Standard Press, 1924), p.60. This book is the most authoritative overview of the history of Queensland racing up to 1924. Unfortunately the records, calendars and guides of the Queensland Turf Club were lost in the flood of 1893. Hence, the descriptions of the early years, that is prior to 1893, are based on the authors' personal memories as well as the recollections of other racing enthusiasts in the 1920s.

68 Nat Gould, *Town and Bush*, (London: George Routledge and Sons, 1896). Facsimile edition by Penguin Books, 1974, p.216.

69 Collins and Thompson, *"Harking Back"*, p.50.

70 G.F. O'Connor, *Souvenir of the Centenary of the Central and Upper Burnett River District of Queensland, 1848 to 1948*, (Brisbane: William Brooks and Co., 1948), p.30.

71 *MBC*, June 12 1852.

72 *MBC*, June 15 1852.

73 O'Connor, *Souvenir of the Centenary*, p.69. For an indepth analysis of W.E. Parry-Okeden, see Chapter: "Sport in the Country: The Elite". The evidence is contradictory as to whether Mr Parry-Okeden merely owned the horse or was its jockey as well. J.E. Murphy and E.W. Easton, in their local history entitled *Wilderness to Wealth: Being a History of the Shires of Nanango, Kingaroy, Wondai, Murgon, Kilkivan and the Upper Yarraman Portion of the Rosalie Shire*, (Brisbane: W.R. Smith and Paterson, 1950), p.26, stated: "At the first Queensland Derby run at Gayndah in 1868, Mr. W.E. Parry-Okeden rode to victory on "The Hermit", a horse leased from Walter Scott of Taramco, whose horses "Zambesi" in 1869 and "Grafton" in 1870 carried off the honours at the famous Gayndah meetings".

74 Ibid.

75 Collins and Thompson, *"Harking Back*, p.51.

76 Leslie F. Slaughter, *Ipswich Municipal Centenary*, (Ipswich: Pohlman-Patrick Advertisers, 1960), p.47.

77 *MBC*, April 2 1853.

78 For a discussion of the controversy see Chapter: "Queensland's First Sporting Industry: Horse-racing".

79 *MBC*, July 10 1852.

80 *C*, July 27 1863.

81 *MBC*, June 19 1852.

82 Collins and Thompson, *"Harking Back"*, p.53.

83 O'Connor, *Souvenir of the Centenary*, p.71.

84 *MBC*, May 10 1851.

85 *MBC*, April 26 1851.

86 *MBC*, May 13 1854.

87 *MBC*, November 11 1854.

88 J.J. McGill, "Authentic Stories of Queensland Racing", *Queensland Racing Calendar*, n.d., p.34.

89 *MBC*, June 2 1855.

90 *C*, March 4 1863.

91 J.J. McGill, "The Brisbane Cup", *Queensland Racing Calendar*, June 1966, p.591.

92. Lawson, *Brisbane in the 1890s*, p.200.

93. J.T.S. Bird, *The Early History of Rockhampton*, (Rockhampton: Rockhampton Morning Bulletin Office, 1904), p.100.

94 *C*, June 13 1863.

95 J.J. McGill, "The Third Decade of Queensland Racing", *Queensland Racing Calendar*, 1966, p.260.

96 Lawson, *Brisbane in the 1890s*, p.200.

97 J.J. McGill, "When the Course by the Creek was first Opened", *Queensland Racing Calendar*, 1968, p.131.

98 McGill, "Authentic Stories of Queensland Racing", p. 36.

99 For an indepth analysis of the 1883 race riot see C.R. Moore, "The Mackay Race Course Riot of 1883", *Lectures on North Queensland History*, James Cook University, 1978, n.p.

100 Ibid.

101 *MS*, as quoted by Moore, Ibid.

102 *QF*, January 12 1984.

103 Ibid.

104 Nat Gould, *On and Off the Turf in Australia*, (London: George Routledge and Sons Ltd., 1895, Facsimile reprint 1973 by Libra Books, Canberra), p.155.

105 *MBC*, June 5 1852.

106 Jack Pollard, *The Pictorial History of Australian Horseracing*, (Sydney: Landsdowne Press, 1982), p.44.

107 For a detailed description of the various amusements see Collins and Thompson, *"Harking Back"*, pp.26–28.

108 J.J. McGill, "The Third Decade of Racing", *Queensland Racing Calendar*, January 1966, p.260.

109 J.J. McGill, "Authentic Stories", p.37.

110 Gould, *On and Off the Turf*, p.37.

111 Collins and Thompson *Harking Back"*, pp.52–53.

112 Ibid., p.36.

113 J.J. McGill, "Topics of the Month", *Queensland Racing Calendar*, November 1968, p.80.

114 Collins and Thompson, "Harking Back", p.70.

115 *BC*, April 25 1873.

116 Collins and Thompson, *"Harking Back"*, p.31.

117 An early newspaper article as quoted in H. Wetherell, *A Short Historical Sketch of the Commercial Rowing Club*, (Brisbane: Commercial Rowing Club, 1947), p.7.

118 *MBC*, May 14 1853.

119 *MBC*, January 24 1857.

120 *MBC*, May 20 1854.

121 *MBC*, January 31 1852; *MBC*, May 27 and May 30 1854; *MBC*, May 30 1854.

122 W.B. Carmichael and H.C. Perry, *Athletic Queensland*, (Brisbane: Diddams, 1900), pp.89–90.

123 *MBC*, December 11 1860.

124 Carmichael and Perry, *Athletic Queensland*, pp.88–89.

125 *C*, October 8 1861.

126 *C*, October 7 1861.

127 Carmichael and Perry, *Athletic Queensland*, pp.3–5.

128 Ibid., pp.94–96.

129 H. Wetherell, *A Short Historical Sketch of the Commercial Rowing Club*, (Brisbane: Commercial Rowing Club, 1945), p.26.

130 Carmichael and Perry, *Athletic Queensland*, p.107.

131 Ron Harvey, *Centenary of Organised Rowing in Bundaberg*, unpublished paper, n.d., p.1.

132   *Q*, December 16 1882, p.863.

133   *AS*, January 23 1875, p.166.

134   *BC*, May 19 1895.

135   Ibid.

136   Gordon Inglis, *Sport and Pastime in Australia*, (London: Methuen, 1912), p.211.

137   *BC*, December 23, 1872.

138   Harvey, *Centenary of Organised Rowing*.

139   *BC*, October 5 1880.

140   Carmichael and Perry, *Athletic Queensland*, p.93.

141   Ibid., p. 88.

142   "Manual Labour Amateurs and Eight Oar Rowing", *The Referee*, May 20 1896, p.1.

143   Grant Pattison, *"Battler's" Tales of Early Rockhampton*, (Melbourne: Fraser and Jenkinson, 1939), p.71.

144   *BC*, August 22 1882.

145   *B*, September 12 1928.

146   The Royal Queensland Yacht Club and the Cleveland Yacht Club are developed in an unpublished paper by Max Howell and Reet Howell, University of Queensland, 1989.

147   Although Carmichael and Perry claim that the first athletic contest in Queensland occurred in the 1860s, there is documented evidence that there were foot races in the Moreton Bay area in the late 1840s. Carmichael and Perry's concern, however, was essentially with amateur athletics.

148   *NM*, June 9 1877.

149   *CTT*, March 23 1889.

150   *BC*, September 18 1871.

151   *CC*, November 4 1872.

152   Bird, *The Early History of Rockhampton*, pp.115–116.

153   *CTT*, May 4 1889.

154   Ibid.

155   *Another Wieneke Wanted: The Book of the Genuine Wieneke Saddle*, n.p., n.d. Jack Wieneke was the great-grandfather of Paul McLean, one of Queensland's and Australia's greatest rugby union players, and the great-
uncle of Bill McLean, captain of the 1947–48 Wallabies.

156   Percy Mason, *Professional Athletics in Australia*, (Sydney: Rigby, 1985), p.76.

157   *CTT*, July 28 1888.

158   Mason, *Professional Athletics in Australia*, p.76.

159   *MBC*, January 6 1859.

160   *BC*, April 15 1873.

161   *BC*, April 22 1871.

162   *BC*, May 17 1871.

163   *BC*, July 7 1871.

164   Carmichael and Perry, *Athletic Queensland*, p.223.

165   Ibid., p.226.

166   Ibid., p.227.

167   Ibid., pp.229–230.

168   See section on "Intercolonial Contests" for a more lengthy discussion of Queensland competing in the Intercolonial Championships.

169   Carmichael and Perry, *Athletic Queensland*, pp.276–279.

Chapter 6. Proliferation of Sports

1   Peter C. McIntosh, *Sport in Society*, (London: C.A. Watts, 1968), p.63.

2   See discussion on the organisation and the formative dates of sport governing bodies in Chapter 5: The diffusion of major sports: 1850 to 1890s.

3   John Daly, *Elysian Fields: Sport, Class and Community in Colonial South Australia, 1836–1890*, (Adelaide: J.A. Daly, 1982), p.131.

4   *R*, April 27 1904, p.6.

5   W.B. Carmichael & H.C. Perry, *Athletic Queensland*, (Brisbane: H.J. Diddam & Co., 1900), pp.133–134.

6   Gordon Greenwood, *Australia: A Social & Political History*, (Sydney: Angus & Robertson, 1955), p.146.

7   R.E.N. Twopeny, *Town Life in Australia*, (Sydney: Sydney Univ. Press, 1975), p.204.

8 See Daly, *Elysian Fields*, pp.54–56, and also John Lacke, "Working Class Leisure", *The Victorian Historical Journal*, 49:1, 1978, pp.49–65.

9 See Anthony Trollope, *Australia*. (Edited by P.D. Edwards & R.B. Joyce), (St. Lucia: University of Queensland Press, 1967).

10 *QCF*, September 15 1893, p.14.

11 J.M. Freeland, *The Australian Pub*, (Melbourne: Melbourne University Press, 1966), p.1.

12 Geoffrey Blainey, "The History of Leisure in Australia", *The Victorian Historical Journal*, 49:1, 1978, p.18.

13 Hector Holthouse, *River of Gold: The Story of the Palmer River Gold Rush*, (Sydney: Angus & Robertson, 1967), pp.141.

14 Ronald Lawson, *Brisbane in the 1890s: A Study of an Australian Urban Society*, (St. Lucia: University of Queensland Press, 1973), pp.236 & 33.

15 Hector Holthouse, *Up Rode the Squatter*, (Adelaide: Rigby, 1970), p.69.

16 Neil Macqueen (ed.), *Back Creek and Beyond*, (Toowoomba: Darling Downs Institute Press, 1981), p.122.

17 *BC*, August 26 1872.

18 *MBC*, December 6 1859 & April 3 1852.

19 *BC*, December 25 1871.

20 *GT*, February 2 1869.

21 W. Ross Johnston, *The Call of the Land: A History of Queensland to the Present Day*, (Brisbane: Jacaranda Press, 1982), p.32.

22 *MBC*, 1855, as quoted in P.G. Leggett, "Class and the Eight Hours Movement in Queensland, 1855–1885", BA(Hons) Thesis, University of Queensland, 1983, pp.57–58.

23 *MBC*, November 1 1856.

24 Leggett, *Class*, p.60.

25 Ibid., p.65.

26 Ibid., p.72.

27 Ibid., p.78.

28 *BC*, as quoted in Lawson, *Brisbane in the 1890s*, p.72.

29 *MBC*, January 8 1856.

30 Nat Gould, *Town and Bush*, (Facsimile edition. London: Penguin Books, 1974), p.234.

31 Leggett, *Class*, p.75.

32 Gould, *Town and Bush*, p.228.

33 *CTT*, March 2 1888.

34 Carmichael & Perry, *Athletic Queensland*, p.221.

35 Twopeny, *Town Life in Australia*, p.203.

36 *MBC*, January 6 1859.

37 *MBC*, October 8 1859.

38 *CTT*, October 11 1890.

39 *NM*, July 25 1891.

40 Daly, *Elysian Fields*, p.51.

41 *BC*, August 2 1870. See also May 17, 18, September 11 1872, May 15 1872, August 3 1872.

42 Jim Fitzpatrick, *The Bicycle and the Bush: Man and Machine in Rural Australia*, (Melbourne: Oxford University Press, 1980), p.17.

43 Ibid., p.32.

44 Carmichael & Perry, *Athletic Queensland*, p.289.

45 Ibid., pp.292–293.

46 Ibid.

47 Frank Lynam, "History of Queensland Amateur Cycling", unpublished paper, n.d.

48 Carmichael & Perry, *Athletic Queensland*, pp.295–296, 299.

49 Ibid., p.306.

50 Keith Dunstan, *Sports*, (Melbourne: Cassell Australia, 1973), p.247.

51 Carmichael & Perry, *Athletic Queensland*, p.316.

52 *BC*, October 28 1892.

53 Carmichael & Perry, *Athletic Queensland*, p.317.

54 *QCF*, May 6 1893.

55 Lynam, "History of Queensland Amateur Cycling".

56 Carmichael & Perry, *Athletic Queensland*, p.373.

57 Ibid., p.326.

58 Lawson, *Brisbane in the 1890s*, p.205.

59 Carmichael & Perry, *Athletic Queensland*, p.327.

60 *Cassell's Book of Sports and Pastimes*, (London: Cassell & Co., 1888), p.29.

61 *C*, December 25 1861.

62 *BC*, June 2 1866. The foundation of this club has been incorrectly stated as being 1867 by Jack Pollard, *Australian Rugby Union: The Game and the Players*, (North Ryde: Angus & Robertson, 1984), p.37.

63 Ibid.

64 Ibid.

65 *BC*, August 24 1868.

66 *BC*, July 25 1870. See also August 23 1870, and August 28 1871.

67 *BC*, August 28 1871.

68 Brisbane Grammar School's records indicate that the football competitions with Ipswich Grammar School begin in 1870. See R.P. Francis (ed.), *Records of the Brisbane Grammar School, 1869–1890*, (Brisbane: Pole, Outridge & Co., 1890) and Stuart Stephenson, *Annals of the Brisbane Grammar School, 1869–1922*, (Brisbane: Government Printer, 1923). However Robert Dudley in his research for "A History of Sport in Moreton Bay District", PhD in the Department of Human Movement Studies, University of Queensland, has found that there were matches between the two schools in 1869.

69 Ibid.

70 *BC*, May 25 1870.

71 Ibid.

72 *BC*, July 25 1870.

73 *BC*, August 20 1870.

74 Carmichael & Perry, *Athletic Queensland*, p.217.

75 Ibid., p.244.

76 *Fifty Years of Football*, (Brisbane: Queensland Rugby Union, 1932), p.5.

77 Ibid.

78 For an indepth discussion of the 1882 season see Chapter 7: Intercolonial Competition.

79 Ibid.

80 For a detailed description of the First Intercolonial Match in 1882, see chapter 7: Intercolonial Competition.

81 Bert Bickley (ed.), *Maroon: Highlights of One Hundred Years of Rugby in Queensland: 1882–1982*, (Brisbane: Queensland Rugby Union, 1982), p.15.

82 Tom Welsby's Diary is held by the Royal Queensland Historical Society.

83 Bickley, *Maroon*, p.17.

84 *Fifty Years of Football*.

85 *Fifty Years of Football*, p.9.

86 *QCF*, July 8 1893, p.7.

87 *BC*, June 15 1893.

88 "Sport in Barcaldine", notes prepared by Barcaldine Shire Council.

89 Ibid.

90 *QCF*, July 8 1893, p.7.

91 *QCF*, August 19 1893, p.5.

92 Bickley, *Maroon*, p.167.

93 Lawson, *Brisbane in the 1890s*, p.203.

94 *NMR*, August 29 1891.

95 Col Hoy, "Australian Code was Here in 1883", *CM*, June 15 1959, p.10.

96 J. Speare, "Soccer Began on Vacant Paddocks", *CM*, June 15 1959, p.10.

97 *MBC*, December 17 1853.

98 *MBC*, December 1 1852.

99 *MBC*, April 18 1856.

100 *MBC*, March 7 1856.

101 *C*, January 1 1863.

102 *C*, February 3 1863; *BC*, February 6 1863.

103 *C*, March 25 1863.

104 *BC*, March 10 1882. See also March 11 1882 and March 25 1882.

105 *BC*, August 17 1872.

106 E. Wetzel, "The Early History of Swimming in Queensland", in *Programme for the 1st Annual Aquatic Gala of the Commercial*

Amateur Swimming Club, n.p., 1914, p.8.

107 Ibid.

108 C.G. Austin, "One Hundred Years of Sport and Recreation in Queensland", *JRHSQ*, VI:1, September 1959, p.283.

109 Wetzel, "The Early History of Swimming", p.9.

110 Bruce Davidson, "The Best Fighters Came From the Country", *CM*, June 15 1959, p.6.

111 Ibid

112 Carmichael & Perry, *Athletic Queensland*, p.154.

113 Ibid., p.155.

114 Ibid.

115 Peter Corris, *Lords of the Ring*, (North Ryde: Cassell Australia, 1980), p.50.

116 Carmichael & Perry, *Athletic Queensland*, p.157.

117 Ibid., p.175.

118 Ibid.

119 Giannini Clerici, *The Ultimate Tennis Book*, (Chicago: Follett Publishing Co., 1975), p.62.

120 Ibid., p.66.

121 Keith Willey, *The First Hundred Years: The Story of Brisbane Grammar School, 1868–1968*, (Melbourne: Macmillan Co., 1968), p.36.

122 W.R.O. Hill, *Forty-five Years Experience in North Queensland*, (Brisbane: Pole & Co., 1907), p.75.

123 *Q*, December 9 1882.

124 *TH*, December 24 1887.

125 Wiley, *The First Hundred Years*, p.36.

126 *QCF*, July 8 1893, p.16.

127 "Tennis: Queenslanders Seek to Bring Back 'the Cup'", *CM*, June 15 1959, p.10.

128 McIntosh, *Sport in Society*, p.64.

129 Terry Smith, *Australian Golf: The First One Hundred Years*, (Sydney: Lester-Townsend Publishing Pty Ltd., 1982), p.15.

130 *Cassell's Book of Sports and Pastimes*, p.58.

131 John Blanch (ed.), *Ampol's Australian Sporting Records*, (Cheltenham: Budget Books Pty Ltd., 1982), p.192. See also, Austin, "One Hundred Years of Sport and Recreation in Queensland", p.281; Keith Brown, "Started Slowly – But How It Grew", *CM*, June 15 1959; Murray Phillips, "A History of the Brisbane Golf Club", BA(Hons) thesis, Department of Human Movement Studies, University of Queensland, 1986, p.29.

132 Jean Harslett & Merwyn Royle, *They Came to a Plateau: The Stanthorpe Saga*, (Stanthorpe: International Colour Production, 1980), p.158.

133 *B*, October 31 1928, p.41.

134 M. MacLaren, *The Australia and New Zealand Golfer's Handbook* (5th edition), (Sydney: A.H. & A.W. Reid, 1975), p.139.

135 *B*, October 25 1933.

136 Phillips, "A History of the Brisbane Golf Club", p.52. See also pp.30, 46 and 55, and Appendix 6.

137 Brown, "Started Slowly", p.10.

138 Phillips, "A History of the Brisbane Golf Club", p.52.

139 "The Brisbane Hunt Club", *TC*, December 6 1890.

140 Daly, *Elysian Fields*, p.140.

141 *BA*, September 23 1867.

142 J.T.S. Bird, *The Early History of Rockhampton*, (Rockhampton: Rockhampton Morning Bulletin Office, 1904), pp.118–119.

143 J. Grant Pattison, *Battler's Tales of Early Rockhampton*, (Melbourne: Fraser & Jenkinson Pty Ltd, 1939), p.72.

144 Ibid.

145 *BC*, April 7 1877.

146 *CTT*, January 19 1888. See Chapter 10: Sport Among the Miners: Charters Towers, description of the Hunt Club.

147 W.E. Parry-Okeden, "Old Queensland Hunt Clubs", newspaper clipping in Mrs Turner's scrapbook.

148 Col. F.G. Newton, "Brisbane Hunt Club", *JRHSQ*, 1957, p.1300.
149 Ibid., p.1299.
150 "The Brisbane Hounds", September 1 1890. Newspaper clipping in Mrs Turner's scrapbook.
151 *BC*, June 26 1890.
152 "The Brisbane Hounds", September 6 1890. Newspaper clipping in Mrs Turner's scrapbook.
153 Newton, "Brisbane Hunt Club", p.1300.
154 *BC*, August 28 1871.
155 Hill, "Forty-five Years Experiences in North Queensland", p.122.
156 Gould, *Town and Buish*, p.64.
157 *MBC*, April 20 1859.
158 A.T. Jackson, *Southern Queensland Rifle Association Jubilee, 1877–1927: A Brief History of the Association During the Past Fifty Years*, (Brisbane, 1927), p.5.
159 *C*, June 1 1861.
160 *C*, December 27 1861. See also December 31 1861 and February 6 1863.
161 *C*, December 23 1861.
162 "Queensland Rifle Association Centenary, 1877 to 1977", *The Marksman*, October 1977, p.14. See also Jackson, *Southern queensland Rifle Association Jubilee*, and Lawson, *Brisbane in the 1890s*, p.210. *Pugh's Almanac of 1865* lists the Queensland Rifle Association.
163 *C*, July 11 1863. See also September 18 1863 and November 17 1863.
164 *BC*, January 31 1870.
165 Jackson, *Southern Queensland Rifle Association Jubilee*, p.7.
166 Ibid.
167 Ibid., p.8.
168 Stuart Stephenson, *Annals of the Brisbane Grammar School*, (Brisbane: Government Printer, 1923), p.103.
169 Ibid., p.104.
170 Jackson, Southern Queensland, p.19.
171 Ibid., p.23.
172 Ibid., p.27.
173 Ibid., p.25.

174 Ibid., p.32.
175 Gordon Inglis, *Sport and Pastime in Australia*, (London: Methuen & Co. Ltd, 1912), p.70.
176 *QCF*, July 8 1893, p.16.
177 *QCF*, August 19 1893.
178 Inglis, *Sport and Pastime in Australia*, pp.235–236.
179 *MBC*, December 25 1858.
180 Blanch, *Ampol's Australian sporting Records*, p.276.
181 Austin, "One Hundred Years of Sport and Recreation in Queensland", p.282.
182 Lawson, *Brisbane in the 1890s*, p.210.
183 Mary Macleod Banks, *Memories of Pioneer Days in Queensland*, (London: Heath Cranton Ltd, 1931), p.16.
184 *BC*, August 27 1872.
185 Austin, "One Hundred Years of Sport and Recreation in Queensland", p.290.
186 *BC*, October 16 1872.
187 *BC*, November 11 1872.
188 *BC*, March 10 1873.
189 Inglis, *Sport and Pastime in Australia*, p. 70.

Chapter 7. Intercolonial Competition

1 W.F. Morrison, *The Aldine History of Queensland*, vol. 1. (Sydney: The Aldine Publishing Co., 1888), p.368.
2 For a detailed analysis of cricket and Australian nationalism see W. Mandle, "Cricket and Australian Nationalism in the Nineteenth Century", *Journal of the Royal Australian Historical Society*, 59:4, December 1973, pp.225–256.
3 *MBC*, October 2 1860.
4 *MBC*, October 18 1860.
5 *MBC*, April 2 1861.
6 *C*, May 28 1861.
7 *C*, May 31 1861.
8 Ibid.

9   E.H. Hutcheon, *A History of Cricket in Queensland*, (Brisbane: V.E. Martin, n.d.), p.21.
10 Ibid., p.18
11 *BC*, April 17 1865.
12 H. Wetherell, *A Short Historical Sketch of the Commercial Rowing Club*, (Brisbane: Commercial Rowing Club, 1947), p.11.
13 W.B. Carmichael and H.C. Perry, *Athletic Queensland*, (Brisbane: Diddams, 1900), p.59.
14 Ibid., p.61.
15 Ibid.
16 Carmichael incorrectly states that Queensland started the Amateur Champion Sculls in Australia in 1892.
17 Ibid., pp.68–69.
18 Ibid., p.267.
19 *Fourth Australasian Championships*. Official Programme, 1899.
20 John Blanch (ed.), *Ampol's Australian Sporting Records*, (Cheltenham: Budget Books Pty. Ltd., 1982), pp.18–25.
21 *BC*, May 29 1882.
22 Ibid.
23 Ibid.
24 *Q*, July 1 1882, p.14.
25 Ibid.
26 *BC*, August 1 1882 and August 7 1882. A reply was published under the pseudonym The Chairman, also on August 7 1882.
27 *Q*, August 28 1882.
28 Maxwell L. Howell and Reet A. Howell, "The First Intercolonial Tour in 1882", *JRHSQ*, XI:4, 126–138, 1983.
29 Ibid., p.135.

Chapter 8. The Country Elite

1   Stephen H. Roberts, *History of Australian Land Settlement (1788–1920)*, (Melbourne: Macmillan, 1924), p.175.
2   Ibid.
3   M.S. order in Chief Secretary's Office, Hobart. As quoted in Roberts, Ibid.
4   Roberts, Ibid., p.178.
5   Ibid., p.179.
6   As quoted in Hector Holthouse, *Up Rode the Squatter*, (Adelaide: Rigby, 1970), p.9.
7   Stephen H. Roberts, *The Squatting Age in Australia 1835–1847*, (Melbourne: Melbourne University Press, 1935), p.212. Hodgson is described as "a cultured *dilettante*...and surrounded himself with a Round Table of well-bred jackeroos, fresh from home Universities."
8   Mary Durack, *Kings in Grass Castles*, (Cordell Park, NSW: Corgi Books, 1983), pp.19–21.
9   Roberts, *History of Australian Land Settlement*, p.371.
10 Ross Fitzgerald, *From the Dreaming to 1915: A History of Queensland*, (St. Lucia: University of Queensland, 1982), p.132.
11 Robert E.M. Armstrong, *The Kalkadoons*, (Brisbane: William Brooks, 1986), p.36.
12 Raymond Stanley (ed.), *Tourist to the Antipodes: William Archer's Australian Journey, 1876–1877*, (St. Lucia: University of Queensland Press, 1977), p.28.
13 As quoted in Fitzgerald, *From the Dreaming to 1915*, p.132.
14 Maurice French & Duncan Waterson, *The Darling Downs: A Pastoral History, 1850–1950*, (Toowoomba: Darling Downs Institute Press, 1982), p.28.
15 Roberts, *The Squatting Age in Australia*, p.369.
16 Edmond Marin La Meslee, *The New Australia*, Translated and edited by Russel Ward, (Melbourne: Heinemann Educational, 1929), pp.70–71.
17 Roberts, *The Squatting Age in Australia*, p.346.

18 Ibid.

19 "Mary Archer, Charles (1813–1862), John (1814–1857), David (1816–1900), William (1818–1896), Archibald (1820–1902), Thomas (1823–1905) and Colin (1832–1921)." *Australian Dictionary of Biography*, vol.1, 1788–1850, (Melbourne: Melbourne University Press, 1966).

20 Letters written between 1833 and 1855 to William and Julia Archer of Tolderodden, Norway, by their sons from Australia. F1665, Fryer Library, University of Queensland, June 30 1842, letter from William to his father.

21 Ibid., Thomas to father, September 10 1843.

22 Stanley, *Tourist to the Antipodes*, p.27.

23 Archer letters, Thomas to sister, August 2 1844.

24 Ibid., Charles to sister, August 6 1845.

25 Ibid., Charles to sister, April 11 1847.

26 This section on William Archer relies heavily on the book *Tourist to the Antipodes: William Archer's Australian Journey*, edited by R. Stanley.

27 Ibid., p.16.

28 Ibid., p.22.

29 Ibid., pp.22–23.

30 Archer letters, John Archer writing to sister, January 2 1842.

31 Stanley, *Tourist to the Antipodes*, p.28.

32 Ibid., p.35.

33 Ibid., p.43.

34 Ibid., p.48.

35 Ibid., pp.48–49.

36 As quoted in Stan Tutt, *From Spear and Musket: 1879–1979, Caboolture Centenary*, (Nambour: Sunstrip Printers, 1979), p.59.

37 The impact of the Bells on the Downs is treated extensively in the work by G.H. Wade, *From Swamp to City, 1863–1963: The Story of Dalby*, (n.p., 1963). This booklet has been used for this case study of the Bells.

38 Ibid., p.13.

39 A.A. Morrison, "Sir Joshua Peter Bell", *Australian Dictionary of Biography*, vol.3, (Melbourne: Melbourne University Press, 1969), pp.134–135.

40 Wade, *From Swamp to City*, p.77.

41 J.L. Collins & G.H. Thompson, *Harking Back*, (Brisbane: The Standard Press, 1924), p.71.

42 Morrison, "Sir Joshua Peter Bell", p.135.

43 W.B. Carmichael & H.C. Perry, *Athletic Queensland*, (Brisbane: H.J. Diddams, 1900), p.7.

44 Ibid., p.46.

45 Ibid., pp.46–47.

46 D.B. Waterson, "Joshua Thomas Bell", *Australian Dictionary of Biography*, vol.7, (Melbourne: Melbourne University Press, 1969), p.258.

47 Ibid.

48 This section is dependent on the work of Mary Durack, *Kings in Grass Castles*.

49 Ibid., p.143.

50 Ibid., p.163.

51 Ibid., p.183.

52 Ibid., pp.183–184.

53. Ibid., p.163.

54 Ibid.

55 We are indebted to the family, particularly Mrs Lehane, for materials they gave us on the Tully as well as the Durack families, and for their various kindnesses, including a most delightful interview.

56 Eve Pownell, *Mary of Maranoa*, (Sydney: F.H. Johnston, 1959), p.179.

57 Materials from the Tully Family.

58 *Nudgee College Annual*, n.d., p.148.

59 Durack, *Kings in Grass Castles*.

60 This analysis is dependent on the work of Harry C. Perry, *A Son of Australia, Memories of W.K. Parry-*

Okeden, 1840–1926, (Watson-Ferguson Co. Ltd, 1928), p.xii.

61 Ibid.

62 Ibid., p.81.

63 Ibid., pp.131–132.

64 Ibid., pp.141–142.

65 "Outlines of History of Polo in Queensland". Unpublished mimeographed paper prepared by N.H. Caswell, Esq., Miss Elaine Cook, C.M. Feez, Esq., Mrs W.K. Gunn, H.W. Hinricksen, Esq., V.J. Rogers, Esq., Allan Gilmore. Also interview with Allan Gilmore at Clifton in 1983.

66 Ibid.

67 F.M.G. Stewart, *The First One Hundred Years, 1863–1963, Centenary of Loyal Pioneer Lodge*, No.3, (MUIOOF, Rockhampton: Oxford Press, 1963).

68 "Mr Adolph Feez", *queensland, 1900*, Alcazar Press, p.160.

69 Col. F.G. Newton, CBE, DSO, "Brisbane Hunt Club, *JRHSQ*, V:5, 1957, p.1300.

70 G.C. Bolton, "The Idea of a Colonial Gentry", *Historical Studies of Australia and New Zealand*, 13:49–52, October 1967–1969, p.322.

71 Holthouse, *Up Rode the Squatter*, p.8.

72 Ibid.

73 Bolton, "The Idea of a Colonial Gentry", p.322.

74 Ibid., p.323.

75 Parry, pp.135–136.

76 Leslie E. Slaughter, *Ipswich Municipal Centenary*, (Ipswich: Pohlman-Patrick, 1960), p.48.

77 David Christie Murray, "Work and Sport on the Darling Downs", *The Daily Telegraph*, Saturday, October 26 1889.

78 Slaughter, *Ipswich Municipal Centenary*, pp.48–49.

79 Murray, "Work and Sport on the Darling Downs".

80 Holthouse, *Up Rode the Squatter*, p.15.

81 Tutt, *From Spear and Musket*, p.66.

Chapter 9. The Stockmen, Drovers, Selectors and Townspeople

1 W. Ross Johnston, *The Call of the Land: A History of Queensland to the Present Day*, (Brisbane: The Jacaranda Press, 1982), p.51.

2 Diana J. Beal, *Rosalie Shire Council, 1879–1979*, (Toowoomba: Cranbrook Press, 1971), p.5.

3 Hector Holthouse, *Up Rode the Squatter: The Savage Beginnings of Queensland's West*, (Adelaide: Rigby, 1970), p.67.

4 Edward Palmer, *Early Days in North Queensland*, (Sydney: Angus & Robertson, 1983), pp.185–186.

5 E.C. Buley, *Australian Life in Town and Country*, (London: George Newness, 1905), p.143.

6 Ian Pedley, *Winds of Change: One Hundred Years in the Widgee Shire*, (Gympie: The Gympie Times, 1979), p.59.

7 M.V. Purdie, *Capella: A Brief History of the Settlement of the Peak Downs*, (Rockhampton: City Printing Works, 1983), p.62.

8 *BC*, January 2 1872.

9 Hector Holthouse, *Gympie Gold: A Dramatic Story of Queensland Gold*, (Melbourne: Angus & Robertson, 1983), pp.102–103.

10 Hector Holthouse, *Up Rode the Squatter*, p.69.

11 Norma Mollar, *History of the Bowen-Collinsville Railway*, Pamphlet printed and published courtesy of the *Bowen Independent*, n.d.

12 *MM&EG*, January 12 1889.

13 See Chapter 10: Sport Among the Miners: Charters Towers; also Dorothy Jounquay, *The Isisford Story*, (Isisford Shire Council, 1975), pp.68–70.

14 J.E. Murphy and E.W. Easton, *Wilderness to Wealth: Being a History of the Shires of Nanango, Kingaroy, Wondai, Murgon, Kilkivan and the Upper Yarraman Portion of the Rosalie Shire*, (Brisbane: W.R. Smith & Paterson Pty. Ltd, 1950), p.182.

15 Hector Holthouse, *River of Gold: The Story of the Palmer River Gold Rush*, (Sydney: Angus & Robertson, 1967), p.143.

16 Isle and Roy Riedy, personal letter to authors, 1983.

17 Palmer, *Early Days in North Queensland*, p.186.

18 Ibid., pp.186–187.

19 Mary Durack, *Kings in Glass Castles*, (Cordell Park, NSW: Corgi Books, 1983), p.186.

20 Palmer, *Early Days in North Queensland*, p.190.

21 A more complete story of Howe and his family is told by Holthouse, *Up Rode the Squatter*, pp.176–179. See also Pam Shilton, "The Story of Jackie Howe", *Sunday Mail Colour*, October 23 1983, p.7.

22 Buley, *Australian Life in Town and Country*, p.3.

23 See Chapter 5: Diffusion of Major Sports, 1850 to 1890s.

24 "Gayndah's (and Qld.'s) First Campdraft", *Burnett Advocate*, 1965.

25 Glenville Pike, *Queen of the North: A Pictorial History of Cooktown and Cape York Peninsula*, (Mareeba, 1979), p.36.

26 Jean Harslett and Mervyn Royle, *They Came to a Plateau: The Stanthorpe Saga*, (Stanthorpe: International Colour Productions, 1980), pp.154–157.

27 Ibid., p.158.

28 Ibid.

29 Information in this section on Winton is gleaned from Vincent T. Corbin (ed.), *Winton: One Hundred Years of Settlement 1875–1975*, (Toowoomba: Harrison Printing Co., 1975), Father Burke (ed.), *Winton Jubilee Souvenir Book 1878–1928*, (Townsville: T. Willmett & Sons, 1982); E.C.P. Phillott, *An Outline History of Winton 1862–1970*, n.d., n.p.

30 From "Nambucca News" Print, Macksville, NSW, as quoted in Corbin, *Winton*, p.49.

31 Ibid., p.58

32 D.F. & J. Ericker (compiled by), *Shire of Flinders 100 Years of Development in Hughenden and District, 1863–1963*, (Townsville: W. Willmett & Sons Pty. Ltd, 1963), p.50.

33 Ibid.

34 *Official Souvenir Publication (Hughenden)*, (Victoria: Hartshorne-Waller, 1951), p.29.

35 G.O. Armstrong, *In Mitchell's Footsteps: A History of the Balonne Shire*, (Brisbane: Smith & Paterson, 1968), pp.145–147.

36 G.H. Wade, *From Swamp to City: 1893–1963. The Story of Dalby*, (Dalby: The Dalby Herald, 1963), p.77.

37 A.M. Tew, *History of Gatton Shire in the Lockyer Valley*, (Gatton: Gatton Shire Council, 1979), p.54.

38 Kathleen Nutting, *Then and Now: The Story of Beaudesert 1874–1974*, (Beaudesert: Beaudesert Times, 1974), pp.39–46.

39 "Grand Final Souvenir", *Logan and Albert Times*, November 24 1980.

40 Johnson, *The Call of the Land*, p.19.

41 Ibid., p.20.

42 Ibid., p.55.

43 Murphy and Easton, *Wilderness to Wealth*, p.318.

44 Wade, *From Swamp to City*, p.25.

45 Mary Macleod Banks, *Memories of Pioneer Days in Queensland*, (London: Heath Cranton, 1931), p.31.

46 Ibid., p.58.

47 *A History of the Burdekin*, Shire of Burdekin, 1982, p.11.

48 Ibid., p.12.

49 W.R.O. Hill, *Forty–Five Years Experiences in North Queensland. 1861–1905*, (Brisbane: H. Pole & Co., 1907), p.101.

50 Ibid., p.21.

51 pp.21–22.

52 Ibid., p.39. It is interesting to note that Willie thanks Archibald Meston for helping with the writing of this book, and Meston similarly organised an Aboriginal escort later on.

53 Ibid., p.75.

54 Ibid., p.26.

55 Ibid.

56 Ibid., p.108.

57 Ibid., p.101.

58 Ibid., p.104.

59 Ibid., pp.99–100.

60 Ibid., p.14.

61 Ibid., pp.118–119.

62 Ibid., p.52.

63 Richard Alford, "Memories of Years Gone By", November, 1908. Ms. 3450, Diary in the National Library, Canberra, p.10.

64 Ibid., p.12.

65 Ibid., p.15.

66 Ibid.

67 Ibid., p.16.

68 Ibid., p.19

69 Ibid., p.13.

Chapter 10. Among the Miners

1 Derrick I. Stone and Sue Mackinnon, *Life on the Australian Goldfields*, (French's Forest: Popular Books, 1984), p.2.

2 Russel Ward, *The Australian Legend*, (Melbourne: Oxford University Press, 1977), pp.137 and 159–63.

3 Geoffrey Blainey, *A Land Half Won*, (Adelaide: Griffin Press, 1980), p.168.

4 Ward, *The Australian Legend*, p.139.

5 L.J. Colwell, "The North Queensland Goldfields", *Lectures on North Queensland History*, James Cook University, 1974, p.73.

6 Raphael Cilento, *Triumph in the Tropics: An Historical Sketch of Queensland*, (Brisbane: Smith and Paterson, 1959), p.199.

7 Colwell, "The North Queensland Goldfields", p.76.

8 Caroline Dunn, "The Town That Wouldn't Die", *The Sunday Mail Magazine*, July 23 1972, p.3.

9 Ross Fitzgerald, *From the Dreaming to 1915: A History of Queensland*, (St Lucia: University of Queensland Press, 1982), pp.66 & 155.

10 W. Ross Johnston, *The Call of the Land: A History of Queensland to the Present Day*, (Milton: Jacaranda Press, 1982), p.65.

11 Ward, *The Australian Legend*, p.147.

12 J. Black (compiler), *North Queensland Pioneers*, (Charters Towers: North Queensland Newspaper, n.d.), p.31.

13 Fitzgerald, *From the Dreaming to 1915*, p.159.

14 D. Stone (ed.), *Gold Diggers and Diggings*, (Melbourne: IPC Books, 1977), p.138.

15 Dunn, "The Town that Wouldn't Die", p.8.

16 "Cheap House Values at the Towers", *Daily Sun*, November 23 1984, p.29.

17 Don Roderick, *The Town They Called 'The World!*, (Charters Towers: Boolarong Publications, 1984), p.43.

18 G. Bolton, *A Thousand Miles Away: A History of North Queensland to 1920*, (Canberra: ANU Press, 1972), p.123.

19 Black, *North Queensland Pioneers*, p.31.

20 Ibid.

21 *CTT*, October 22 1890.

22 *CTT*, November 5 1890.

23 *NM*, July 14 1877.

24 *NQR*, December 10 1877.
25 *CTT*, October 15 1888.
26 *CTT*, December 5 1890.
27 *CTT*, November 4 1889.
28 *SM*, August 17 1895.
29 *CTT*, June 15 1894.
30 Elena Springel, *Glimpses of Glory: Charters Towers 1872-1972*, (Charters Towers: Northern Miner, 1972), p.51.
31 Black, *North Queensland Pioneers*, p.34.
32 *CTT*, August 11 1890.
33 *CTT*, January 14 1888.
34 *CTT*, March 27 and March 28 1889.
35 *Charters Towers Centenary 1872-1972*, (Charters Towers, 1972); *Charters Towers 1872-1950*, (Townsville: T. Willmett & Sons, 1950); Robert H. Davies ("Merlin"), *Sporting Flashbacks*, (n.p., December 1975).
36 Laurie Arthur, "When Charters Towers was the World", *North Australian Monthly*, March 1958, p.8.
37 *NM*, Saturday July 21 1877.
38 *CTT*, June 20 1888, p.2.
39 *CTT*, June 28 1889.
40 *CTT*, July 17 1888.
41 *NM*, March 13 1877, p.2.
42 *CTT*, March 9 and April 11 1889.
43 *CTT*, April 13 1889.
44 *CTT*, February 18 1889.
45 *CTT*, February 12 1890.
46 *CTT*, April 18 1890.
47 *CTT*, April 17 1890.
48 *CTT*, July 12 1890.
49 *NM*, December 5 1877.
50 *NM*, June 18 1877.
51 *CTT*, June 28 1888.
52 *CTT*, March 18 1891.
53 *CTT*, March 10 1888.
54 *NM*, December 5 1877.
55 *NM*, March 3 1877.
56 *NM*, June 9 1877.
57 *NM*, June 16 1877.
58 Ibid.
59 *CTT*, September 17, 18 and December 5 1888.
60 *CTT*, April 23 1889.
61 *CTT*, June 4, 1890.
62 *CTT*, June 6 1890.
63 *CTT*, June 11 1890.
64 *CTT*, March 8 1889.
65 *CTT*, July 3 1890.
66 *CTT*, August 10 1890.
67 *CTT*, October 10 and October 21 1890.
68 Jack Pollard, *Australian Rugby Union: The Game and the Players*, (Sydney: Angus & Robertson, 1984), p.673.
69 *NMR*, July 25 1891.
70 *CTT*, May 26 1888.
71 *CTT*, June 20 1888.
72 *CTT*, May 2 1890.
73 *NMR*, August 8 1891.
74 *NMR*, June 15 1892.
75 *CTT*, May 1 and May 13 1890.
76 *CTT*, May 26 1890.
77 *CTT*, July 7 1890.
78 *CTT*, June 6 1890.
79 *CTT*, April 23 1890.
80 *CTT*, June 11 1890.
81 *CTT*, September 20 and October 7 1890.
82 *CTT*, November 13 1890.
83 Norman Mossman Millar, personal interview with the authors, Charters Towers, December 20 1983.
84 *NMR*, April 25 1891.
85 *NMR*, May 16 1891.
86 *NMR*, September 12 1891.
87 *CTT*, June 14 1890.
88 *NMR*, June 29 1892.
89 *NMR*, April 26 and May 25 1892.
90 Thomas Welsby, unpublished manuscript, Royal Queensland Historical Society, n.d.
91 *Charters Towers 1872-1950*, p.34.
92 *NQR*, June 15 1892.
93 *NQR*, June 22 1892.
94 Ibid.
95 *NQR*, June 29 1897.
96 W.H. Bickley (ed.), *Maroon: Highlights of One Hundred Years of Rugby in Queensland*, (Brisbane:

Queensland Rugby Union, 1982), p.2.

97 Millar, personal interview.

98 Bickley, *Maroon*, p.28.

99 *Charters Towers 1872–1950*, p.12.

100 Davies, *Sporting Flashbacks*, p.29.

101 Springel, *Glimpses of Glory*.

102 *CTT*, January 7 1889.

103 *CTT*, November 13 1889.

104 *CTT*, December 24 1888.

105 *CTT*, December 14 1888.

106 *NQR*, May 4 1891.

107 *CTT*, March 13 1891.

108 *NQR*, October 1892.

109 Davies, *Sporting Flashbacks*, p.30.

110 *NMR*, May 12 1892.

111 Davies, *Sporting Flashbacks*, p.31.

112 *CTT*, July 28 1888.

113 *CTT*, October 4 and October 9 1888.

114 *CTT*, October 9 1888.

115 *NMR*, May 11 1892.

116 *NM*, December 15 1877.

117 *CTT*, March 29 1890.

118 *NM*, May 12 1877.

119 *NM*, May 21 1881.

120 *CTT*, June 28 1888.

121 *CTT*, October 4 1889.

122 *CTT*, January 26 1889.

123 *CTT*, March 8 1890.

124 *CTT*, December 2 1890.

125 *CTT*, November 12 1890.

126 *NMR*, March 16 1892.

127 *CTT*, December 3 1888.

128 *Supplement to the NM*, October 9 1899.

129 *CTT*, August 21 1888.

130 *CTT*, September 3 1888.

131 *CTT*, May 7 1888.

132 *CTT*, June 20 1888.

133 *CTT*, April 14 1890.

134 *NMR*, September 12 1891.

135 *CTT*, June 18 and August 24 1888.

136 *CTT*, January 18 1888.

137 *CTT*, January 30 1888.

138 *CTT*, August 7 1888.

139 *CTT*, September 13 1888.

140 *CTT*, August 8 1888.

141 *CTT*, October 17 1888.

142 *CTT*, April 8 1890.

143 *CTT*, June 6 1888.

144 *CTT*, May 25 1888.

145 *CTT*, April 22 1891.

146 *CTT*, July 12 1890.

147 *CTT*, August 9 1890.

148 *CTT*, April 29 and May 3 1890.

149 *CTT*, July 25 1890.

150 *CTT*, July 26 1890.

151 *CTT*, July 20 1890.

152 *CTT*, November 29 1889.

153 *NMR*, May 30 1890.

154 *NM*, February 3 1877.

155 *CTT*, January 14 1890.

156 *CTT*, January 6 1891.

157 *CTT*, January 20 1888.

158 *NMR*, December 16 1891.

159 Springel, *Glimpses of Glory*, p.57.

160 *CTT*, October 20 and December 4 1890.

161 *CTT*, March 22 1902.

Bibliography

Alford, Richard, *Memories of Years Gone by*, November 1908, MS 3450, Diary in the National Library, Canberra.

Another Wieneke Wanted: The Book of the Genuine Wieneke Saddle, n.p., n.d.

"Archer, Mary, Charles (1813–1862), John (1814–1857), David (1816–1900), William (1818–1896), Archibald (1820–1902), Thomas (1823–1905), and Colin (1832–1921)". *Australian Dictionary of Biography*, vol. 1, 1788–1850, (Melbourne: Melbourne University Press, 1966).

Armstrong, G.O., *In Mitchells' Footsteps: A History of the Balonne Shire*, (Brisbane: Smith and Paterson, 1968).

Armstrong, Robert E.M., *The Kalkadoons*, (Brisbane: William Brooks, 1986).

Arthur, Laurie, "When Charters Towers was the World", *North Australian Monthly*, March 1958.

Austin, C.G., "One Hundred Years of Sport and Recreation in Queensland", *Journal of the Royal Historical Society of Queensland*, vi:1, September 1959.

Bailey, P., *Leisure and Class in Victorian England*, (London: Routledge & Kegan Paul, 1978).

Banks, Mary Macleod, *Memories of Pioneer Days in Queensland*, (London: Heath Granton Ltd., 1931).

Beal, Diana J., *Rosalie Shire Council, 1879–1979*, (Toowoomba: Cranbrook Press, 1971).

Bickley, Bert (ed.), *Maroon: Highlights of One Hundred Years of Rugby in Queensland: 1882–1982*, (Brisbane: Queensland Rugby Union, 1982).

Bird, J.S., *The Early History of Rockhampton*, (Rockhampton: Rockhampton Morning Bulletin Office, 1904).

Black, J. (compiler), *North Queensland Pioneers*, (Charters Towers: North Queensland Newspaper Co., n.d.).

Blainey, Geoffrey, "The History of Leisure in Australia", *The Victorian Historical Journal*, 49:1, 1978, p.18.

Blainey, Geoffrey, *A Land Half Won*, (Adelaide: Griffin Press, 1980).

Blanch, John (ed.), *Ampol's Australian Sporting Records*, (Cheltenham: Budget Books Pty. Ltd., 1982).

Bolton, G.C., "The Idea of a Colonial Gentry", *Historical Studies of Australia and New Zealand*, 13:49–52, October 1967–69.

Bolton, G., *A Thousand Miles Away: A History of North Queensland to 1920*, (Canberra: ANU Press, 1972).

"Brisbane Hunt Club, The", *Town & Country*, December 6 1890.

Brown, Keith, "Started Slowly – But How It Grew", *Courier–Mail*, 15 June 1959.

Buley, E.C., *Australian Life in Town and Country*, London: George Newness, 1905).

Father Burke (ed.), *Winton Jubilee Souvenir Book 1878-1928*, (Townsville: T. Willmett & Sons, 1982).

Carmichael, W.B. and H.C. Perry, *Athletic Queensland*, (Brisbane: Diddams, 1900).

Cassell's Book of Sports and Pastimes, (London: Cassell & Co., 1888).

Caswell, N.H., Elaine Cook, C.M. Feez, W.K. Gunn, H.W. Henricksen, W.J. Rogers, Allan Gilmore, "Outlines of History of Polo in Queensland", unpublished paper.

Charters Towers Centenary 1872-1972, (Charters Towers, 1972).

Charters Towers 1872-1950, (Townsville: T. Willmett & Sons, 1950).

"Cheap House Values at the Towers", *Daily Sun*, November 23, 1984.

Cilento, Raphael, *Triumph in the Tropics: An Historical Sketch of Queensland*, (Brisbane: Smith & Paterson, 1959).

Clerici, Giannini, *The Ultimate Tennis Book*, (Chicago: Follett Publishing Co., 1975).

Collins, Jas. L. and Geo. H. Thompson, *"Harking Back": The Turf: Its Men and Memories*, (Brisbane: Standard Press, 1924).

Colwell, L.J., "The North Queensland Goldfields", *Lectures on North Queensland History*, James Cook University, 1974.

Corbin, Vincent T. (ed.), *Winton: One Hundred Years of Settlement 1875-1975*, (Toowoomba: Harrison Printing Co., 1975).

Corris, Peter, *Lords of the Ring*, (North Ryde: Cassell Australia, 1980).

Crawford, Scott A.G.M., "A History of Recreation and Sport in Nineteenth Century Colonial Otago", PhD thesis, University of Queensland, 1984.

Daly, John, *Elysian Fields: Sport, Class and Community in Colonial South Australia*, (Adelaide: J.A. Daly, 1982).

Davidson, Bruce, "The Best Fighters Came From the Country", *Courier-Mail*, 15 June, 1959, p.6.

Davies, Robert H. ("Merlin"), *Sporting Flashbacks*, (n.p., December 1975).

Dowse, Thomas, "Old Times", *Brisbane Courier*, 18 September 1869.

Dudley, Robert, "A History of Sport in the Moreton Bay District", Ph.D thesis, Department of Human Movement Studies, 1989.

Dunn, Caroline, "The Town That Wouldn't Die", *Sunday Mail Magazine*, 23 July 1972.

Dunning, Eric and Kenneth Sheard, *Barbarians, Gentlemen and Players*, (Oxford: Oxford University Press, 1979).

Dunstan, Keith, *Sports*, (Melbourne: Cassell Australia Ltd., 1973).

Durack, Mary, *Kings in Grass Castles*, (Cordell Park, NSW: Corgi Books, 1983).

Ericker, D.F. & J. (compilers), *Shire of Flinders 100 Years of Development in Hughenden and District, 1863-1963*, (Townsville: T. Willmett & Sons Pty. Ltd., 1963).

"Mr. Adolph Feez", *Queensland 1900*, Alcazar Press, 1900.

Fifty Years of Football, (Brisbane: Queensland Rugby Union, 1932).

Fitzgerald, Ross, *From the Dreaming to 1915: A History of Queensland*, (St Lucia: University of Queensland Press, 1982).

Fitzpatrick, Jim, *The Bicycle and the Bush: Man and Machine in Rural Australia*, (Melbourne: Oxford University Press, 1980).

Fourth Australasian Championships, Official Programme, 1899.

Francis, R.P., (ed.), *Records of the Brisbane Grammar School, 1869-1890*, (Brisbane: Pole, Outridge & Co., 1890).

Freeland, J.M., *The Australian Pub*, (Melbourne: Melbourne University Press, 1966).

Maurice French and Duncan Waterson, *The Darling Downs: A Pastoral History, 1850-1950*, (Toowoomba: Darling Downs Institute Press, 1982).

"Gayndah's (and Qld's) First Campdraft", *Burnett Advocate*, 1965.

Gould, Nat, *Town and Bush*, (London: George Routledge & Sons, 1896).

Gould, Nat, *On and Off the Turf in Australia*, (London: George Routledge & Sons, 1895).

"Grand Final Souvenir", Logan & Albert Times, 24 November 1980.

Greenwood, Gordon, *Australia: A Social and Political History*, (Sydney: Angus & Robertson, 1955).

Harris, H.A., *Sport in Britain: Its Origins and Developments*, (London: Stanley Paul, 1975).

Harslett, Jean and Mervyn Royle, *They Came to a Plateau: The Stanthorpe Saga*, (Stanthorpe: International Colour Production, 1980).

Harvey, Ron, *Centenary of Organised Rowing in Bundaberg*, unpublished paper, n.d.

Hill, W.R.O., *Forty-five Years Experience in North Queensland*, (Brisbane: Pole & Co., 1907).

History of the Burdekin, A, Shire of Burdekin, 1982.

Holthouse, Hector, *Illustrated History of Queensland*, (Brisbane: Rigby Ltd., 1978).

Holthouse, Hector, *River of Gold: The Story of the Palmer River Gold Rush*, (Sydney: Angus & Robertson, 1967).

Holthouse, Hector, *Up Rode the Squatter*, (Adelaide: Rigby, 1970).

Holthouse, Hector *Gympie Gold: A Dramatic Story of Queensland Gold*, (Melbourne: Angus & Robertson, 1983).

Howell, Reet and Max Howell, *Foundations of Physical Education*, (Brisbane: William Brooks, 1984).

Howell, Maxwell L. and Reet A. Howell, "The First Intercolonial Tour in 1882", *The Royal Historical Society of Queensland*, xi:4, 126–138, 1983.

Hoy, Col, "Australian Code was Here in 1881", *Courier-Mail*, 15 June 1959, p.10.

Hutcheon, E.H., *A History of Queensland Cricket*, (Brisbane: V.E. Martin, n.d.).

Ingham, A.G., and R. Beamish, "The Maturation of Industrial Capitalism and the Bourgeoisification of America's Ludic Interests", unpublished paper, 1982.

Inglis, Gordon, *Sport and Pastime in Australia*, (London: Methuen, 1912).

Jacks, S.W. Cutting Book, No. 37, Oxley Library.

Jackson, A.T., *Southern Queensland Rifle Association Jubilee, 1877–1927: A Brief History of the Association During the Past Fifty Years*, (Brisbane, 1927).

Johnston, W. Ross, *The Call of the Land: A History of Queensland to the Present Day*, (Brisbane: Jacaranda Press, 1982).

Jounquay, Dorothy, *The Isisford Story*, Isisford Shire Council, 1975).

Knight, J.J., *In the Early Days: History and Incident of Pioneer Queensland*, (Brisbane: Sapsford, 1895).

Lacke, John, "Working Class Leisure", *The Victorian Historical Journal*, 49:1, 1978, pp.49–65.

Lawson, Ronald, *Brisbane in the 1890s*, (St Lucia: University of Queensland Press, 1973).

Leggett, P., "Class and the Eight Hours Movement in Queensland 1855–1885", BA(Hons.) Thesis, University of Queensland, 1983.

Lynam, Frank, "History of Queensland Amateur Cycling", unpublished paper, n.d.

McGill, J.J., "Authentic Stories of Queensland Racing", *Queensland Racing Calendar*, n.d., p.34.

McGill, J.J., "The Brisbane Cup", *Queensland Racing Calendar*, June 1966, p.591.

McGill, J.J., "When the Course by the Creek was First Opened", *Queensland Racing Calendar*, 1968, p.131.

McGill, J.J., "The Third Decade of Racing", *Queensland Racing Calendar*, January 1966, p.260.

McGill, J.J., "Topics of the Month", *Queensland Racing Calendar*, November 1968, p.80.

McIntosh, P.C., *Sport in Society*, (London: C.A. Watts Co. Ltd., 1968).

MacLaren, M. *The Australian and New Zealand Golfer's Handbook* (5th edition), (Sydney: A.H. & A.W. Reid, 1975).

Macqueen , Nell (ed.), *Back Creek and Beyond*, (Toowoomba: Darling Downs Institute Press, 1981).

Mahoney, J.R.D., *Wide Bay and Burnett Cricket, 1864-1908*, (Maryborough: Alston, 1908).

Mandle, W., "Cricket and Australian Nationalism in the Nineteenth Century", *Journal of the Royal Australian Historical Society*, 59:4, December 1973.

Mason, Percy, *Professional Athletics in Australia*, (Sydney: Rigby, 1985).

Meslee, Edmond Marin La, *The New Australia*, translated and edited by Russel Ward, (Melbourne: Heinemann Educational, 1929).

Mollar, Norma, *History of the Bowen-Collinsville Railway*, pamphlet published and printed courtesy of the *Bowen Independent*, n.d.

Moore, C.R., "The Mackay Race Course Riot of 1883", *Lectures on North Queensland History*, James Cook University, 1978.

Moorehead, Alan, *The Fatal Impact*, (London: Reprint Society, 1966).

Morrison, A.A., "Sir Joshua Peter Bell", *Australian Dictionary of Biography*, vol. 3, (Melbourne: Melbourne University Press, 1969).

Morrison, W.F., *The Aldine History of Queensland*, vol 1 (Sydney: The Aldine Publishing Co., 1888).

Murphy, J.E. and E.W. Easton, *Wilderness to Wealth: Being a History of the Shires of Nanango, Kingaroy, Wondai, Murgon, Kilkivan and the Upper Yarraman Portion of the Rosalie Shire*, (Brisbane: W.R. Smith & Paterson Pty Ltd, 1950).

Murray, David Christie, "Work and Sport on the Darling Downs", *Daily Telegraph*, Saturday, 26 October 1889.

Newton, F.G., Col., "Brisbane Hunt Club", *Journal of Royal Historical Society of Queensland*, 1957, p.1300.

Nutting, Kathleen, *Then and Now: The Story of Beaudesert 1874-1974*, (Beaudesert: Beaudesert Times, 1974).

O'Connor, G.F., *Souvenir of the Centenary of the Central and Upper Burnett River District of Queensland, 1848 to 1948*, (Brisbane: William Brooks, 1948).

Official Souvenir Publication (Hughenden), (Victoria: Hartshorne-Waller, 1951).

Palmer, Edward, *Early Days in North Queensland*, (Sydney: Angus & Robertson, 1983).

Parry-Okeden, W.E., "Old Queensland Hunt Clubs", newspaper clipping, Mrs Turner's scrapbook.

Pattison, Grant, *"Battler's" Tales of Early Rockhampton*, (Melbourne: Fraser & Jenkinson, 1939).

Pedley, Ian, *Winds of Change: One Hundred Years in the Widgee Shire*, (Gympie: The Gympie Times, 1979).

Perry, Harry C., *A Son of Australia. Memories of W.K. Parry-Okeden, 1840-1926*, (Watson-Ferguson Co. Ltd, 1928).

Petrie, Constance Campbell, *Tom Petrie's Reminiscences of Early Queensland*, (Victoria: Currey O'Neill, 1981).

Phillips, Murray, "The Development of Sport in Gympie during its First Decade, 1867-1877", unpublished paper, University of Queensland, 1984.

Phillips, Murray, "A History of the Brisbane Golf Club", BA(Hons) Thesis, Department of Human Movement Studies, University of Queensland, 1986.

Phillott, E.C.P., *An Outline History of Winton 1862-1970*, n.d., n.p.

Pike, Glenville, *Queen of the North: A Pictorial History of Cooktown and Cape York Peninsula*, (Mareeba, 1979).

Pollard, Jack, *The Pictorial History of Australian Racing*, (Sydney: Lansdowne Press, 1982).

Pollard, Jack, *Australian Cricket: The Game and the Players*, (Sydney: Hodder and Stoughton, 1982).

Pollard, Jack, *Australian Rugby Union: The Game and the Players*, (North Ryde: Angus & Robertson, 1984).

Pownell, Eve, *Mary of Maranoa*, (Sydney: F.H. Johnston, 1959).

Purdie, M.V., *Capella: A Brief History of the Settlement of the Peak Downs*, (Rockhampton: City Printing Works, 1983).

"Queensland Rifle Association Centenary, 1877 to 1977", *Marskman*, October 1977, p.14.

Reynolds, H., "Racial Thought in Early Australia", *Australian Journal of Politics and History*, 20:1 (April 1974).

Roberts, Stephen H., *History of Australian Land Settlement (1788-1920)*, (Melbourne: Macmillan, 1924).

Roberts, Stephen H., *The Squatting Age in Australia 1835-1847*, (Melbourne: Melbourne University Press, 1935).

Robertson, John, *Uppies and Doonies*, (Aberdeen: Aberdeen University Press, 1967).

Roderick, Don, *The Town They Called "The World"*, (Charters Towers: Boolarong Publications, 1984).

Roth, W.E., "Games, sports and amusements", *North Queensland Ethnography*, Bulletin No. 4, (Brisbane: Government Printing Office, 1902).

Roth, W.E., *Ethnological Studies among the North-Western Central Queensland Aborigines*, (Brisbane: Government Printing Office, 1897).

Roth, W.E., "Games, Sports and Amusements of the Northern Queensland Aboriginals", *Report of the Australian Advancement of Science*, 9 (1903).

Salter, Michael Alber, "Games and Pastimes of the Australian Aboriginal", M.A. Thesis, University of Alberta, 1967.

Shilton, Pam, "The Story of Jackie Howe", *Sunday Mail Colour*, 23 October 1983.

Slaughter, Leslie, *Ipswich Municipal Centenary*, (Ipswich: Pohlman-Patrick Advertisers, 1960).

Smith, Peter, "Evan Mackenzie", paper presented at the Brisbane Historical Society, Kilcoy Homestead, October 1986.

Smith, Terry, *Australian Golf: The First One Hundred Years*, (Sydney: Lester-Townsend Pty Ltd, 1982).

Speare, J., "Soccer Began on Vacant Paddocks", *Courier-Mail*, 15 June 1959, p.10.

"Sport in Barcaldine", notes prepared by Barcaldine Shire Council.

Springel, Elena, *Glimpses of Glory: Charters Towers 1872-1972*, (Charters Towers: Northern Miner, 1972).

Stanley, Raymond (ed.), *Tourist to the Antipodes: William Archer's Australian Journey, 1876-1877*, (St Lucia: University of Queensland Press, 1977).

Stephenson, Stuart, *Annals of the Brisbane Grammar School, 1869-1922*, (Brisbane: Government Printer, 1923).

Stewart, F.M.G., *The First One Hundred Years, 1863-1963, Centenary of Loyal Pioneer Lodge*, No. 3, (MUIOOF, Rockhampton: Oxford Press, 1963).

Stone, D., (ed.), *Gold Diggers and Diggings*, (Melbourne: IPC Books, 1977).

Stone, Derrick I. and Sue Mackinnon, *Life in the Australian Goldfields*, (French's Forest: Popular Books, 1984).

Strutt, J., *Sport and Pastimes of the People of England*, (London: William Tegg, 1875).

Tew, A.M., *History of Gatton Shire in the Lockyer Valley*, (Gatton: Gatton Shire Couoncil, 1979).

Trollope, Anthony, *Australia*, (St Lucia: University of Queensland Press, 1967).

Tutt, Stan, *From Spear and Musket: 1879–1979, Caboolture Centenary*, (Nambour: Sunstrip Printers, 1979).

Twopeny, R.E.N., *Town Life in Australia*, (Sydney: Sydney University Press, 1975).

Wade, G.H., *From Swamp to City, 1863–1963: The Story of Dalby*, (Dalby: The Dalby Herald, 1963).

Ward, Russel, *The Australian Legend*, (Melbourne: Oxford University Press, 1977).

Waterson, D.P., "Joshua Thomas Bell", *Australian Dictionary of Biography*, vol. 7, (Melbourne: Melbourne University Press, 1969).

Weedon, T., *Queensland Past and Present*, (Brisbane: Government Printer, 1897).

Welsby, Thomas, diary, held by Royal Queensland Historical Society, Brisbane.

Welsby, Thomas, unpublished manuscript, Royal Queensland Historical Society, n.d.

Wetherell, H., *A Short Historical Sketch of the Commercial Rowing Club*, (Brisbane: Commercial Rowing Club, 1947).

Wetzel, E., "The Early History of Swimming in Queensland", in *Programme for the 1st Annual Aquatic Gala of the Commercial Amateur Swimming Club*, n.p., 1914.

Willey, Keith, *The First Hundred Years: The Story of Brisbane Grammar School, 1868–1968*, (Melbourne: Macmillan Co., 1968).

Wilson, R.K., *Australia's Resources and Their Development*, (Sydney: Department of Education, University of Sydney, 1980).

Newspapers and Magazines

Brisbane Courier, 1864–1895

Burnett Argus, 1867

Burnett Advocate, 1865

Charters Towers Times, 1888–1902

Courier–Mail, 1959, 1983–1990

Daily Sun, 1984

Gympie Times, 1869

Logan & Albert Times, 1980

Moreton Bay Courier, 1846–1861

Mundie Miner & Etheridge Gazette, 1889

North Queensland Register, 1877, 1891–1892, 1897

Northern Mining Register, 1890–1892

Northern Miner, 1877, 1881, 1891

Queensland Figaro, 1883–1884

Queensland Cricketer & Footballer, 1892–1894

Sunday Mail, 1972, 1983–1990.

Sydney Mail, 1895

Sydney Morning Herald, 1843–1845

The Referee, 1896, 1999–1920

The Bulletin, 1928, 1933

The Courier, 1861–1864

Town & Country, 1890

Townsville Herald, 1887

WA/TC, 1866

Warwick Times, 1868

Letters

"Letters written between 1833 and 1855 to William and Julia Archer of Tolderodden, Norway, by their sons from Australia". F1665, Fryer Library, University of Queensland, June 30 1842.

Isle and Roy Riedy, personal letter, 1983.

Index